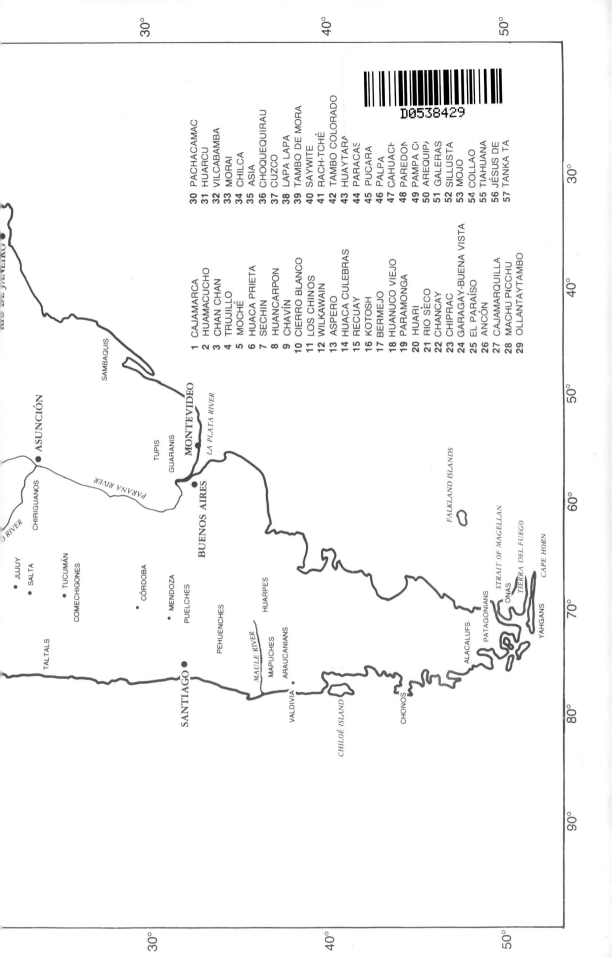

An Ancient World Preserved

Relics and Records
of Prehistory in the Andes

An
Ancient
World Preserved

Relics and Records
of Prehistory in the Andes

Revised and Updated
by Frederic André Engel

translated by Rachel Kendall Gordon

Crown Publishers, Inc., New York

Designed by Manuela Paul

Printed in the United States of America

Published simultaneously in Canada by General Publishing Company Limited

Library of Congress Cataloging in Publication Data

Engel, Frederic André, 1918-
An ancient world preserved.

Translation of Le monde précolombien des Andes.
1. Indians of South America—Andes—Antiquities.
2. Andes—Antiquities. 3. Indians of South America—
Peru—Antiquities. 4. Peru—Antiquities. I. Title.
F2229.E5313 1976   980'.004'98   76-19793
ISBN 0-517-51874-0

CONTENTS

INTRODUCTION

The Andes, backbone of South America, constitute an immense and thrilling world, as marvelous as it is diverse, with astonishing landscapes, at times very beautiful, at times terrifying, a world as alluring as it is unknown.

There are, to be sure, histories of Peru, histories of the Incas, already old though excellent in their time. But these works are mostly out of print now, and are in any case obsolete because American prehistory studies have progressed since they were written. If certain texts on Peru are still obtainable, it is very difficult, outside of some specialized libraries, to secure information regarding the episodes that marked the history of regions such as Ecuador, Argentina, or Araucania, to cite only a few examples.

This work follows up two of mine: *Elements of Peruvian Prehistory* and *Elementary History of Ancient Peru,* both published in Lima in Spanish and now out of print.

In a book not intended for specialists, detailed references to the different authors cited would make the text too heavy. The reader who wishes to delve more deeply into certain aspects of the history I have sketched should simply head for the library of the nearest large city or university, where he will find the titles of many of the works by authors I have mentioned. The reader will thus have at his disposal all the complementary documentation he could wish for. At any rate, it will be to his interest to go through a few basic works, among which I shall mention:

—For geography of the Andes, volume XV of *Géographie Universelle* by Vidal Lablache, edited by P. Denis;

—Concerning the central Andes and the Incas, first, the *Handbook of American Indians*, volume II, published under the direction of Julian Steward by the Smithsonian Institution between 1940 and 1945. The *Handbook* contains almost all that is known on the prehistory of the Andes, except for recent discoveries. The reader will also find there the texts of authors he should know, like Lévi-Strauss, Metraux, Rivet, Kubler, Bird, Willey, Kidder, Ford, Bennett, and others. This list is not exhaustive, of course.

Second, a book by John Hemming, *The Conquest of the Incas.*

—Concerning the other Andean societies, volumes II, III, and V of the *Handbook* given above.

—Concerning the history of the preagricultural high Holocene, my texts and those of Rex Gonzales, Augusto Cardich, and Richard S. MacNeish.

—Regarding comparisons with Mexico, texts by Jacques Soustelle (such as *The Daily Life of the Aztecs on the Eve of the Spanish Conquest*) and, relating to North America, the works of Alden Mason and the Smithsonian Institution on the natives of that continent, or encyclopedias such as Collier's.

Several years of study devoted to Peru and the cordillera, from Venezuela to Chile, both through excavating and through exploring mountain and desert, encouraged me to make better known the history of the Andes and the importance that should be attached to it, for this history constitutes one of the fundamental pages in the history of mankind.

Indeed, we shall find in the Andes monuments erected in the course of extremely varied periods of history; first, pre-Columbian societies; then the civilization of Spain of the Renaissance and Counter-Reformation. The latter has left us unforgettable baroque and rococo works of art of a quite peculiar character, the work of indigenous artists adding the touch of their native inspiration to the European models they were copying.

My theme is limited to the pre-Columbian world of the Andes. Therefore, I shall allude to what took place during the Hispanicization of South America only to define the former life, whose demise sets in with the arrival of Europeans.

I shall do my utmost, on the other hand, to draw out of the shadows and bring again to light these Andeans of the past who contributed, and in large measure, to the development of civilizations. Let us not forget that in the Andes was born, independently, just as in the Near East, India, China, and Mexico, a modern world of farmers, of men who produced food and were no longer parasites and predators and who created the conditions necessary for the invention of writing, thanks to which the sciences are preserved and diffused. I have always considered Western Europe as marginal in this respect, because its civilization was indebted from the outset to eastern Europe and the Near East. A young archaeological school is trying to introduce concepts contrary to this viewpoint, making efforts to prove that Europe created its metallurgy and cyclopean structures quite early. I am willing to believe this, but Europe invented neither the cultivation of cereals nor the domestication of animals, nor arithmetic nor the sciences, all of which were devised by the inhabitants of the Near East, India, China, Mexico, and, in part, by the inhabitants of Peru. And in creating sufficient nutritional resources, agricultural production favored the birth of groups of artisans and artists to whom we owe the jewels of art that times gone by have left us.

It is the Andes, and the Antilles that, according to geographers, constitute a prolongation of the cordillera emerging from the Atlantic, which have played a cultural and economic role in the history of the South American continent. The great grassy plains of the East, the lowlands of the hot and rainy Amazonas, the pampas of Argentina, even the temperate plateaus of the Guianas and Brazil, do not appear to have contributed substantially to the history of the continent.

It therefore seemed logical to devote a book to the cordillera, but provided that I treat the subject in its entirety, that I observe what occurred from the Antilles to Tierra del Fuego, and not only among the Incas of Peru. As soon as one approaches the history of the Andes, one realizes, as a matter of fact, that the modern political borders are irrelevant to that history. So it is, for example, that the princes of Cuzco exerted their influence from the modern boundaries of Colombia to the middle of Chile. One may state that the Andean world constitutes a whole, peopled with the same human material, and revealing, beneath diversified appearances, a very ancient foundation of common ancestral customs.

The Andes, once heavily populated, were emptied of their inhabitants as a result of the intervention of European invaders. The Andeans who survived the terrible shock resulting from the meeting of the New World and the Old lost, over the centuries, all creativeness. Until the nineteenth century, which witnessed a reversal of forces, only some populations practically reduced to slavery or taking refuge in the most inaccessible regions managed to survive in the cordillera.

The populations that came back to life after the South American territories had acquired their independence from the Spanish crown were, therefore, different from those that formed the pre-Columbian world; first, as a result of crossbreeding with Europeans, Chinese, and Africans; then, owing to the destruction of the pre-Columbian social structures; finally, because of four centuries of indoctrination carried out in the name of a new religion and new ways of thought.

Thus, in order to understand the pre-Columbian Andes, we are obliged to envision a world that has almost entirely vanished, an immense edifice that has collapsed (certain sections of which have fortunately survived), a world that has contributed significantly to the history of mankind and known one of its most glorious epochs: despite their isolation and totally autonomous development, the Andean societies were able to conquer for man one of the roughest territories in the world, and turn to advantage a particularly hostile environment; to deliver to us, finally, plants so precious that we still use and consume them throughout the world. Let us not forget that it is the Andeans who gave us corn, cotton, the pota-to, and the peanut, to cite only their most widely known products.

At the moment of their destruction, the Andean societies had attained a sociointellectual level comparable to that of preliterate and protodynastic Egypt and Mesopotamia of five thousand years ago. They seemed to be on the point of starting on the road to progress.

In order to understand these societies, we should begin by restoring them to their rightful place in the history of the development of civilizations.

Anthropologists generally accept the notion of a dynamic that prevents human groups from remaining immobile and makes them tend to evolve, to pass progressively from a stage of life in bands (which stage one may call primary) to a more complex stage of tribes that join to form confederations of various sorts. Only later are chiefdoms, kingdoms, and states born, the existence of a state being revealed by the presence of a regular army in the service of the nation or prince, and of a body of artisans working for society. Then comes the mechanization of the Western world and, finally, the space age.

But all men did not evolve in the same way. Certain groups remained im-mobile, organized at the stage of bands. Such was the case with tribes who sur-vived without ever practicing agriculture: Eskimos, natives of Australia, Pygmies of central Africa, of the Philippines, or of certain forests of Asia, and small groups in the tropical forests of America and Patagonia.

Other groups, however, regressed. Thus, for example, the remnants of the peoples that live today along the low eastern fringe of the Peruvian Andes, where the Amazonas begins, once knew a more developed social status and a better life.

Let us adopt for a moment this generalized notion of the evolution of socie-ties in terms of complexity. Where, then, shall we place the pre-Columbian populations? So as not to make a mistake, we should compare them to another civilization that has similarly evolved from life in tribes to that of an empire.

I could adopt as elements for comparison China and India, which very early created original agricultural civilizations, as did Mexico. But it is the Near East that cultivated readers know best, so I shall therefore adopt the ancient Fertile Crescent as a point of reference. Bearing in mind what happened in predynastic Egypt around 3300 B.C. and in Mesopotamia, Palestine, Iran, and the area that is now Turkey a little earlier (around 3500 B.C.), I shall examine the acts and in-tentions of the princes of Cuzco and the history of Andean societies in general. In doing so we shall be studying two comparable worlds, both preliterate and on the point of entering the age of metals, writing, and science; and we shall not make the mistake of comparing the world of the Incas with that of the states of Europe and the Renaissance, heiress to five thousand years of literate and protoscientific culture, rather than looking at Ur upon the arrival of the Sumerians in Mesopo-tamia. In adopting these precautions, we shall avoid establishing absurd compari-sons between pre-Columbian societies composed of fishermen-peasants and head-hunters, and the inhabitants of sixteenth-century western Europe. To understand the pre-Columbians it is safer to observe the present inhabitants of New Guinea, who themselves practice agriculture, drink out of the skulls of their enemies, and do not know how to write.

The cultural and agricultural nuclei of the Near East seem to have emerged as early as the end of the last ice age, during the beginning of the Holocene period, after which they progressed slowly. (The Holocene epoch is the geological period that began with the end of the last ice age, around 10,500 years ago, as opposed to the Pleistocene, the period of the ice ages. The Holocene and the Pleistocene together constitute the Quaternary. All the large animals typical of the Pleistocene had already disappeared when the Holocene began.) The Near East's nuclei took some twenty-five hundred years to reach the stage I have adopted as a point of reference—that of states already established but still preliterate, well on their way to becoming protoscientific and literate civilizations.

From that moment the blossoming was rapid, and around 2000 B.C., Egypt, Mesopotamia, Palestine, Turkey, and Iran had already attained the height of their ascension, after which they went through a long period of quiescence, then fell into decadence.

Mexico and the countries of the Andes, after a start that was almost contemporary with that of the Near East, underwent a distinctly slower development.

In the year 6000 B.C., some populations of the Andes were already living in conditions comparable to those of groups who were at that time living in the Near East. All these Andeans were not yet farmers or shepherds, but a good many of them were already living a sedentary life and occupying (at least during some month every year) well-defined territories in which they obtained their food by gathering, fishing, and hunting. The settlement patterns we observe in those days, at least in the central Andes, do not correspond to a nomadic life but, on the contrary, to the existence of villagers living in hamlets and villages of from five to a few hundred huts. This sedentary existence is further proved by the fact that a heavy milling stone is usually found in every hut, together with the graves of the inhabitants.

The term *Neolithic revolution,* coined by V. Gordon Childe to describe this level of development, has been criticized, because the phenomenon would have constituted an evolution, not a revolution. The effects of it, however, have been revolutionary—the production of food permitted the creation of surpluses that liberated the work of certain men for new activities. However this may be, the Neolithic revolution, or better said, the evolution from the stage of predators-parasites living off what the environment could offer to that of agricultural production, was considered a rare and precocious phenomenon that had happened only in the Near East, where it dates back to at least 6000 B.C. Now it seems (in the light of the most recent discoveries, notably those of Richard S. MacNeish in Mexico and more recently those of Thomas Lynch) that a similar phenomenon had been taking place at the same time in the eastern Andes, in the Santa Valley in Peru, and from there had penetrated the highlands. On the western slopes of the Andes, nevertheless, neolithization seems to have taken shape later, about six thousand years ago, and from then on the evolution was slow. We

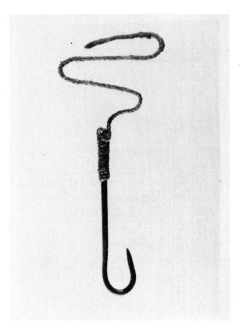

A fishhook made of a cactus spine. Such fishhooks are the earliest ones yet found in Peru, but they were still used in late pre-Columbian days in Chile. About 4000 B.C.

shall have to wait until the fifteenth century of our era to find among the pre-Columbians of the Pacific Coast achievements comparable to those one observes in Mesopotamia, Palestine, Turkey, Egypt, and Iran—achievements that in the Near East had taken shape some five thousand years ago. Having set out in the race under nearly comparable conditions, the two American nuclei then let themselves be outdistanced.

The terms *Paleolithic*, or Old Stone Age, *Mesolithic*, or Middle Stone Age, and *Neolithic*, or Age of Polished Stone, in vogue in the nineteenth century, and which some anthropologists persist in using, seem to me to be totally unsuited to what they are supposed to reflect, namely, an evolution of preagricultural peoples that led to a transitional period followed by the birth of agricultural societies.

We know, by way of operating in the arid Andes, where everything is preserved through thousands of years, that before using metal, men did not use stone only. Implements made of such diverse materials as wood, bone, or shells played just as important a role among the pre-Columbians. Twelve years of excavations have allowed me to assemble some fifty thousand objects of firmly established provenance, nearly all placed in time. Now stone objects do not constitute a fifth of this collection, and if one remembers that wood is more perishable than stone, one will see the relatively small role that lithic material must have played. Besides, to cut a string one does not need a beautiful flint knife; one need only place it on a small stone and strike it with the edge of a pebble flake. To kill a deer, a javelin with a hard wooden point does its duty as well as an obsidian-tipped arrow. It may be that one used one material or another according to a tradition, perhaps born of the environment in which one lived and the resources of a region, or maybe even according to considerations of a magical order. And, of course, traditional techniques get lost and the art of making certain objects falls into decay.

If other prehistorians were willing to reevaluate their analyses of the European Pleistocene epoch from this point of view, they would have to arrive at similar conclusions. Thus, for example, U.S. researchers have already noticed that millstones and mortars, tools that formerly one would not have thought of finding outside of Mesolithic or Neolithic sites, were already used in Pleistocene times, in times in which theoretically only nomadic bands of paleo-Indian hunters were wandering about the northern continent. As far as South America is concerned, experience quickly taught me the antiquity of this sort of equipment, and I have never respected the theory that formerly man would have lived solely by hunting. One can roast game only after it has been killed. While waiting, one must take nourishment, and that is where provisions of berries, rhizomes, bulbs, and roots intervene, for the consumption of which, grindstones and mortars are necessary.

Just as far from reality, it seems to me, is the terminology used by most authors in the United States: paleo-Indians, archaic Indians, and meso-Indians. What difference can there be between a paleo-Indian, an early Indian, and an archaic Indian? I think societies differ according to the resources they have at their disposal, the techniques applied to their exploitation, and the inherent genius of the groups that compose them, all things that these names do not reflect at all.

On occasion, however, I shall use the two classical terms *Mesolithic* and *Neolithic,* not in their technological sense, but for their convenience and brevity. When I use the word *Mesolithic,* it will be to designate tribes living in a sedentary fashion, at least during some months of the year, in a territory and in villages where one finds the millstones, mortars, and pestles that the inhabitants used to crush the seeds, roots, and tubercles that they gathered, but without having planted them beforehand. *Mesolithic* is therefore opposed to *Neolithic.*

I shall use the term *neolithization* to describe the passage from the life of a preagricultural, parasitic nature to the life of producer-peasant. A *neolith* is a man who cultivates his field or raises animals but does not employ metal.

This terminology has its practical usefulness, but we must be aware that my concern is mainly to convince the reader that the prehistory of man may in fact be reduced to two great chapters: that of preagricultural times, during which man lived as a parasite of nature, and that of agricultural times, in which man was a producer.

Furthermore, I divide agricultural times into two periods: the archaic, in which one took advantage of the natural resources of the region in which one lived, and the period of intensive and extensive agriculture during which one settled (with the help of great hydrological works) the new lands necessary for the existence of big cities. All the rest is only nuances and details, certainly interesting, but of purely technological significance.

The reader will have observed that I prefer the term *society* to those of *civilization* or *culture.* Classical authors spoke of the Chibcha or Nazca civilizations and so forth. To me the term seems poorly chosen to describe the life of small groups of farmers or fishermen-peasants who were still headhunters. Moreover, *civilization* implies that the "civilized" skirted the "uncivilized." The term introduces a notion of degree and depreciates that which does not meet certain criteria, highly imprecise in themselves and to which one refers in order to justify the use of the word *civilization*. *Culture* is even worse. How many definitions have been formulated for the word? One hundred fifty, perhaps, which plainly indicates that the concept is not very clear. *Society,* on the other hand, seems to me to suit any group exceeding the level of a few families.

Another classical term I shall use is *horizon*. It designates a span of time during which several societies existed side by side, revealing common cultural traits but without our yet knowing the nature of the ties that might have existed between these societies.

Indeed, in reality the process of development that the societies of the Near East and Andes underwent was parallel, and it is only on the chronological chart that differences appear. As René Grousset expressed it so well, with respect to a comparison between the Americas and Asia, "It is simply a question of anteriority." And my thought joins that scholar's when he says that "even if we have sprung from the Mesopotamian seed and Mediterranean classicism, we cannot, nor should we, neglect India, China, and the Americas as sources of cultures." If science was born between the Tigris and the Euphrates, was not art born in western Europe, in the Magdalenian caves of Lascaux and Altamira?

The causes of the slow development of the Americas have remained unexplained to this day, but various hypotheses have been formulated on the subject. The most plausible, in my opinion, is the one that gives responsibility for the phenomenon to their remoteness. The next chapter will describe the Andean environment in greater detail. For now, let me say that it is extremely harsh, in good part very arid, and that it confronts man with serious obstacles in matters of communications; that agriculture there is difficult, subject to variations in climate —gradual, to be sure—but dramatic in effect, because they affect the water resources.

Moreover, the Near East constituted a center of communications among peoples and a focal point for the diffusion of thought and experimentation, born of contacts between very diverse groups. Contact between two societies acts as a stimulant when the groups that come into contact with each other are sufficiently large and dynamic. This phenomenon is not observed among very small groups, which may be too weak to provide dynamism, the will necessary to try to modify their way of life. But the desire to copy one's neighbor is evident practically everywhere, whether in Europe or in America. There are fashions: the mestizo copied the Spaniard, the forest group copied the cultural traits of the Inca societies. The rape of women, a constant and reciprocal operation between two neighboring groups that is rendered necessary by the requirements of exogamous rules of living, also favored the diffusion of inventions. But, unlike the Near East, the Americas were cut off by two vast oceans, with the world of the Andes even more isolated. The Andes world was barred from the sea to the east by the "green hell," the Amazonas, so conditions there were not propitious for exchanges and contacts, and America had to create its original civilization autonomously.

The majority of Andeans today, our contemporaneous citizens of the South American republics, are offended when one reminds them that their pre-Columbian ancestors lived in prehistory—that they formed societies which did not write. This is a psychological situation that curbs the study of the pre-Columbian past: an ancient prejudice considers the contributions of preliterate peoples to world culture to be essentially negligible, and there are still numerous scholars specializing in the ancient history of the Mediterranean world who refuse to attach the slightest importance to what American prehistory has to offer. We have forgotten that our nineteenth-century masters themselves took a hundred years to accept the idea that our ancestors—Gauls, Germans, or Scandinavians—had some worth, and that their entrance into history was not the consequence of their Romanization. The fact of not writing did not, moreover, prevent the ninth-century Normans from conquering a good part of western Europe, and the great Mongol Khans, who reached the very threshold of Vienna, never wrote.

History or prehistory, what does it matter? The finality of our labor is man. We do not judge societies, and above all, not in an ethnocentric fashion. We are content to observe facts. Besides, such an approach to problems enriches us further: by avoiding the introduction of degrees of value, of comparisons founded on a notion of "good," "bad," or "better," we shall escape the dangers of a graduation in the appreciation of facts that astonish us, but which seem strange to us only because they result from different concepts.

It is essential, in the domain of applied anthropology, to avoid anything that might be felt by someone we are speaking with as a loss of prestige. The defect of our anthropology is, moreover, that it suffers from Europeocentrism, that it judges problems in terms of the education *we* have been given.

In reaction, to avoid this fault we are at times inclined to rush forward, to formulate premature judgments, and to irritate the person with whom we are speaking, because of an untimely zeal. Thus, only a few years ago it was difficult in South America to overcome the prejudices existing against that which was pre-Columbian. For example, even if the Peruvian declared himself proud of his Inca predecessors, he recoiled from the opportunity to make contact with that which could give him a precise and concrete vision of the existence of the populations from which he was descended. He detested archaeological excavations, therefore, and did not understand their meaning.

Generally speaking, even if an Andean belongs to a cultivated milieu, he is unaware that he is either a Eurasian or, according to his degree of crossbreeding, a nearly pure Asian. Therefore, he suffers from complexes that result from the contempt the Spaniards have always shown for the Indians, a contempt that the nouveaux riches and those South Americans who have "made it" socially still affect in our time. The Indian has unconsciously remained the vanquished. It is not a question of skin color but of social status; a poor man will remain an Indian or a *cholo*, a mestizo; a rich man will no longer be one. The word *Spain* has more deep-seated resonance than one thinks—to be Spanish is to be a civilized person and not a barbarian. The rich Indian who speaks Spanish will become a gentleman. I am acquainted with people who would be insulted if one praised the merits of the pre-Columbian societies to them. "He is telling me that because he takes me for an Indian," they think. But the wound would be, if not as acute, at least as deep if I were to show contempt for what is not Hispanic.

It is possible to stop these complexes by recalling, for example, that the Gauls were not writing two thousand years ago; that the Russians learned to write only a little while before the American peoples; that Pizarro and Almagro themselves could neither read nor sign their names; that Europe and the Near East witnessed continual upheavals, invasions, and crossbreedings. The Spanish invasion of the Andes constituted only one episode among all those that have affected the stability of societies throughout the world. One should therefore not agonize over the fact that one is not of pure Hispanic blood, but should on the contrary be proud, as are for example the Japanese, to belong to the Asiatic world.

The Andean's distrust of archaeological excavations also stems from the fact that, his country having always been exploited by strangers, he was never convinced that the aim of excavations was not the pillaging of hidden treasures. And the mania to uncover treasures is still rampant. Twenty years ago, adventurers in Lima frequently used to ask you to finance expeditions to discover gold. They sold you dead lodes; they offered you treasures stolen from graves. Now they are searching for booty sunk with galleons in the Caribbean Sea.

It was necessary to come to the present young generations, to the students of today (mostly products of the new cities surrounding Lima and the other capitals), or the sons of emigrants who came down from the high Andes to look for work in the cities, to make them agree to contemplate their ancestors in the perspective of actual historical events. And in order to do this we had to teach them that the Gallic houses of Alesia were no more beautiful than those of the inhabitants of the Peruvian coasts of two thousand years ago.

In short, the evolved Andean insists he is considering himself the descendant of an illustrious race, but he refuses to look at the ruins of his pre-Columbian past.

With regard to Hispanic monuments, it is the anticolonialist and anticlerical prejudices that interfere; only a literate minority and some fervent Catholics escape them. For the majority of Andeans, a beautiful baroque church is identified with the hated colonial regime. Also, among simple folk (be they workers, city people, or peasants) it seems completely natural to replace these old things with something new, to bury the Indian grandmother under a nice concrete tenement. The farmer in the Andes will thus replace his tile roof with corrugated iron, and the village priest will sell the baroque decorations of the temple to a passing merchant in order to install neon lights.

Despite four centuries of Spanish indoctrination, Andeans maintain a repulsion for Cartesian thinking. They only appear to reason like Europeans; it is always difficult for us to foresee their reactions. With time, one ends up guessing the code of good manners, interpreting the hidden meaning of sentences, of certain deceptions that we mistakenly call lies, for they are, rather, diplomacy, a science of savoir faire, the means to escape while saving face. Saving face is a major preoccupation of Andeans. For example, a leader must never appear weak;

if he is in trouble, one pretends not to notice it. I remember being on a balky horse, isolated among the rocks of the high cordillera, and my foremen continuing their journey, without turning around.

As they have always been totally swindled by foreigners, why should we expect Andeans to have other feelings for us than those ranging, according to the circumstances, from distrust to hate? Even the sincere affection that we may have for them, and all the friendly and disinterested gestures that we may attempt will most often be wrongly interpreted. Cooperation will remain difficult, for instinct tells the Andean that the European is incapable of a gratuitous action—if he pretends to give something, it is really to make a theft in other respects. This idea is so deeply rooted that in certain social groups a man is not respected unless he shows himself to be *macho,* or virile, by succeeding in playing a nasty trick on his competitor, the government, or the community.

Fortunately for the archaeologist, the Andes are dry, totally arid even on the Pacific Coast. Thus, the excavations there yield many more documents than do Europe and Asia, in the form of clothing, wooden objects, remains of food, plants, and a host of materials that would have disappeared somewhere else. Therefore, the absence of written documents is somewhat compensated for by the very rich booty yielded by the buried villages.

In the Andes, the first years of Hispanicization may be called protohistoric, since scribes, or chroniclers, as they were called, noted down the last convulsions of the indigenous civilizations. I shall, therefore, refer to their texts as much as possible, but with due caution, for writing prehistory is even more difficult than writing history. Even in history, it is hard to remain completely objective, to avoid any commitment. In prehistory, we are writing secondhand, since we are interpreting the information that we procure from excavations. As François Braudel says, "True history begins with the document." But here the document is unwritten, and, what is more, it is fleeting, for even in careful excavating, one destroys. Thus, I shall be cautious first because most chronicles were written well after the Conquest, when the societies of the pre-Columbian world had already been destroyed; then because of the obvious prejudice of the writers, men whom no instruction in ethnology or history had prepared for objectivity, the basis of all anthropological study. Thus, their works reflect either their passions or a mission, and serious misrepresentations of the facts have resulted. Besides, a multitude of details relating to the thought, poetry, and art of the natives, which would have interested us prodigiously, were never transmitted.

I shall refer more to the documents offered by ethnology. Tribes scarcely touched by Europeanization have survived until recently. Groups of natives still live in the northern Andes as their ancestors lived, or nearly so. Other groups have unfortunately disappeared, but ethnologists in the beginning of the twentieth century still knew them and wrote studies of great interest about them. It would, therefore, be absurd not to instruct ourselves, not to try to understand the motivations and actions that are incomprehensible on first sight by observing the behavior of these likable fossils of a completed past.

Before dreaming of writing syntheses and painting great historical frescoes, we should, then, patiently gather and analyze facts and force ourselves to paint, with small strokes, a succession of tableaus.

Many people still do not understand that the problem can be approached only from this angle. How many times have I not been asked, at the beginning of a conference or a university course, "What did such and such a people think? What was their religious conception of the universe?" How should I reply, when we hardly know who were the people in question, and where, how, and when they lived?

It is not the time, therefore, given the present state of archaeological research, to do more than put in place, in a geographical environment that will first be sketched in its broadest outlines, a certain number of facts, valid because they are supported by concrete documentation that can already be dated.

Moreover, after reading this work, the reader will fully grasp the acuteness of the problem created by the painful lack of documentation that we suffer. He will discover the long hiatuses, the obscure voids of several centuries that quite frequently separate the few events we know.

With respect to the very early periods, information regarding social organization is still completely lacking. We can only proceed in this domain, therefore, by comparison with ethnological studies of simple societies, of nonagricultural tribes that have been studied recently.

With respect to the high Holocene period, we know practically nothing at all about the migrations of peoples, the invasions. In matters of art, we are still to observe the first stammerings. For all that is very far from us in time. Therefore, I shall mainly make observations of an economic and ecological character, using what excavations of encampments and villages yield to us, in view of learning more about habitat, dietary customs, and agricultural techniques. For want of something better, information of this order will already permit us to place the people whose life we are studying in an environment, in a geographical and climatic framework, and, thanks to radiocarbon dating, into a chronology.

For the more recent periods, we are apparently better informed, but perhaps only apparently. In fact, the information is most often based on archaeologists' studies of only certain aspects of life. Sadly, up to recent years, investigators were particularly fond of observing the evolution of pottery decoration and of devoting themselves to the pursuit of nice objects to put in their museums. Hence the pillaging of graves, which a famous anthropologist ironically called sepulchrology. Generally, it is the violation of tombs that has furnished the essential documents that have served to construct a sketch of South American prehistory.

Now tombs alone are far from providing us with all the elements we need to form an idea of what may have been the life of the pre-Columbians. I have, therefore, elaborated the plan of my work in the Andes while bearing in mind the differing natures of my sources and accepting the necessity of collecting data of a very diversified character: environmental, technological, statistical, and so on.

After the introduction and a description of the geographical environment, I have devoted a chapter to the Andes of the sixteenth century. In it I shall briefly relate the history of European penetration into the continent, and then discuss the existing population and social organization according to the Spaniards' description of them. Finally, I have added several pages relating to the thought of the Andeans in matters of philosophy, cosmogony, and religion, based on ethnological reports and my own personal contacts. Not until Chapter Four will the contributions appear of field archaeology of the excavations themselves, insofar as they have produced valid results.

That being said, this work has only a modest claim to originality. So many things have already been written about the Andes, in a thousand forms and by highly talented authors, that my personal contribution will be but minimal with regard to the existing documentation. My aim is essentially to facilitate for everyone an easy and sufficiently broad understanding of a world whose past no cultivated person should fail to appreciate.

After devoting years to explorations, laboratory work, and excavations, one wonders if one's most valid contribution will not result quite simply from his mere presence on the soil, in the most diverse landscapes, ranging from the snowy peaks of the high Andes and the *puna* (bleak tablelands) to the tropical forests and great coastal deserts, and from one's knowledge of the mentality of its inhabitants. I have traveled through this land on foot, by mule, and by jeep in the course of long tours totaling more than thirty thousand miles. I have planted my shovel and trowel into many thousands of pre-Columbian sites, and raised the plans of buildings, huts, houses, and villages almost everywhere, with the exceptions of Patagonia and the Argentine eastern Andes. It is this direct contact with the Andes that has best allowed me to appreciate the grandeur of this vanished world and the human worth of those who built societies there.

I have acquired my experience of the Andes in various ways:

• Through explorations realized notably for the United Nations, explorations whose aim was to create an embryonic inventory of the pre-Columbian and Hispanic cultural patrimony of the countries in the Andean bloc. Thus, I had the opportunity not only to visit, but also to investigate the majority of the archaeological sites on the west of the continent.

• Through excavations. For the last twelve years, supported financially by the Department of Cultural Relations of the French Ministry of Foreign Affairs, occasionally by the French National Center of Scientific Research, and constantly aided also by the national Peruvian university, I have continuously maintained working excavation sites, as much in the high and middle Andes as in the oases and deserts of the coastal plains.

These excavations have led me to live long months in the field each year in the company of a team of Peruvians who were Europeanized to extremely varied degrees, and I am happy to declare that in my life I have had few experiences that have been so pleasant. The native of the Andes, once one has gained his confidence, shows himself to be a very hard-working individual, endowed with great qualities of endurance, good will, and politeness, skillful at living on little in the most frustrating situations; in short, the ideal companion for conducting expeditions in arid and difficult territories.

• Finally, through education at the university level, and laboratory teamwork. Perhaps it is this university experience and permanent contact with young students, most of whom are little or not at all Europeanized, that has given me, along with the excavations, the greatest satisfaction.

·1·

THE ENVIRONMENT

GEOGRAPHY

The South American continent covers an area of approximately 7,200,000 square miles and may be schematically divided into geographically well-marked zones.

The Andean range or cordillera constitutes the backbone of the continent. (It seems that the term *Andes* comes from the Quechua word *anti*, meaning *east*, or maybe from *antasuyo*, meaning *zone of metals*.) The cordillera stretches over more than six thousand miles, from the archipelago of Tierra del Fuego in the south to the Antilles and the Caracas chain in the northeast.

The Andes wind around. If they form a continuous chain, it is not rectilinear. Starting at the seventeenth parallel of north latitude, they curve to form a sort of lunar crescent encompassing the continent. The highest summits reach twenty-three thousand feet. The Atrato River, which separates the cordillera from the Isthmus of Darien, forms a boundary conveniently separating South America from Central America, but actually the cordillera continues toward Panama, beyond the Gulf of Uraba.

Utterly peculiar geographical conditions prevail along a lengthy stretch in the lowlands of the Pacific slope of the cordillera. I shall return to this point in greater detail, for this region played a prominent role in pre-Columbian history. For the moment, let me say simply that the coast here is rainy and cold as far as about thirty degrees of south latitude, then completely dry and temperate, then tropical from the equator onward.

To the east of the cordillera there stretches out almost uniformly an immense domain of hills and plateaus; dry, semiarid, or grassy low plains; or the terrain is very humid and wooded, according to the exposure and latitude. These plains originate in the Orinoco Basin and run as far down as Patagonia. The hills and plateaus of the Guianas and eastern Brazil rarely attain six thousand feet in elevation.

The maritime fringe of the continent is split into a great number of islands. I shall cite here only the principal ones. In the south are Tierra del Fuego and an archipelago whose principal member is Chiloé. Off the coast of Peru there are only some rocky islets, but off the coast of Guayaquil the puna has played a historic role. In the Caribbean Sea we may recall the presence of Aruba, Curaçao, Bonaire, Margarita, the Lesser Antilles, and Trinidad. Finally, Maracá and Marajó, at the mouth of the Amazon, have been equally inhabited since ancient times.

The Falkland Islands, facing Argentina 250 miles offshore, have been known since 1591, but they were apparently unpopulated. However, Louis Antoine de Bougainville points out the presence of a fox-dog reminiscent of the yellowish dog I have found in pre-Columbian graves. These dog bodies should be studied further and compared to those still found in the Chaco.

The Galapagos Islands and Easter Island must have played a role in the prehistory of this part of the globe, be it only as ports of call, voluntary or otherwise, in the course of transpacific voyages, but tradition incorporates them into Oceania. Pre-Columbian pottery has, however, been found in the Galapagos, and it is difficult not to make comparisons between certain South American statues and those of Easter Island, as between the polyhedral walls of Cuzco and those of the Marquesas Islands.

The theme of this work being the Andes, I shall speak only occasionally of that which does not constitute the cordillera, on which all our attention will focus. Less elevated along the Atlantic, from Trinidad to Lake Maracaibo, the Andes rise massively as soon as one penetrates the Sierra de Mérida and into Colombia. The Sierra Nevada de Santa Marta plunges into the ocean from a summit reaching eighteen thousand eight hundred feet and situated scarcely twenty-four miles from the Atlantic shore.

Before reaching the Isthmus of Darien, where the Andes start turning abruptly toward the south, the cordillera divides into two or three chains, separated by valleys or plateaus. This division lasts, with fleeting interruptions, until about the thirtieth degree, at the latitude of Valparaíso. One should thus remember, when I mention later in this book episodes referring to a crossing of the

Andes, that such adventures did not only mean the crossing of a single high barrier but, according to the route adopted, of two or three cordilleras separated by very deep canyons. At about the twenty-fifth parallel, salt lakes, *salares* or salt marshes, and deserts like that of Atacama further complicated the route.

This is what the traveler crossing the Andes along the twelfth parallel, approximately east of Lima, will observe: The capital of Peru extends between 300 and 850 feet above sea level, and its port, Callao, is scarcely higher than the level of the high tide of the Pacific. But 66 miles farther east, one is at almost the same height as the summit of Mont Blanc in the Alps, since it is at 16,000 feet that one goes through Ticlio Pass, which permits one, after crossing the puna, to reach (at about 10,000 feet) the Andean valley of the Mantaro. After that, one must cross the white cordillera at 16,500 feet, then finally the eastern cordillera, before descending to the Amazonas.

To get to Cuzco, following the coast and passing through Nazca, the traveler will find the same extremes: After 345 miles of desert coasts intersected by oases, he will ascend to about 16,500 feet before going down again, almost to sea level, at the bottom of the Apurimac canyon, from which he will have to go up again to Abancay, descend again, then finally ascend once more to go down into the Cuzco Valley.

At Cuzco he will in no way be on the eastern slope of the Andes. He will have to cross the puna once more, then go down again to 6,600 feet in the Urubamba Valley, from which he will have to climb up to the Larès Pass to skirt the snowy Veronica massif at 15,840 feet.

The width of this system can in no way compare to its expanse. At the center, only four hundred fifty miles separate the Amazonian lowlands from the Pacific shores, penetrated by the last spurs of the Andes. At its narrowest the cordillera barely measures sixty to ninety miles. In Ecuador, the extreme crests of the two cordilleras, dotted with volcanoes, are only sixty miles apart. On the Pacific slopes, the contrasts are such that if we trace a line from Taltal to Chile we would find, sixty miles to the west, an oceanic trough 23,100 feet deep and, 120 miles to the east, the Falso Azufre Glacier, 22,400 feet high, making a change in altitude of about eight and a half miles.

A great proportion of this territory is made up of extreme highlands, exceedingly tortuous and cut up almost everywhere by deep fractures. The mean altitude of Andean territory exceeds ten thousand feet. Fifty-seven peaks exceed eighteen thousand feet. Most of the cultivated surfaces are between seven- and thirteen thousand feet.

It is not unusual in Peru to travel roads overhanging sheer abysses from fifteen hundred to three thousand feet deep. Few situations leave a more intoxicating memory than traveling in the Andes in the black of night on a mule, going along a track bordering precipices 1,650 feet deep, without parapets. The mule doesn't walk in the middle of the track, rutted by the rains—she chooses to advance along the little outer crest, very narrow, which separates the abyss from the muddy trail. There is nothing left to do then but close one's eyes.

Sometimes the crupper holding the saddle gives, and abruptly the rider flies toward the abyss, happily stopped on the way by a tuft of bushes. At other times the mule is blind, or almost so. Then she sniffs at the obstacle, and when a fallen tree bars the way, she presses her nose against it. Then suddenly, without warning, she clears the whole thing with a great flying leap, hardly agreeable to the rider on her back carrying heavy equipment that bangs into him.

On the western slope of the cordillera, flat surfaces are found only in a few relatively small zones: in the north, around the Gulf of Maracaibo, along the banks of the lower Magdalena River, around its low tributaries, and finally, around the Atrato River. Farther south, these low, flat areas may be found at the equator, in the vicinity of Buenaventura, Tumaco, and the Daule River. Some forested lowlands are also found in the Guayaquil Delta. After that, one must go down to the fifth parallel of south latitude and reach the Sechura Desert to find again an altitude below three hundred feet. Finally, in Chile, the atlases show little green spots indicating low altitudes only south of Santiago, below the thirty-third degree, and at the tip of Chiloé Island. Elsewhere, the Andes penetrate into the ocean almost everywhere, the tormented Andes, with their lofty summits, where intense volcanic activity still prevails in some areas.

Geologically speaking, the volcanoes are of recent origin, whereas the cordillera is ancient and has experienced periods of subsidence and elevation during which the seas penetrated far into the continent. This explains why one finds the remains of marine animals in alpine landscapes and whale bones near Cuzco. Very powerful folds, which supervened 70 million years ago, gave the cordillera its present face.

To contemplate from close up the volcanoes in eruption, it is enough to go to Ecuador. Near Quito one can see them in numbers: Cotopaxi, Chimborazo, Cotocachi, Sanguay, and Tunguragua are mentioned most frequently. In Peru, El Misti, which dominates the city of Arequipa, is still wreathed with smoke. Volcanic activity resumes at the sixteenth parallel. In Chile, where the summits again reach twenty-three thousand feet, the line of volcanoes extends as far as to the south of Santiago, after which the cordillera becomes progressively lower, to plunge finally into the ocean. The snow line drops in the same way, going from sixteen thousand feet to zero. The chaotic character of the Andes appears even in the island of Tierra del Fuego, where there again rises a peak eight thousand feet high.

We know that a long and narrow fringe subject to continual seismic movements surrounds the North Pacific. The South American cordillera is part of this unstable system, and the earth there is always being jolted. Landslides that result then form natural barriers, and these are smashed on the occasion of another quake, thus liberating torrents of water and mud that eliminate all life in their passage. The coasts, on the other hand, are periodically affected by tidal waves. The Andes are thus one of the most tormented and bruised regions in our universe, and their inhabitants must have been extremely attached to their land not to have abandoned it.

Arequipa, Lima, Trujillo, and Cuzco have by turns several times been either totally destroyed or seriously affected by earthquakes. Valdivia in Chile was ravaged in 1960 by an earth tremor followed by a tidal wave that penetrated the bay of Paracas, in Peru, after returning from Japan. In 1970, fifty thousand persons perished in Peru in cascades of mud or rockslides in the inter-Andean valley of the Santa. In Lima and Santiago, the earth trembles at least once a week, and the Peruvian capital has experienced during the last thirty years three quakes exceeding the seventh degree on the Richter scale.

CLIMATE

Latitude and altitude are not the only factors dominating the climate of the Andes. In Caracas, the northern cordillera is at the tenth degree of north latitude, and Lima, the capital of Peru, is still at only twelve degrees south latitude, a position comparable to that of Martinique. The lowlands of the territory that interests us should therefore have for the most part an equatorial or tropical climate. Even Santiago, at the thirty-third degree, should enjoy a much higher mean temperature.

The actual situation is quite different. The Pacific Coast, from the seaport of Bahía de Caráquez, situated on the equator just below the zero parallel, to the Santa Elena Peninsula, two degrees lower, should be torrid; but in fact it is cool and foggy in winter and temperate in summer, with totally abnormal maximal temperatures of eighty-four degrees Fahrenheit.

After passing the jungle of Guayas, one again finds the same climate the whole length of the coast, from the third parallel of south latitude in Peru to about the twenty-seventh parallel in Chile. All along this long fringe, and except for some exceptional spots I shall mention below, it practically never rains. (At an altitude of 12,210 feet, in Chile and Bolivia, only 2.4 inches of rain fall annually, as opposed to over 40 inches in New York.) This is true up to an altitude that varies with the latitude and oscillates between thirty-three hundred and fifty-seven hundred feet. This second fringe receives a little rain, but it is still arid. But in the lowlands, life is possible only in the oases, where springs flow, or in the vicinity of a river or watercourse.

These unexpected climatic conditions are caused by the general atmospheric circulation that brings hot air over the coastal area, whereas the winds, which blow permanently from the south-southeast, favor a northward movement of the cold ocean waters. This is called the Humboldt Current. In fact, the waters are cold not because they are carried up from the Antarctic, as was thought in earlier days, but because they are brought up from a great depth—the Pacific reaches depths of twenty-three to twenty-six thousand feet at various places along the southern continent.

The cool air brought over the lowlands by these winds is damp, but it cannot condense and change into rain, because of the hot air that circulates above the phenomenon, called a temperature inversion. So, during the southern winter, from May to November, meteorological conditions are such that the sky is most often foggy. In Lima, where one sometimes goes a week without seeing the sun, and the humidity reaches almost 100 percent, this fog forms only a light, fine drizzle, and in total no more than four to eight tenths of an inch of water are collected during a whole year. Winter temperatures vary between fifty-five and sixty-four degrees Fahrenheit. Above twenty-six hundred to thirty-three hundred feet, the sky remains completely blue, with the sun dazzling all year round. No rain or fog can form, which causes the lower Andes to remain completely arid.

In summer, the inverse happens: the coast is sunny and clear, but rains brought over from the Atlantic by the easterly winds darken the sky over the high cordillera, which then suffers hail and snowstorms, but these rains are not felt much beyond the line of crests. As soon as one moves away from the high summits, the annual rainfall is reduced to no more than about eight inches. In the central Andes, it does not rain in useful quantities until over ten thousand feet.

It is true that a short and heavy squall sometimes hits the coast, but such a phenomenon is very occasional, when meteorological circumstances permit a larger volume of rains to pass over from the Atlantic. During the last hundred years, episodes of this nature have been observed only in 1970, 1925, and 1891. Man can thus not count on rain to survive.

Beyond the twenty-seventh degree of south latitude, the coastal climate remains temperate for a few hundred miles, but it gets increasingly rainy as one approaches the Pole. The vicinity of Chiloé Island still constitutes a zone propitious to agriculture, but the extreme south of Chile, called Patagonia, is too cold for farming. The climate is unpleasant, with violent winds blowing and glaciers finally plunging into the ocean.

The climate is evidently quite different in the regions not subject to the effects of the corrective factors just described. For example, the Gulf of Guayaquil, which separates Ecuador from Peru, constitutes a warm enclave between two temperate zones. Here the effect of tropical waters brought by rivers counteracts that of the cold marine waters.

In Ecuador, northward of the province of Manabí and Bahía de Caráquez around the equator, the cold current gives way to the equatorial countercurrent, and the coast becomes tropical, covered with a luxuriant vegetation that penetrates right into the ocean, with palm trees being unearthed by waves. The rain here falls in abundance, reaching up to twenty-five feet annually in the Colombian Chocó, in comparison to the eight feet accumulated in Jamaica. Cities like Cartagena and Barranquilla, situated on the Atlantic at sea level, suffer from an annual mean temperature of eighty-four degrees Fahrenheit.

The hinterland of these tropical shores, however, has been favorable to man. Agriculture prospered and great fields of maize were sown there in pre-Columbian times. But today, deforestation has led to a drying out of the soil, and the valleys of the Atrato, the Sinú, and the lower Magdalena are in the process of being overrun with high grasses, introduced by settlers breeding cattle, hybrids of zebus (Asiatic oxen) and European cows.

Eastward of the cordillera, the climate of the Amazonas is entirely tropical —very hot and more or less humid according to the region. Once one has crossed the cordillera and walked through the forests covering the eastern slope of the Andes, one penetrates (at an altitude of about twenty-five hundred feet) into a jungle landscape with undulating hills, where one must withstand temperatures exceeding eighty-six degrees Fahrenheit, and where the humidity, heat, and insects create unhealthy and unpleasant living conditions, especially because there are no breezes to refresh the air during the night. The vegetation, luxuriant and overgrown, forms a dense cover under which everything stays damp and rots. Only a few large species, like American oaks and palm trees, point toward the sky: this is the "green hell."

To find refuge in more normal climatic conditions, the immigrants regained altitude, climbing back up the Andes. But there again, the nearness of the equator intervened to undercut the usual mechanisms. In towns like Tingo Maria, at twenty-five hundred feet, it is still very hot, even at night, and typhus and other diseases are endemic. Even in the middle and high Andes, local geographical conditions create unexpected situations. Thus, for example, glaciers continue to exist today only above fifteen thousand feet in most of the cordillera, and as a result of warm air climbing up from the Amazonas, tropical forests are found along some eastern slopes until an altitude of ten thousand feet. This is what geographers call the cold forest, or tropical woodland.

Even situated between thirteen thousand and sixteen thousand feet, the high, grassy plateaus, the puna, and the *paramos* (alpine meadows) of Ecuador, Peru, and Bolivia are never covered by snow. Temperatures are not severe in the high Andes; one suffers there from the cold because of the lack of oxygen. But in the inter-Andean valleys, cities situated at more than ten thousand feet, like Quito and Cuzco, do not have the low temperatures that affect Europe in winter. The thermometer descends little below freezing, and only during some nights in July and August. Very strong insolation (exposure to sun rays) is at work there, even through foggy skies, when one gets sunburned by ultraviolet rays.

The lack of a real winter is also manifested in another form. Because of the nearness of the equator, there is little difference between the lengths of day and night. Even southern Chile is far from long polar winters. In Lima, along the twelfth parallel, the discrepancy between day and night attains a maximum of forty-five minutes.

We would understand pre-Columbian history much better if we knew more about the past of the cordillera. Unfortunately, we are very poorly informed on the subject of Andean paleoclimatology. No correlation has been established between the climatic cycles that might have affected South America in the past and those that Europe and the United States have experienced. Thus, we can only make guesses about the effects that might have been produced in the cordillera by the cyclic cold periods that marked the other continents, interrupted with more-temperate stages. We all know that in Europe, the Himalayas, North America, and the Near East these cold cycles gave rise to ice ages during which glaciers and snows spread very widely. In the U.S.A., glaciers covered the ground as far as

Virginia. New York is built on basalt striated by ice. Central Europe did not escape the ice, and the Alps extended as far as Lyon.

But what would have happened during these periods in Africa and South America? Regarding Africa, one speaks of correlative pluvial phases. Apropos of the Andes, geologists inform us that glaciers, of which we now see the vestiges above sixteen thousand feet, were much more extensive. One speaks of eleven thousand five hundred feet as the lower boundary of ice floes. But the effects of glaciation are difficult to observe here because of the continual restructuring of an unstable, chaotic ground as a result of tectonic movements and the torrents of mud, water, and stones that are their usual result.

In order to establish a valid climatic curve, if only for the last hundred thousand years, it is necessary to turn to paleobotany. We know that the floras of warm periods are never the same as those of cold periods, in no matter what region of the globe. Now although the plants of past times survive only rarely, the pollens of these plants usually escape destruction. Thus, one finds them intact in marshes, peat bogs, and even in domestic hearths. Extending the study of these plants in South America, as done already for North American and European plants, and establishing a collection of types of present-day pollens, would enable us to compare these samples with those one finds in geological strata belonging to the Pleistocene period or, with respect to the last twenty thousand years, in sites formerly inhabited by man. As a climatic scheme for the Andean Late Pleistocene and Holocene epochs does not exist today, we frequently have recourse to a document established by Rhodes Fairbridge, the well-known geologist who devised a curve relating to the eustatic levels of the oceans. (Let us recall that the levels of the seas, leaving out the movements of the tides, stay the same in all oceans as a result of the effect known as "the principle of communicating vessels," in accordance with which the waters of adjoining vessels or seas will find an equilibrated, or eustatic, surface everywhere.)

During the last few million years, the seas have alternately known periods of high and low waters. To the periods of low waters correspond, though perhaps a little in advance, the colder periods. A cold period in effect signifies an absorption of water by glaciers and clouds and, consequently, a subsiding of the level of the sea, or a marine regression; that is to say, a recession of the water, which disengages itself from the beaches and makes shoals appear. Thus, the Bering Sea separating Asia from North America could be crossed on dry land, and New Guinea was united to the Asian continent during the peaks of the cold episodes.

To the warm periods, on the contrary, correspond the periods of high waters. The level of the sea rises, coastal towns are swallowed up, fishing villages too near the shore disappear. Investigators who intend to study the prehistory of the populations of the coastal Andes have to remember that the Pacific coastline experienced considerable variations throughout the period characterized by the ice ages: fifteen thousand years ago, the Pacific's waters were found some three hundred feet below the present level. They then progressively climbed to an elevation exceeding the present level by sixteen feet, and finally began a series of oscillations causing variations of from sixteen and a half to twenty-three feet before reaching the level we see today, which will of course not remain stable in the long run, but which we use as a geologic marker.

One understands, therefore, that all early pre-Columbian sites situated at the edge of the sea have quite simply disappeared. It is useless to search, below a line joining all the points situated at sixteen to nineteen feet below the level of present-day high waters, for establishments more than thirty-five hundred years old, the date of the highest and last of the known rises, which occurred about fifteen hundred years before the Christian era.

The Andes must not have known profound climatic upheavals during the formation of the cordillera, some millions of years ago. Geologists and archaeologists are agreed on this point. The Peruvian desert is very, very old. Traces of great stability in the macroclimate (the overall climate) are observable almost everywhere. As far as the Holocene epoch is concerned, I have found on the dry coast of Peru villages more than ten thousand years old, which have preserved, frequently intact, organic matter and the skeletons of the inhabitants in their cerements. Individuals are often found wrapped in numerous pieces of clothing, with the flesh in place and sometimes even the eyes in their sockets. If it had rained, all these remains, buried close to the surface, would have been swept away.

Archaeology shows us, on the other hand, that though the macroclimate remained stable, the Andean territory experienced localized climatic crises. One will recall the seven years of plenty, followed by seven years of famine, in Egypt, as described in the Biblical story of Joseph.

I have already alluded to the torrents of mud as a consequence of an exceptionally heavy rain in the high cordillera. Such events may create catastrophic conditions in the low valleys, which are then ravaged by flooding. The cultivated fields painfully created by pre-Columbian farmers must thus have been washed away in a fashion similar to what I have observed today. This means that an excess of water could have dramatically affected the life of Neolithic populations just as much as a period of drought.

I suspect, furthermore, that oscillations of the marine level could also have disturbed the lives of the pre-Columbians. At the edges of beaches, fresh waters are kept from seeping deep into the earth by the denser sea waters. It is therefore possible that a subsiding of the saltwater level could have produced a seeping away of the freshwater sheet and rendered a coastal territory sterile by drying up the wells or rendering inaccessible the subterranean waters feeding the oases. On the other hand, a marine transgression could have introduced salt water into the freshwater sheets.

Like all peasants in arid lands, the pre-Columbian farmers must have known periods of happy living followed by periods of famine. This hypothesis is supported by the fact that certain coastal territories were subject at different times to long periods of abandonment.

For want of something better, students of pre-Columbian America who need to know in what climatic framework this or that event revealed by archaeology occurred should refer to the Fairbridge curve and imagine that a period of low waters might have corresponded to a cooler cycle, and that a period of high waters corresponded to a more temperate cycle. They may also refer to the curves established for the United States, northern Europe, and the south of France that place the last retreat of the ice at about ten thousand five hundred years ago, in the high Holocene period, at the beginning of a warming up or "anathermal" period. This would have lasted three millennia, to reach its maximum or "alithermal" peak some seven thousand years ago. Subsequently, the world would have known a more temperate climatic stage, the so-called Atlantic phase, during which only slight cyclical variations would have affected the local climates, with the macroclimate remaining stable.

Here are the Andean climates, according to one commonly used system of classification.

Af:	Tropical rains	Llanos		Af
Aw:	Savannahs, dry winters	Manabí, Manta,		
Bsh:	Hot steppes	Guayaquil, Ayabaca		Aw
Bwhn:	Hot desert, thick fogs	Cool coast of Ecuador and		
Bwk:	Desert, cold winters	Peru		Bwhn
Bwkn:	Desert, cold and foggy winters	High central Andes and southern Chilean archipelago		E
Bsk:	Cold steppes	Santiago, Chile		Bsh
Cwk:	Mesothermal, dry summers and cool winters	Peru and Chile between parallels 18 and 30		Bwkn
Csb:	Mediterranean	Northern Araucania		Csb
Cfb:	Humid mesothermal, cold winters	Southern Araucania and Patagonia		Cfb
Cfc:	Humid mesothermal, very cold winters	Eastern slopes of the Andes from Venezuela to the		
E:	Tundra	twenty-third parallel in		
	Andes of Venezuela and northern Colombia	Aw	Chile	Cwb
	Cartagena, La Guajira	Bsh	Farther south	Cfc
	Lower Magdalena	Aw	Below	Bsk
	Atrato	Af	Farther south	Bwk
	Andes of Colombia, Ecuador, and Peru	Cwb		

HYDROGRAPHY

The Andes are crossed by numerous rivers, some of which are very large, but the only one that is navigable is the Magdalena, which reaches the Caribbean after traversing all of Colombia. And even the Magdalena does not become navigable until it reaches the lowlands, at an altitude of about three thousand feet.

A small number of rivers, notably those of the central Andes, flow in a general north-south or south-north direction before turning to begin their abrupt descents toward the Pacific in the west or the forests in the east. This is the case with the Santa, the Mantaro, and the Apurimac in Peru.

But on the contrary, other rivers, like the Cauca and the Magdalena, traverse more than one thousand miles from south to north before reaching the Atlantic, as if the Rhone were to have its source in Marseilles and flow into the North Sea at Hamburg.

It is essentially the large rivers of Peru, Ecuador, and Colombia that create the enormous Amazon, fed also by the Atlantic's rains. I shall not speak of the Amazon here, for though it is born in the cordillera, it is not, strictly speaking, an Andean river.

All the South American rivers that empty into the Pacific are dangerous, torrential, and subject to considerable jumps in volume. Many of them remain dry a good part of the year. Even under the equator, and as a consequence of deforestation, the rivers coming down from the Andes toward the temperate coast of Ecuador are today no more than wadis or gullies, channels with intermittent flow. One must reach Esmeraldas, farther north, to find large rivers.

Past the warm waters of the Guayas and the Gulf of Guayaquil, only half of the sixty or so Peruvian rivers flow throughout the year. All the others are subject either to annual flooding or to cycles of complete dryness alternating with occasional years of torrential discharge.

In arid Chile the landscape is the same. Streams do not even reach the coast during normal years. One must go down below Santiago to find rivers in the strict sense of the word.

Another important element in the hydrography of the Andes is Lake Titicaca, which extends, at twelve thousand five hundred feet above the sea, over one hundred miles in length, and forms a sheet of water of about three thousand square miles. This plane of water is complemented by that of Lake Poopó, about twelve hundred sixty square miles. Titicaca is deep and navigable, filled with fresh water, whereas Poopó is salty and in the process of drying up, with a maximum depth of ten feet and bordered by *ciénegas*, or marshes. Neither of these lakes has an outlet to the sea; they are "inland seas."

LANDSCAPE

The Andean landscape is commonly described as the reflection of three large climatic zones: the coastal desert, the bare high Andes, and the Amazonian forest. This portrait, too schematized, calls for completion.

The dry coast, from Tumbes to the twenty-seventh degree of south latitude, is a peculiar mixture of deserts and human anthills. Far from the banks of rivers and streams, where the water sheet does not come near enough to the surface to create a savannah of acacias and mimosas, the earth is bare, without vegetation, covered with immense sand dunes wafted by the winds coming from the ocean. Elsewhere the soil is made of a mixture of pebbles and dust, from which emerge the rocks of the Andes.

Every twenty-five miles or so, this desert is cut by a stream or river, some of which dried up millennia ago, probably much earlier than the last ice age. As soon as a stream, a river, or a plane of water exists, it creates an oasis, and human life becomes possible.

Trees are rare in these oases today. The farmers think trees exhaust the ground and create unproductive surfaces. What a mistake! A plant cover would reduce evaporation and oppose the arrival of winds laden with salty marine sands, which invade the soil as soon as it is not protected by screens of trees.

Before Hispanicization, the coastal oases gave life to tufted savannahs. They were also the sites of very large cities. During Hispanicization, however, provincial life turned away to the central Andes and the coast remained practically bare.

The colonial administration and the insecurity of the times did not favor the development of cities in Peru. From the sixteenth century to the present, the coastal areas have remained empty, inhabited only by the poor laborers of the large farms that practiced industrialized agriculture. The elite lived in Lima, and the provincial towns (except for small cities like Trujillo, Cuzco, and Arequipa) were nothing but little markets. It was a very different situation in Mexico, which has always had an intense provincial life. Colombia also created large and lively towns almost everywhere.

Except for Lima and the city of Trujillo, life during Hispanicization was limited to the big farms, the *haciendas*. It was only in modern times that the reverse happened once more; Lima has grown in size so much in 125 years that it now has, with its harbor, Callao, more than two million inhabitants. Santiago, the capital of Chile, is also a large city, but it is situated far from the sea, at an altitude of sixteen hundred feet.

It is not enough to climb up into the dry Andes, into the gorges through which the rivers descend, to come upon a friendly landscape. Until one has reached the climatic floor that receives some rain, one sees nothing but dust and rocks.

More-pleasant surroundings created by grass, cultivation, and groves of eucalyptus imported from Australia are found in the high inter-Andean valleys, the high plains, or the foothills that form the piedmonts of the high summits. It is on this level that the cities of historical fame developed—Bogotá, Quito, Cajamarca, Cuzco, Arequipa, and La Paz are all situated at altitudes between ninety-two hundred and twelve thousand eight hundred feet.

In Colombia the evolution is different. A fringe of tropical forests isolates the ocean from interior lands. Then, once the coastal chain is crossed, one penetrates into the warm and relatively dry valleys of the Cauca and Magdalena. The mountain heights, here even more tortuous, create extremely varied and changing landscapes. Farther east one again finds the high Andean plateaus from which the glaciers and volcanoes emerge. Then, after crossing the last cordillera, one descends again toward the *llanos*, or plains.

Once one has passed beyond the cool desert coast of Chile to the south, below the twenty-seventh parallel, the landscape becomes Mediterranean. The valleys surrounding Santiago may remind one of Provence or Tunisia.

Farther down, Araucania is a land of lakes, forests, and fields. And at the very south, the coastal fringe becomes extremely narrow. One goes from forest to forest as far as Patagonia.

FLORA

Because of the highly varied climatological conditions prevailing in the Andes, one encounters there one of the richest floras in the world, one that is unfortunately very poorly studied. Only a few pioneers have begun to catalog it, and they have not been followed. This flora is furthermore characterized by a great variety of useful or edible plants producing fibers, bulbs, rhizomes, seeds, and fruits.

Among the plants with rhizomes, roots, and tubers, let me mention several species of potato—the sweet potato, manioc or cassava, jiquima (a rhizome), and ullucu.

Among the plants bearing edible seeds, let me note the alder, a kind of spinach (*quinoa*), as well as peanuts, beans, various species of mimosa, the pacay, acacias, and so forth. The graminaceous plants bear corn.

The edible fruits are quite numerous: tomatoes, pineapples, mamey (tropical apricot), guayavas (guavas), papayas, chirimoyas (similar to pawpaws), avocados, calabashes, Amazonian pomegranates, cactus fruits called *tunas*, lúcumas, and many others, such as mangoes, which were of colonial importation.

With regard to spices, let me cite the *aji*, or red pepper.

Useful fibrous plants abound. Cotton has been used for at least five or six thousand years in the Andes. It succeeded many other plant fibers that one could spin and employ in making clothing: rushes, cactus, *achupaya*—a Tillandsia that grows on sand—kapoks, and so on. Wool appeared late, when the pre-Columbians had learned to domesticate the auquenidés, a branch of the camelids.

Hallucinogens and innumerable medicinal plants were employed very early. The best-known and most widespread of all was the coca shrub, the source of cocaine. Alcoholic beverages were prepared with corn and the seeds of mimosas.

Three thousand years ago, Peruvians were already smoking cigars. Before that they took snuff, but used leaves unknown to us. It does not seem that smoking tobacco was known in the pre-Columbian Andes, where, on the other hand, other species of *Nicotiana* grow that were used for medicinal purposes.

Let me cite, finally, the existence of a great number of plants used to prepare dyes. The pre-Columbians obtained from them the most beautiful and varied tones.

I cannot describe here the flora of the tropical forest; it is too rich.

The cold and cool Andes are totally bare. Only some stunted bushes survive in the puna. Even in the coastal oases, trees have become scarce. The remaining species are mainly acacias, mimosas, pepper plants, willows, and a few bushy varieties.

It seems that this bareness of the Andes is the result of deforestation that started with the pre-Columbians, who were short of fuel and did not use coal and fossil fuels. Even today, to provide fodder for ten cows or so, farmers will set a whole forest on fire. I have witnessed a scene of this kind in the cold forest.

The deforestation undoubtedly accelerated with the arrival of the Spaniards, since they developed the mines in which, for want of fossil fuel, they consumed wood. Besides, the Spaniards introduced to America such destructive agents as cows, goats, and sheep.

Our contemporaries have completed the disaster for the needs of their mines and railroads. Even today, inhabitants of the Andes sometimes travel miles to bring back a little wood (be it only some withered cactus trunks) to feed their stoves, for charcoal is still not used. In the cities they use kerosine, transported first by truck, then manually from distribution center to house. Fortunately, the mean temperature is mild on the Peruvian coast.

FAUNA

The lack of an abundant fauna composed of large animals, especially domesticated ones, may have constituted one of the weak points of Andean ecologies.

The pre-Columbians had domesticated only dogs, two species of camelids (the llama and the alpaca), the guinea pig or cavy, and a type of duck. Dogs were domesticated very late, perhaps two thousand years ago, which means that the prefarming hunters had to operate in large bands, using nets to encircle the game. Even the turkey cock, a pet of the Mexicans, was absent from Andean farms, and the domestic cat seems to have been unknown there.

It is possible that the absence of pack and draft animals retarded the area's economic development. The llama carries a maximum of fifty-five pounds, so cannot carry a man. The ox and horse were unknown. Besides, even today, certain regions of the high Andes are accessible only with the help of mules and donkeys, so bad are the trails that lead to them.

Formerly, everything had to be carried on the backs of men or, in the case of construction materials, dragged along the ground. Only powerful personages could have themselves transported in litters.

Since two or three millennia ago, well before the arrival of the Spaniards, hunting seems to have played no more than an accessory role in the diets of Andeans, and to have maintained its importance only in the psychological sphere, as a masculine activity, a sport, probably of a magical character. The chroniclers tell us that the Inca princes reserved hunting rights for themselves, but it must have been a different situation in the chiefdoms. In hot lands where corn was cultivated, deer harassed the farmers and destroyed their harvests.

In terms of wild fauna, it is again necessary to distinguish between the hot and wooded Andes and the cold Andes. The hot, tropical Andes were the domain of small tigers, pumas, peccaries, monkeys, caimans (alligators), and sloths (the opossum), to cite only the principal species. The puma ranges up the eastern slopes as far as the edge of the cold forest. Thus I lost one of my dogs, which rushed to attack a puma in the high valley of Huanta.

Furthermore, the puma plays a large role in the iconography of the pre-Columbians. Stylized faces of felines were constantly modeled or painted on pottery, temple walls, and fabrics. Representations of felines were even woven into the garments of the Tiahuanacos. The Chavíns painted them on their garments (see Chapter Four).

Small bears have survived even in the central Andes. I have seen them in trees in the cold forest, feeding on fruits and honey. During the damp southern hemisphere winter, bears sometimes even go down as far as the coast, to within a few miles of the ocean, to browse in the fog oases.

One may hunt deer and roe deer in the arid Andes, but it is necessary to station oneself near water holes, where a fault makes the water sheet accessible. Driven by thirst, the game is obliged to approach.

In the rivers were different species of aquatic mammals and fishes. Today, terrestrial fauna are clearly less abundant. Birds, however, are quite numerous there, as are, of course, insects.

The cold Andes are sparsely populated. Surviving there are deer, roe deer, a few bears, opossums, rodents such as the vizcacha of the Chinchillidae family, llamas, guanacos, alpacas, vicuñas, and numerous birds—stilt-legged birds on the ponds, quails, partridges, and ring doves on cultivated land.

For want of abundant heavy game, the pre-Columbian populations had recourse to parrots and flamingos for their feathers, and to ducks, doves, pigeons, and partridges for their nutritional value. But it was actually the sea that constituted the pre-Columbians' most important food source, the one richest in proteins —in the form of shellfish and seafood: mollusks, sea urchins, crabs, and crustaceans—and of course in the form of the innumerable edible fish of the Pacific: rockfish, sandfish, anchovies, flounders, gray mullets, coalfish and cods, rays, torpedoes, and even sharks. Tortoises and sea lions also played an important dietary role. The mounds of detritus of certain ancient periods are a compact mixture of ashes, shells, and the burned bones of marine mammals.

The contemporary Andean has lost the habit of eating fish. For example, he used to refuse to eat tuna, which abounds and would have provided him with cheap meat. Peru is a country where one could eat cheaply, with rice, sugar, bananas, cottonseed oil, and tuna, if the publicity directed by sellers did not thwart the habit. Let me give an example. Peruvians have a tendency to consume during the same meal (in addition to their traditional beans) bread and noodles for which it is necessary to import wheat, whereas formerly they ate corn that each picked from his own garden. Today, propaganda is urging the population to consume fish, but it has become as expensive as meat.

Archæology has not supplied proof that dolphins, sperm whales, and whales were hunted by the pre-Columbians of this southern continent, who were less valiant in this respect than their seafaring brothers of the Canadian Northwest.

Sea mammals looking like sperm whales appear painted on Nazca vases. Was the animal hunted, or did it just terrorize fishermen? The dolphin is absent from iconography, as are the large whales. Dolphins abound, however, off the coast of Peru, and just twenty years ago, whales still used to come to give birth close to shore in Sechura Bay.

The fauna of the Andes does not seem to have been affected by profound changes since the beginning of the Holocene epoch. The last large predators and large herbivorous fauna of the Pleistocene period—the mammoth, the mylodon, the megatherium, the horse, and the camel—had disappeared in the course of the last glaciation. Of the large birds, only the ostrich and the nandu (rhea) survived in the plains of the southeast. The sloths became small animals the size of beavers.

Two theories clash with regard to the obliteration of the large fauna. Some attribute it to a climatological factor, to a drying up of the prairies necessary to the diets of large herbivores. Others see in it an increase in the number of carnivores that, themselves lacking food as a result of the drying up of the cordillera, would be responsible for the disappearance of the larger species of herbivores.

Since the beginning of the Holocene period, therefore, the Andes must have been populated by a fauna of the type described by the Spanish chroniclers, though perhaps a little better stocked in the categories of felines, bears, deer, and roe deer. This fauna survived until industrialization and the intensive utilization of land, phenomena we have witnessed in the course of the past few years. Today it is disappearing rapidly, but some twenty years ago, innumerable sea lions and elephant seals still kept their harems at the foot of cliffs and on islets near the coastal desert. Sea otters fished around the rocks there, and vicuñas, now quite threatened, were counted by the thousands in the puna.

To see serpentlike creatures, let alone snakes, one must go down to the hot forest. Everywhere else, serpents are a rarity. In the dry Andes they are replaced by sand tarantulas, iguanas, lizards, and a kind of salamander that, though harmless, instills a magical terror in the people of the country. Amphibians must have a magical significance that is no longer remembered. The natives are not afraid, on the other hand, of the numerous scorpions and large centipedes, which rather amuse them. These amphibians are also found painted on Nazca pieces.

The Pacific coasts are still the crossing points of hundreds of thousands of migratory birds coming, according to the seasons, from north or south. Compact flights of terns maneuver in rapid groups on the sand, where they forage for small shellfish. Flamingos cover some lagunas with a pink veil as they take wing, accompanied by cranes and herons. Parrots form green clouds, even in the coastal valleys. In the bay of Paracas in southern Peru, I once estimated several hundred thousand sea birds, accompanied by flights of pelicans.

Guano, the excrement of these birds and of pelicans, cormorants, and *piqueros*, a type of gull, has constituted for centuries one of the resources in the countryside. The pre-Columbians were already exploiting the thick beds of this powerful fertilizer, deposited by the billions of birds that had nested successively in the rocky islets near the coast.

Today even these birds are greatly diminished in number. In order to produce more fish meal, fishermen exhaust the anchovy beds, starving the birds but also, in addition, killing those that come near their nets. Economists say that it is better to fertilize the soil with fish than with the excrement of the birds that consume them, excrement of which a large percentage falls into the sea. But the natural equilibrium is close to dissolution. It has already been necessary to establish periods when fishing is forbidden, for the fish have almost disappeared.

The condor, a legendary bird, is now in the process of becoming extinct. Its lack of agility makes it too easy a target. It is due to a zoological mistake that so much magical importance was given in pre-Columbian folklore to a bird that feeds on dead flesh, as do sea gulls, the common vulture, the griffon vulture of mountainous southern Europe, and the turkey vulture. The condor describes great circles at a high altitude and was likened on this account to a messenger of the sun or a messenger to the sky from souls of the dead. In fact, the mythological bird of the Andes was not the condor but the harpy, physically much alike but an eagle, feeding on live prey. What is represented in Chavín art and so on is the harpy, not the condor.

The birds that deserve admiration, on the other hand, are the truly rapacious hunters of the falcon family, represented in the facial painting of the Nazcas some two thousand years ago. Many Peruvians still are called *huamani, huaman* being the local word for *falcon.*

MISCELLANEOUS RESOURCES

Among mineral resources, I shall of course cite gold, the element that gave the Spanish Conquest the look of a novel by Kafka. (To reread certain episodes in the history of the Conquest makes one understand Voltaire's statement that one cannot open a history book without being horrified by the human race.) Apparently, little gold was extracted from veins, for lack of explosives and hand-churn drills. It must have been nugget gold, gold washings, extracted from the sand of tropical rivers, that essentially made up the pre-Columbian production.

Veins of zinc, silver, lead, and copper were more accessible, often exposed to the air. One could, therefore, obtain pieces of ore that one could cold hammer.

It was another problem if one wanted to proceed by fusion. Gold and copper melt at a little more than twenty-two hundred degrees Fahrenheit. Thus, we may wonder how the pre-Columbians were able to attain such temperatures. It was probably when they noticed that bringing two metals face to face lowered the melting point that metallurgy developed. The chroniclers tell us that the Andeans blew on the fire. But they did not use bellows, so one thinks they must have had difficulty in attaining high temperatures. The chroniclers also tell us that the Andeans had the wind help them—they installed their hearths on hilltops.

However this may be, they proved to be great experts in the domain of fine metallurgy. The systematic pillaging that has been carried on in pre-Columbian sites for four hundred years makes the task difficult for those seeking to find the production centers for the delightful jewels that may be seen in the museums of Bogotá, Quito, and Guayaquil, and in private collections in Lima and the United States. But we know that, technically speaking, fine Columbian metallurgy (for example, that of the Taironas and Quimbayas, who used the lost-wax method) far surpassed in quality that of Peru and Mexico.

Mexican metallurgy developed late, only about the year one thousand of the Christian era. However, about 300 B.C., the inhabitants of northern Peru were already melting gold and copper.

In Colombia, copper was rare, and the use of silver was unknown. These two metals were particularly exploited in the south. Platinum was exploited only in Ecuador, and by hammering, because of its high melting point. Iron was used only very rarely, in the form of hammered, then filed, meteorites.

The manufacture of jewels seems to have been the object of small-scale production at the village level. We are still far removed from the royal workshops of Egypt and Mesopotamia.

The use of wood for construction must have always posed problems owing to the lack of metal saws. The Andeans sawed with bones, stones, and shells, but that did not go far. The result was the almost complete absence of wooden trays exceeding the size of what we would call a very small board. Small boxes made of boards have been found in tombs on the central coast of Peru, but the tombs in question were so late that one wonders if what we are finding is not the result of contact with Europeans.

All over South America, stone tools, complemented by tools of wood, bone, and shell, played an essential role until the arrival of Europeans. Metal was just beginning to be used in the fifteenth century, for maces, knives, chisels, needles, and sledgehammers, and I think that the majority of copper objects were used more as exchange money than as genuine tools.

When hard stone was lacking, shell tools often substituted for it. We have numerous examples of this around the Caribbean Sea.

It is in the field of dyes, pigments, and colorings that the pre-Columbians attained a high degree of proficiency. Few of the colorings they used to paint ceramics before firing have yet been identified. The nature of certain vegetable pigments used long ago for the paint applied after firing, when the technique of painting before putting a piece in the kiln was not yet known, remains a mystery. Certain pale and olive greens and certain turquoise blues leave us wondering. Other techniques of pottery decoration have likewise remained difficult to imitate, like the float finish, the wet look of certain vases, or the mirrorlike shine, the shiny-smoked finish, and the graphitized one.

A small school for crafts set up in Bolivia, in Jésus de Menchaca near Tiahuanaco, is trying to revive the ceramic art of pre-Columbian ancestors, with success in the realm of the processing and colors of pastes. Only the creative talent is missing; forms and decorative themes are for the moment just imitating the two-thousand-year-old models.

The colorings used by pre-Columbians to enliven their fabrics remain among the most beautiful the preindustrial world has produced. Purple mauves were obtained, as in the Mediterranean, from a base of shells and cuttlefish. Shells that served as bowls, and little paintbrushes imbued with a violet dye are found in most prehistoric villages.

Red was obtained with achiote, a bush whose crushed seeds one finds on the millstones and which stain the pestles of almost every village since at least ten thousand years ago.

Yellow was obtained with a kind of saffron, palillo. Green tattooing was practiced using another plant. To decorate buildings, recourse was had to inorganic colorings, primarily red or yellow ochers. Vivid blacks and whites were also used. Ceramists obtained white tints with the kaolin found in the Andes of Cajamarca.

Flints were rare, so abundant use was made of obsidian, which must have constituted an advantageous material for exchange. Several Peruvian coastal societies (those of the Paracas and Nazcas) were equipped with obsidian for some five centuries. The inhabitants of this region must have had access to a vein of blocks of this vitrified lava, for obsidian is found only at very precise points in the Andes.

Lacking obsidian, the pre-Columbians used basalt so hard that one can barely manage to break it. Lacking basalt, they worked quartz or pink porphyries, of poorer quality. When slatelike hard sediments were accessible, the pre-Columbians seized the opportunity to polish it in the shape of arrowheads, and anthracite was used for polished mirrors.

Certain techniques seem to have remained traditionally associated with a single society. Thus, only the Chavíns polished anthracite mirrors and slate arrowheads (see Chapter Four). The situation with objects of polished stone is even more peculiar. The Chavíns sculpted and polished stone vases and mortars, which were consequently copied in Inca times, leading one to think that the Incas had looted temples and perhaps also graves. The Chavíns also polished war clubs and hatchets. Afterward, objects of this sort do not reappear until the society of the Paracas brought them back, two thousand years ago, to disappear again and reappear for the last time in the fifteenth century A.D.

Certain stone objects made during the late fifteenth century are very likely

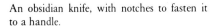
An obsidian knife, with notches to fasten it to a handle.

copies of metal implements or weapons. This phenomenon is familiar from the Neolithic revolution in the Near East. In Peru, one thinks in particular of certain Chavín war clubs, helical in shape, made with such precision that they could not have been carved that way unless the artisan had a metal model to copy. Likewise, in Peru we find star-shaped maces made of stone, but equipped with a raised edge or a central groove, faithful reproductions of typical copper maces introduced by the Incas.

The case with arrowheads having deeply serrated edges also makes one stop to think. Such weapons appeared in the central Andes ten thousand years ago. Then they disappeared, to reappear only once, seven thousand years later, with the Chavíns. These weapons are small, but still are comparable to the large, sometimes gigantic, ones found in Central America.

·2·

THE ANDES IN THE SIXTEENTH CENTURY

DISCOVERY AND CONQUEST

The existence of a New World, first called the West Indies, then America, was generally unknown to fifteenth-century Europeans. China and Tibet had been known since the journeys of the Polo brothers, made between 1271 and 1295.

Only a few geographers suspected the existence of unknown lands that one would come upon in traveling westward. The memory of contacts established around the tenth century by the Vikings and others with the northern, and maybe even the southern parts of these lands apparently survived only in the form of a map buried in the archives of a convent, and even the authenticity of this document is in dispute. On the other hand, it seems that Portuguese fishermen later not only knew of the existence of the Azores, but also of the coast of what was to become Brazil.

The search for a new route to the Indies and the Spice Islands had become absolutely necessary. The Turks and Arabs, in control throughout the Near East, were cutting off Europe from the rest of the Old World. Genoa, Castile, and Portugal started to compete in conquering new commercial routes.

Thus, the aim of Columbus's explorations was not to discover a new continent but to establish contact with the Far East by sailing westward. Columbus thought he would land in China or Japan. (America was reached with the help of three vessels 128, 59, and 56 feet long, respectively.) His first voyage took place in 1492, fifty years after the Ottomans took over Constantinople. Constantinople, or Byzantium, was then the number one trading center in the world, where all the products of the Orient were gathered, then to be distributed throughout Europe by the Catalans, Genoese, and Venetians.

The West Indies were the first part of America to be found. The rivalry between the Spaniards and the Portuguese then took on such scope that as early as 1494 the pope had to divide the world into two zones. The one given to the Spaniards extended westward approximately from the twenty-fifth meridian. The one granted to the Portuguese extended eastward. Other conflicts were born, of course, on the other side of the globe, concerning first the southern Far East, then later Oceania.

In fact, Columbus had discovered the mainland in 1498, but he did not realize it, thinking the Venezuelan coast was just another island. Alonso de Ojeda was the first European to walk on the soil of South America, in 1499. Later he visited Maracaibo, the Guajira Peninsula, and the Isthmus of Darien. The coasts of Venezuela and Brazil had been explored around the year 1501 by Cabral.

While Columbus was searching for a westward passage and getting stuck in the Gulf of Darien, Amerigo Vespucci, a clear-headed Renaissance man and not a mystic like Columbus, was more realistically making every effort to circumvent what he guessed was the formidable obstacle of a continent. In 1508 he was reaching far enough south (to the fortieth parallel, in fact) to persuade his colleague Magellan to explore the Indies route by circumventing the land via the southern hemisphere. Magellan and his 265 companions rounded Cape Horn as early as 1520 and entered the Pacific, the existence of which had been known since 1513, the year in which Nuñez de Balboa crossed the Isthmus of Panama on foot.

The chronicler Antonio Pigafetta, from Vicenza, Italy, accompanied the Magellan expedition. Therefore, we have a good account of it and are indebted to him for the first description of a guanaco and a *patagon* that is, a man with big feet. The natives, very handsome people in some tribes, seemed like giants to the small Portuguese sailors.

Thus, it was Vespucci finally who gave his first name, Amerigo, to the continent. This name appeared for the first time in a text of 1507 and then on a map of 1514, the so-called map of Leonardo da Vinci.

The history of the northern continent is outside the context of this work; let me recall only the essential facts.

The northern continent was known to the Scandinavians, the Vikings, who tried to establish themselves on the East Coast, starting from Greenland, but were expelled from it by the Eskimos. After that, North America led an autonomous life up until the arrival of the Spaniards in the Caribbean. North America, like the southern continent, was populated by Asians forming numerous groups and speaking very diverse languages. It is the counterpart of the southern continent, with its cordillera, vast plains, and an empire, the Aztec one, comparable to the Inca empire. There is, however, a big difference between these two worlds. In the northern one, a large proportion of its population had always lived in a preagricultural stage, and it was to disappear without adopting another way of life. But the southern continent was a world of farmers. As late as the nineteenth century, the entire northwestern United States and California were still populated by fishermen and seed collectors. Agriculture developed late in the Southwest, from techniques acquired probably in Mexico and the Caribbean, as a result of the migration of Arawaks. The southwestern tribes finally became quite successful at irrigating and lived essentially on corn, but in the east, cultivated plants played only an auxiliary role.

The use of native nugget copper, possibly a Siberian tradition, appeared very early in the central northeast, but no metallurgy developed there.

The northern continent produced no monuments of any importance. Only the Southwest has left us compact settlements, with houses made of unfired clay bricks. The indigenous peoples who have survived on the reservations still build their villages in the same fashion as did their ancestors. The Southeast has left us very large mounds embellished with molded representations of animals.

The current idea one may have of the Great Plains of the North American West does not, however, correspond in any way to the actualities of pre-Columbian life. James Fenimore Cooper described for us the Sioux cavalcading on horseback and hunting the buffalo, scalping their enemies on the way. But one should remember that the horse had disappeared from the Americas at least ten thousand years ago and was only reintroduced by the ships of Columbus. The Sioux, formerly farmers, became buffalo hunters only shortly before being exterminated by the white man.

At any rate, for the first sixteen years, Columbus and the Spaniards controlled only islands: Cuba, Puerto Rico, and Hispaniola, or Santo Domingo. And when in 1508 Ojeda tried to settle on the mainland, on the Isthmus of Darien, he met with total disaster.

In 1519, Cortez rushed to attack Mexico, which took six years to pacify. In the meantime, Ponce de León was visiting Florida. Explorers were trying to disembark in the Yucatán Peninsula, on the coast of Honduras—almost everywhere around the Gulf of Mexico.

The first explorations of the northern continent date from 1531. In 1539, Hernando de Soto discovered the Mississippi. In 1540, Colorado and California were reached. The approaches to the Rio de la Plata, the future Argentina, were explored by Diego Garcia as early as 1526, at the same time as journeys were being made toward Cape Horn. But it was only in 1534 that Pedro de Mendoza attempted to found what was to become Buenos Aires.

Different motivations, of diverse origins, must have given birth to the desire to mount these expeditions. We used to be taught that the completion of the

Reconquest, the expulsion of the Moors from Spain, had liberated soldiers of adventurous spirit for whom the Italian campaigns were no longer enough. But more-modern studies seem to indicate that the professional soldiers were few in number. The troops in the American campaigns basically consisted of simple folk fleeing extreme poverty in Spain.

Men like Columbus and Vespucci evidently belonged to a more highly developed intellectual level, and their motivations were different from those of the captains. As for the Spanish crown, we may wonder if it was fully conscious of the vastness of the movement taking shape. In the beginning, at least, one senses it to be impelled more by the will to maintain its authority over a world that should not escape it. The Spanish king intended to go on playing the role of an absolute and centralized Christian monarch supposed to remain the only one in command.

Reading the history of this period helps us understand the concept of an authoritarian monarchy and the power exercised by the centralized kingdom of Spain. The king intended to rule from as far away as nine thousand miles. In actual practice, he could not determine the details, nor, despite all his efforts, could he protect the natives against the cupidity of the colonists. But up to the end, the Spanish monarchy sought to maintain its control over its overseas domains. Everything was institutionalized; all decisions were made by the Council of the Indies in Seville. Even such minor matters as the building of a church had to be approved, with the plan being signed by the king. The conquerors were not allowed to keep inheritable estates. In Mexico, the heirs of Cortez managed to keep possession of large estates serviced by up to ten thousand Indians, a seemingly justifiable reward, considering their achievements. But this was an exception. Soon after the Conquest, the monarchy took over control of the state. And as soon as he could, the king reestablished order in Peru, after he had liquidated the leaders of the Conquest, whose lack of discipline he could not tolerate.

It is unthinkable that we shall ever succeed in finding out the deep motivations, not of the troops of adventurers that constituted the field forces of the Conquest, but of its leaders. In the great majority, the troops came from very modest milieus: artisans, small farmers, or people of no profession; even the leaders were not of high lineage. Not a single member of any important Spanish family took any interest financially, militarily, or intellectually in the Conquest of the Indies. The *virreyes* of Peru were in fact merely the Spanish king's agents, usually medium-rank civil servants. Cortez, the conqueror of Mexico, and Pizarro, the conqueror of the Andes, had only the word *religion* in their mouths. Were they perfectly sincere, and did they honestly believe they were serving God? Or had they studied Machiavelli and were disguising their thoughts? Columbus seems to have vowed a cult built around treasures recalling that of Baal and the golden calf. Cortez was more modern, more artful, less mystical, with solid juridical notions; he wanted power and glory. Pizarro seems great especially in his courage, his rage to succeed in the most diverse circumstances. Gold was evidently an attraction, but above all, one senses in him the need to vanquish and dominate.

What was the Spanish king doing in all this? Profoundly religious, fundamentally imbued with his Catholic mission, he dreamed as much of Christianizing as of exercising his prerogative of absolute monarchy in all realms. But Christianizing was expensive—the king did not disdain gold.

Deep down, His Majesty would have wanted to receive gold without extortions being committed with regard to the natives of the Indies, and he showed himself to be very sincerely pained when he got to know in what manner the "fifth" of gold, the part belonging to the crown, had been obtained. After the gold had disappeared, all shipped to Seville and squandered in disastrous wars, the captains started building domains for themselves, to the detriment of the Indians, and enslaved them. How otherwise could the conquerors have been rewarded? The gold was quickly used up, but manpower was needed again when the Spaniards discovered how to process silver ore. Manpower was needed in any case to cultivate the fields the natives had abandoned. Recourse to forced labor thus accelerated the destruction of the indigenous societies.

The conqueror, the *conquistador,* nonetheless remains the principal figure in these bloody and grandiose adventures. For having successfully carried out enterprises into which they dashed with ludicrous resources compared to the difficulties to be overcome, these conquerors must have been very gifted, morally and physically. The monarchy did not contribute to any of the conquests; all the expeditions had to be financed by private individuals. Those who embarked set out without pay and without guarantee as to their future. To sail meant either to succeed or to die. Courage and bodily resistance were predominant in them. One could add harshness, but it was that of the times, when the infidel or heretic did not deserve mercy. (Manuel Ballesteros praises the conquerors for an additional quality, that of loyalty to the king. Perhaps . . . but the facts seem to indicate otherwise.) One was cruel because one was conducting a harsh war, not because of sadism. Besides, the risks these adventurers took in leaving at their own expense for the Indies were so great that one understands their drive to make a fortune, to create domains for themselves, to have slaves.

Thus, it was not projects of colonization that animated the first conquerors, but the attraction of gold and jewels, the lack of which obliged them to establish domains. The missionary spirit, the so-honorable desire to Christianize, formed a corollary of the enterprise. It emanated from the good elements of the clergy and the crown of Madrid, which did not let any vessel depart for the Indies that did not have at least two monks aboard, charged with instructing the natives in the Christian faith. But the religious brotherhoods, however rich, did not finance the expeditions, all of which were mounted by partners united to carry out business transactions. This was rather like when, later, among the inhabitants of Saint-Malo in France, one entered into partnership in order to finance raiding operations, the pillaging of enemy vessels and places.

First the Indies, then the mainland, even Mexico, were a disappointment to the conquerors. When the monarchy offered them landed property they grumbled, "We did not come here to till the earth like peasants."

When the first explorations to cast out along the Pacific Coast in the direction of the equator led the conquerors to suspect the existence of a vast southern empire and other great riches, new expeditions were organized. Twenty years later, all the Andes had come under Spanish rule.

The first voyage toward the south was commanded by Pascual de Andagoya. Leaving Panama in 1522, this sailor barely passed beyond the Chocó, the tropical coast of Colombia, but even so brought back from it the name *Biru*, the future *Peru*.

During the second voyage, which took place in 1524, Pizarro was aboard with eighty men and four horses. The expedition reached the Atrato River in 1525, but without success. Almagro lost an eye there, and no gold was brought back.

The third voyage was undertaken in November 1526, with 160 men and a few horses. The chroniclers tell us that it was during this voyage that the Spaniards came across a raft filled with objects for barter, and gold and silver appeared. Pizarro therefore decided to continue, and his pilot, Ruiz, conducted him to the coast of Tumaco. But some soldiers had already succumbed to hardship and tropical pestilences, so the chief could persuade only thirteen men to stay with him.

Pizarro's determination brought him success. Pushing farther south, he reached the Gulf of Guayaquil, then Tumbes, the first built-up area subject to the Incas, and suddenly we find him climbing up the Santa Valley, in the heart of the northern coast of Peru.

In 1528 Pizarro was in Spain, and in 1529 he obtained the *Capitulacion*, the charter authorizing him to administer his future conquests.

The third expedition left Panama in 1530 but lost time and forces in Ecuador and on the island of Puná. Arriving in Tumbes, the conquerors found the area in ruins, probably in consequence of a revolt against the Incas. Pizarro had to return to Panama.

Thus, it was only in 1532 that he was able to start exploring the north coast of Peru and to found the first colonial city, San Miguel de Piura, next to the indigenous city of Tangarara.

In November 1532, accompanied by 62 horsemen and 106 foot soldiers, Pizarro launched his dramatic offensive. Penetrating the heart of the Andes and crossing the cordillera, he met the Inca, Atahualpa, in Cajamarca. This sparked the explosion that would make the native societies of the continent disappear, a subject I shall momentarily neglect, as I shall come back to the conquest of Peru in the chapter devoted to the Incas.

The conquest of the lands that later became the republics of Ecuador and Colombia was also marked by blighted hopes, massacres, and fighting between conquerors. The first voyage along the coasts of Colombia, by Bastides in 1525, achieved nothing. The first strongholds created on the continent had much to endure during their first decades. The port of Santa Marta, the first to be founded, succeeded in holding on, but Cartagena (which was to become the largest port in

the West Indies), founded in 1532, was first besieged by the natives, then immediately following that and constantly thereafter was the object of attacks by
raiders, then by the French and English navies.

In 1536, Jimenez de Quesada dashed toward the interior. One of his contin-
gents was advancing by land, the other going up the Magdalena River. He had
heard it said that the *cacique* or *zipa* of Bacata, the *zaque* of Tunja (Hunsa), and
another religious chief, installed at Sugamuxi, were quarreling over their rights to
rule the highlands. So Quesada seized the high Colombian plateau as well as
some very rich booty, and founded Santa Fe de Bogotá. He thought he had found
the land of gold, El Dorado. Once the natives' resistance had been liquidated,
therefore, he started to search for other sources of riches, but upon learning that
competitors were rushing after the same scents, he had to prepare to resist his
own compatriots.

In 1534, Captain Alvarado, who had acquired great renown in Mexico and
Central America, had the idea of mounting an expedition starting from Guatemala and Nicaragua, whose aim would be the conquest of what is now Ecuador. Rumor had it that Quito contained even more riches than Cuzco had yielded. Therefore, Alvarado landed on the tropical coast at the zero parallel and from
there, accompanied by thousands of Guatemalan soldiers and natives transformed
on the spot into bearer slaves, he rushed across the jungle to storm the cordillera,
thinking he would reach Quito from the west.

Hearing of this, Benalcázar, a lieutenant of Pizarro who was stationed in
Piura, did not hesitate. He organized an expedition of two hundred men and
sixty horses and advanced as quickly as possible toward Quito. News of this
reached Pizarro, who sent Almagro in pursuit of Benalcázar. But the latter was
already far from Peru, and once again the native resistance proved insufficient to
stop the little force. As a result, Benalcázar reached the high plateaus, passed by
the Inca fortress of Tumibamba, and made an alliance with the Cañari tribe.
Only the ruins of Tumibamba have survived, under the name Ingapirca, "the
stones of the Inca." These ruins are in the process of being restored and will constitute an additional tourist attraction around Cuenca, a charming little colonial-
style city.

This situation led to the most terrible of all the battles of conquest between
invaders and natives, the battle of Teocajas, in the *paramos* (alpine meadows) of
the high Andes. The Spaniards survived vigorous attacks, but the outcome remained indecisive, and the invaders were obliged to resort to trickery, to go back
down the western side of the cordillera, then back up onto the plateau. Four
months after their setting out, in June they entered Quito, extremely disappointed
to find there nothing more than the smoking ruins of a built-up area that had
been destroyed. A little while later, they again had to sustain the shock of a battle
—the first one to be delivered at night by the natives—but the Spaniards came
out the victors.

While Benalcázar and his men were dressing their wounds, they were
overtaken by Almagro. He reminded the captain of his duties of loyalty with

respect to Pizarro, who had been given his powers from the king of Spain, and of whom Benalcázar was the lieutenant. Alvarado, who had chosen the bad route and decimated his troops in his climb through the forest, as a result arrived too late.

Three conquering groups thus found themselves face to face; it was a grave situation. The confrontation between the Spanish armies could, however, be avoided by negotiation. Almagro and Alvarado withdrew, and Benalcázar kept command of the operations with regard to Ecuador and Colombia.

In Ecuador, it took him several months of campaigns to capture and put to death the generals defending the country. Then he dashed to the conquest of southern Colombia, where he founded Popayán and ravaged Tierradentro. After this, anti-Spanish resistance ceased for two and a half centuries in this part of the continent.

In all of this, Benalcázar had forgotten the presence of Quesada, installed at Santa Fe (now Bogotá). Now a third robber, the German Nikolaus Federman, ravenous from hardship, was coming out again from one-hardly-knows-what jungle. German bankers had financed an expedition that set out from the Caribbean and founded Maracaibo. Charles V of Spain, in need of money, had granted them the lands of Venezuela, the starting point of Federman's explorations of Colombia. It was therefore necessary to have the dispute settled by the Spanish crown, so the king distributed rewards and left the government of Popayán and the extreme south of Colombia to Benalcázar.

The first expeditions launched against the lands located south of the Inca empire were hardly successful. Almagro, whom Pizarro wanted to get rid of, advanced against Chile, but he only gave himself up to pillaging and extortion, after which he came back to Peru and took possession of Cuzco for a brief period before being beheaded.*

The second attempt was no more successful. Pedro de Valdivia was killed in 1540 by the Araucanians while trying to penetrate Chiloé Island. There followed fifty years of suffering, martyrdom, famine, and death for the colonists who persisted in remaining in Chile.

Only much later, around 1598 under Garcia de Loyola, were the Spaniards able to hold their ground with the help of fortresses, some of which had already been constructed by Valdivia. They were still not able to penetrate Araucania, and had to remain entrenched behind the forts separating central Chile from the southern part of the continent. It ultimately took them three hundred years to pacify the whole of Chile. The disorganized appropriation of lands that we witnessed in the course of the administration of President Allende in 1971 is only one aspect of the vengeance of the natives, who want to take back their property.

Finally, in 1540, eight years after the confrontation of Pizarro with the Inca in Cajamarca and after millennia of isolation, all the northern Andes entered, subdued, into the European orbit.

*For more details regarding these expeditions, see Chapter Three.

In Peru, by 1574 the viceroy, Toledo, had practically eliminated the Incas. The survivors of the royal family of Cuzco sought only to be forgotten and to manage the little that was left to them of their patrimony.

The unannexed regions: the Amazonas, Argentina, Patagonia, and southern Chile, did not play a role in the history of the continent until much later. One can consider, therefore, that by the third quarter of the sixteenth century, pre-Columbian societies had on the whole disappeared as autonomous entities, the protohistoric period had ended, and a period had already begun which is not our present concern, that of colonial history.

THE POPULATION OF THE ANDES

In the first quarter of the twentieth century, we were still being taught that the Americas had been populated very late, during the postglacial period, by immigrants who came from Asia already neolithized, practicing agriculture. Since then, scholars have understood their error and admitted that the populating of the New World dates back to a much earlier epoch.

Today, all specialists agree in considering the essential populating of the two Americas to be the result of a migration on foot across the Bering Strait, made into dry land during the course of a glacial period. The marine regression* that was the result of a cold climatic cycle would have created a bridge uniting the two continents by lowering the level of the ocean by three hundred feet.

Specialists estimate that, despite the extension of glaciers, two access routes remained open in the north of the continent. One would have allowed access to Alaska to immigrants from Siberia, by way of the Amur River, Kamchatka, and the Bering Strait. These immigrants would have then gone around the Rocky Mountains to the east and would have reached Central America and Mexico by way of the Great Lakes and the Mississippi. From Central America this migration would have penetrated South America as far as Patagonia.

Another route would have led immigrants from central Asia to Alaska by way of Japan and the Aleutians. From Alaska these immigrants would have followed the Pacific Coast, and they too would have reached Patagonia.

New Guinea was then part of the Asiatic continent, and the Isthmus of Panama formed a wider passage. Paul Rivet even designed a map in which Oceania appears almost joined to the South American continent by way of the Antarctic.

It is now firmly established that man was already living in North America in the Pleistocene epoch, before the last glaciation. Even in the southern conti-

---

*See page 22.

nent, the presence of humans thirteen thousand years ago is attested in Venezuela, Argentina, and Peru.

Agriculture of course did not exist in those days, even in Asia or the Near East. Men then formed groups devoted to hunting, fishing, and gathering products of the earth, lakes, rivers, and seas. But we should not assume that men subsisted only on hunting and fishing. These were important activities, but only once the basic nourishment had been obtained, for seeds, edible plants, and shellfish represented up to 85 percent of the diet of preagricultural peoples. And, as Richard S. MacNeish has stated, agriculture became customary only slowly, as cultivated plants replaced wild ones.

The reader will possibly be surprised to find immigration habitually cited as the only possible source of the population of the Americas. I am uncomfortable myself when discussing this point. Paleontologists maintain that an American man dating back a hundred thousand years or more will never be found, arguing from the fact that skeletons of apes, the cousins of man, have not been found in the New World. The environment, which would not have favored the development of apes, would similarly not have permitted the birth of human beings.

To me this reasoning has always appeared unconvincing. Man seems to have developed, like any other mammal, independently of the ape, and I speculate as to whether this theory is unaware of some ethnocentrism and whether it is not influenced by the old biblical notion of the single source from which all men would have issued. We cannot brush aside the possibility of the human species developing in multiple centers at several points on the globe, and then exclude the American continent from the number of possibilities. Who would have dreamed of Africa being one of the cradles of mankind, before the discovery of skeletons of Africans dating back to the beginning of the Pleistocene period and more than a million years old? Who can affirm that the remains of a very early *Homo americanus* will not be discovered someday?

Whatever may happen in this field, the fundamentally Asiatic character of most of the inhabitants of the Andes is beyond doubt. This character is confirmed by the physical appearance of the majority of those who have not been crossbred since the Conquest.

The Andeans of today are most often brachycephals, men with a head wider than it is long. All the small tribes of the Andes present indices equal to or above 83, whereas dolichocephalism starts at an index of 75. To find indices below 83 (that is to say, mesocephals or dolichocephals), one must go to Patagonia, into the Amazonas, or along the Orinoco.

The most dolichocephalic skull known at present is that of a man of Lagoa Santa, who lived in Brazil during the high Holocene epoch—his cephalic index reached 71. Current studies by the University of Missouri regarding skeletons five to ten thousand years old that I have found in the Andes may reveal similar features. One of the skeletons measured between 68.4 and 69.2 inches in height and seemed extremely dolichocephalic. (The index is the ratio of the maximum width of the head to its maximum length, multiplied by 100.)

In terms of height, the variety is great, ranging from pygmoids 51.2 inches tall to the Bororos of southern Brazil, who reach 69.6 inches. But very tall men of the African or Australian type are rare.

Sexual dimorphism is marked. The women are distinctly smaller than the men.

The South American's cranial capacity is normal, on the order of .9 cubic inches.

The hair of purebred Andeans (if they can be found!) is rarely wavy, practically never frizzy, almost always thick, straight, wiry, and black. Body hair is absent or very much reduced. Beards are rare.

The color of the skin is extremely variable, ranging from a grayish whitish yellow to a purple brown or a greenish coppery brown. In Venezuela, the Yaruros, though extremely Mongoloid, are practically black, whereas some Tupis of Brazil are practically white. In Cuzco I am acquainted with people having extremely dark skin, and among these people, as in Otavalo, Ecuador, the children have bright red cheeks.

Eye color ranges from hazel to very dark brown. I have never seen gray or blue eyes, except as a result of crossbreeding. But some anthropologists maintain that children may sometimes have blue eyes and red hair at birth.

According to Paul Rivet, Asiatics belong most frequently to blood groups A and B, and rarely to group O. Albinos are infrequent. The epicanthic or eye fold is seen frequently, and the Mongolian or blue spot is common. One of my pupils at the university, to whom I was describing the Mongolian spot, let out a cry of joy when he understood that the children of his village, with whom he had played naked as a child, were not the victims of a shameful disease, but simply presented a physical characteristic indicating their Asiatic origin.

Their metabolism is very good almost everywhere (better than in Europeans), even above average, except perhaps in Peruvians, who are weaker. For example, the Mayas, who are not carnivorous and live on a diet of 85 percent corn and other hydrocarbonic foods, have excellent metabolism, as do the Mapuches of Chile.

This Asiatic foundation once firmly established, one cannot help observing that strong foreign influences appear practically everywhere in the Americas. This was already true in pre-Columbian times, without considering the crossbreeding that followed the Conquest. Asia, some tens of thousands of years ago, was herself a melting pot where highly diverse components—Caucasians, Asians, and Negroes—mingled. To be convinced of this, one need only recall the existence of the Dravidians of India—"Austrians," as the modern Indian anthropological school calls them, or the Pygmies or Negrillos of the Andaman Islands and Philippines, the Australians of large stature and of the African type in Oceania, the Polynesians with some Caucasian blood, and the bearded Ainus of Japan.

Everything of a somewhat African character in the world of the Andes is not, therefore, necessarily the product of importing labor from Africa and the result of the slave trade practiced on a large scale from the seventeenth century onward. It is generally unknown that, according to statistics found in the archives of the viceroyalty, at least three hundred thousand Africans were brought into Peru, whereas two hundred fifty thousand were taken to Mexico. If one remembers that, according to the census ordered by the last viceroy, about 1780, the number of Indians had fallen to seven hundred thousand, one will understand the nature of the impact created by the African newcomers. The lowlands of Ecuador and Colombia have been Africanized to a degree that cannot be denied, but Andean nationalism generally prefers to ignore it.

African traits found in the Andes are rather the mark of a substratum from the tropical Asiatic or Australoid fringe, perhaps even of Africans who crossed the Atlantic a very long time ago. Everything that indicates crossbreeding with Nordic elements (Caucasians) is not necessarily the result of an intermixture subsequent to the arrival of Europeans; that is to say, dating back to the sixteenth century. Caucasian elements might have been introduced from Asia by way of Polynesia or the extreme north of the continent.

Natives of the two Americas are, furthermore, of extremely varied types. All crossbreeding dating back to European colonization aside, one finds in the southern continent individuals with a Caucasian appearance but with dark brown skin, next to Mongolian types or men with African faces, but of a pale or sallow complexion. Big, straight, nonaquiline noses are frequently seen among inhabitants of the Cuzco region, where non-Mongolian characteristics mix with true Asiatic ones. A straight nose appears clearly on the sculptured faces on the Gate of the Sun at Tiahuanaco. On Sundays, at mass in Chinchero, eighteen miles from Cuzco, one would think he was in Tibet, in spite of the fact that the present-day costumes of Andeans are not their own; they are dressed like Spanish peasants in the eighteenth century. If we were to see the natives of the cordillera in their original clothes, they would look much more Asiatic.

The notion of a migration that entered America only by the Bering Strait is not unanimously accepted by researchers. Scholars such as Rivet have not hesitated to set forth their reservations on this subject and to maintain that the influence of transoceanic voyages has been neglected, that peoples have come from southern Asia, Polynesia, even Australia or Africa, by way of the ocean. The Polynesians certainly crossed the Pacific, some two thousand years ago. Why not imagine that other groups could have succeeded, voluntarily or otherwise, in comparable voyages?

The scholar Julian H. Steward recently wrote that he now accepts the idea of a mixed population that was of maritime as well as terrestrial origin. Writers like Miguel Covarrubias and Heine Gildern have devoted their lives to researching factors capable of solidifying the thesis that physical contacts subsequent to the land migration via the Bering Strait must have existed between the peoples of southern Asia and those of the two Americas, and as a result of ocean voyages. The notion of the arrival of successive waves of immigrants having traveled differently is therefore gaining a foothold in the literature. I do not specialize in the field of transpacific contacts, but I can nevertheless not stop wondering how dark men of southern Asiatic and even Negroid types could have walked around what amounts to half the world, all through China and Siberia, to end up in Patagonia.

The only point on which everyone agrees is that the whole influx of immigrants belonged to the variant *Homo sapiens* (modern man), a product of all the components blended in the Asiatic and oceanic melting pot, the natives of Australia and Tasmania included.

Julian Steward goes as far as to admit that cotton, calabashes, and corn would have entered America as a result of a transoceanic migration. He gives examples of objects whose appearance in Asia and the New World is not easily attributable in his opinion to a multilineal evolution. Maces of polished stone, blowguns used to shoot poisoned arrows, fabrics with a negative decoration or batik, to cite only three examples, can only be products of a diffusion in the Americas resulting from a migration from southern Asia.

But the extinction of whole societies has blurred our sources of information. The natives of Tasmania have all disappeared, and those of Australia number about two hundred thousand, surviving in the continent's interior. But their essentially nomadic way of life does not teach us much regarding the Andes. Only a blind man or a person of bad faith could deny the southern Asiatic traits visible in Maya art, the Indonesian reminiscences in the architecture and decoration of Central America and even in the Chavín society in Peru.

Archaeology will help us unravel this skein of the population someday. Skeletons from the high Holocene epoch that I have been able to find in the course of my excavations are going to oblige specialists in physical anthropology to restudy this problem of multiple migrations. It seems, in fact, that the classical Andean whom the Spaniards came upon in the sixteenth century—a man of average or mediocre height, mesocephalic or brachycephalic, with short limbs and frequently a slender frame—differed from the ones I have unearthed in archaeological strata six to ten thousand years old. The early men would have been, on the contrary, dolichocephals, prognathous, big boned, and tall.

The development of agriculture, a phenomenon that occurred in the southern continent between eight thousand and five thousand years before our time, as will be seen later, may thus have been the result of another, later migration, the arrival of a new wave that would then have been responsible for the disappearance of the earlier groups through crossbreeding or destruction through illnesses.

The bands that first set foot on the South American continent invaded all the lands, even the most remote. As early as the high Holocene period, we find remains indicating the presence of little groups that were settled almost everywhere and as far as Cape Horn at the extreme southern tip of the continent.

When ethnologists at the beginning of the twentieth century began to inventory what remained of these bands, grouping them into tribes, they counted as many as two thousand such groups. But how many groups of immigrants had crossed the Bering Strait? Certainly not two thousand; probably a much smaller number. A dividing up would then have occurred in the course of the ensuing millennia, a likely result of an increase in the number of inhabitants usually practicing exogamy.

The Andes, like the South American continent as a whole, must have been sparsely populated in the high Holocene. The vestiges we find seem to indicate the existence of scattered little villages grouping together at most a few hundred inhabitants. The natives of Tierra del Fuego and the Chilean archipelago, for example, still numbered only a few tens of thousands in the sixteenth century.

Prehistoric demography or the history of the evolution of this population is making hardly any progress. It is one of the branches of history that advanced least during the second quarter of the twentieth century. When one raises this subject, one notices very soon that the specialists, after citing the few bands that would have made up the first migration to the new continent, proceed abruptly to another problem, that of the population of America at the time of the arrival of Europeans. Even in this domain, these specialists have never succeeded in reaching agreement and in giving us uniform figures. The figures that have been formulated vary to such a great degree that one no longer knows whom to trust. They range between 2.5 and 75 million!

With regard to the whole continent, the most reasonable figure (though a bit low in my opinion) is the one expressed by Steward in 1959: on the order of 10 million inhabitants. We may break this down as follows:

3,500,000	for the Inca empire; that is to say, the cold and temperate central Andes
1,500,000	for diverse chiefdoms of the northern Andes
1,150,000	for the southern Andes: Diaguites, Atacamanians, and Araucanians
2,200,000	for the tropical forests
650,000	for the Chaco and eastern Brazil
100,000	for the Chilean archipelago and Patagonia
225,000	for the Caribbean*
150,000	for northern Venezuela
75,000	for the Isthmus of Darien

The density per square mile would thus have varied from .4 to 1 inhabitant, according to the area. Rivet saw the southern continent as being much more populated, and estimated 25 million inhabitants there.

In the absence of written documents, which we will never have at our disposal, I think it will only be possible to get a more serious answer to the problem by tackling it from a different angle—by going, so to speak, from the base up to the summit. The method being applied in this field for small pilot studies consists of trying to account for the surface of the lands that were cultivated, for example in the course of the fifteenth century. By evaluating the average productivity of

---

*I would have imagined the Caribbean to have been more heavily populated and the tropical forests of the continent to have been less so.

these lands in hundredweight of corn or in potatoes per acre, and adopting a figure that we suppose corresponds to the annual mean consumption (so many
hundredweight of corn per family of five), we come to know not the number of
families that lived in a region but the number of people who might have lived
there at a given time, bearing in mind the nutritional resources the territory en-
sured.

At first glance, to accomplish such a program seems to involve interminable
labors. In practice, to obtain usable results within a reasonable time is easier than
one would think. One can, in fact, proceed by extrapolating. After creating categories of cultivable land, one proceeds to study in close detail an area considered
prototypical of each category. Results can then be extended to other territories,
but of course only to ones in comparable categories.

Regarding the annual consumption per family and the productivity of the
soil per acre, one can use information provided by ethnology and be inspired, for
example, by the needs of a Guatemalan family living on corn cultivated on terraces according to the *milpa* (slash-and-burn) system.

This kind of research is made difficult by the fact that the measurements
employed are not only not standardized, but are not even defined. Measurements
of surface area are most often expressed in the number of working days necessary
to reclaim a plot of land. Such a figure naturally varies according to the topography and the quality of the soil. Moreover, who can tell us the value of the *tupu*,
an Inca unit of area? All the researchers have cracked their teeth on it. And
what's more, the measures of weight, concerning forage of edible plants, are
replaced by measures of volume. A sack of beans will be smaller, because of the
beans' greater density, than a sack of *quinoa* (pigweed), and so forth. Therefore,
it is easy to know what the peasant had at his disposal in the time of the Incas
in order to feed his family, nor is it easy to evaluate his actual annual food consumption. This is especially true in coastal regions, where the nutritional contributions of marine origin played a considerable role and probably compensated
for the lack of carbohydrates in lean times.

The partial results I have obtained from proceeding in this way have already allowed me to form an idea of what might have been the population of
some Peruvian valleys in the central Andes. So we now have at our disposal a
few coefficients allowing us to formulate working hypotheses, remembering, of
course, to take into account variables that intervene in this type of equation. We
note, for example, that whether it be the domain of the Incas in the high Andes,
or the desert coast, up to 10 percent of a given territory was utilizable for men
who knew how to live in an arid zone, whereas today only 1.2 percent of all
Peruvian lands are under cultivation, leaving out the Amazon area.

If such percentages were to be confirmed, they would indicate that the
un-Hispanicized Andeans had at their disposal thirty-five times more arable land
than do the Peruvians and Bolivians of our day, illustrating the decadence of our
contemporary ecologies. Present-day Peru is obliged, in order to feed some 13
million inhabitants, to spend fortunes annually to import food.

My first observations relate to points that are still too localized for me to be able to add more than a grain of sand to the research concerning pre-Columbian demography. But they already let us catch a glimpse of Andean areas that could have been more populated in pre-Hispanic times than they are today.

LANGUAGES

The study of languages hardly helps us resolve the problem of migrations. At the beginning of the twentieth century, linguists had cataloged nearly two hundred families or groups of dialects spoken by natives of the South American continent. Linguistics (such as glottochronology, explained later) teaches us that the existence of so many families of languages seems to be just the consequence of the immigrants subdividing into a multitude of groups and of their adopting distinct territories. A multitude of languages does not in itself prove that the first immigrants were divided into a great number of tribes.

Then again, there is no necessary link between a society, its culture, and its language. Certain languages (such as Maya, which is still spoken by some two million people) become a lingua franca, a common means of communication, as did Quechua in the central Andes and Tupi and Guarani in the eastern part of the continent.

After wars that end in the fusion of two clans, sometimes the victims, sometimes the victors impose their language. Finally, a good many languages have simply disappeared.

All that specialists can do here is to apply the methods of glottochronology, the science that allows one to evaluate how many centuries or millennia have elapsed since one group separated from another, both groups having belonged to a single linguistic family but since having each developed a different language.

The diffusion of languages reveals migrations, of course. As examples, Arawakan and Cariban instead of Ciboney were spoken in the sixteenth century in the West Indies, on the plateau of Bogotá, on the Pacific Coast, on the Isthmus of Darien, on the grassy plains of eastern Colombia, and even in the forest east of Lima. Chibcha, on the other hand, had penetrated the Pacific slope, the shores of the Caribbean, and even along the Orinoco.

In northern Peru there were two languages: Puruhá of the Mochicas (also spoken by the Mantas of Ecuador), and Yunga, the language of the Chimus of Chan Chan, today Trujillo. One finds traces of Yunga from Ayabaca, north of Piura, to Yauyos, in the high valley of the Cañete in central Peru.

The Diaguites spoke Kakan; the Atacamanians, Kunza, a type of Arawakan.

Finally, Quechua had penetrated all the central Andes and as far as Quito, possibly as the result of intervention by the Incas—who would have imposed population transfers and set up colonies almost everywhere—then later by the Spanish clergy, who would have used this diffusion as a means of continental communication. But on the contrary, other linguists maintain quite a different thesis. They see Quechua as a central Andean language that would have subsequently reached Cuzco, where formerly Aymara would have been spoken, as Aymara was spoken all around Lake Titicaca.

We are generally taught that all the American languages belonged to the Mongolian group of polysyllabic agglutinate dialects. (Specialists have classified languages into three big groups: inflected polysyllabic, such as the European and Semitic languages; monosyllabic, such as Chinese; and agglutinative polysyllabic, in which one joins syllables without using inflections to indicate tense, number, or gender.) Some authors, like Alden Mason, for example, maintain that on the contrary it is impossible to catalog the American languages as one unit, that some show tendencies toward inflection, others toward polysyllabism. According to Mason, one can therefore attempt only to classify these dialects on a genetic or a historical basis, a basis of origin or of the relations between them. Paul Rivet reminds us, moreover, that Franz Boas would not have accepted the classification of all the American languages in the agglutinative polysyllabic group. According to Boas, it would be impossible to indicate the common character of these languages solely on the basis of an analysis of sounds. To do so, one would have to take into consideration the use of such grammatical parts as suffixes and prefixes. This would indicate an American achievement in matters of language, but not a common character.

Nor can one classify the South American languages by referring to the names of surviving tribes. These names have been handed down to us deformed and Hispanicized, and have in many cases a double, triple, or even quadruple use. Thus, for example, the term *motilon*, which means *primitive*, was utilized in the eighteenth century apropos of quite diverse groups living in territories far apart from one another. One would have thus thought this to be the effect of migrations, whereas it is actually the result of poor taxonomy.

In practice, linguists now recognize the existence of four great groups of South American pre-Columbian languages. These are subdivided into thirteen subgroups and into a hundred or so families. I mention here only the families to which allusion will be made in this work, without entering into all the details.

MACRO-CHIBCHA

CHIBCHA

Muisca, Cundimarca, and Chibcha spoken in Bogotá, Tunja, Cundimarca, and Pasto.

Today, Chibcha survives only among the Arhuacos, the Cunas of Panama, and on a few islets, as well as among the Barbacoas of Esmeraldas Province in

Ecuador, the Tarascos of Colombia, the Ikas of the Sierra de Santa Marta, and in the islands of San Blas.

PAEZ

Paez is still spoken by several groups in Colombia, in Tierradentro, in Popayán, along the upper Cauca, by the inhabitants of the forests of the Chocó, by the Colorados of equatorial coastal Ecuador, and by the Warraus of the lower Orinoco, but the latter are placed by Mason in an independent family.

MACRO-CHIBCHA

The range of this language was very extensive, including Nicaragua, Costa Rica, Honduras, and Panama. In the east one finds it among the Timotes of Venezuela and in the west on the cool coast of Ecuador, where it was the language of the Mantas, Huanacavelicas, Mochicas, Tallans, Sechuras, and the Yunga-Puruhás of northern Peru. In eastern Peru one finds it again among the Baguas and Chinchipes.

ANDEAN

ANDEAN OF THE CENTRAL ANDES

Quechua was spoken by the Chachapoyas in Huánuco and the Cajamarcas in the Ancash district of Peru, in the heart of the Peruvian Andes from Huamachuco to Ayacucho, and again, farther south, in Cuzco, Puno, and Arequipa, also in Peru.

Aymara is the language of the Collaos and Lupacas. It was formerly spoken as far as Sora, Arequipa, Chanca, Vilcas, and Sicasica, in Peru.

SOUTHERN ANDEAN

This group includes Atacaman, Diaguite, Huamahnaca, Charrua, Huarpe, Araucan, Chono, Puelche, Het, Tehuelche, Yahgan, Alacaluf (considered by Rivet to be an Australian language), and Ona.

ARAWAK

ARAWAK IN THE STRICT SENSE OF THE WORD

Steward places Arawak, along with Quechua and Aymara, in an Ecuadorian Andean group.

This is one of the most important groups, spoken from the West Indies to as far as southern Brazil. Let me note here only a few examples, from north to south: Antillean, Goajiro, Caquetio, Guayape, Arawak proper, Orinoco, Rio Négro of the Amazon, Gaicuru and Juruá Purús in the Andean piedmonts, Piro,

Campa, and Chuncho in the Peruvian *montaña;* Moxo and Chiquito in Bolivia, Puruna, and Xingu.

AFFILIATED LANGUAGES

Jivaro. Spoken by a largely un-Quechuanized forest people living from the Marañón Valley to east of Guayaquil.

Uro-Chipaya-Puquina, the speech around lakes Titicaca and Poopó, and of the Puquinas in central Peru, and also Chongo, spoken by the fishermen of coastal Chile.

Caribbean was almost as widely spread as Arawakan. It was spoken from the lower Antilles to Maracaibo in Venezuela, in the Chocó, among the Cenus in the lower Magdalena, in the Cauca Basin, and among the Pijaos of eastern Colombia. Steward places there the Chiquitos who, according to Mason, would have spoken Puno, and he groups Caribbean with Panoan and Jivaro in the Ecuadorian group, along with Arawak.

Tupi and Guarani are still living languages, spoken from the Guianas in Uruguay and eastern Brazil to the foot of the Andes. (Mention will be made in Chapter Four of the westward migrations of the Guaranis.) Steward places these in the Ecuadorian group, together with Arawak.

Tucanan or Macro-Tucanan are languages still spoken by several groups in the northwestern Amazonas. We may hear there the Chamicuo, Shipibo, Cashibo, Setibo, and Bororo dialects.

GE-PANOAN

These are essentially the languages of central Brazil, like Botocudo, Macro-Ge, and Ge. Most of these are now extinct. Steward adds two families to Ge-Panoan-Caribbean: Nambicuara of central Brazil, and Taruma of the Orinoco.

HOKAN

This idiom seems North American. It is spoken in the Isthmus of Darien.

SOCIAL ORGANIZATION

I have already alluded in the introduction to a dynamic of societies that would generally cause them to evolve from the simplest to the most complex, but with each society evolving according to a different rhythm. Thus, the territories we are studying were populated in the sixteenth century by a mosaic of societies living in very different stages. In moving around the South American continent before the arrival of the Spaniards, one could have visited an empire (that of the Incas), a kingdom (of the Chimus), chiefdoms and feudalities, societies that were barely stratified and hardly structured according to a social plan (generally in the hot lands), those of villages (in the forests), and finally, what anthropologists have named the "marginal" tribes, or tribes grouping together bands of families linked simply by relationship.

Today, only a few of the marginal tribes have been able to maintain their particular life-styles. All the other pre-Columbian social structures have collapsed, even those of the forest villages. The groups of natives that have survived in number, such as the inhabitants of the high plateaus of Ecuador or the Araucanians of Chile, have had to yield to the exigencies of modern life.

The marginal tribes were the object of serious studies by researchers in the beginning of the twentieth century, and fortunately so, because the majority of the groups described have since disappeared. Without these so patiently elaborated texts, we would be ignorant of even the existence of a great number of tribes, whose very traces are now lost.

The information about marginal tribes is also very useful to those trying to understand the mentality of the Andeans, their conception of the world, the mechanism of their ties of relationship, their animistic religions. Studying their material life also explains their use of everyday objects that archaeologists unearth in the course of their excavations.

Despite these studies regarding the marginal tribes and despite the excavations, we still lack many of the elements we need to make the societies of the past come to life. To describe a society is, moreover, one thing, and to make it come to life in a sociopolitical framework is another. For the moment, the most we can do is to draw the broadest outlines.

The societies of the central Andes are those best known to us. Furthermore, they are the ones that seem to have reached the highest degree of sociopolitical and economic maturity. These societies existed from Tumbes, in northern Peru, to around the twenty-second degree of south latitude, and they were incorporated into the empire of the Incas. Therefore, the chroniclers paid more attention to them than to others. Moreover, the Spaniards knew the Incas and had a hard time subduing them. The abundance of documentation we have at our disposal in this respect has thus led me to devote the first half of Chapter Four wholly to the central Andes.

These societies were characterized by a set of cultural traits such as the implementation of a technicized agriculture, maintenance of a network for communication and transport, the existence of urban centers, the practice of a religion calling for public ceremonies, and the conducting of wars whose aim was territorial conquest and not just raiding to obtain trophy heads or prisoners to sacrifice.

Like those of the Near East and China, the societies of the central Andes evolved toward what have been called "hydraulic societies," or societies in which the dominant factor was the control of water resources. Let us remember that it does not rain in the lowlands of Peru. Life there was possible only for communities capable of organizing an irrigation system sufficient for large cultivated areas. Now in arid lands, as seems to have been the case in Mesopotamia, Iran, and Egypt, he who controlled the water became omnipotent. According to the specialists who have studied these problems, hydraulic societies would therefore have taken an autocratic and monolithic form. The same phenomenon would have occurred in China, where the problem was less one of aridity than of controlling the overflow of the great rivers. The necessity to create dams and embankments, to drain multiple canals, would have led the inhabitants to submit to an imperial and unified regime of the same type as the one the Peruvian Incas attempted to establish.

In taking up the study of the central Andes, in order of decreasing complexity, we shall obviously encounter the Inca empire first. Then we shall find factors allowing us to assume that there existed, at least in Peru, a kingdom: that of the Chimu princes, whose capital was Chan Chan, at the threshold of the modern city of Trujillo on the northern coast. The Chimus dominated some twelve coastal valleys and a territory of some 125,000 arable acres. Other kingdoms may have existed, such as that of the Chinchas on the middle southern coast, but the facts to prove it are lacking.

Less complex were what we call chiefdoms. We know the chiefdoms through what the chroniclers have told us, but also thanks to evidence provided by excavations. In the low central Andes, the dry desert sand has preserved for us vestiges permitting reconstitution, down to the smallest detail, of certain aspects of everyday life.

The Muiscas or Chibchas of the high Colombian plateaus, who lived in the region where the cities of Bogotá and Tunja have since been built, constitute a good example of what anthropologists mean by chiefdoms.

In scrupulously reading the chronicles, I shall guess that two kinds of chiefdoms seem to have existed, one being militaristic societies subdivided into distinct hereditary classes and governed by war chiefs, all ruling similar regimes that differed only in characteristics of rather minor importance: a more or less favorable environment, more or less abundant nutritional surpluses, more or less elaborate equipment of everyday life. The number of classes was generally four, sometimes three: that of *caciques* or chiefs, sometimes a female; that of people of rank; that of farmers, and that of slaves. We have known ethnological examples of such stratification among the Maoris and the natives of western Canada.

Another type of chiefdom was that of theocratic societies. Among them, wars seem to have played a less important role. A common cult was practiced by several villages under the spiritual guidance of a shaman who functioned in a sense as a minister of religion and officiated in a temple, a building reserved for

A carved frieze at Chan Chan.

this purpose. In chiefdoms situated in hot lands, this temple would have been a simple building of bamboo and straw, but quite large. The chroniclers described some that were three hundred feet long. In the cool central Andes, theocracies created stone temples and represented their gods and sacred personages in sculptured monoliths. It is in the villages of these peoples that have been found the heavy stone abdominal girdles reminiscent of the ceremonial garments formerly worn in the southern East Indies.

Here war remained necessary at times to maintain cannibal practices and to assure the procurement of trophy heads* or of prisoners. These prisoners served two purposes, either as slaves (manpower), like among the advanced clans of western Canada; or as victims to be sacrificed in the course of great religious ceremonies, as in Mexico.

When it concerns early prehistoric periods, for the study of which we can have recourse only to excavations, it is very hard to place a given society in one or the other category, militaristic or theocratic. We shall probably never know if the personages carved in stone that these societies have at times bequeathed to us represented war chiefs, or magician-priests. Regarding protohistoric societies, on the other hand, it has at times been possible to guess somewhat the type of organization existing at the time of the Conquest.

Let us bear in mind, moreover, that these chiefdoms, whether warlike or theocratic, seem to have been clearly distinguished by one of the traits typical of three categories of societies: those living in the central Andes; those of the circum-Andean regions, influenced by the first; or those of societies called circum-Caribbean, which lived around the Caribbean Sea and in the islands, in Honduras, northern Colombia, and Venezuela. All these societies were endowed with socially stratified organization and practiced a cult in a building used for the purpose.

Other traits typical of chiefdoms are desiccation of the corpses of high-ranking individuals, construction of funerary mounds, wars of conquest in order to obtain tribute and additional resources, and an advanced material culture marked as much by usages typical of the Andes (like hammering metal and chewing coca) as by those of forest people, like hunting with blowguns, bows, and poisoned arrows.

The use of the spear thrower and cremation of the corpses of the common people are, on the other hand, very ancient cultural traits whose origin is hard to establish.

Chiefdoms had developed in very diversified environments: hot forest or steppes, cordilleras overhanging the Atlantic, arid coastal valleys of Peru, the cool coast of Ecuador, and so on.

The Spanish chroniclers noted the presence of military chiefdoms among the Tolus, Turbacos, Calamaris, Monpoxes, Cenus, and Taironas in hot Colombia,

---

*See the next section: "Thought Processes, Philosophy, and Religion."

in lands bordering the Atlantic as well as the Pacific; among the Arawaks of the Caribbean, and among societies living in temperate or cold lands, such as the Muiscas, Buritacas, Antioquias, Paezes of Colombia, and Cañaris of Ecuador.

Theocratic societies, on the contrary, were recognized in the Greater Antilles, Venezuela, and in eastern Bolivia, among the Mojos.

Chiefdoms were also characterized by the existence of nutritional surpluses permitting life for a relatively dense population. A marked sociopolitical organization would not, moreover, have developed if the resources had been too reduced and everyday life too difficult. The chiefdom therefore commanded if not cities, at least villages of some importance, inhabited by up to three to four thousand persons, sometimes in clusters of six to eight hundred houses protected by fences. Such villages were quite often enclaves in areas where farming villages that had remained independent survived. From this tangle there therefore resulted (especially in the lowlands) a high population density, and a great number of edible and useful plants were cultivated intensively.

A heavily fortified retreat village often complemented the village of everyday life. Every big village had nutritional needs. The chief thus had to assure the protection of the village in order to provide for establishing food reserves and the defense of the farmers on whom the life of the community depended.

Cieza de León describes a peasant of the lower Magdalena as ". . . digging the earth with one hand, the other ready to seize the bow to defend himself against the invader."

I think that a formal relationship must have existed between the chief and the warriors on the one hand, and the common farmers on the other. In my opinion, the word *feudalities* would be as fitting as *chiefdoms* here.

Cieza's description reminds me of what a Congolese African said when a Belgian asked how independence would change his way of life. The Congolese replied, "That will oblige me to carry my gun when I go to the village, as my grandfather used to do." We can also imagine that the pre-Columbian defending his field would have been happy to fertilize it, when the opportunity presented itself, by shedding an enemy's blood.

The process of protecting villages led fatally to the formation of confederations of tribes, to the domination of a territory by a more powerful chief, the establishment of states, the creation of a codified and stratified social system, and such would have been born in the central Andes if the Europeans had not destroyed everything.

Chiefdoms were not formed solely in hot lands developed according to slash-and-burn farming, called *milpa* in Central America and *roza* in Peru. They were found as well in the lands where intensive and extensive agriculture was practiced on terraces, on the basis of rains. Other chiefdoms dominated the lands where irrigation was necessary, as in the territory of the Cañaris or the Muiscas of Colombia and of upper Ecuador, in the Caribbean islands, and in the mountains of Venezuela.

On the other hand, there generally were not chiefdoms in the forest. This kind of society penetrated there only occasionally, and probably by acculturation. The best-known exceptions in this respect are those of the Mojos, Paressís, Baurés, and the Mananis of Bolivia, all important chiefdoms in the hot forests.

At the time of their arrival, the Spaniards were able to observe vast fields of corn in the lower Magdalena Valley and the Caribbean. The Caribbean seems to have been very prosperous. On Hispaniola, six chiefdoms were counted—one Taino and five Ciguayo—all Arawakan, grouping on the order of one hundred thousand persons. Each chiefdom was subdivided into territories administered by subchiefs who divided up the lands among blood-related groups of five to six hundred persons living according to the principles of matrilineal endogamy.

But it is possible that the domain of feudal lords had at that time already been heavily cut into by invaders from the east. We shall see, further on, the possible causes of the weakening that would have permitted these invasions.

What was the respective order of appearance of the two types of societies, of the Andes and of the forest? Did one of the two (or both) evolve from the primitive tribes, some of which survived as marginal tribes? The classical anthropological school considers the Andean societies to be the culmination of a long "cordillera tradition," the traces of which may be noted from Mexico to the central Andes. It considers the forest societies to be recessive, formed by groups that would have fled toward the less heavily populated hot lands, where they would have lost a good many of their Andean or circum-Andean cultural traits.

I think it fitting to await the results of more advanced excavations before taking a position on this issue. If the very early skeletons beginning to be discovered in the Andes turn out to have belonged to a type different from that of the Andean farmers, the position of the defenders of the theory of successive waves of immigration will be strengthened, and one will be led to suppose that the more highly developed cordillera tradition was superimposed on a simpler foundation that subsequently survived here and there in the form of what have been called the marginal tribes.

Outside of the feudal chiefdoms, there existed simpler societies remaining at the stage of independent villages. One found this type of village as much in the forest as in the sub-Andean region, around the Caribbean, in the Orinoco Basin, and among the farmers and shepherds of the southern Andes: Atacamanians living in the oases, Diaguites in the arid cordillera, Araucanians in humid and wooded Chile.

The villages of the pre-Columbians of the southeastern Andes have all been abandoned now, and the Mapuches, Diaguites, and Araucanians have been integrated into the life of modern Chile. (The Araucanians formed a nation composed of three tribes: the Mapuches, the Huillichés, and the Picunchés.) We must, therefore, appeal to archaeology in order to find out anything of the life of the pre-Hispanic inhabitants of these regions.

It is the farmers of the hot lands, who have survived here and there down to our time, who have provided us with the most complete information regarding the life of these forest villages.

Thanks to the natives who still live in the *llanos* (the grassy savannahs of the plains), in the grassy pampas of the Amazonas in Brazil, and on the hot Pacific Coast, we know that the forest villages were made up of consanguineous bands. (The term *relationship,* in societies of this type, does not have the same meaning as in the classical Mediterranean world. In the societies we are discussing, one is a relative because he is the offspring of a common ancestor, at times a very distant one, usually hypothetical.) Social relations there were reduced to their simplest expression, to the domain of familial relations. Classes and social stratification were unknown. Sometimes there was a secret society, but cults were not practiced. The mysteries were controlled by the shaman.

The villages were often important, fortified, surrounded by stockades. The federation of several villages was an unusual thing, and war raged permanently among neighboring groups. Hunting for trophy heads remained a necessity of a psychological order as well as for obtaining prisoners.

Having returned home after hunting, fishing, or fighting, these warrior-farmers lived in the nude, their bodies painted, in beautiful houses covered with thatched roofs made of laths from long bamboos cut with a stone axe. For hunting and fishing they used the bow, pronged harpoons, and boats.

The first European immigrants described for us the life of the Caribans of the Lesser Antilles, the Guajiros of Colombia, the tribes of the Guianas plains, and the *montaña* (the hot Andes piedmonts) of Ecuador and Peru, as well as the Tupis of the Amazonas and the Guaranis of southern Brazil and the Bolivian Chaco. Their agriculture was prosperous, centered simultaneously on harvesting manioc and corn, harvests obtained in clearings made by burning trees, on land fertilized by the ashes. Thus, forest societies searched for and followed the vegetal covering. But they also needed water; therefore, when the soil in a given place lost its fertility or the water supply diminished, they moved to a place that had the resources their lives depended on.

Let me add that the equipment of material life hardly differed here from that of chiefdoms, and that numerous typically Andean traits were present in these villages: looms, baskets, boats. But other cultural traits, like that of using poisoned arrows, were typical of the forest.

Next to bands grouped in independent agricultural villages lived the marginal tribes, consanguineous bands of Shipibos, Jivaros, and Piros. These tribes likewise practiced agriculture, but they lived either as seminomads in the montaña or settled in simple forest villages in the northwestern Amazonas and in the llanos. The surviving Ge-speaking groups of the high Brazilian plateaus—the Yaruros of the Orinoco, the Comechingons of the Chaco, and the Huarpes— were ancient hunters from marginal tribes who had become farmers, devoted to cultivating plants with rhizomes in the forest. If need be, therefore, one can categorize all these groups as semimarginal.

More simply still lived the genuinely marginal tribes, those who formed bands that did not practice agriculture. Europeans encountered some of them in cold lands (such as the Patagonians, Puelches, and Tehuelches in the southern part of the continent), but equally in hot lands—Ciboneys in the Caribbean, the Bororos of Brazil, and other groups in the Chaco.

These truly marginal tribes also lived in bands of individuals united by ties of consanguinity. Their material life and technology were rudimentary. The equipment observed among the marginal tribes by twentieth-century ethnologists indicates an obvious decadence, compared with what the archaeology of previous periods reveals. Before this last regression, all these tribes would have used equipment of the same value, without marked changes over a period of at least ten thousand years, and perhaps much longer.

The social organization of the marginal tribes was reduced to that of family life. The rules of living were transmitted and applied in terms of the tradition of each tribe. Anthropologists call a tribe a cluster of groups that may be politically independent, but are united by a certain number of common traits of a cultural and linguistic nature.

The nutritional resources of marginal tribes, obtained by picking, gathering, beachcombing, hunting, and fishing, were generally limited and did not permit the accumulation of reserves. Their bands therefore remained necessarily reduced in size.

The lack of means of transportation must also have created limitations. The marginal tribes lived as they could, each group in terms of its tradition, either of hunting, like the Onas of Tierra del Fuego, or the gathering of mussels, like the Yahgans, who lived aboard boats.

The accommodations of the marginal tribes were reduced to a strict minimum. Some of them, like the Ciboneys of the Caribbean, were even reputed to live with neither huts nor shelters, but that is certainly inaccurate. Other groups used only simple shelters against the wind, or transportable tents. Finally, others constructed huts of various shapes and, according to their traditions, domes or conical tepees. Among them, a big multifamilial house was a rarity. At times they built semisubterranean huts or huts surrounded by low stone walls, a mark of Andean influence. Whereas in the forest villages one slept on a platform or in a hammock, the marginal tribes slept on the ground on mats. Some of them had, however, adopted the use of the hammock or of a bed set on a platform, copying the usages of the forest people.

Little is known of the social organization of these bands. It must have barely exceeded the stage of families living isolatedly in little nuclei of one to five huts. At times, the necessity of protecting themselves against dangers such as witchcraft or invasion led families to form themselves into bands under the direction of an *ancient* who became the head of a group. But the situation most frequently noted is that of a state of fears of magic from which all these populations suffered, leading them to stay away from their neighbors to protect themselves from the evil eye. Today, natives from the tribes living on the peninsula of Guajira, Venezuela, still live in isolated huts protected by cactus spines and at a bow-shot's distance away from the nearest neighbor.

All this was, moreover, vague and variable enough. Groups were known that had organized secret societies and practiced rites of passage. Others were known that did not indulge in these practices. Some groups were patrilineal, others matrilineal, and there were composite groups, at times even associations of bands of people having no ties of relationship with the others.

Some bands united as many as a hundred persons, the medley of four or five consanguineous families. When they became too numerous, they divided into two exogamous halves. This exogamy continued even if the two halves no longer lived together.

As the number of group members increased, direct and natural affiliation ended up being lost. A common mythical ancestor then re-created an artificial relationship and there was born what is called a totemic clan, the totem being the representation of the common ancestor.

In summary, these were simple societies, dominated by their shamans, with no class distinctions, burying their dead simply, but already having an evolved conception of cosmogony and the problem of the hereafter, already familiar with the notion of a principal divinity such as the moon or sun, using hallucinogens and practicing games, music, and ritual sacrifices like gashing a finger, pulling out a nail, receiving flagellation, and so forth. The equipment of everyday life here is reduced to a strict minimum: the spear thrower, spears, and bolas, perhaps borrowed from Andean societies. Baskets were unknown.

THOUGHT PROCESSES, PHILOSOPHY, AND RELIGION

Nothing is harder to know than the deep motivations governing the thought of natives who are strangers to our mentality and education, whether this be in matters of thought, philosophy, religion, or cosmogony. The same observation holds for some aspects of their daily life, like taboos on food and medicine.

First, the native feels reluctant to tackle these problems. When questioned, he does not like to reply; initially because the inquisitor instills in him a magical fear, then because often he has forgotten the deep, true meaning of his gestures and no longer explains them except by rationalizations. Just as our hesitation to go under a ladder, a hesitation whose real reason we have forgotten (the possibility of having a can of paint fall on us) is explained by creating the myth of the ladder that brings misfortune, so will the native have forgotten the true reasons that incite him to refuse to eat his meals in a dish belonging to other people. He will speak of hygiene, whereas in fact he is afraid of insulting the evil spirit that has come with the stranger.

To speak of the thought and religion of the Andean peoples is therefore an act of audacity that a historian should normally avoid, and this chapter will be the one that will risk the most criticism in this work. But can one avoid treating this theme? Through experience acquired in higher education, I know that the first questions that an audience of students ask will generally refer to the soul of these Andean men of the past. "What was the religion of the Mochicas?" I shall be asked in Peru. It is with disbelief and scorn that the audience will listen to me while I explain that in this area we shall never have written texts at our disposal and that we can search for the solution only in completely indirect ways such as excavations, chronicles, and ethnology.

Excavations will never tell us what the pre-Columbian natives thought, but they will orient us to some of their preoccupations. Thus, the study of their sepulchers will reveal their fear of death to us. The presence of objects for sorcery will indicate their anxieties regarding the cure of diseases and indicate the presence of a shaman or sorcerer-healer in their villages.

In fact, all the authors of the Spanish accounts considered the natives of the Andes to be living in a blameworthy state of heresy, given to idolatry and indulging in demonic practices. This was a natural reaction on the part of men animated by a great faith but brought up in the ambience of a Spain just coming out of the Middle Ages. To the conquerors, even for those who were true ruffians, animated by the most shameful spirit of profit, and for the clergymen who accompanied them, the beliefs of the natives represented only evil.

Fortunately, the chroniclers have nevertheless provided us with some observations regarding the rituals practiced by the natives: ceremonies, festivities, burials, prayers to the dead, intervention because of diseases, superstitious terrors, and so on. Some of this information can, moreover, be corroborated by the information we can procure from excavations, and many rituals have survived notwithstanding the effects of so-called modern education.

In this field, Mexico offers us many more resources, on account of the survival of some protohistoric texts. But it would be dangerous to transpose directly to the Andes what Mexico reveals to us.

Finally, let us not forget that although the majority of the natives were crossbred and converted to the official religion of Spain, there survived on the two American continents groups still living like their ancestors, as non-Europeanized and free-thinking individuals influenced very little by our customs. Ethnologists have thus been able to learn from such of these groups as the natives of western Canada, Eskimos in the Far North, and tribes living in Mexico and Central America.

For South America, one may consult texts describing the Jivaros and other tribes of the Amazonas, the Guajiros of Colombia, the Paezes of Tierradentro, and certain tribes from the Chaco, Patagonia, and Tierra del Fuego.

Even among the groups that underwent crossbreeding (like those of Otavalo, or the Manabís in Ecuador, or those of the high plateaus of Peru and Bolivia), the present mentality is the product of traditional pre-European concepts blended with concepts acquired since Hispanicization. To realize this, all one has to do is be present at a festival in Otavalo or in the province of Huarochiri in the heart of Andean Peru where marriage, though blessed by the priest, is still practiced according to the millennial rites and where appeal is made on this occasion to the ancestral spirits.

As a last point, let us not neglect the few useful bits of information bequeathed to us by the oral traditions of the Polynesians, whose social pattern, after all, was that of chiefdoms, when Europeans met them.

THE PRE-COLUMBIAN MENTALITY

The study of those who populated the un-Hispanicized American world gives rise to the following reflections.

The native of the Americas seems to have been fundamentally animistic. For him, and even for the South American mestizo or mixed-blood today, not only man but also animals, plants, inanimate objects, and natural phenomena have a soul. This soul does not die; it travels.

This animistic conception of the known and unknown worlds leads progressively to that of metempsychosis—the soul travels, therefore it wanders around to find its new lodging, which is usually thought to consist of a part of the body of the deceased, especially the cranium and bones. It is peoples with a more developed philosophy who believe that the soul finally reaches nirvana. Among simple folk, the soul always remains migratory and dangerous. Halfway between these two extremes, there takes shape the notion of the soul finding repose by fixation in a tree.

When the notion of resurrection has taken shape, one will as much as possible preserve the human corpse; first, that of chiefs, persons useful for leading the group; then that of the most humble fisherman. In Paracas, almost-intact buried bodies of humble fishermen are found by the hundreds. If possible, one will preserve the corpse by drying it in the sun, in order to facilitate the rebirth of the individual. The body will be given a fetal position in its tomb, which should facilitate its second birth. Other people, on the contrary, will strip off the flesh and burn or reinter the bones of the deceased, dyed with red urucú or achiote, since red is a symbol of life and blood. Vermilion constitutes a love potion. One likewise paints his body red before going into battle, in case of injury, sickness, and the like. The nails and hair play an important role in this process. According to Inca Garcilazo de La Vega, "Andeans carefully buried all remains of hair and nails, in order to facilitate resurrections; and venerated this type of remains of the Incas."

In the Chaco, some misfortunes were attributed to the lack of care taken for the hairy parts of the body—eyebrows, eyelashes, and the like. Thus, one could not eat fish until one had arranged one's hair in a certain way.

A general practice was to take special care in decorating the graves of little children, whose health is always delicate and should thus be protected in view of their second birth.

In Peru, our excavations show that it is the bodies of stillborn or very young children that received the most attentive care and that were accompanied by the richest funerary accoutrements.

Some groups also believed that when the soul was reborn, it would be reincarnated in an inferior being by way of punishment, not to return to the state of being a man until later. Or they believed that the soul had taken refuge in a certain animal, who then became the protector of a group of people related by blood. This practice is called totemism, the totem representing the animal protector of the group.

In some cases, a more complicated mechanism was conceived. The soul was supposed to end up living in a territory inhabited by the divinities who protected such and such a group: pumas, ostriches, foxes, and so forth. This territory was either a rock, the bottom of a lake, the base of a mountain, or the like. Regarding the Andes, this concept is directly known to me by information given by contemporary Araucanians in Chile.

Finally, among the natives of the Andes there existed the concept of an association of thought between man and the animal world, be it lower (like that of insects) or higher, like that of the big or intelligent mammals or birds. Thus, the soul of a Chiriguano of the Pilcomayo Basin, in the Bolivian Chaco, first had to visit its god before being reincarnated in a fox, an animal feared for its artfulness and swiftness. From the fox, the soul could pass to the body of a mouse, finally to find repose in a tree trunk.

A good many animals became untouchable in this way: birds, for example, because "they came from the land of the ancestors." Broadly speaking, it was thought that all animals had been men.

Simple beings never cease to live in fear, since they move in a dangerous world, one in which they feel themselves surrounded by the souls of their ancestors and by those of their enemies. Now it is these souls that they hold responsible for their ailments and for death. They attribute all their misfortunes to the vengeance of the deceased. The first reflex of the native will as a result be to protect himself against disease. He will smear himself with oil and paints. To say that one coats himself with oil in order to keep the insects away is a rationalization, an apparently logical explanation of a gesture whose deeper meaning has been forgotten. The native will deform his child's skull to protect him, since in elongating it one gives less of a hold to a demon who would want to carry the baby off. This later rationalization says in effect that in creating a pear-shaped skull, one helps to make a child healthy.

After killing an enemy, one must have the murder forgiven by the soul of the deceased. Long ceremonies are thus practiced with an eye toward placating the evil spirit that might venture—oh horrors!—to be reincarnated in an animal one might inadvertently come to eat. Therefore, one will bless the animals one is about to eat or hunt, to try to purify them. The natives of the archipelago of southern Chile, for example, feared Ayayema, the spirit of evil, the persecutor; and Kawtcho, the spirit who prowled in the night. One could not throw a mollusk back into the sea for fear of making all the shellfish hostile.

In other societies, the warrior tries to attach the soul of the vanquished to himself, to make it his slave. But he does this as much to absorb its force as to neutralize it.

The orifices of the body constitute dangerous portals through which spirits can penetrate the individual. Against these possible intrusions, one uses the most diverse defenses, the most common of which are ones such as the wearing of plates covering the lower part of the face and attached to a perforation of the septum, the bone of the nose. Such plates were frequently made of gold. They were also copied in highly polished semiprecious stones. Most of them have been found in graves, but they can also be seen represented on the Nazca painted vases in Peru, or in Mexico.

Other defenses are used, such as attaching big plates to the ears (the lobes of which are deformed for this purpose), the use of labrets or tubes passed through the lower lip, the wearing of necklaces made of tubular bones or the teeth and claws of animals, or of small bells and rings on the arms, and protective bindings on the legs as well as girdling with a rope the lower abdomen of pubescent girls. Everything is done to conquer fear. Hiding one's sexual parts is obviously to protect them from attacks by flies and from cuts by lianas in the forest, but above all it is to block the apertures through which the evil spirits might enter. Thus, for example, it is feared that a demon may enter a woman during coition. Before going near a man, a widow must wait a year so that the soul of her husband first has time to become appeased.

Since ashes and waste from fires are considered to be prophylactic, they are rubbed into the tattooing incisions with which one adorns girls. In this way, the propitiation wounds inflicted during puberty will not disappear and will have a durable protective effect.

The idea that a misfortune overtakes you following the unfriendly gesture of an enemy returns at every moment. This, for example, is how the sudden attack of a jaguar is explained.

The notions of *taboo* and *mana* are very likely derived from generalizing about spiritual conditions of this nature. Certain objects or actions are taboo; that is, they must be avoided, since they would be liable to bring diseases. Thus, using glasses and plates used by white men risks favoring the introduction of evil spirits into the bodies of natives and ruining their health.

In Lima, I have seen my excavation foreman use his own dishes for fifteen years. He carefully transports them wrapped up in a napkin knotted at the four corners. Another man on the team used a special cup to drink his tea "because Japanese porcelain is the healthiest." Was it that my dishes seemed suspect to him? Catching the eye of a stranger, of whatever race, always risks bringing evil. This is why one never looks anyone in the face, especially while speaking.

Today, the fear of causing oneself to be snubbed—treated as an Indian and thus backward—holds Andeans back from offering you recourse to exorcism. They only risk it with respect to people in whom they have great confidence.

Probably it was timidity on this order that kept a man on my team, an Andean from San Pedro de Lloc in northern Peru, from offering me his services when I was the victim of a serious accident. This foreman had formerly been a *curandero*, a healer, and even knew how to deliver babies.

Once when I had returned from the clinic after an operation, I was back at work one day when the man waited for all the members of the team to leave, then came over to me to say, "Why didn't you tell me, boss, that you were so sick? If you had told me, I would have taken you to a willow which, when one embraces its trunk on a moonless night, draws the sickness out of your body. . . ." "How I regret, Don A——," I replied, "that you did not tell me about this sooner."

To protect oneself is one thing, but evil often succceeds in entering. Therefore, it must be treated and exorcised. Then appeal is made to one of those who possesses *mana*, a supernatural power capable of resisting the evil spirit. In Peru, mestizos ask the priest to exorcise their home when anything suspicious is happening. The Andean appeals to the witch doctor, the *curandero*, the medicine man, and generally to any person he thinks able to help him, either to cure or protect him or to bestow particular forces and opportunities upon him. The result of this is a kind of circuitous route that may be represented as follows: Sickness equals demon. Hence, an appeal is made to the witch doctor, with an eye toward obtaining the intervention of other, beneficial demons. This intervention appears in the form of purifying ceremonies, sacrifices, offerings and, in certain cases, in enforcing a taboo—an obligation to abandon or burn the house or even the village, to proceed at times to human sacrifices, most frequently of babies.

Certain instruments used for incantatory or propitiatory ceremonies remain taboo themselves: flutes, blood, and so on. Naturally, one cannot let them be seen by women, always impure and dangerous elements on account of their menstruations. After a long absence, I found all the avocado trees in my garden in Lima dead, withered. When questioned, the gardener refused to reply, until one day a heavy dose of rum having given him the audacity, he confessed that my trees had died because the maidservant had climbed them to steal fruit while she was "impure," which is to say during her period.

Operations of a magical character pursue various objectives, the essential one being to transfer the evil onto a scapegoat, to purify, to bring the good forward. The propitiatory ceremony tends to ameliorate contact with the divinity. These ceremonies also aim to obtain a transfer of powers in favor of the individual or group for whom the witch doctor or priest is officiating.

Even more than cannibalism, the object of deep horror on the part of Renaissance Europeans, who did not understand that this action was a part of the magic ritual, hunting for trophy heads was practiced by numerous societies of the New World, as by those of New Guinea and Polynesia. In Peru, the trophy head played an important role in the iconography of farmer-warriors in Chavín, Paracas, Nazca, and Tiahuanaco. This head-hunting activity astounded the conquerors, who had come from a continent where this means of acquiring virile virtues and assimilating those of an adversary had long since been forgotten. However, the Europeans should have remembered that the Mongolian and Chinese princes next door to them boasted of raising pyramids composed of as many as a hundred thousand heads (at times more) and that the Vikings, some five centuries earlier, were still drinking from the skulls of their enemies.

In South America, several groups living in the hot lands still hunt human heads and reduce them to the size of a toy, after fasting and enduring the privations intended to obtain the pardon of the soul of the deceased. But then why kill the enemy and make him into wind bags stuffed with straw, which the Spanish chronicler Cieza de León saw, hung and animated by the wind, at the entrance of Colombian villages? The idea is the same everywhere. The scalp, the easiest part to attach to the saddle, could be the symbol of the trophy head, with the same rite adapted to the use of a horse and of a tomahawk, a metal axe with a sharp cutting edge. Another theory suggests that scalping was introduced by whites, who paid the natives a reward for each Indian killed. Scalps were counted instead of skulls, which were too heavy to carry. What one wants in killing a man is of course on the one hand to prove one's valor and thus one's virility. Hunting for heads and prisoners must have been indispensable for maintaining, by selection, the aristocracy of warriors.

But on the other hand, one tries to assimilate into oneself the strength and courage of the vanquished. Thus, in order to go to war one covers oneself with the skin of a tiger or fox, symbols of strength and astuteness. One drinks from the skulls of enemies in order to absorb their courage. Once the battle is ended, one munches his bones and eats his flesh.

In thinking he wants a skull or its symbol the hair, the warrior is in fact making a rationalization. He thinks he wants to prove his valor, whereas in actuality it is the power of the enemy that he unconsciously desires to appropriate. And we have perhaps forgotten it, but we find a comparable image in the Bible with the parable of Samson, who loses his virile strength through losing his hair.

In tropical Asia, as in pre-Columbian America, one even hunted heads in order to assure the fertility of the harvest. Thus, Filipinos practiced this sport twice a year. When they were about to harvest, they planted a skull on a post at the edge of the field.

The trophy-head cult, therefore, proves to be not only a virility rite but an aspect of a cult of the fertility of nature as well. In the lower Andes, it appeared only with the cultivation of corn and then invaded the iconography of the Chavín society, to last nearly fifteen hundred years. Among the Incas, who were more highly developed, this rite disappeared. On the other hand, the Incas preserved corpses of their direct ancestors and carried them with great pomp on days of religious ceremony.

On the painted vases from Nazca, the trophy head was used next to corn and symbols of rural activities. At times, the man was holding a skull in one hand and ears of corn in the other. In defending his field, he was fertilizing it.

The bird of prey also played a role in this domain. The French even have a saying that translates literally as "defend oneself with beak and nails." Caps and cloaks were decorated with their feathers, certainly for beauty, but also to assimilate the powers of falcons and eagles. The faces of men painted on the Nazca vases are often tattooed with two spots called *falconides*, since they have been copied from spots observed on the faces of Andean falcons.

Feathers also symbolized hair, of men and animals; the use of feathered ceremonial garments would have arisen from this. The magic flute and the arrow that cannot miss the enemy were also decorated with feathers.

Another method of purification was mutilation. One proceeded by bleedings and suckings to draw the disease out of the body. One whipped, pierced a limb with thorns, and cut the body. One tortured at puberty and mutilated the genitals by circumcision or excision, by piercing the urinary duct. One had a young woman deflowered before marriage by an old woman, by the witch doctor, or even by her mother, Garcilazo tells us.

Preparation for marriage required many precautions. To perform coition with a young woman who had not been purified could lead to death.

One also mutilated one finger or toe, in order to mourn or to prove one's strength, like the old Australian who at forty removed the nail of his second thumb with a bamboo chisel in order to prove that he was as virile as when his first nail had been removed at puberty.

Magical force was obtained not only with the help of the shaman's intervention, but also with the intermediation of symbols, for example in the form of ornamental decorations with secret meanings. I have already cited in this respect the designs painted on the human body. But the same idea is found in the decoration of objects from daily life, and this perhaps favored the birth of art.

Some groups paint their plates and dishes; others do not. Should one see in this the reflection of a difference in philosophical concepts? Some authorities consider art to be just a magic ritual. Here is an idea to puzzle over.

During periods in which one decorates ceramics and objects from daily life, the artist will draw bodies, faces, or stylized representations of beings who personify the souls of several personages whom one needs or, on the contrary, whose spirits one wishes to conjure. The masks typical of the Far East and the Andes, and which represent demons, were very likely born from such a concept. The Onas of Patagonia, for example, used to initiate youngsters to the life of men with the help of masks symbolizing dangers: those of the sky having a red mask with white dots; those of the clouds, a white mask, and that of the demon of abysses, a black mask.

The forest people also thought that by painting drums with symbolic colors or figures one was increasing the magical power of their sound, and thought that in painting the image of a serpent on his legs or house, one would neutralize the serpent's deadly bite; that one could avoid being shipwrecked by painting on the boat the sperm whale that might throw him into the ocean.

Among the Aymaras, serpents were the enemies of thunder. A serpent was sculptured on one of the stones of the walls of their houses or of their *chulpas,* their funerary towers. With Christianization, one will protect oneself from thunder and lightning by invoking Santiago, Saint James, the master of these elements.

One still comes upon flocks of llamas with their ears decorated with pompons of red wool. This is done to honor the spirits. But when the spirits are evil, one must go further. For example, one greatly fears the larilari, a bird with the face of a rat, that steals the souls of its victims. Against these demons, the Aymaras place on the frame of the house, under the roof, the *toyru,* a cross made of threads, an object that has also been found in graves four thousand years old.

Certain fears have survived until now, such as fear of the *pistacco*, the white man who seizes little boys in order to extract the fat from them. Fifteen years ago there were still numerous villages in the cordillera in which not only the young women used to flee upon the arrival of a European (one can guess why), but so did the children, who would signal the presence of danger by crying *"Pistaccos!"*

The artistic effort exerted in order to give to ceramics artistic decoration responds to a secret and particularly subtle need. "The vessel contains water, and water is the source of life," the Pueblos of Arizona used to say. But the clay of which the pot is made is also life, since clay is earth. Therefore, one decorates the pot in order to honor the earth, but not with closed lines, since one cannot hold life a prisoner. Pots, after the death of their users, become not offerings but life charms or amulets, like the rest of funerary furniture. One smashes them or places them whole in tombs, according to custom. Other societies, like the desert cultures of the American Southwest, used to break the family's grindstone when the father died.

Cave paintings are also exorcising or propitiatory images. Today the natives do not like to come near them. They are gods, they say, believing that to touch them brings disease.

With the development of agriculture, one witnesses a modification of notions regarding the respective roles of man and woman in society. Knowledge about birth and the different roles of the parents at the time of coition remain vague. The notion of copulation is often not associated with that of conception, which is attributed to the moon or to plants. One of my employees in Lima complained that she was expecting a baby "because she had consumed too many vitamins."

For a long time, the man will remain the bearer of the egg that the woman will enclose, and in some groups the male will practice couvade. He will take care of himself and purify himself after childbirth, in order to assure the health of the newborn child. But when agriculture takes the lead, it is on the fecundity of the earth, the goddess mother of vegetation, that one will count in order to be assured of a normal life, a life that will not be embittered by the horror of famine. The sorcery of hunting then becomes of secondary importance, as does the role of hunting itself. Men take refuge in *kiwas*, in their underground clubs, to smoke and gossip in secret, far from the women. The role of women in society thus becomes more important, partly because it is the woman who works the fields, but mainly because woman cannot be dissociated from the image of the earth goddess, the mother of the group. Feminine votive statuettes thus appear everywhere, with the help of which one tries to assure the fecundity of the earth.

And legends are born. Thus, the Jivaros think the earth goddess, called *Pachamama* by the Andeans of Peru and Bolivia, once appeared to them and taught them how to cultivate the soil. Then she abandoned her ungrateful children.

Certain plants have a beneficent character, but others, on the contrary, are pernicious. Thus, the chonta palm, a hard and obstreperous wood, was used to make spears, whereas achiote, which has a red dye, was considered beneficent. In agriculture, plants will become either male or female; one will honor the edible ones with a cult. Thus, Father Cobo tells us regarding corn that "one used to choose the finest ear, and place it in an earthenware jar covered with the finest fabrics, and worship it for three days; then one guarded it preciously like a *huaca,* a sacred object, in the house, until the shaman said this corn had lost its force; then one started over again with other ears."

The religious concepts seem to have evolved in the last pre-Columbian centuries. In the Andes, one still worshipped as *achachilas* (venerable and sacred objects symbolizing the ancestors) the sun, moon, stars, thunder, rainbows, clouds, rocks, and all the cosmic manifestations that generally preoccupied all peoples living close to nature. (Even the very humble hunters in the interior of Australia are preoccupied with cosmogony. They know how to recognize the seasons and how to tell time with the help of a rudimentary gnomon, a simple stake planted in the ground.) Titicaca itself was the red rock, the refuge of the sanguinary feline, one of the most sacred places in the high Andes.

But the earth, the water, the sea—Mamacocha, the mother of waters, the creator of all things—took a more and more important place in religious thinking. One adopted the cult of Viracocha, a god who had come out of the waters of Lake Titicaca, and the island of Koati was considered to be the dwelling place of the moon. Upon the arrival of the Spaniards, Viracocha seemed on the way to assuming an anthropomorphic face. Are we not approaching a concept comparable to that of Zeus?

The modifications that little by little came to affect the ways of practicing religion also affected social life, as, for example, bonds formed between villages as a result of their practicing the same cult. Such cases have been observed among the Caribbeans in the Antilles, in Venezuela, and in eastern Bolivia, where the shaman practiced rites in a ceremonial house reserved for the men. But on the contrary, in other Caribbean countries the concept of ancestral spirits, guardians of the group, remained vivid.

It is possible that the moon, Venus, and the Pleiades had played, long before the sun did, a preponderant role in the religious conceptions of these peoples. The lunar calendar seems to have been conceived first, the solar calendar being adopted later. The two systems were often maintained together. I cannot prove it, but I suspect the Nazcas of Peru of having devised a Venusian calendar. It is only later, and progressively, that the Incas of Peru seem to have tried to attribute to the sun an increasing importance, perhaps with an eye to creating a theocratic state. The notion of the Inca incarnating the sun god perhaps facilitated obtaining the submission of other princes, who also called themselves son of the sun and therefore did not think they were losing prestige in forming an alliance with a personage of the same race.

But when he has been taught that the sun is the divinity and that the Inca incarnates the sun, a man will soon understand that he needs a strong sun; his own life depends on it. Therefore, he must help to reinforce the power of the sun as much as that of the prince. The loss of power of the god will constitute a calamity to be avoided at all costs, since, as Sir J. G. Frazer remarked, "The gods are not immortal." It used to be said that certain Africans were in the habit of killing their kings as the result of a decision by the warriors assembled in council, to replace him by a stronger sovereign; but modern anthropology rejects this concept.

One will seek to make the god strong by instituting sacrifices in his honor. One will offer him flowers, shells, gold, little woolen garments, llamas, red pepper, and *chicha*, a beer made from fermented maize. One will hide votive objects in the corners of buildings under construction, generally baskets in which one has brought his contribution of materials for the construction of the building—gravel or blocks of stone. When the seriousness of the situation demands it, one will even offer human sacrifices.

Other peoples have also sacrificed human beings. The Sioux did so until about 1837. The Cañaris of Ecuador used to sacrifice as many as a hundred children in order to ensure a good crop, and during battles the women used to collect the blood shed by the men in order to spread it over the fields. At times a son would be sacrificed to save a father, and the idols used to be wetted with blood obtained by sacrifices.

But this kind of sacrifice, which played a considerable role in Mexico, remained unknown in the eastern Andes and was hardly practiced in the high Andes. It was the llama, especially white ones, a domestic animal directly linked to man, that was offered to the sun. The sacred character of llamas and alpacas appears in certain episodes of everyday life. For instance, by invoking the pretext that the animals experienced difficulty coupling by themselves (perhaps on account of their being domesticated), the inhabitants of the high Andes would justify the habit of helping them manually to practice coition. One will note a typical rationalization here, the true but forgotten meaning of the action probably being to cooperate with the fecundity of a sacred animal.

Therefore, even when he became a farmer the Andean remained essentially an animist. He used to make dolls of corn covered with amulets and worship Zara-mama or Mama-zara, the goddess of this plant; or Cocamama, Quinuamama, the goddesses of coca and quinoa, and so forth. Near Cuzco, Father Cobo tells us, there was a hill where corn was worshipped and children were sacrificed.

The Andeans were so imbued with animism that finally everything became sacred for them—a place of worship, a votive place: tombs, high summits, volcanoes, thunder, everything was *huaca;* that is, either a representation of the divinity, the divinity itself, or the place where it dwelled. All of this indicates, moreover, a great need of spirituality and probably the search for a faith. As an indication of this need, it suffices to refer to the fervor with which Andeans of today still practice, in their own way to be sure, the Christian religion. The mass said for the natives in Chinchero, near Cuzco, is, for example, one of the most moving spectacles one can witness but must not be confused with the ugly farces organized for tourists, such as the mass at Pisac.

The Andeans had already invented purification in order to diminish the

An early farmer's skull. The fact that the skin and hair are still visible and the eyes are in the sockets indicates an extremely dry environment.

A rare object of unknown use (possibly a sieve), found up to now only in Paracas during one short period. Nothing similar has been found anywhere else. It dates from around two thousand years ago.

dangers of an unhealthy and dangerous situation. To purify was also to bring forward good. In ameliorating contact with the god, one obtained a transfer of divine powers in his own favor. Incantations and sacrifices were not the only remedies in this respect—in the high Andes, the search for protection against diseases, death, cataclysms, had already attained very spiritualized forms. Thus, for example, confession was practiced in the Inca empire, and it was taught that the transgression of moral rules brought defilement, that evil action leads to affliction. One therefore sought to neutralize evil by confessing it. Even in only confessing an evil thought one exorcised the defilement, and the affliction would be cured.

But one confesses only what is necessary to ward off the evil spell. It is not a matter of a general confession in order to purify the soul of the sinner. The mechanism remains specifically animistic; the wound is believed caused by a demon.

Because in all the arid zones of the world the gravest affliction that may overtake a man is lack of water, I thought I would give a conclusion as poetic as it is logical to this chapter by citing here the prayer addressed to the god Viracocha by an Andean of high Peru, as it was reported by Father Cobo. This invocation reveals a high level of spirituality and a conception of the divine nature of things.

"Lord, you who have created all things and who have judged well in creating me among those you have made, as well as the water of this source, in order to ensure my survival, I humbly ask of you: Do not allow this source to dry up, but make it trickle over the earth, as it did the other years, so that we shall be able to reap what I have sown . . ."

But the foundation of animistic thinking is never far, and the good countryman adds, while offering a sacrifice: "O you, source, origin of the water which has irrigated my field for so many years, you by whose grace I receive my food, do this year, too, what you have done until now; and better yet: give us more water, so that my harvest will be more abundant."

·3·

TEN THOUSAND
YEARS OF
ANDEAN HISTORY

I could have adopted a plan for this chapter reflecting the subdivisions that ethnologists have devised for social organization. Thus, I could have successively treated marginal bands, forest villages, chiefdoms, and, finally, kingdoms and the Inca empire. But at the end of pre-Columbian history, South America was a mosaic of overlapping groups enclaved one in another and usually endowed with different patterns of social organization. Adopting sociological criteria of classification would thus cause us to zigzag through the continent and develop a difficult reading sequence.

I have for this reason chosen instead to follow a plan of a geographical character, a plan that is, moreover, more logically adapted to the nature of the information available to us. Our documentation is clearly most nearly complete with respect to the heart of the Incas' domain, Peru and Bolivia. This history will thus be the subject of the first section.

When I take up the life of other societies, on the other hand, we shall be less well informed. So I have grouped everything referring to them in the second section, for which I have adopted a geographical order, from north to south.

THE CENTRAL ANDES, PERU, AND BOLIVIA

The cold and temperate Andes extend from Tumbes on the Peruvian coast near the Ecuadorian border, from Cuenca and Loja in the Ecuadorian mountains, around the third parallel, outside the zone of influence of the hot waters of the Guayas River, to the twenty-seventh parallel in Chile. These cold and temperate Andes are arid or subarid according to the altitude. They were the home of the most-developed South American societies and gave birth to the Inca empire. It was a remarkable political system, if one bears in mind the state of isolation in which it developed and if one considers it in its proper context in the history of the evolution of peoples. Indeed, the imperial attempt of the Incas constitutes the only known example of a Neolithic and preliterate empire. Copper metallurgy was beginning to develop in the Andes when the European conquerors arrived, but metals seem to have played only a minor role in this history. It would be incorrect to state that the Andes had known a genuine Copper or Bronze Age.

The territory dominated by the Incas covers the highest and, even more important, the widest part of the cordillera. Here we are in the heart of the Andean lands, of which the lowlands represent only a minute part.

However, of all the lands of the cordillera, it is the central Andes that, though they are very arid or simply arid according to the altitude, offer man the highest proportion of usable soil compared with the total land surface. By usable soil I mean not only arable lands but also alpine and subalpine pastures and *lomas,* the fog oases. Stockbreeding, which I shall speak of further on, was practiced in the upper Andes as well as in lomas in the coastal gorges and seems to have played an important role in the ecological balance of Andean societies during the last pre-Columbian centuries.

The extent of the usable soil in the upper Andes seems to have escaped archaeologists. They have spent too much time in the coastal oases and have neglected the study of the upper Andes. Evidently it was easier and less exhausting to excavate the hot sands of the lowlands than to work in caves at an altitude of thirteen thousand feet. The result is that with regard to the cordillera one was usually content to recall the existence of the ceremonial centers such as those in Chavín and Tiahuanaco, all complexes known since the nineteenth century, if not earlier.

The modern archaeological team has now understood that at the present time a serious study of the upper cordillera is needed much more than more study of the lowlands, and we are getting brilliant results, thanks to the fieldwork of men like Thomas Lynch, who found eight-thousand-year-old beans in a highland cave, or like Augusto Cardich, who established a full chronological sequence from 1300 B.C.

One has only to move about in the cordillera to verify that the tortuous character of Andean topography did not necessarily constitute as much of a hindrance for the pre-Columbian inhabitants as one might imagine at first sight. Here we are dealing with populations that worked and traveled on foot, with neither wagons nor draft animals.

I am often asked why Andeans did not use the wheel. I think they had little use for it. Trails in the mountains are so obstructed by boulders, so difficult (often even cut into the rock) that a wheel would be of no use. And wheels would hardly have been useful in the coastal deserts, where they would have sunk into the sand. I know from experience that a good walker can travel faster from one Peruvian coastal valley to another by taking a side route across a mountain and over a crest than I can in a car that must take the road, which follows the valleys, skirts the mountains, and goes down as far as the seashore before being able to enter the next basin.

My excavations have also taught me that immense territories, now abandoned, were at one time either cultivated or used as pastures. The innumerable and vast villages in ruins that I have found almost everywhere in the upper Andes confirm a dense human occupation of presently deserted lands. The study of these settlements and the agricultural systems surrounding them is vital to the progress of American prehistory. It tends to prove that the cordillera offered considerable resources to clever societies, even ones with weak technological means.

Classical authors described Peru and Bolivia as "the cradle of the high civilizations of the Andes." This phrase seems obsolete to me. Why give certain prehistoric societies priority over others? At most, I shall admit to having observed different degrees of complexity among them, and I shall gladly recognize that the central Andes produced more complex societies than those of the Chibchas in the north, for example, or of the Araucanians in the south.

We may wonder, incidentally, where the men came from who contributed to the formation of these more developed Andean societies. So far there is not the slightest proof that they were indigenous to the highlands. They may very well have climbed over the cordillera and come from a land far to the east, as did many tribes during the later pre-Hispanic centuries, which has been historically verified.

Stating that the Incas were more "civilized" than the Chimus would be like suggesting that the Romans were more civilized than the Greeks. They were living in different worlds, the Romans closer to mechanization and ready to invent new sources of energy, had they not had slave energy at their disposal.

Today the central Andes, which could have formed a powerful economic unit with very complementary resources, are politically divided into five countries that hardly help one another at all. Ecuador holds a little portion in the north, then comes Peru. South of Lake Titicaca one enters Bolivia, and the two slopes of the cordillera are then divided between Argentina and Chile.

The name given to the territories that have become the Republic of Ecuador does not pose a problem. Quito is close to the zero parallel, the equator.

Bolivia takes its name from Simon Bolivar, the liberator, one of the heroes of decolonization.

Argentina is a translation of Rio de la Plata, "the silver river."

Chile seems to have come to us from the groups that lived in the rainy lower Andes. This name may perhaps be compared with that of the island of Chiloé.

And *Peru?* The lands now making up the territory of Peru have been known by this name since the sixteenth century, probably as a result of extending the traditional name of a region to all the territory around it.

Rivet and other scholars have been studying the problem of the origin of the name of Peru, but no one has solved it. The most sensible hypothesis is the one given by Sigvald Linné. He thinks it became customary to call all the territories explored by Pizarro and his companions, and located to the south of the seventh parallel, by the name for a cacique or chieftain, *Piru* or *Beru,* from the region of Darien, the Chocó, or the Atrato.

Father Blas Valera wrote in the sixteenth century: "Pelu, the name given to the Natives who live between Panama and Huyaquil . . ." Rivet, like Sigvald Linné, considered *Pelu,* which became *Piru* and then *Peru,* to mean *water.* The inhabitants of Pelu were apparently Chibchas who had moved over from the eastern part of the continent and then had come down from the Andes, pushing the Cunas back toward the Atlantic Coast. After doing so they transformed the coastal strip of the Chocó into a rich and prosperous land. Moreover, Pizarro cites the fact that the people of Pelu used poisoned arrowheads, and he mentions two Carib chieftains, one of whom, Bizuquete, had ruled a land called *Peruqueta.* The sound reappears once more, in the middle of the seventeenth century, to designate the Viru Valley, which extends south of Trujillo.

Of all the regions of South America, the central Andes have been the subject of most of the thorough studies. Their aridity, which preserves the remains of the past, has readily attracted archaeologists. But the history of the central Andes is still at the level of a collection of episodes separated by long hiatuses, sometimes by periods several centuries long, which have remained completely obscure.

I am most critical of certain authors who have lately written histories of Peru or other such fantasies for their failure to reveal these "holes," these periods that are still devoid of concrete facts. Such authors have not hesitated to formulate peremptory declarations that are in fact just masking reality. Thus, for example, they affirm that in such and such a region "the society of the X succeeded the society of the Y." But they neglect to tell us that five hundred or a thousand years elapsed between the two events. It is almost as if someone told us that Louis XVI succeeded Charlemagne.

I am in no way criticizing the classical authors of the 1940s, such as Junius Bird, Julian H. Steward, or Alden Mason. Nor am I criticizing Gordon R. Willey, who prudently entitled his latest, massive, work *An Introduction to American Archaeology.* Rather, my criticism is addressed to the works that only restate facts known for fifty years, while refusing to acknowledge the poor quality, generally, of our information and not admitting that we are not ready to write the history of the Andes. Such failings were acceptable thirty years ago but cannot be forgiven today.

Given the present state of documentation, I have preferred to keep to the rough sketch of a provisional spatial and chronological plan in which already known or still-to-be-discovered events can be placed. I shall stay at the level of simply reporting several less poorly known events that I have chosen from among the most significant ones when trying to form an idea about what could have happened.

In order to develop this plan I have used various kinds of materials. When dealing with very early times, about which we know little, I have based the discussion on information of an essentially ecological order: adaptation to the environment, diet, and so on.

As we approach the period of Hispanicization, more-complete information is available. The middle periods reveal not only details regarding ecology but also facts of a sociocultural nature such as ground plans and settlement patterns for villages, as well as architecture and artistic expression. Later on, indications of social stratification make their appearance, and it is possible to assign a territory to several tribes. The documentation will only begin to fill out, however, during the protohistoric period, the period of contact with Europeans.

By extrapolation, this plan will be usable as a guide for other Andean regions, for ultimately the development of all the peoples of the cordillera followed similar patterns, but with differences in rhythm. Thus, certain groups stopped developing at the level of simple, unstratified sociopolitical systems. These are the groups that U.S. authors call marginal and that seem to have lived in much the same way as the central Andean preagriculturalists of the high Holocene, the Andeans of ten thousand or eight thousand years ago.

When agriculture came into use, a noticeable break seems to have occurred, the causes of which remain unknown, as we shall see. Certain groups became constructive, organized, and stratified, whereas others remained headhunter-farmers or warrior-farmers like the ones who have survived in New Guinea or in the forests of the American hot lands.

In the constructive groups, kingdoms were created like that of the Chimus, which was very soon threatened by bands of warriors who probably came down from the cordillera and divided up the lowlands to create feudalities. Then, as if they were the last in a display of fireworks, the Incas tried to consolidate an empire that they did not actually have the means to dominate.

It has been said at times that the Mayas in Central America were "fossilized" holdovers of an earlier social system, a system that was still viable after its time. The system of the Incas was, on the contrary, ahead of its time; they were unfortunate precursors.

PREAGRICULTURAL TIMES

Several discoveries made at very different points of the two continents, in the western United States, Mexico, Colombia, Venezuela, and Peru, have allowed us to establish that man was already living all over the New World before the end of the last ice age.

With respect to the central Andes, Richard S. MacNeish was the first to find, in their original place, the tools of Pleistocene men who hunted animals: camelids, perhaps the horse, certainly sloths.* The tools were at the bottom of a rock shelter in a semiarid valley on the western slope of the cordillera.

Unfortunately, we do not yet know anything about the physical nature of these early inhabitants, for so far only their tools, rubbish, and hearths have been found. We are better informed with respect to the following period, the one corresponding to the high Holocene of geologists.

According to geologists, the lower edge of the glaciers, which today is found at an altitude of about 16,000 feet in the cordillera, had gone down as low as 11,550 or 10,890 feet during the last phase of the Wisconsin ice age. The melting of these ices produced serious upheavals, and the rarity of human sites found that belonged to the Pleistocene epoch is due, perhaps, to the resulting chaos.

It is now widely confirmed that since the end of the last phase of the Wisconsin ice age, known in the United States as the Valders glacial period, the central Andes have been inhabited by numerous bands whose ways of life may already be partially reconstructed. These bands led an existence typical of so-called archaic societies, to use a term from North American authors. European authors would in this case employ the term *Mesolithic* societies.

The existence of such societies has been established by several researchers: Alberto Rex Gonzalès in Argentina; Augusto Cardich, M. Gonzalès, and the present author in Peru; Junius Bird, Lautaro Nuñez, José Emperaire, and others in Chile and Patagonia.

Traces ten and a half to seven millennia old have been found in caves as well as in outdoor sites. In the central Andes, the caves that have already been explored are mainly those of Lauricocha, near the source of the Marañon River, at an altitude of 12,900 feet, where thirty-nine inches of rain fall annually; that of Toquepala, in the very arid Far South of Peru, also at a high altitude; and, finally, those of Chilca, in central Peru.

The caves of Chilca have provided us with the most interesting information about the lives of the men of that epoch. We discovered them at altitudes around twelve to thirteen thousand feet in the arid Andes, where only some eight inches of rain fall annually. These caves had remained dry, so we were able to sift as many as fourteen superimposed archaeological strata, representing alternating cycles of occupation and abandonment stretching out over ten thousand years. Modern herdsmen still shelter their livestock there on stormy days.

Livestock do great damage to archaeological sites. We had walled up one of the caves in order to protect a ten-thousand-year-old settlement, but some shep-

*For details relating to analogous finds in Colombia, Venezuela, Argentina, and Chile, see "The Other Andean Societies" below, which discusses each region. Let me also note that in 1973 Hermann Trimborn obtained an age of thirteen thousand years for some charcoal he recovered from the Far South coast of Peru.

The Tres Ventanas caves in the Central Andes, the site where burials eighty-five hundred years old were discovered.

herds reopened it to take in their cows, so everything we had left untouched for future study was destroyed.

These caves, moreover, sheltered the perfectly preserved corpses of two men, a woman, and two children. Now we know as a result what individuals of that epoch looked like and even how they dressed, since their clothes survived. Their bodies were those of stout people of tall stature, varying in height from 65.2 to 69.2 inches, according to sex, with long heads, very protuberant jaws, and strong bones.

Their clothes were made of cactus plant fibers or of twined or looped reeds. Up until the appearance of pottery and corn, which occurred in the central Andes around 1500 or 1300 B.C., the inhabitants wore clothing made of "twined" fabrics; in other words, made like mats, by encircling each warp, or sometimes a pair of warps. When the side of the piece was reached, the wefts were knotted, then brought down an inch or less and knotted again. Then one began twining again, but in the opposite direction, and this continued the whole length of the piece. In this way the Andeans made mats that were up to seventy-two inches long, the maximum length of the rushes, and sometimes more than six and a half feet wide. By bringing the wefts close together, one could even make tapestries, close-textured fabrics. By using cottons of different shades of white and brown, or by dyeing the yarn, they obtained stripes or bands.

By modifying the course of the warps or wefts, the preceramicists obtained decorative patterns like stylized birds and fish or serpents with interlocking heads. The latter motif, apparently one of the archetypes of the coastal mythology of Peru, lasted until Hispanicization.

"Looped" fabrics were made in addition to twined and netted ones. Looping was done by making a circle out of a succession of more or less loose loops, using a single thread. These were then picked up by the loops of the next circle, and so on. This technique permitted making not only bags and cylindrical caps but also flat fabrics. Adjusting the tension of the loops to create ribbed patterns and regular spacing made it possible to achieve various pleasing decorative effects. For example, by leaving appropriate openings, one obtained a geometric design, a fili-gree bird, and so forth. One could also insert several superimposed loops before having them picked up in the next circle, or could twist them, shift them, or whatever.

The third basic technique was netting, which was also executed with a single continuous thread, but in this method the loops were knotted, creating regular rectangular meshes. In one preceramic village I found *malleros,* little wooden or bone rectangles used by fishermen to give a regular shape to the meshes of nets.

Weaving was introduced with the arrival of the first wave of corn eaters, and it replaced twining and looping except for making bags and mats. The evolu-tion that occurred then might have foreshadowed the end of the preceramic period, for some villages of the bean planters during their final stage already con-tained up to 5 percent woven fabrics. True, all these fabrics were very small, just narrow bands usually used as edges on twined pieces.

In weaving, the weft thread passes alternately above, then below the warp threads, to form a square motif. If one wanted a closely woven fabric, one brought the threads closer together. If one wanted a "dishcloth," one wove loose-ly.

At present, the evolution I have described is valid for the coastal territories, but we do not yet know much about the history of weaving in the upper Andes, where humidity has destroyed practically all ancient fabrics. But it is likely that the evolution had been the same in the cordillera, for so far all the pieces that have been found in refuse containing pottery were woven, whereas the fabrics worn by preagriculturalists that have survived because their owners had been buried in dry caves were twined or looped.

I have also noticed a comparable evolution among the Neolithic tribes of the Swiss lakes, whom I have closely studied. There also, fabrics were first twined or looped and later woven, an interesting coincidence that should be studied careful-ly. Is the adoption of weaving the result of diffusion, or a synchronous, multilin-ear evolution, the result of neolithization? In the Andes, neolithization preceded the adoption of weaving by several thousand years, a point that speaks in favor of a diffusion of the technique.

Looms were of no use in twining or looping. Ethnological reports indicate how these techniques were used. Two posts driven into the ground supported a few horizontal threads that made up the upper edge of the fabric. This was enough for twining to start, after one had arranged the warps to hang loose over the edge. In order to loop, one used a needle without an eye.

It was possible to weave in the same way as one twined. Two posts were enough to assure the tension of the sheet formed by the warps, which could even be held between the knees. Therefore, weaving did not imply the existence of a loom, but looms took shape, as a means to speed up the process, when weaving began to develop. I have found two looms in a twenty-eight-hundred-year-old village of corn planters. At present, these are the earliest-known ones in the Americas.

A child's body found in a cave. Note the shell pendant, the bone needle, and the straw bed. This body is unique in being so old and so well preserved. Central Andes, 7000 B.C.

Two types of looms may be seen today in the Andes: the vertical one, attached to a tree or post, the use of which is typical of the Arawaks, in Asia, and in Central America; and the horizontal one, attached to a post in front of the weaver, who sits on the ground.

On some bodies found in the Chilca caves, cloaks of vicuña skin painted with blue stripes and sewn in very fine stitches with the help of cactus spines were used to keep the body warm, worn with the fur next to the body and the skin outside. (But in other villages we have found bodies wrapped in skins that were placed against the body with the fur on the outside. Was this another tradition, or another climate?) A leather sling encircled one of the heads, possibly indicating that an unsuccessful attempt had been made to cure a sick person. A large mesh bag accompanied one of the corpses, as well as bits of tanned leather dyed with red pigment. Lying next to a child was a little bird with still-intact multicolored feathers, wrapped up in a little straw packet.

What's more, we have found in these caves the objects that constituted the equipment of the inhabitants' everyday life, such as weapons and tools necessary for the preparation of food and of certain basic materials.

Their weapons were slings and spear throwers (the *estolicas* of the Quechuas and *atlatls* of the Mexicans) and probably also weapons that were thrown, made of split pebbles with blunt edges. The spear thrower was used to throw javelins with points made of such stones as obsidian (a natural glass, an aluminum silicate melted down during a volcanic eruption), basalt, and quartz, but only rarely of flint.

The axe with a handle, the knife, and the dagger, typical of subsequent epochs, were not yet present. Instead there were beautiful big amygdaloid bifaces (two-sided igneous rocks with cavities containing various minerals) that could have come from a European site and were formerly called hand axes. The similarities between the tools found in these caves—end and side scrapers, notched scrapers, and basins, denticulated ones and so on—and the implements made by the European Mousterians are all the more striking when one realizes that the two cultures were separated by a gap of some twenty to thirty thousand years.

Of the tools, let me cite the following:

• Digging sticks used to extract from the earth the edible rhizomes, roots, bulbs, and tubers found in the cooking refuse.

• Needles, awls, scrapers, punches, and spatulas of bone used for working leather and to make mats, fabrics, and mesh bags, which at that time were used instead of baskets.

At the present time, we do not know of any baskets prior to the agricultural periods. The earliest baskets I have found are fifty-five hundred years old. I found them near cotton and beans, which indicate farming activity.

• Calabashes cut in the shape of bowls, plates, or flasks, used as dishes.

• Antlers of buck and roe deer, used to prepare projectile points, stone points placed at the tips of javelins.

Hardwood javelins and spears were also used in the Andes, but in later periods, when the techniques of cutting stone tools had fallen into disuse.

For food preparation, immovable milling stones were not yet used, but some volcanic blocks had served as anvils, maybe for preparing chipped-stone tools such as scrapers and drills, and as mortars to pulverize red pigments. It is the red pigment produced by the achiote plant that seems to have been most commonly used, as well as a black pigment whose origin is unknown to us. From the Caribbean to Chile, the natives smeared themselves with achiote and attributed a magical role to red coloring. Even today, one can see the Colorados of Ecuador walking about naked, their bodies painted with polychrome but essentially red dyes.

Red pigment was also used to decorate walls. One began by drawing on the rock geometric decorations—stylized shapes whose meaning is unknown to us— or hunting scenes in which the hunters are shown armed with spear throwers, busily driving game out of cover, with vicuñas visible in front of long nets. Contrast between the wall and the drawing was obtained by means of black, red, or siena pigments.

Cave paintings are always hard to associate with the refuse carpeting the floors. There is nothing to prove that they are as old as the refuse littering the ground, for good shelters were constantly being reoccupied.

The need for artistic expression appears in several forms in the high Andes as early as the high Holocene, which of course is quite normal, but the achievements in this realm are still limited. I have already mentioned painted clothing. Let me add necklaces, bracelets, carved pendants, and bones engraved with geometric motifs painted green. Musical instruments have not yet appeared.

We must now take a look at the diet. Through the study of the excrement and kitchen remains that carpet the huts, we know that the people of this epoch ate many vegetables. Seeds of alders and tomatoes (the latter being a South American plant rather than a Mexican importation as formerly believed) and the *tuna,* the fruit of the opuntia or prickly pear cactus, constituted basic foods, as did plants with rhizomes and tubers: jiquimas, potatoes, the ullucu plant, and possibly manioc and sweet potatoes.

Botanists I have consulted, as for example Dr. Douglas Yen of Hawaii, have suggested that the plant remains mailed to him for examination probably belonged to a wild species, this being understandable considering the age of the settlement. One may nevertheless wonder if farming could not have been practiced much earlier than thought on the eastern slopes of the cordillera, from which it would have spread first to the highlands, then rather later to the Pacific shores. Since farming in arid lands is much more difficult than dry farming, or unirrigated planting with merely the help of rains, one can easily understand the reasons for this delay.

The refuse also contained a great many bones of land mammals: bucks and roe deer, vizcachas (similar to rabbits), camelids (guanacos, llamas, etc.), and rodents. These animals must have been hunted for their meat as well as for their skins.

We also found remains of fishes, probably from fresh water, and marine mollusks, although the caves in question were sixty miles away from the ocean. This appearance of blue mussels from the Pacific in the upper Andes leads me to think that the visitors to this area belonged to migratory bands who lived part of the year at the seashore, probably in the *lomas,** and who retired to the cordillera to hunt there during the southern winter. The months from June to November are cool and damp on the coast. In the upper Andes, on the contrary, these months are colder but dry and sunny.

The caves in Chilca were eight and a half feet in diameter and sixty-six feet long on the average. In view of their size, therefore, these caves could not have sheltered a transhumant or migratory band. They could have served only as temporary shelter for one or two families; a more numerous group must necessarily have lived in an outdoor village. My explorations and excavations have enabled me to locate several of these villages, in the upper Andes as well as in the coastal plains. One finds them by looking for beds of ashes and stone flakes littering the ground. After scraping the surface, one may observe the circle of a hut with the holes in which the posts stood, and frequently, the bases of the posts themselves.

In the cordillera, villages have generally left traces only in the form of hut foundations, ashes, food, and tools. The huts themselves have disappeared. In the dry lower Andes, however, one finds villages that are practically intact. Huts do not appear on the surface, but one often finds them whole, simply hidden beneath detritus, with the bases of the posts that supported the walls still firmly set in holes. When the posts are gone, we can still find the outline of the hut by following the postholes dug in the plain or in previously accumulated refuse.

The walls of such huts and the interiors seem to have been carpeted with mats generally made of bunches of straw twenty-four inches thick at the base.

Lomas are oases where vegetation lives by means of condensed fog. See page 86.

The small cords binding such straw mats have often survived, and sometimes even the door and debris from the walls and roof can be found.

Such villages certainly indicate a preagricultural life, but one that was sedentary for at least part of the year. In the lower Andes, I have found villages that extended over three-tenths of a mile and must have been inhabited by as many as several hundred families, each living in one or two huts. Later I discovered that several thousand dead were buried in such villages, which further confirmed that people had lived there for long periods.

Circular and small, the huts were usually thirteen feet in diameter. One has to step down into them, for the floor was slightly lower than the surrounding soil. The posts supporting the walls were made either of willows or of reed canes, bound together in groups of three or four. The verticality of the posts, held in the soil by pebbles acting as wedges, leads me to think they were not conical huts, tepees like those in the United States, but rather, mushroom-shaped huts with straight walls and probably conical roofs, like the huts one still sees today in numerous regions of the upper Andes. In this respect one should visit the villages of pure-blooded natives in Colombia and Ecuador, as for example San Miguel in the Sierra Nevada de Santa Marta.

A semiellipse of ashes found in the hut's center shows that there was a hearth in the interior, probably for warmth on cool nights. A circular platform, which must have been used for cooking, made of stones set next to each other on the ground is visible outside the huts. It is also covered with ashes, and with some unburned plant material such as grass. Let us remember that the inhabitants did not yet make pottery, and thus could not use vessels for cooking. They could thus only roast food on the embers or on burning-hot rocks, a better solution for sparing fuel.

In the central Andes, such villages are generally associated with a *loma*, a fog oasis or well-delimited zone in which specific topographical, weather, and soil conditions prevail because fogs from the ocean condense water there. Some six inches of rain fall annually in a loma over open lands, which a savannah may condense up to twenty-four or even thirty-six inches. This easily explains why the lomas were densely populated up to Hispanic days.

In the present context, a loma can exist only fairly near the ocean. Vegetation becomes able to live at an elevation of 660 feet, but only below 2,600 feet. Above this elevation the sky stays blue and there is no rain, since rains from the

A fire drill of the type present in most early houses of the prefarming, early farming, and early corn-eaters periods. Coastal Peru.

Atlantic only very rarely reach the Pacific slope of the cordillera. The water produced by fog rolling up the canyons during the winter penetrates into the soil and forms, in the middles of these desert oases, subterranean springs and brooks that explain the existence of savannahs and sometimes forests, but in any case make possible an abundant flora.

All this sounds very logical, but let me confess that we still do not know exactly what it was that people were seeking in the lomas. We do know for a fact that they lived there. Perhaps the savannah provided them with edible seeds. But why choose to transport tens of thousands of tons of marine mollusks from the beaches to the lomas, which were often twelve to twenty-four miles away from the ocean, instead of carrying down the seeds? I suggest that the pre-Columbians chose the lomas because they supplied them with both fresh water and edible plants, whereas the beach only supplied them with brackish water and perhaps during some periods with no water at all.

Underground sheets of fresh water come near the surface at many points on the central Pacific coast. The easiest to recognize are those surfacing at the edges of beaches, where the sheet of fresh water forms a layer that won't mix with the denser salt water. Similar underground sheets surface on the coastal plateaus, between 165 and 1,650 feet above sea level, and in the piedmonts of the upper cordillera, between 9,240 and 9,900 feet.

We still have to determine which food plants the lomas provided. A study of the inhabitants' excrement, which contains seeds, shows that they did not live on meat exclusively. At best, sea mammals, fish, and shellfish could have constituted only a third of their daily needs in calories, and the bones of land mammals are very rare in the refuse. So let us assume for the time being that these early ecologies were centered around the gathering of certain species providing rhizomes, seeds, and tubers, as well as around seafood. So far we have found only seeds of Graminaceae and no acacia or mimosa seeds. Fruits are represented by cacti, and tuberous plants by begonias.

Hunting constituted only a complementary food source, providing meat occasionally, to be sure, but even more importantly, the vicuña skins used as clothes and bones used to make tools. We now suspect that herding could have been practiced very early in the western Andes, earlier than farming. MacNeish says that llamas and alpacas began to be domesticated on the eastern slopes of the cordillera perhaps eight thousand years ago. A camelid mandible I recently found in the six-thousand-year-old village of Paloma could indicate a similar situation.

Only long mammal bones, which were used to make needles, punches, or leather scrapers, are found in the kitchen middens. Thus, the meat was apparently eaten in the upper Andes and only the most useful materials were brought to the coast.

An excellent example of this sort of ecology is provided by the complex discovered at Pampa Colorado, a plain three and a half miles long that stretches out in the Far South of Peru, around the sixteenth parallel, between the spurs of the Andes and a chain of hills thirteen hundred feet high that separates the pampa from the beach.

A grinding stone. Prefarming period, south coast of Peru.

Some eight to seven thousand years ago, the hundreds of dwellings inhabited around this plain must have received the waters of the now dry wadis. These waters must have attracted animals hunted by the people who lived in the plain. I have found the foundations of their huts on some five hundred mounds strewn with thousands of javelin points. But I also found milling stones, mortars, and pestles practically next to each hearth. The eastern slopes around "Pampa" Colorado are, in effect, covered by loma vegetation. In addition to hunting, the pre-Columbians must have collected seeds there, if not some sort of wild potato of the type that still grows in some oases in the Lima area. At first glance, the area appears ultra-arid, and today the vegetation is clearly regressing. Now it is reduced to low plants and mosses in the lomas. But fossilized debris is found in savannahs under the sand, and some trees have still survived in inaccessible spots. This desert is nevertheless much alive, with deer, foxes, owls, and countless other birds.

I have also discovered villages of the same period at the seashore, the inhabitants of which lived on fishing and by gathering seafood, but also on plants they obtained from a neighboring loma. In such encampments the dead were buried, dressed in vicuña skins, right inside the huts or just next to them.

The most representative of these villages is the one I excavated from the sand with the help of a brush and trowel in the Paracas Desert, some 160 miles south of Lima. The Paracas Desert, followed by the Marcona Desert, begins on the southern bank of the Pisco River and extends more than 150 miles, as far as the Acari River. Separated from the Ica and Nazca valleys by a coastal range twenty-six hundred to thirty-three hundred feet high, this desert constitutes a well-defined regional entity that is of the greatest interest from the viewpoint of prehistoric human geography. It has no surface water, but I found about one hundred pre-Columbian sites there. In all likelihood, these were camps, and in later times villages of fishermen, but as far as early preagricultural times are concerned, I do not know yet if the inhabitants lived there all year round. If this was the case, they must have obtained some edible plants through bartering. One can also imagine that they may have visited the area along the beaches only once a year, for several months or for just a few weeks. If this was so, it would mean they were in control of areas in the highlands and, during later centuries, in valleys watered by streams. Here was a territory in which they could practice either gathering or agriculture, according to their degree of cultural development.

While brushing the sand-covered plain, I discovered Paracas Village 96. The presence of a savannah in the process of drying up, very nearby, had alerted me to the possibility of finding traces of human life there.

Brushing then revealed circular huts with a diameter of about thirteen feet. A spot of ashes was again noted inside each hut. Dead persons dressed in vicuña skins were buried either in the huts or in the surrounding sand. Here foods were essentially composed of alder or tomato seeds, seafood, and fish. Furthermore, in this village (which was dated by the radiocarbon method at about nine thousand years) I found the earliest fishing net that is presently known. Its meshes were just under an inch square, and it was made of a plant fiber other than cotton.

The burials showed that great care was taken to prepare corpses for disposal. I found them wrapped in several mats and layers of clothing, decorated with necklaces, caps made of leather or looped plant fiber, and sometimes holding a dangerous bone dagger bound to the palm of the right hand.

The life of these Andeans must have undergone few changes between ten thousand and six thousand years ago. At most we may note an evolution in their

An adult buried wrapped in a vicuña fur robe, with a bone dagger bound to his right hand. Note the cap on the skull. From Paracas, 7000 B.C.

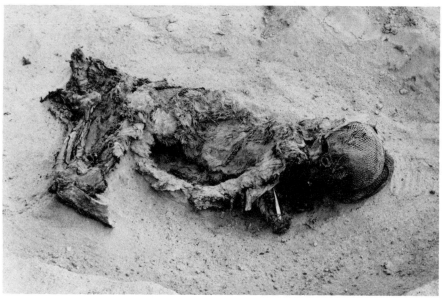

chipped-stone tools, an evolution similar to the one observed in Europe, Africa, and the Near East: from being pretty, elegant, and of medium weight, the projectile points became over the millennia small, even microlithic, and light. Or they became more and more poorly made—the art of flaking stone must have been lost. At the end of the period when agriculture began, fine stone implements disappeared, giving way to poor knives made of basalt or pink quartzite. The shape of projectile points changed according to the age of the sites, which once more indicates migrations, with new societies taking the place of older ones.

In order to learn more about such episodes, we shall have to study these sites in much greater detail and sift a large volume of refuse. But assigning an age to a site by taking into account its stone industry has proved risky, for people reinvent previously known shapes of tools or use old ones they find on the ground.

For the time being, the sites of Chilca, Pampa Colorado, and Paracas still serve as prototypes, as a sort of background for the kind of life led by the Andeans of the high Holocene, from Venezuela to Chiloé.

Apparently the western Patagonians and the inhabitants of Tierra del Fuego and the archipelago lived differently and had learned very early to use boats. I think they should be kept in a separate category, which will be discussed again in the next chapter. In Paracas, fishing must have been done from the shore. Except for a large rope, I have not yet found any object in the very early sites of the southern coast of Peru that gives reason to suspect maritime activity. Even in the time of the Nazcas, two thousand years ago, fishermen were still depicted on ceramic vessels swimming in the water with a net in their hands. On the northern coast, however, the use of reed rafts is confirmed at least as early as the time of the Mochicas, two thousand or twenty-five hundred years ago. Scenes painted on pottery represent rafts like the ones the fishermen on the north coast use today.

In 1974 I discovered the remains of a raft twenty-three feet long hidden under sand covering a village in the Peruvian Far South, in the middle of the desert. It was composed of several probably cylindrical rollers made of reeds held together by small ropes. These rafts, which must have been stabilized by the wooden staffs that were buried with the long rollers, date back to the Tiahuanacoid period, one thousand to eleven hundred years ago. The Tiahuanacoid character of the rafts is attested by the fact that the staffs were decorated with amulets consisting of little dolls made of multicolored wads of cotton and fragments of warm-water bivalve mollusks.

With respect to the middle Holocene, to the last centuries of the preagricultural horizons, Village 613 of the loma at Paloma seems to me to be the best prototype site. This village extends over nineteen hundred feet in length, in a little plain located at the entrance to a dry gorge of the lower Andes, at an altitude of 660 to 825 feet, where the vegetation fed by ocean fogs begins. Thus, the village is clearly associated with the flora of the lomas. Actually, I expected nothing new of this village, which had been indicated, like all its brothers of the desert lower Andes, by mounds of detritus mixed with ashes and shells emerging like rounded cones from the dust that had accumulated all around. Consequently, I was greatly

A doll made of reed-and-cotton fabric. A typical Paracas braided turban was wrapped around the head.

surprised when, in making the first probes, we came upon an unexpected concentration of graves, all found in or around huts, as preagricultural villages did not yet have cemeteries. The fact that the graves were found packed tightly together indicated a population density that no investigator would have dreamed of uncovering. I decided, therefore, to go on to make two perpendicular cuts, each twenty feet wide, crossing each other in the center of the mound.

This undertaking allowed me to sketch the contour of the area covered by the detritus and to figure out its volume by applying the formula that applies to semiellipses. Unfortunately, though my hopes were amply met with respect to interesting discoveries, this mound created many problems in terms of manpower, time, and financial resources. Finally, in order to complete the two trenches, we had to remove about 35,000 cubic feet of rubble, using only trowels and brushes so as not to destroy the remains of the huts. Mixed with this debris we found 90 graves and around 45 superimposed huts, for the shelly heaps of Paloma actually cover three villages, not just one. Now if we extrapolate these figures and apply them to the entire mound, which represents a volume of 350,000 cubic feet, we see that we would have to unearth about 900 graves and 450 huts just to excavate one mound, which corresponds to a complex of dwellings. And if we were to excavate the entire village, composed of about 20 similar mounds, we would undoubtedly find some 9,000 skeletons distributed in and around 4,000 to 5,000 houses. Such are the surprises that Andean prehistory holds in store for us.

Careful examination, faithful reproduction, and the placing in three dimensions of all the objects and situations observed or found in a block 1,260 cubic feet in size (20 by 20 by 3 feet thick on the average) is an operation that takes at least 15 working days for a team of several people. Thus, a single investigator cannot think of acquiring a thorough knowledge of a village like Paloma. He would have to devote some five years to it, and where would he find the necessary subsidies? Here one puts his finger on the limitations from which prehistory suffers and the reasons for the slow development of its important branch, prehistoric demography. For in Paloma we are in a position, perhaps for the first time, to arrive at a reasonable estimate of the number of inhabitants in the village by counting the bodies buried there; to find out the exact number of huts they had built and inhabited; to find out the composition of a preagricultural village in terms of its inhabitants' sex and age; to determine the average height of the Andeans of seven thousand years ago; and finally, to evaluate the energy content of their food debris, which would open new horizons to us with respect to the duration of the sojourns that took place in similar settlements. Unfortunately, the carrying out of such programs is a utopian dream. Who, other than specialists and enlightened amateurs, would see any point in undertaking them?

For the time being, therefore, we are reduced merely to formulating hypotheses, as soon as we approach such essential problems as finding out how many inhabitants actually lived in Paloma, for how long a time, and what they ate.

Now—and again I am only speculating, basing my conjectures on extrapolations of a few concrete facts I have established—I suggest that about two thousand people lived in Paloma during three to twenty-year periods. However, in order for this figure to agree with the energy value of the food wastes, the number of graves, and the number of huts, I must add three qualifications to this figure. First, the sojourns could not have been only seasonal ones, for we do not find in Paloma the paraphernalia necessary to spend a hunting season in the mountains. Second, shellfish could only have supplied about 50 percent of the protein in the diet, the remainder being supplied by fish, crustaceans, and sea mammals. And third, edible plants must have been eaten in normal quantities. If we do not introduce qualifications such as the second and third, we find ourselves facing totals of days, calories, and years that are not enough to account for the number of deceased and the number of houses.

Otherwise, life in Paloma seems to have differed hardly at all from life in any other villages of the sixth millennium B.C. It was a very simple way of life that probably consisted of gathering shellfish and fishing during the summer, and gathering seeds of trees and graminaceous plants during the winter.

Apparently, art did not yet have a place in everyday life. Only the mats used as beds, blankets, and clothes were sometimes decorated.

THE BEGINNINGS OF AGRICULTURE

The raising of crops and herding of animals are indicated in the Near East by the presence of grains of wheat or barley and by the bones of domesticated animals in the debris of villages. But in South America it has not yet been proven, though I suspect it is the case, that animal husbandry would have been contemporaneous with the beginnings of agriculture. Establishing the presence of cultivated plants in the debris of a village is usually considered proof sufficient to declare that the settlement in question was already inhabited by farmers.

Of the plants that botanists admit into the category of American cultivated plants, and that one finds in the very early sites, let me cite cotton, beans, peanuts, red pepper, and fruits such as guavas, *lúcumas* or eggfruit, *paltas* or avocados, and chirimoyas. Calabashes appear even earlier and are the subject of controversy. They are found in the earliest sites, which are ten thousand years old. Were these calabashes the fruit of wild plants, or had man cultivated them? Botanists incline toward this second hypothesis, but since these same botanists classify as wild species the edible plants that are found mixed with these calabashes in the bottoms of huts, one does not know what to do—push back the threshold of the appearance of agriculture? This solution was offered by Thomas Lynch, who found beans that were eight thousand years old in the upper Santa Valley.

Let us remember that some natives in Arizona knew how to water plants in order to obtain fruit from them but did not know the art of growing them from seed. One could suppose, then, that Andean calabashes propagated themselves the same way and that they were especially cared for because of their great usefulness. Indeed, depending on how they were cut, they served as bottles, cups, and plates, or as coffins for stillborn children. As for plants with edible tubers and rhizomes, they would simply have been dug up in their wild state.

Thus, the history of the origin of cultivated plants in the Andes is still in its infancy. It is not my business to participate in botanical debates, so I follow the advice everyone has given me. I consider all those sites whose debris contains either beans or cotton or both to be huts, houses, camps, or villages that were inhabited by farmers. These cultivated plants are the first to appear. Corn was not eaten until much later, as we shall see.

From radiocarbon datings we know that cotton and beans were already present in the upper inter-Andean valleys eight thousand years ago, but in the coastal villages they have never appeared before six thousand, or at the most, fifty-five hundred years ago. After that time, villages that do not contain the remains of at least one of these two plants are nonexistent. Thus, it seems that agriculture was established in the lower central Andes as early as the sixth millennium B.C.

Why would the situation seen in the upper Andes appear to be so different? Because investigations in the highlands are less productive on account of the rains, I can only hypothesize. So far, except for the site discovered by Lynch, I have a feeling that farmers had penetrated only the upper Andes during the second millennium B.C.

Some authors have suggested that farmers had reached at the same time the highlands and the north coast of Peru, those reaching the former having come from the Orinoco Basin and Central America, the latter from Colombia and Ecuador. The existence of such double currents would explain the simultaneous development of Amazonian manioc farming and of Central American corn farming. For the time being, such suggestions remain theoretical.

Other scholars (for example, Bird) look toward Chile as the cradle of South American farming, and remind us that wild potatoes are found on Chiloé Island. All speculation aside, in keeping strictly with the facts we still seem to face an agricultural penetration that first crossed the Andes from east to west and then followed the coast from south to north. (I found all the earliest farmers that are presently known to be in the central part of the Peruvian coast. No other investigator has pointed out sites of this kind yet.) The Far North has not yet revealed anything, and in the south, beyond the Nazca watershed, agricultural activities become scarcer and later the closer we move toward Chile.

Furthermore, the early development of agriculture in Central America and around the Caribbean could be proven by the fact that pottery, a typically Neolithic craft, shows up much earlier around the Gulf of Mexico, the Caribbean, Venezuela, the Guianas, Colombia, and Ecuador, than it does along the coast of Peru. At Garbanzal, a site located in the Tumbes Valley, Izumi has obtained a carbon 14 age of fifty-five hundred years for a pottery-yielding site. Such an age corresponds to the beginnings of preceramic farming on the central coast of Peru. According to some authors, the neolithization of the Caribbean occurred after the inhabitants of the area were already using pottery.

In Peru, I have discovered so far only five villages belonging to the early farmers' period, and no other author has mentioned the existence of others. All five sites contained cotton and beans, and dated back (according to the radiocarbon process) to 3500 B.C.

Two of these villages, Chilca 1 and Rio Grande de Nazca 49, were located on a terrace bordering a stream and facing a freshwater pond that permitted life beyond the few weeks when the river flooded. The annual flood, on the other hand, permitted the sowing of cottonseed and beans in the moist riverbed after the flood had receded.

Two other sites, one of which seems to have been a cemetery, were located in the desert. (I discovered and described it ten years ago under the name of the Paracas Ossuary, since it contained more than fifty burials.) The other site was Village 514 of Paracas, near the preagricultural Village 96. It was located between an acacia savannah and the beach, where the water sheet came close to the surface and permitted horticulture on a small scale.

These first farmers still lived in villages formed by huts similar to those of the preagriculturalists, with walls of straw or mats, supported according to the environment by reeds or by trunks of young willows. The floor was slightly lower

The excavated floor of a prefarmer's hut in the Paracas Desert. Diameter, fifteen feet. Note the remains of a door, the postholes, wooden implements, grinding stones, and other artifacts lying on the ashy refuse.

A grave with the bodies of a mother and child lying in the sand, wrapped in reed mats. Paracas, south coast of Peru, 7000 B.C.

A prefarmer's hut with whale ribs to push the walls out and wooden posts for support. The hut was buried in refuse left by later settlers. Central coast of Peru, 3 500 B.C.

than the surrounding plain. In two cases I found a small, low, yoke-shaped doorway at the side opposite the prevailing wind.

Although these people were already sowing three species of beans, they were still eating the fruits or seeds of wild plants. Alder and tomato seeds and the chewed roots of rushes are found in their excrement.

From this time on, certain elements of everyday life clearly indicate the development of artistic tendencies. Clothes became decorated with colored threads forming geometric motifs, with shells sewn onto the fabric. Carved bones, pendants, and big beads of green malachite were no longer rarities, as well as musical instruments like flutes and toys like animals made of reeds or carved out of coral. Red pigment played a role, of course, but I have found no trace of it on the skeletons, perhaps as a result of carbonization of the vegetable pigment that was in contact with the decaying body.

The funerary customs seem to indicate a great fear that the deceased person's soul would return. For instance, women's bodies were held in their graves by means of five pegs nailed through different parts of their bodies. And men's bodies were held down with the help of big millstones placed on their chests. I also found the skeletons of babies attached to a post by a small cord.

The graves of very young children and stillborn infants were the ones that received the greatest care. They usually contain objects such as jewels and of course clothing, of the best quality. In two graves, the fetuses were covered by pliable basket cradles of the type that allowed the mother to carry the baby strapped on her back.

Skulls usually had been deformed by frontal and occipital pressure that gave an elongated shape to the head.

Burying the dead in cemeteries, in places reserved especially for the dead, became a common practice, though it had not existed in earlier periods. One can observe such a transition in all old villages that have been reoccupied or been inhabited by many generations. During the earliest period, the deceased were buried inside or around their huts, and stillborn babies and fetuses can be found practically everywhere in the village's soil. The habit of placing bodies in one area to form a cemetery may have been introduced by different tribes.

In Village 1 of Chilca, located forty-five miles south of Lima, the cemetery contained about a hundred graves, wrapped in mats and dressed with many-layered varied garments. Here again the children and fetuses had been treated with the greatest care, which may suggest a desire to protect weak beings with objects whose artistic nature is apparent to us but which the users perhaps valued more for their usefulness as amulets.

At least half of this village had been carried off by a torrential flood, so we shall never know the exact area it had covered. What remains of it forms a flattened gray and white semiellipse of about seven and a half acres, sparkling in the sunlight, a compact one or two yards thick, made of organic matter, ashes, and shells which, because of erosion, have covered the huts.

A cubic yard of kitchen midden refuse made of organic matter, ashes, shells,

An early necklace of stone and shell sewn on leather. From the prefarming and early farming periods.

sand, and stone weighs about twenty-six hundred pounds. Thus, sifting a village seven and a half acres in area that forms a mound one yard thick on the average means removing and sifting some thirty-six thousand tons of debris, the equivalent of a train a thousand cars long.

Our excavation had to be held to an area of only a few hundred square yards out of the existing thirty-three thousand. In other words, we have examined only a few hundred cubic yards out of the fifty-eight thousand that should have been dealt with. Consequently, I can only make suggestions as to how many huts could have existed in the village.

Furthermore, stratigraphy shows that this village had not been occupied permanently. Radiocarbon datings indicate successive periods of occupation and abandonment.

Layers containing granulated sand reveal colder periods corresponding to winds blowing from the south-southeast, whereas layers of fine yellow dust indicate a milder climate with very light winds from the north.

The composition of digestive remains also changes with the periods. Some layers are made up of ash and plant remains mixed with a few seashells. Others are richer in organic materials and contain a large amount of seashells. In most of the preceramic coastal villages some layers are black, greasy, and full of sea lion bones, which seems to indicate that there was a cooler climatic episode between forty-three hundred and thirty-eight hundred years ago. If we accept the results of carbon 14 dating, we may suggest that the first settlers arrived around fifty-five hundred years ago, then left and returned many times until the site was finally abandoned around 2300 B.C., or forty-three hundred years ago. A reoccupation occurred some fifteen hundred years later, but this episode had nothing in common with the early farmers. The new settlers were corn eaters who used pottery.

Large mollusk colonies of big monovalves and mussels living stuck to rocks, and of bivalves living in the sand, must have existed near the site at the time the village was inhabited. Today these mollusks are no longer to be found. Perhaps the sand mollusks such as the Mesodesma populated a vast saltwater pond that was formed behind a sand bar separating it from the sea and that has since dried

A fire-engraved decorated wood flute. From the early farming period.

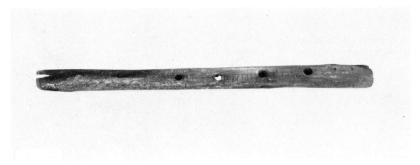

up. I suspect that six thousand years ago the shore was much to the east of where we see it today. The extinction of a mollusk colony might have led to the abandonment of a site like Chilca 1.

Another settlement that had been occupied by early farmers, or at least by fishermen who had been using cotton and eating beans, is Village 514 of Paracas, which consisted of about a dozen huts situated several yards apart to form a circle around a central structure, described below. No refuse mound has survived here. The debris had been blown about by the winds common in this area of southern Peru and had covered all the archaeological remains with a thick layer of sand. But the investigator with enough patience to brush away this sand will soon find remains indicating a human presence, such as bottoms of posts wedged into their holes with stones, silos often containing food, and ashes from hearths.

The central house measured thirty-six feet in diameter and was surrounded by a hundred willow posts forming a slightly oval circle, with a depressed floor slightly lower than the surrounding ground. Countless caches and silos, filled with the remains of the most diverse objects, had been dug inside and around the huts. Postholes showing that porch roofs had probably sheltered the kitchen hearths could be seen outside the huts.

A hearth was also noted in the center of each hut, a semielliptic ring of ashes, sometimes with a bundle of little sticks stuck into the ground next to it that could have been used to revive the fire. It looks like the interior hearth was used to warm the hut and the exterior one was used for cooking.

The presence of these two types of structures, the usual fifteen-foot-wide hut and the large central hut, might indicate a life-style similar to that of other natives we know from ethnology, such as in the Amazonas or New Guinea. The Paracas 514 large hut could have been either a meeting place for male inhabitants or a house used as a dwelling by various families.

Here the deceased had still been buried inside huts or around them in the sand, and not in a cemetery.

Studies in physical anthropology and measurements not yet having been completed, not much can be said about the physical peculiarities of the inhabitants except that they were tall with strong bones and had died there at every age, but generally young—a mixture of fetuses, young children, and young adults. But I also found the bodies of a few individuals who were fifty years old when they died. All had beautiful teeth filed down very low, probably as a result of chewing mollusks that contained sand, and shells crushed into powder and mixed with fish. On the other hand, their bones were in bad condition, with porousness, lateral curvature, and spinal pathologies. Several broken bones indicated a setting of the fracture and joining of the two elements. Signs of violent death, which were to become so abundant in later periods, seem to have been absent, unless we did not recognize them. Spear throwers were, however, present in these villages, as were slings and wooden hunting lances. We even found a very small spear thrower that must have been a toy or a small-scale model intended for children to use.

I favor Junius Bird's conclusion that these people led a peaceful existence. I have, furthermore, noticed several secondary burials that probably indicate a sedentary way of life, the inhabitants wishing to be buried in their home village. This would mean that the body of a man who had died in a remote place had to be brought back.

Up until now, no author has identified agricultural sites in Peru more than five or six thousand years old. It could well be, then, that the fifth millennium B.C. constituted the threshold of agricultural times in the lower central Andes. We are still completely ignorant as to the agricultural techniques these first farmers might have used. Had they come down from the upper Andes, or from the eastern Amazonas, from rainy hot lands where they might have practiced an agriculture based on rain, which specialists call a dry, or nonirrigated, agriculture? Migrating from a rainy climate to totally arid lands, where nothing grows without irrigation, would have constituted quite a brutal change. Furthermore, we know that prehistoric peoples were very much anchored to their traditions and that when they could no longer practice their accustomed farming techniques in a given territory, they abandoned the area. I would, then, be more inclined to think that a colonization of the arid lowlands was brought about by peasants from other equally arid regions, where they had already learned to farm on the basis of flood irrigation.

In the light of the excavation evidence now available to us, it does not seem that the early settling of farmers in the lower Andes was successful. Although I have located several hundred preagricultural villages between the eighth and fourteenth parallels, I have so far been able to identify only very few villages of the first planters. A revival did not occur until much later, some two thousand years after the end of the great burgeoning of nonagricultural villages.

THE BEAN PLANTERS' SOCIETY

Beginning about four thousand years ago, the lower central Andes were populated by many villages whose kitchen middens abound in beans and debris of cotton clothes and underwear. What I call the bean planters' society apparently came into being at this time.

This name has been criticized. Several archaeologists have pointed out to me that beans were not the only vegetable eaten in the villages we are about to consider. True, jiquimas were being eaten then, as a thousand years later, and new fruits and vegetables had appeared. But in my opinion, this period was best characterized by the consumption of beans and the use of cotton to the exclusion of wool.

A few sites occupied by bean planters were described for the first time around 1945 by North American investigators such as Bird, Bennett, Willey, Ford, and Strong. When I arrived in Peru, nothing earlier was known. Bird had worked in the village of Huaca Prieta, at the mouth of the Chicama River. The other archaeologists mentioned sites in the Viru Valley. Huaca Prieta was subsequently dated at 1500 B.C. by the radiocarbon method, and the appearance of the earliest pottery known on the northern coast of Peru was dated at 1300 B.C. These results agreed perfectly with Bird's predictions.

Subsequently, good fortune has permitted me to carry the age of the earliest sites back to four thousand, then five thousand, seven thousand, and finally, ten thousand five hundred years ago. Since then, MacNeish has joined the game and discovered a site on the eastern slope of the central Andes dating back to the Pleistocene.

The development of this society was relatively rapid, if one compares it to the twenty-some centuries devoid of any apparent changes which constitute the first agricultural phase. The first phase of this bean planters' society is characterized by the accumulation of large refuse mounds, black, oily, and consisting of ashes mixed with organic matter and the bones of sea lions. Because of erosion, this refuse has covered villages, the sizes of which may be checked by the postholes of the huts. It may quite well be that the inhabitants had belonged to a new group of emigrants whose customs differed from those of the first planters. Anyway, little by little, in the course of some two hundred years, an evolution occurred that led to a second phase, characterized by the existence of two kinds of villages.

One type had improved, rectangular structures or houses built aboveground, with clay floors. The houses were now bordered by low stone walls faced with clay. In the large villages corresponding to populated areas, these houses generally were surrounding one or several high, oval, refuse mounds surmounted by a flat platform where I imagine people got together on various occasions, as I observed there the existence of many hearths. To avoid degradation of the sides, slabs and cobbles had been stuck against the refuse to form a stone belt encircling the structure.

The second type of village had underground houses dug into the refuse of earlier occupations. A rectangle was cut down to about five feet deep, and the four sides of this hole were then faced with stone slabs held in place with clay. Some of these houses had small blind niches in which objects were stored. The roofs have disappeared, but we know from the debris that they were made of rushes or reed mats supported by branches or whale ribs.

These underground houses were very close together and formed combined units constituting a highly compact village. Some five hundred people could have lived there on some three to five acres.

Our studies are not yet advanced enough to allow us to establish the exact ages of these two types of villages. They may have coexisted and corresponded to two distinct societies or, on the other hand, may have existed at two different times.

During a third and final phase, which I date from 1800 to 1500 B.C., a blossoming seems to have occurred. We know of dozens of villages belonging to this phase, with the biggest having been inhabited by possibly as many as several thousand people. Furthermore, the houses now surrounded big buildings that undoubtedly must have had a communal or ceremonial function and were probably used as storehouses and temples.

About twenty years ago, I discovered a vast settlement, the most spectacular known achievement of this epoch, near Lima in the final stretch of the Chillon River Valley three miles east of the ocean, and gave it the name El Paraíso, after the name of the area.

According to radiocarbon datings, El Paraíso was abandoned around 1500 or 1400 B.C. The thickness of the refuse, a mixture of ashes and food remains extending over the few acres of flat land surrounding the monument, indicates that occupation of the site must have lasted at least one hundred and possibly two hundred years.

On the basis of research by Gordon Willey, I would say that we can now guess at the existence of a somewhat stratified society whose leaders had been able to enlist community efforts to create complexes that could be built only under centralized supervision. Today El Paraíso consists of seven architectural units, all dating back to the same period, but more units must have originally existed. Six of the remaining units are to be found grouped on the south bank of the Chillon River in a side canyon where a rich spring permanently yields fresh water. The Chillon, which here runs in a deep gorge, is dry nine months out of twelve.

El Paraíso must have been a large settlement with plenty of manpower available. The architectural units were enormous buildings made of two rows of heavy quarried and roughly shaped stone blocks cemented with unfired clay, the gaps between blocks being filled with rubble. The walls were faced with various layers of clay, the last one being polished and painted black, red, ocher, and white. The buildings were of various sizes and shapes. Some were rectangular, a thousand feet long; others were almost square, 165 by 132 feet. Some of the structures were quite massive, made of two parallel walls as just described to form a passage 8 feet wide. These massive outer walls surrounded some rectangular halls and rooms joined by doorways that do not seem to have had lintels. At times these doorways were staggered to hide the interior from view.

I restored Unit I according to the anastylosis method. This process consists of putting back into place the blocks of stone that have fallen from the walls. In the case of El Paraíso, there is no doubt as to the ground plan of the building and the rooms that made it up, for the bases of the walls have survived in every case. We just picked up the blocks that had fallen in each room and put them back on the walls. On the other hand, errors may have been made with regard to the proper height of each wall. These may not all have been the same height in the way we rebuilt them. Some rooms may have varied in height, becoming lower as one moved away from the back of the building.

Unit I was a square building surrounded by platforms that formed tiers. Three wide staircases, two made of stone blocks, one of clay, led to it. The unit had been rebuilt and enlarged at least five times, but we were able only to reestablish the halls and rooms on the upper story, corresponding to the last occupa-

The oldest architectural complex known in the Americas—Unit I, El Paraíso, on the central coast of Peru. Abandoned around 1500 B.C.

tion. It alone contained twenty-five enclosures, whose functions have not yet been determined. In my view they were used for storage and festivities, with the other long rectangular units used as living quarters. Once we had removed the rubbish from fallen walls, we found the clay floors in all the rooms to be perfectly clean. Garbage had been thrown out of the building. At least one of the halls must have been intended for ceremonies. Vast and rectangular, it contained a square basin in the center, surrounded at the four corners by conical cavities that had been coated with clay and blackened by fire.

The main staircase, the clay one, was monumental and led to this hall. After that, one walked through various rooms forming a suite joined by doorways. The last of these rooms was furnished with a kind of clay altar.

The whole building reached a height thirty feet above the plain. It seems to have been covered not by a permanent roof but perhaps simply by mats supported by willow posts, only one of which was found still erect.

It is hardly likely that humble farmers in the Chillon Valley made the great effort that the building of these units must have required, just to live in them. The architecture corresponds, moreover, to work of inexperienced builders, to tentative efforts, innovations, and probably failures. But beyond a doubt, we are here confronted with an attempt to achieve a grandiose work.

Some Peruvians have conceived that the main body of the population inhabited the plain in wattled, dank huts, and that the stone buildings were reserved for communal functions and as dwelling places for religious or military leaders. As yet we have found no weapons or projectile points at El Paraíso, and nothing in the debris of the settlement indicates warlike activity. Up to now, the only indication of a socially stratified society is the existence of these monuments that could not have been built without a great communal effort, the achievement of a vast farming community that led a peaceful existence but was led by rulers. In this alone, the face of the Andes had changed a great deal since the first farmers had faded away.

Unit II was comparable in size to the first one, and its ground plan was the same as that of Unit I. We have not restored it. The other buildings were much bigger, with two being as much as a thousand feet long, enormous beehives that contained many little halls or rooms.

If El Paraíso had been one of the first Peruvian examples of a command center annexed to a temple, the tribes' leaders, whether elders, priests, or soldiers, would have controlled the whole lower Chillon Valley, accumulating food reserves in the enormous storehouses. In fact, a few years after discovering El Paraíso, I found a complex with similar architecture and belonging to the same period but located higher in the Chillon Valley, at what is now thirty-six miles from Lima. This site, called Buena Vista, could confirm that a single tribe was actually in control of the entire lower Chillon watershed.

This viewpoint was first expressed several years ago. It was subsequently reinforced when I discovered, first, that the enormous building of Garagay had a preceramic foundation, and then that a little higher up in the Chillon Valley there was a second big complex of the same type as El Paraíso. When I unearthed Buena Vista, I recognized the preceramic architecture of the walls, which had been decorated with several layers of clay, the last being polished and painted. Dating the straw extracted from one of these walls yielded further results similar to those obtained at El Paraíso: 1500 B.C.

Aside from the architectural work, El Paraíso has left us nothing spectacular. The material life seems to have been humble in those days. The diet was composed of fish, marine shellfish, and seafood. It seems to have been a poor diet, with consumption of chitons (mollusks), little sea urchins, and other unpleasant-tasting creatures. The food plants were beans and jiquimas. Clothes were made of cotton, according to the techniques typical of preceramic horizons: netted (a single yarn held in place by knots), looped (a single yarn but not knotted), or twined (made of two or more yarns). The weaving of small pieces made only a timid appearance in other late preceramic villages. On the other hand, mats made of rushes or other reeds still played an important role. They were used as partition walls, roofs, beds, and winding-sheets for the dead.

Fabrics for garments were abundantly decorated, either by using different techniques in the same piece (one went from looping to twisting and vice versa), by shifting warps or wefts, by adding or removing wefts and creating openings or double fabrics, or finally, by using colored pigments or different-colored cottons. Wool was not used yet.

Decorative themes had already reached a high level of complexity, ranging from simple geometric patterns to very stylized zoomorphic (animal-like) motifs. The theme of inverted serpent or fish heads had already appeared in the last preceramic phase. This "interlocking" theme was to last (with some temporary disappearances) throughout the pre-Columbian history of Peru.

Here again, the deceased were treated with great care. Trepanation and the deliberate deformation of skulls were practiced frequently as early as this period, and maybe even earlier. However, let us not fall into the error of thinking that the practice of trepanation indicates the existence of a complex society. Ethnology shows that some natives of Oceania and New Guinea were trepanned several times, and that even mothers trepanned their children, who evidently had a much better resistance to infection than do European children. But the latter have better resistance to other diseases, such as measles, scarlet fever, and whooping cough, which readily kill Asians.

Corpses were usually wrapped either in several layers of garments (maybe blankets or cloaks), in a great looped sack, or in a net. A small looped bag pulled down to the chin served as a cap. This little bag was sometimes replaced by a basket, and apparently it was in this period that baskets first appeared. On the other hand, shoes were not used yet. I have also noticed the presence of clothes made of pieces of cotton cloth sewn together, but the carbonized state of these fabrics, destroyed by the decaying bodies, has not permitted us to reconstitute what must have been shaped clothes.

Village 1 of the preceramic complex of Asia, which I discovered in the lower Omas Valley sixty miles south of Lima, has provided us with more details as to the way of life of these last preceramicists. (This village was abandoned around 1400 B.C.)

Here we also have entered the horizon of aboveground houses: rectangular ones with stone walls faced with clay, only thirty-two inches high. Here again we find double walls separated by rubble of ash and shells in which willow trunks supporting the roof were planted.

The weapons used were the rod-shaped spear thrower with a hook but without a ring, and the sling. Projectile points were made of quartz or lava, and often of obsidian. Being small, they must have been fastened to light reed arrows. We have also found hunting spears, countless objects and tools made of wood or bone, and a mirror—the first one known in the Americas—a small piece of very shiny hard stone fastened to a clay tablet. These wooden objects, found in great abundance in dry preceramic Peruvian villages, remind us how dangerous it is to

Maybe the earliest mirror found in South America: a flake of hard stone glued on an unbaked clay tablet, with shell inlays. Late preceramic period, central coast of Peru.

form a picture of a prehistoric complex while taking into account only its stone objects.

Female statuettes of unfired clay, typical of an agricultural world in the process of being formed, were also found. Such statuettes have appeared in Village 1 of Chilca. Hardly shaped at all, they are the earliest ones I know of. Thus, they seem to accompany settlers already practicing agriculture.

Finally, I recovered a shaman's small bag containing all the paraphernalia of a witch doctor, including a skunk's paw and tablets and tubes for taking snuff.

In Asia 1 I also found the earliest seal that has been discovered so far in the Andes, a small plate of unfired clay with a mythological theme engraved on it, a bird with two heads facing each other.

Art had already taken several different forms: flutes, spindle whorls sculpted with zoomorphic motifs, and magnificently ornamented fabrics.

For planting and sowing, a digging stick was used to make a hole and fill it with earth after dropping a seed into it.

Dishware was still made of calabashes, but baskets were now in general use.

Cooking was done on circular platforms made of stones placed on the ground. Once the stones were heated, they remained hot enough to broil meat and make shellfish open up. Through ethnology, we know that a burning-hot stone was also used to warm up soup contained in a calabash, which was an inflammable material that could not be put over the fire, of course.

In Río Seco, fifty-four miles north of Lima, on a terrace facing the ocean, I unearthed another village that may have been one of the earliest settlements of this third and final phase of the preceramic bean planters' society. Here radiocarbon datings have yielded ages ranging from 3,750 to 3,600 years ago.

The only and maybe the earliest seal found in South America, engraved on an unbaked clay tablet. Late preceramic period, central coast of Peru.

A flute from Paracas. Two thousand years old.

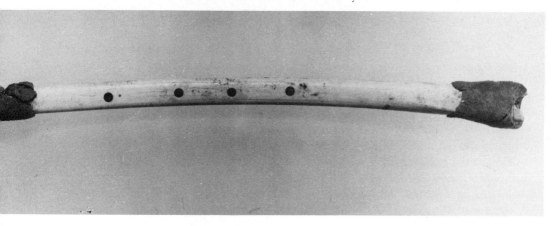

Río Seco was a village composed of a multitude of small rectangular huts bordered by low walls of unfired handmade bricks surrounding several large buildings that must have had a communal function. These buildings were made of large cobbles that had been carried up from the dry bed of an ancient wadi, and of large blocks of coral brought from the beach. They were circular and half-underground in that the floors of the rooms were lower than the surrounding plain. One entered these rooms from the top of the walls, which were very thick, thus giving the structure the appearance of a cone. Partition walls that subdivided the buildings into several rooms were decorated with a geometric arrangement of stone blocks alternating with blocks of unfired clay. It was in Río Seco that I first noticed the existence of doorways surmounted by wooden lintels made from cactus trunks, and this reminds me again how careful one must be not to fail to consider the possibility of cultural traits existing, though no traces have yet come to light. Cactus lintels may well have existed in El Paraíso, but they could have decayed.

From what we were able to see, seven communal buildings must have existed distributed throughout the village. This indicates its size, for refuse is found for several hundred yards in each direction, forming an oval of some twenty-five acres.

Río Seco must certainly have been a fishermen's village. I found it in a completely deserted area along the Pacific, far from any visible source of drinking water and not suited to agriculture. Up to now, I have not been able to rediscover the inhabitants' sources of drinking water. Anyway, even horticulture seems out of the question. Therefore, its inhabitants must have either exchanged seafood for edible vegetables that they obtained from the farmers of the rich Chancay Valley, nine miles away, or they must have dominated this valley themselves. They probably also gathered food in the nearby lomas of Lachay and Doña Maria.

Río Seco has provided us with a large collection of extremely varied fabrics, but very few objects of everyday life. The stone tool industry was completely decadent in this period, to the point that all I could find were a few little basalt knives that had been roughly made by percussion and then glued with resin to a handle.

The refuse in Río Seco, unlike that in Asia 1, was filled with objects whose use escapes me, like little bundles of small sticks and straw sewn into small cotton bags. Peruvians call the objects I brought back *offerings*. In my belief, the materials were prepared to reactivate a hearth, or to make a fire upon returning to the village after a seasonal abandonment. Villages like Río Seco may have been deserted, for example, during the sowing and harvesting seasons, while the inhabitants worked in the neighboring valleys or in the lomas. We are still reduced to hypotheses in this regard.

I cannot describe here all the bean planters' villages I know, most being located on the coast. Archaeologists are just beginning to discover the preceramic age in the cordillera. In the eastern Andes, in the Huallaga Basin, the Japanese scholar Izumi was the first to bring to light the preceramic village of Kotosh, made of little rectangular aboveground houses built of stone embedded in clay, joined into very compact units or quarters. A little ceremonial area apparently also existed there in the form of a rectangular room decorated with anthropomorphic figures made of unfired clay and molded against the walls. This room was called "the temple of the crossed hands."

Kotosh, like Garagay in the lower Chillon Valley, at the edge of the Rímac Basin, was reoccupied in later times. As a result, sites of this kind were formerly considered to be late pre-Columbian. Peruvians have a hard time accepting the idea that the Incas did not invent everything in their country.

On the northern coast, I have worked in Culebras, Bermejo, Los Chinos, Guañape, and many other villages of this period, which must have been an age of prosperity and progress.

North of the eighth parallel, on the other hand, I have found only the remains of what must have been small camps. Henning Bischof, who explored the dry coast of Ecuador thoroughly, found a similar situation. If it could be confirmed that the cool coast of Ecuador had remained uninhabited, this could provide useful information in the field of climatology. One possibility would be that the equatorial countercurrent may have made itself felt farther south than it does now. If this had been the case, the coast would have been wooded not only as far as Esmeraldas but as far as Piura in northern Peru, and the rain would have washed away the mounds and villages, thus depriving archaeologists of their pasture.

Archaeology indicates that all the bean planters' villages were abandoned at about the same time, apparently around 1500 to 1400 B.C. Maybe the event was not contemporaneous everywhere, but there is no doubt that the entire society suddenly disappeared without leaving a trace, their villages never being reoccupied. They were still intact when discovered. Some preceramic sites were reoccupied, but not until much later, after a period of abandonment lasting several centuries.

Up to now, no explanation has been suggested for the sudden and complete disappearance of the preceramicists of Peru. One naturally is tempted to imagine that some corn eaters who used pottery destroyed the preceramicist bean eaters and occupied their territory. However, the results of excavations do not confirm this hypothesis. Rather, they indicate that the Peruvian coast probably remained deserted for one to three centuries and that the process of reoccupation could have been very slow.

The presence of a different ethnic group in the vicinity of the last preceramicists is attested, however, by the crossbreedings that specialists in physical anthropology have observed by studying the skeletons I have provided them. Brachycephalic and mesocephalic skulls are now found in addition to the dolichocephalic ones of the past, the mesocephalic skulls becoming common.

Such events also remind us of the important role played by diseases. The collapse of the Andean world in the sixteenth century A.D. can partly be linked with their contact with Europeans and Africans bringing along diseases against which the American natives had no genetic defenses. One could imagine that foreign ethnic groups had brought along a plague that killed the bean planters, just as smallpox and malaria killed the Andeans after the Spaniards got a foothold on the continent.

A climatic crisis could also have driven away the preceramicists. One of the periodic recessions of the sea level could also have made the fresh-water springs inaccessible to the inhabitants of the coast. But if this is so, where did they go? We never find them again. It is a fact that in an ecology of arid lands as fragile as that of the bean planters, living conditions could have become unbearable following the arrival of a little more or a little less water at the time of the rivers' annual flooding. Their agriculture totally depended on the behavior of such streams. Now the volume of the floods was in turn a function of a slightly cooler or slightly warmer season in the upper Andes; more water meant violent floods that washed away the farmlands that these peoples, not knowing how to build canals, were obliged to establish at the same level as the riverbeds. A dry period, moreover, meant famine for tribes who did not have cultivable land enough to build up food and seed reserves.

The great complex of El Paraíso, with its collective granaries, may have been built in reaction against the danger of famine. While I was working on its restoration, I saw the flow of the Chillon River rising in one day from 2.6 cubic yards to 156 cubic yards of water per second, with its level reaching several yards above its normal summer height. What today would end up as only a costly incident would have constituted a real disaster for the peasants of thirty-five hundred years ago.

THE BEGINNINGS OF CORN GROWING

From 1500 B.C. onward, the central Andes, both in the cordillera and on the coast, were peopled with villages whose inhabitants ate corn and cooked their food in ceramic vessels. Corn remains are not found in all the villages of this epoch, for vegetable matter is destroyed wherever the soil is slightly moist. But even in the absence of corn, it is easy to verify the arrival of a new wave of immigrants, for they brought pottery with them and their presence is characterized by a host of new cultural traits.

Pottery was apparently not used in the central Andes before corn consumption began. Some authors contend that the evolution had been different in the Far North of the continent, but I have doubts about this theory. Apropos of Valdivia, located on the cool Ecuadorian coast, Clifford Evans and Betty Meggers state that the inhabitants of this site, who used pottery, did not know how to grow corn. I do not agree with these distinguished authors. Rather, I support the thesis of Izumi, who thinks that corn disappeared in the Valdivia kitchen middens because of ground water, whereas pottery survived. Valdivia, with its countless female statuettes, is more Neolithic than Mesolithic. It seems to me to be typical of an agricultural society.

The earliest-known villages of pottery users who ate corn were, and still are, located around the Caribbean Sea. Next came Valdivia in Ecuador, and Panama, where pottery has been found in sites four thousand years old or older. In Peru, however, pottery does not seem to have been introduced until about 1300 B.C. At first it was thought to have been brought down through Ecuador. I have discovered various villages in the central Peruvian lower Andes that yielded pottery as well as carbon 14 ages in the 3300 to 3500 B.C. range. So one wonders whether corn and pottery could not have been brought over from the eastern slopes of the cordillera. A village like Chanapata, now on the outskirts of Cuzco, was using pottery thirty-five hundred years ago. However, from this date onward, practically no Peruvian villages are found that do not contain pottery.

As mentioned, all the bean planters' settlements were abandoned around thirty-five hundred years ago and were not rebuilt. This fact, as well as the appearance of new cultural traits, gives reason to believe that we are observing here the effects of a migration and not simply of the adoption of a new product by settled populations.

If a migration had taken place, we must once more seek its source in arid lands. One can hardly imagine a more discouraging environment for peasants used to dry farming than that of the central Andes coastal oases, where nothing can grow without irrigation.

What I call the first wave of corn-planting invaders has been studied very little. I was the first to locate several of their villages, first on the coast, then in the upper Andes. This revolution should have attracted more interest, for these innovators changed Andean eating habits for the next three thousand years.

It is also possible that the adoption of corn as a basic food played a fundamental role in the evolution of the Andean peoples. Corn resists drought better than beans, keeps better, produces more per acre, and is easy to cook. Perhaps it was the adoption of this plant that permitted the accumulation of food reserves and favored the development of advanced societies.

The polemics regarding the center where corn farming developed have lasted thirty years and are still in progress. Less theory and more good archaeology are badly needed in this field. It would be especially appropriate to establish a detailed list of cultural traits for the countries adjacent to Peru, to compare with those that appeared in the central Andes at the same time as corn. For example, several of the somewhat peculiar shapes of Peruvian pottery are found as much in Ecuador as in Central America, whereas Caribbean or Amazonian decorations entered Colombia in the north, the eastern Andes in the continent's center, and the Argentine Andes in the south, but did not reach the Pacific Coast between Ecuador and Chile.

Another profound change that accompanied the appearance of pottery was the disappearance of the twining technique of weaving. Looped bags and caps and twined mats were still made, but underwear, blankets, and cloaks were no longer twined but were woven, with the loom being invented soon afterward.

Furthermore, wool as well as cotton was now used to make clothes. The *unku,* a shirt with neck and arm openings, the existence of which I could not prove in the preceramic period, may have been brought by the second wave of corn farmers. Since we lack clothes belonging to the first wave of corn planters, we do not know for certain if the *unku* was introduced into Peru at the same time as pottery. What is certain is that the preceramicists did not wear garments cut and sewn to shape.

The changes brought about by the corn planters were also deep in the areas of architecture and settlement patterns. The compact, agglutinated villages of preceramic times did not survive. Now people lived very differently, and in a less confined way. In the coastal sands we find them living on top of small artificial mounds bordered by two to four tiers, inside a rectangular hut of mats kept in place by a low stone wall. Similar low walls, usually one row of planted cobbles, divided the hut into little rooms. Other mounds are topped by ruined stone build-ings that could have been ceremonial structures.

In the dry gorges of the lower Andes and in the upper cordillera I have found villages belonging to the same period, with circular houses dug halfway into the ground and surrounded by low walls made of stones set in clay. The roofs have generally disappeared, but from what remains in places we know that they were conical, made of straw, and supported by branches and tree trunks.

The villages of this first wave of corn planters are so poorly known that I think it will be useful to describe in some detail the ones I have mapped out.

LAS HALDAS

The plain of Las Haldas, located on the northern coast of Peru, forms a crescent seven and a half miles long and fifteen hundred yards wide in the center. It borders a marine zone that abounds in good-quality fish. This plain had al-ready been inhabited in preagricultural times by fishermen who had built villages of huts there. Then it underwent a very dense occupation in the middle phase of the bean planters' civilization, which was probably thirty-eight hundred years ago.

After a period of abandonment that lasted five centuries, the corn eaters who used pottery appeared there around thirty-three hundred years ago.

As a result of destruction caused during later reoccupation of the site, it is hard to estimate the number of inhabitants who lived in Las Haldas at the time. I would say there were at least several hundred families, or several thousand peo-ple, who must have obtained their vegetables from the adjacent rich Casma Valley, perhaps by bartering fish for vegetables.

When I looked for the place or places where the inhabitants would have been able to obtain their drinking water, I noticed bunches of purslane and salt-marsh plants at certain spots on the beach. So I probed at these points and found some brackish water less than six feet below the surface. Very likely it was this water that made possible the existence of Las Haldas, as similar water sheets made possible so many other Andean coastal villages, very remote from all visible surface water resources.

Las Haldas is a vivid example of the drastic change that occurred when corn was introduced. Beans, manioc, peanuts, and jiquimas seem to have come into disuse, only to reappear a few centuries later. Corn had indeed become the basic food of Americans. At a given moment, however, one does witness the diffusion on the coast of potatoes and other plants with tubers. But here again, it is only a question of such complements to the main item as just listed. Basically, from thirty-three hundred years ago onward, the American ate corn, as the European ate wheat and the Asian ate rice. Corn still represents around 80 to 85 percent of the diet of the present farmer populations of Yucatán.

Now contrary, it seems, to what happened in Central America, in Mexico, and among the Mayas, seafood always played a major role in the Andes. Despite the formation of agricultural societies, fish (especially shellfish) retained a dominant place in the diet until the time of the Incas. Seafood provided protein for a population that lacked meat, living as they did in lands providing very few large mammals and where hunting must have become a luxury; where the llama, a beast of burden and an animal of a magical character, would hardly have been eaten, where only the guinea pig provided a small amount of meat for the small farmer living at a distance from the sea. The princes of Cuzco had seafood brought up as far as their capital. But such imports could not have been considered by ordinary citizens.

The use of pottery undoubtedly constitutes a new cultural trait, but one of ultimately secondary importance; the diffusion of corn was a much more important event. In the beginning, pottery remained primitive. Badly fired to colors of brown, chocolate, or gray, it was often freely scored with a semipolished spatula, decorated with incisions or little modeled appendages, or with some red paint applied in restricted areas after the vessel had been fired. Not until the arrival of a new wave of immigrants, around 800 B.C., did a highly stylized pottery appear, with an imaginative and entirely new decoration.

ANTIVAL AND HUARANGAL

It was in the Chilca Basin that I first discovered the existence of villages indicating the sudden arrival in the central Andes of newcomers who used pottery and ate corn. The Chilca ends up where the coastal plain begins, forty-seven miles south of Lima, but to the east it reaches the high cordillera around thirteen thousand feet. It thus provides us with a good profile through the western slopes, with its usual climatic floors: extremely arid, then semiarid in the lomas, then quite arid again, semiarid once more where rains occur, and, finally, rainy.

In the upper Chilca Valley I found the caves described later, then I ran across Antival, a large settlement with beautiful stone houses located on a crest at eleven thousand feet, in a good defensive position. One can still see a spring there, which is dried up now except for a few days in winter.

The study of such sites is rendered particularly difficult as a result of the absence of drinking and cooking water. Just providing drinking water for a small team camping on a site will keep two men constantly busy, so long and painful is the path they must travel each day to reach a spring that has not dried up.

Formerly, the countryside around Antival must have been wooded. Farming terraces, now abandoned, are spread out on the sides of the hill. The whole complex is now in ruins and is very hard to get to, but it must have been a splendid, well-defended refuge before deforestation dried out the environment and obliged the inhabitants to abandon the place. The pottery-yielding refuse gave radiocarbon ages in the thirty-three hundred to three-thousand-year range.

Walking down toward the sea, I found the Huarangal dry gorge, today entirely uninhabited but still partially carpeted in winter, between 660 and 2,640 feet in altitude, with a loma flora. Now practically everyplace where such a flora exists, one will find, by brushing away the modern soil, villages of huts belonging to the preagricultural horizons. In many places, villages of houses made of low

A stone house in Antival in the central Andes. It probably belongs to the Nazca period.

stone walls half buried in the ground are found over the villages of older huts. The newcomers were using pottery. One even finds fragments of their vessels in the village *kiwas*, the "clubhouses" of the prefarmers that seem to have been reused.

Huarangal is apparently one more piece of evidence that groups belonging to the first wave of corn eaters entered the lower Andes from east to west.

A *kiwa*, a ceremonial or communal structure, after excavation. Diameter, sixty feet. Early corn period, Huarangal canyon, lower-central Andes, Peru.

Radiocarbon datings agree, being in the range of thirty-five hundred to thirty-three hundred years ago.

Several villages similar to Huarangal can still be seen in the neighboring canyons. All of them consist of low houses made of big blocks or small stones, and all are surrounded by terraced gardens and hundreds of subterranean stone-roofed storage bins.

Some villages are widely spread out in the bottoms of the gorges, without any defense. But others occupy hard-to-reach strategic positions on narrow crests.

One may wonder if the latter may not have been contemporaneous with the end of the period, built by inhabitants who were threatened by new invaders, the people I shall soon describe who formed the second society of corn planters or, on the contrary, built by the first arrivals, who were even so threatened by earlier occupants of these canyons.

THE APPEARANCE OF POTTERY IN THE EXTREME UPPER ANDES

Ramiro Matos was the first to point out to me the existence of the Disco Verde type of pottery around glacial lagoons at an altitude of sixteen thousand five hundred feet, above Castrovirreyna, Peru. Since then, I have found examples of the earliest pottery in numerous points in the puna, as well as near Lake Titicaca and in the Cordillera de la Viuda, northeast of Lima. We know now that this type of ceramics—three thousand to thirty-five hundred years old—is to be found almost everywhere in the caves and rock shelters of the upper Andes.

Other villages with ancient pottery were found by investigators in the upper Andes as early as twenty or thirty years ago. The most typical are Chanapata, located in the suburb of Santa Ana in Cuzco; Chiripa, on the shores of Lake Titicaca, and Pucara, in the puna forty-eight miles north of the lake. Some brown pottery coated with white slip was also extracted from a twenty-eight-hundred-year-old site at Qualuyu, near Lake Titicaca.

Chanapata has never been properly excavated. Now it is too late to do so, because the village has been destroyed, the soil used for making bricks. I luckily obtained an age of thirty-three hundred years from charcoal found in a hearth. The ruins here consisted of small houses encircled by low walls one or two yards thick. Rains and erosion had covered the area with stratified refuse. Graves were also found, as is normal in any village. Many camelid bones were found in the middens. The inhabitants must already have been stockbreeders, as they were making their clothes of llama wool.

We know as well that the Chanapatas had javelins with obsidian points. But which were they using to propel them—spear throwers, or bows?

Bone tools and little figurines carved out of stone or modeled out of clay were also found. The pottery was very elegant, with shiny black dishes. The cups had straight sides and were highly polished and decorated with incisions depicting animals. A postfiring white-on-red decoration that was similar to the one found in Las Haldas and in Disco Verde on the coast had also been in use. The white paste was probably obtained from kaolin. Chanapata pottery has been found from Maras, 18 miles north of Cuzco, to Ayaviri, some 180 miles south of Cuzco.

In Chiripa, which dates back to 300 B.C., and at a few other points in the vicinity, one can observe different architectural styles. The walls were built with unfired clay bricks painted red, green, and white and resting on a pebble base. All of them were double, with storage spaces or niches in between. In my opinion, these bins, with their square doors topped with lintels, must have been stables for guinea pigs of the type I found in Paracas and other sites. The roofs must have been of straw held up by posts planted across between walls.

The first investigators of Chiripa found graves under the floors. These contained no pottery, only small green malachite-and-shell beads decorating the corpses. Among other items found in the graves were small fragments of gold hammered into thin sheets. If it could be confirmed that the gold actually belonged to the preceramic period, and not to later reoccupations that yield samples of corn and pottery, this would be an important discovery.

Chiripa pottery has a very stylized decoration using Greek step patterns and other geometric forms in addition to small appliqué figurines. Large flat-bottomed dishes were used, as well as drinking utensils with straight, tapering sides.

Pucara is a highly unusual site, with vast buildings still standing on a system of planting terraces there. It is astonishing that this site, on the main road joining Cuzco to Lake Titicaca, has not attracted the attention of serious researchers.

Until scientific excavations are undertaken, it will be hard to place in time the various ruins that have survived there. From what I could see, it seems that something basically analogous to Chiripa had existed at Pucara, but the different temples, terraces, and dwellings have not been dated.

J. C. Tello and the classical authors considered as an achievement of the second wave of corn planters the society then known as Chavín (see below). I think this may be an error and that Pucara was not Chavinoid. Furthermore, not a single creation of the Chavín society has yet been pointed out around Lake Titicaca. In my opinion, Pucara was either earlier, contemporary with the Chanapata period, or later, a product of the Marcavalle period.

Other objects found in Pucara clearly show the influence of Tiahuanaco. Therefore, they must be five hundred to a thousand years younger.

The carved stelae and the monoliths with high-relief decorations are something totally different. They remind me of the monoliths planted on top of the big mounds of Mocachi in Bolivia. The site is located at an important strategic point. *Pucara* means fortress; it could have been a fortress that changed hands several times. A little wood, called "the Incas' wood," may still be seen on hills overlooking the site at an altitude well over thirteen thousand feet, and this is a rarity in the upper Andes.

THE SECOND WAVE OF CORN PLANTERS: THE CHAVIN HORIZON

In 1943, the Peruvian anthropologist J. C. Tello announced the discovery of a fascinating new culture that had created imposing buildings. In fact, it was well after treasure looters had put objects of an unprecedented style into circulation that Tello decided to visit the place the strange-looking pottery came from. Incidentally, similar pieces had already been reported by Charles Wiener in the nineteenth century.

At the very beginning of the twentieth century, Max Uhle had excavated the coastal settlement of Ancón, near Lima, whose upper layers date back to the last pre-Hispanic centuries. Uhle reported the existence of older shell mounds, but he attributed them to the cooking middens of simple fishermen. He did not suspect that these remains (though they did indeed cover the ruins of humble fishing villages) in reality contained objects and fragments of pottery vessels interchangeable with those subsequently extracted from the Great Temple of Chavín de Huantar, the chief site of the Chavín society.

Tello arrived at last at the vast edifice that has survived at the entrance to the village of Chavín de Huantar, located in an inter-Andean valley on the west bank of the Mosna River. Set into the walls of the building were monoliths carved in the round. Tello noticed that these were decorated with the same motifs as certain wooden, bone, or ceramic objects he had already recorded as products of an original and unknown society. This society was thus called Chavín.

From then on, Tello became enthusiastic and devoted the last years of his life to studying it. He finally defined the Chavín society as "the matrix culture of the Andes, the creator of a megalithic empire."

Chavín was undeniably a highly original phenomenon in the central Andes. So, with praiseworthy patriotic sentiment, Tello and his collaborators made every effort to have its achievements known as those of a society that had played a predominant role in Peruvian prehistory. They emphasized both Chavín's civilizing and its innovating roles. The thesis that the Chavín society had an innovating role, before which nothing worthwhile existed, was subsequently defended with desperate eagerness by Tello's associates until the 1960s. It is with the greatest difficulty that I have been able to convince not foreigners, of course, but Peruvians themselves that an important preceramic society had already taken shape fifteen hundred years before Chavín appeared. I shall never forget the disbelief, then anger, of some of Tello's friends when I took them to the excavation site and showed them a completely preceramic village buried under a settlement containing Chavín pottery.

Tello wanted to take a view opposite that of the classical one taught at San Marcos University in Lima. According to this school, there had been no splendid achievements in the pre-Hispanic period except for those of the princes of Cuzco, the Incas. And in those days, even the achievements of the Incas did not arouse much enthusiasm.

Thanks to Chavín, Peruvians found they had ancestors they could trace back to very ancient times, ancestors who had created a civilization that was comparable, according to them, to that of Mycenae.

It was probably with the idea of bringing about such a comparison that the adjective *megalithic* was applied to Chavín, which was supposed to have invented architecture in stone. No one knew in those days what I discovered twenty-five years later, that the preceramicists were already building with heavy stone blocks, as in El Paraíso. The walls of most pre-Columbian buildings in Peru are, moreover, made of stone, but since they are faced with clay that survives for centuries in the absence of rain, the public is convinced that Chavín was a unique megalithic period, the only one using stone instead of unfired bricks.

Now apart from such considerations, which belong to the past, Chavín deserves our attention just as much as the bean planters' society. These two groups should be kept in mind, though they were some seven hundred years apart in time and were extremely different. Both had influenced a vast territory. The preceramicists left their mark on the entire coast of central Peru, the highlands, and probably also on the eastern slopes of the cordillera. Chavín influenced much of what is now modern Peru, including what is called the cold forest.

But in the field of social structures, the differences are extreme. With only their beans and jiquimas, the preceramicists succeeded in feeding numerous populations clustered in big, densely populated villages that already incorporated communal centers.

Chavín, on the other hand, created monumental complexes typical of stratified theocratic or militaristic social organization. But on the other hand, its villages were next to nothing. The population apparently lived scattered at the edges of fields and beaches, and seemingly supplied immense fortress-temples that doubled as granaries. The two systems must have been heirs to very different traditions.

It is customary to speak of a Chavín horizon, the anthropologists' term describing different groups among which a number of common cultural traits appear in the course of a given span of time. These traits, however, are foreign to each of these groups taken individually. The horizon may thus be the product of intellectual or religious influences without there having been political influence over a territory or physical occupation of it.

I do not think the term *horizon* should be applied in this case. All the sites marked with the Chavín stamp show us cultural traits that are so profoundly Chavinoid that one wonders if groups that were unconnected with the movement would have been able to exert any influence.

According to radiocarbon datings, the first manifestations of Chavín began to appear in 800 B.C., some 2,750 years ago. The same date is arrived at throughout the territory affected by the phenomenon. Therefore, it must have developed rapidly, perhaps in a single generation or less. Furthermore, it seems to have influenced strongly all the territory under consideration, for no sites contemporaneous with Chavín and belonging to the area influenced have yet been found that did not yield at least one cultural trait typical of the society.

These traits are, moreover, so original that it is hard not to notice them. With Chavín appear:

• Low-relief ornaments made on hammered gold leaf
• Cigars, but ones not made from tobacco leaves
• Carved and polished-stone vessels and stone tools of various shapes. We have already found polished-stone objects that are ten thousand years old, or Mesolithic. But they were only little rings some two inches in diameter, and not notched axes or cylindrical maces such as we have found in Chavín sites.

I once saw a helical stone mace attributed to Chavín in a museum in the United States. This piece is so perfect in its execution and design that it must be a stone replica of a metal object made in a mold. This piece, whose place of origin is unfortunately unknown, links Chavín art directly to a region that was already living in the Copper or Bronze Age. But the Chavíns did not use copper, a situation that reminds me of the Polynesians migrating eastward and forgetting the use of pottery.

• Stone sculpture in the round, and carved stone stelae
• Anthracite mirrors. These mirrors did not survive the Chavín society. We

should note that the known anthracite mines in Peru are located right in the heart of the territory of this society. The Chavíns also used polished slate projectile points, which ceased being used when Chavín died.

• Very large architectural units, some of which are several hundred yards long

• Portrait vessels, vessels with phytomorphic (plantlike) decorations, and vessels with demoniacal decorations completely foreign to earlier traditions

The decorative themes were almost always derived from five basic subjects:

• An African-style mouth with thick lips

• Fangs shaped like curved swords, with those of the upper jaw often crossing those of the lower

• Several snakelike bodies protruding from the heads of demoniacal beings or from human figures. Such bodies have heads of an animal that is hard to identify, with a prominent round nose, that could have been a feline just as well as a crocodile.

One also sees these snakelike figures protruding from a body, like an elephant's trunk, on Mexican objects. Is this an Asian archetype? One is also reminded of a crocodile snout, which is considered sacred in Africa. Maybe the caiman was held to be sacred in the Americas.

The Tiahuanaco society later took up this decorative theme again and gave a square, more feline shape to the snout. I am also reminded of the "life lines" painted on human bodies in Chinese medical treatises.

• Crenellations, staircases, or other architectural or geometric forms recalling models of buildings or fortresses

• Vessels representing human or demonic heads, animals, and plants such as corn, red pepper, and even chirimoya, for example.

At least one of these themes is found on the majority of decorated objects found in the places inhabited during the period, and often also in the decorations of buildings constructed by the Chavíns.

Contrary to the very widespread and hard-to-uproot belief that everything involving an artistic effort is essentially ceremonial, reserved for the temple or the palace, the fine Chavín pottery was in actual fact intended for everyday use. I found it in the hearths of the humblest fishermen on the coast. The broken fragments in the ashes were equal to in workmanship and interchangeable with those found in the big temples, as in the one called the Gallery of Offerings at the eponymous site of Huantar.

This tendency to consider archaeological objects sacred is universal. It survives even among the French, despite the efforts of Eugène Viollet-le-Duc. Who, even among a cultivated public, does not maintain that Romanesque architecture had only a religious function? One need only walk around the streets of the French city of Cluny, however, to observe private houses decorated with the same windows and little columns as those that adorn the abbey.

In villages bearing the Chavín stamp, even objects found in the dirtiest kitchen middens always show, when decorated, one of the themes typical of the period, as just described. Even vases painted according to the technique of negative decoration depict crenels and geometric motifs. This rule applies, moreover, to all forms of decoration: engraving or carving on stone, wood, shell, or bone; repoussé work on gold leaf, and patterns visible on fabrics. In the last case, the pattern appears in filigree in the weaving or painted on it, for embroidery was apparently not yet practiced.

Chavín pottery is usually fascinating and strange, sometimes beautiful, often noteworthy from the technical point of view. The usual colors of the paste were

A typical Chavín bottle.

black, greenish gray, or pale beige. Cooking dishes were generally chocolate colored. On the south coast such pieces were highly oxidized and fired to an orange pink. Bottles often had long necks of a kind brought back in style in France around 1900. In Huantar, some bottles found in the Gallery of Offerings could have come from Gallé. Some bottles had two straight spouts that extended from the vessel at about forty-five degree angles, with a solid extension between the spouts that formed a handle.

I have practiced copying pre-Columbian clay vessels, but my efforts to reproduce these highly polished blacks of the Chavíns, some of it mirror shiny, have failed. Chavín pottery is hard to imitate.

The portrait vessels often depict two half faces joined in the middle, uniting a man, a demon, or an animal, a trait common to both Chavín and southern Asia.

Decoration was obtained either by polishing; by obtaining a black, smoky surface; by reproducing stylized motifs by making wide incisions with a spatula; by engraving fine incisions on the half-dried paste with a pointed tool, or by pressing a tube, a fingernail, a wedge-shaped reed, or a shell into the soft, wet clay. (The best source for learning how to study and classify pottery is undoubtedly a work by the late Ann Sheppard, *Ceramics for the Archaeologist*, available from the Smithsonian Institution in Washington, D.C.)

The art of painting pottery was not yet known. To enliven the vessel, red, green, white, or yellow pigments were applied in areas bordered by incised lines or into circles, but only after the piece had been in the kiln. These incisions seem to have been made with a kodakia shell, but this shellfish, which is typical of North America, apparently does not live in Peruvian waters.

When there was not enough space for more, a mouth with swordlike fangs, or a single element of the complete theme, was sculpted on the piece with a spatula. Some motifs are found engraved with a pointed tool on the dry paste before firing the pot. This would indicate that local potters had been copying original vessels, the models for sculpturing already being lost.

Chavín pottery is the only kind in Peru that included oval, square, rectangular, or triangular vessels. Sometimes they had three or four feet, sometimes strictly flat bottoms, or with bases surrounded by annular rings that were sometimes pierced at the side, as in the perfume vessels of the Far East. Dishes with an annular base appear very early in Ecuador and as far as Tumbes. In central Peru, however, one finds them only in the sites that show Chavín or earlier influences.

I should also mention that I have found, in some Chavinoid fishing villages on the central coast of Peru, the molded and painted portrait of a smiling little animal with three fingers, which zoologists have identified as a xenarthra, a small forest sloth. Sometimes the animal is chewing coca and a lump appears in his cheek. At other times he holds a bow, a spear thrower, or both weapons. His head is generally covered with a big tuft of feathers or with a parrot. This combination of traits immediately brings to mind the Amazonian forest. Let us not for-

A Chavín doll of red, fired ceramic. From Curayacu, central coast of Peru.

get, however, that fifteen years ago we still used to see opossums (the local name of which is *muca*) living right down to the outskirts of Lima, even in my garden, and also that parrots still fly there in dense flocks over cornfields. Coca, on the other hand, is now chewed in the highlands.

The natives of the country attribute to a local type of opossum great aphrodisiac power, as do the natives of Australia. A wounded *muca* I had sheltered in my garden thus ended up in the cook's frying pan. He had not been able to resist the temptation to give himself strength.

Let us now study the problem of the origins of the Chavín movement, a problem that has not yet been solved.

Tello and his school saw Chavín as a culture that was essentially central Andean, a culture of the Peruvian cordillera. Very well; I have nothing against this idea. But is it normal for an art and decorative themes to appear in a definitive—one is tempted to say classical—form, without archaeologists succeeding in finding somewhere in the vicinity (or even far away) villages in which one can observe an evolution leading from the origins of this art to its developed forms, its apogee? As long as archaeologists have not found an Andean site yielding pieces showing a stratigraphically established evolution in decoration, I shall refuse to reject the idea of Chavín art being the product of foreign immigration. Stratigraphic excavations at Las Haldas, and those done by Izumi at Kotosh, reveal Chavín motifs showing up over non-Chavín decorated pottery.

After Tello, various authors studied the problem. Several of them see Chavín as the product of a foreign immigration to Peru, but each suggests a different center, one saying South Asian; another, China under the Chou Dynasty. According to these writers, several migratory groups from either of these places landed in the Americas, where they reproduced on gold, wood, bone, pottery, textiles, and stone, mythological themes that had previously been reserved for reproduction on copper or bronze. Izumi and his Japanese associates, on the other hand, do not hesitate to envisage an evolution of the Chavinoid culture in Peru itself, an evolution they think occurred on the eastern slope of the central Andes.

I should also point out the analogies that may be seen between the Mexican art of Oaxaca or Vera Cruz and the art of Chavín. If one compares the dancers carved in stone in Monte Albán, Mexico, with those adorning the temple of Sechin, Peru, he will be impressed by the similarities. Three-dimensional statues

These engraved monoliths surrounding the Sechin temple bear a resemblance to the Monte Alban monoliths of Mexico. North coast of Peru, Chavín period.

representing round heads with big Negroid mouths are to be seen in Vera Cruz. Such mouths are typical of Chavín as well as of southern Asia.

A temple has been found in Mexico that is topped with a feline with saberlike teeth, the lips being sewn together by a narrow band. Now the exact same theme appears on a stone object from Peru that was first revealed by Tello. A similar theme also occurs in a slightly different and simplified form in Oceania as well as in the forests of eastern South America. In both regions, the natives kept the skulls of some of their enemies, attached the lower jaw to the cranium with narrow crossed bands, and carried the whole thing on the end of a small cord. The Mexican or Chavín motif of the bound lower feline jaw is clearly a highly developed and sublimated form of a very archaic practice.

In the same field, let me note also the head of a feline placed between two paws showing their claws, which has been found in a Mexican temple, and a similar motif decorating the temple of Punkurí Bajo, in the Nepeña Valley of Peru.

Finally, I should point out (as Covarrubias did) that I noticed resemblances upon looking closely at the decorative themes of Chavín and of Chou bronzes from China.

I could, of course, lengthen this list of examples by appending it to the one given by Steward with regard to possible transpacific contacts and to Clifford Evans's and Betty Meggers's observations apropos of comparable traits that these investigators see as much in the Jomon pottery in Japan as in works from Valdivia, Ecuador.

If we are completely ignorant of the origins of the Chavín movement, we know hardly anything more about its deep meaning. Was the movement the result of territorial conquests, or of religious conversion? of theocracy, or a warrior aristocracy? The figures carved on the stelae adorning the building in Sechin, the molded figures of unfired clay one could also see until a few years ago on the walls of Moxeque on the Peruvian coast, and the figure carved on a stone lintel with its head crowned by a tuft of feathers, which I found at Huancarpon in the middle Casma Valley, do not allow us to settle the question one way or the other. It is instead a carved vessel now on view at the Lambayeque museum that could indicate the existence of an organization of warriors. It is decorated with a portrait of a man carrying a bow in one hand and a spear thrower in the other.

The trophy-head motif appears in Peru along with the Chavíns. I have never found it represented in earlier societies. After Chavín it reappears from time to time, particularly among the Paracas and Nazcas of the Peruvian Middle South and among the Tiahuanacos of Bolivia. In the north, the Mochicas have left us battle scenes with bound prisoners, but without trophy heads.

Whatever the answer, military and secular or theocratic, it is likely that there was a marked social stratification in the Chavín world. The large buildings this society built could not have been the mark of farming communities alone operating without any leadership. One senses here the existence of a master craftsman.

This sculptured limestone polychrome fresco, a Cerro Blanco temple in the Nepeña Valley of northern Peru, is typical of the Chavín period.

Moreover, the Chavíns did not leave us cities, even large villages, and they probably never built any. Their monuments are immense, grandiose, but we find them isolated in the countryside, surrounded by very humble dwellings that might have been the homes of peasants, servants, or officials in possibly fortified storehouse-temples.

I usually describe Huancarpon, also called Cochipampa, found in the middle Nepeña Valley, as having been an assembly point, a refuge, and a fortified storehouse. A monolithic lintel with a decoration engraved in the purest Chavín style has survived there, and what seems to have been a temple with underground galleries can be seen in the middle of a system of terraces built around a nearby hill. Huancarpon could be a second Chavín de Huantar. Pallka, in the nearby Casma Valley, could also have been a fortress defending a temple and a storehouse.

Punkurí Bajo, also in the Nepeña Valley, was made entirely of clay where the bases of round columns made of unfired clay have survived, and gives the impression of being a religious building. Around Asia, in the lower Omas Valley on the central coast of Peru, I had the surprise of unearthing a small clay temple with round clay columns that is a faithful replica of the one in Punkurí.

It will be hard to categorize Moxeque, an enormous building that has been badly plundered, in the Casma Valley. Here again I opt for the hypothesis of a fortified storehouse-temple complex.

All this hardly speaks in favor of a peaceful existence but suggests rather a society dominated by caste. But there ends the comparison with chiefdoms in the northern part of the continent, as the chronicles described them, for the Chavíns were builders. Their monuments remain among the largest in the world, equaling or exceeding in size, if not in height, the monuments of the Romans, and as far as area is concerned, comparable to the monuments of the Mayas of Yucatán and Petén, Guatemala. But here the resemblances do not go beyond the size of the structures. I shall return to this point

Although the edifice has been very poorly studied, no one doubts that Chavín de Huantar was a temple. Located at an altitude of ten thousand feet, the building is rectangular, five hundred feet long, massive, and pierced with dark subterranean galleries. One gallery is decorated with a *lanzón*, an elongated monolith carved in the round as a demon's face and engraved with diverse motifs meant to inspire terror, perhaps during religious ceremonies. This monolith could not date back to the beginnings of the movement. Its sides are covered with disparate decorative themes that do not seem to have been placed in a logical order and certainly were copied from more-ancient models.

The top of the main edifice formed a terrace reached by a monumental staircase. This terrace may have served as a stage for outdoor ceremonies.

Another platform, now partly destroyed by the river, extended to the east on a level with the floor of the building. It is on this platform that stelae, big monolithic slabs, and carved and engraved columns have been found under rubble fallen from the walls.

Stone blocks carved in the round representing faces of men with saberlike fangs, their foreheads encircled by what may be serpents, have survived, planted into the outer walls of the main building.

Wilkawain, in the upper Santa Valley, may also have been a temple-fortress. The building was square, high, and massive, pierced with underground galleries and air shafts.

The pre-Columbians of both continents, Mayas as well as Chavíns or Incas, did not know how to construct an arch. Thus, they could build only narrow rooms and passages that were never wider than what could be roofed with corbeled slabs.

Cerro Blanco, in the lower Nepeña Valley, may have been a small temple. There one may still see, after removing the covering earth, a remarkable decoration made of unfired clay moldings painted in varied colors and representing stylized motifs of Chavín, but also of the purest southern Asian effect. The Mochicas unfortunately reoccupied this edifice and marred it, but not as much as the sugar manufacturers, who cut it in half while enlarging the road leading to their factory.

Chavín art shows clearly that new gods were feared and invoked at this time. Felines and men with feline heads were introduced into the iconography. The ancient tradition of the fish or serpent with two interlocking heads had temporarily disappeared. Only the harpy, representations of which are found in Chavín, can be connected with earlier Andean tradition. Junius Bird has identified one drawn in filigree on a garment of the Huaca Prieta bean planters.

If I had to formulate a hypothesis, I would be inclined toward one of an immigration of foreign origin, by groups dominated by priests who led warriors. Such groups would have seized the valleys that were vital from the food production point of view. The Chavíns colonized the best lands and fishing territories they could grab, and that was where they built their big ceremonial and economic centers. Life would then have continued in the little villages of the farmers and fishermen. They would then have become Chavinoid as the Sudanese became Moslem.

Outside Maya lands, the only elements of American decoration that one can vaguely compare to those of Chavín are on the one hand those appearing in the early pottery of Florida, produced by groups that authors in the 1940s called the cultists. On the other hand are those that can be observed in some potteries in the Argentine Andes. But all of this is unconvincing.

Why, then, has no one found the villages that would have been occupied during the period immediately preceding the invasion? As already indicated, we have unearthed a few of the settlements from the first wave of corn planters. But they date back to 1300 or 1500 B.C., whereas Chavín dates back only to 800 B.C. at the most.

Would, then, the Chavíns have settled in a territory that had already been largely abandoned by its inhabitants? One may ask the question.

Although Chavín is not superimposed on earlier villages, one very often finds its debris mixed with undecorated pottery of a chocolate brown color. I have named this pottery *Disco Verde,* after the name of the village where I first identified it, along Paracas Bay.

In the site by this name and in the village of Puerto Nuevo de Paracas, very close by, Disco Verde pottery is mixed with Chavín pottery as early as the deepest strata, which are twenty-seven hundred years old. *Disco Verde* means in Spanish

A Disco Verde, pre-Chavín bottle. From the early corn-planter period, south coast of Peru.

"a green disk." On the beach, at the foot of a cliff overhanging the ocean on Paracas Bay, I suddenly saw a bunch of purslane, sixteen miles from any visible source of water. The existence of these plants indicated the presence of an underground but accessible water sheet and gave me the idea of visiting the cliff, where I found the pre-Columbian village overlooking the green disk.

As one rises in the site (that is to say, as one approaches modern times), the Chavinoid elements diminish, to disappear at the surface of the mounds.

In some cases the Chavíns resettled preceramic villages, for practical reasons: to reuse posts for building, and other such materials as fuel, mainly because a refuse mound was easier to dig into than the soil of the plain. But the two occupations were of course very distant from each other in time. It was only a matter of coincidence.

One may thus suppose that non-Chavinoid groups had lived in the area, and probably also in the lower coastal valleys as well as in the upper Andes. One may further suppose that the ones living in the lowlands had been Chavinized by contacts with other people living along the shore.

Many researchers are inclined, however, toward a second hypothesis, according to which the populations of that time used two types of pottery—one reserved for ordinary use and one intended for the cult. Only the latter would have been decorated with Chavinoid motifs. I do not agree, for as said before, I have found richly decorated ware in the most humble fishing villages inhabited during that period.

Tello, as mentioned, saw Chavín as a civilization of the central Andes. Today we have much more information at our disposal, and we cannot discard the possibility of a migration originating north or northeast of the central Andes and reaching the Pacific slope to conquer some valleys in northern Peru by brute force. Later, the migration would have been followed by a southward penetration that may have been more difficult.

Looking at a map, we find the Chavinoid complexes and villages concentrated in a triangle. The apex of this triangle is at the edge of the mid-south of Peru, in the Nazca Basin. Its base is at the Lambayeque Basin on the northern Pacific shores. From there it penetrates into the forest at least as far as Moyobamba in the eastern Andes, approximately along the sixth parallel.

Although numerous in the north, Chavín establishments diminish in size and number as one goes south. The northern valleys—Chicama, Moche, Casma, Sechin, Nepeña, and Huarmey—still contain a great number of very large buildings. But in the Lima area, I can report only a few buildings, of more modest dimensions, such as a small, terraced structure in Iguanil near Huaral, the platforms of the La Fortaleza temple, and the Pucara fortress in the Lurín Valley. Farther south, traces of the coastal society have survived only in small villages, but a round head carved in stone and similar to the Huantar ones was found in Palpa in the Rio Grande Basin. Had the southern complex been destroyed by the Nazca society?

Several centers have survived in the upper Andes. La Copa, on the road to Cajamarca; Wilkawain, in the Santa Valley, and Huantar, beyond the central cordillera, are the best known.

In the eastern Andes, Izumi discovered Kotosh, and Tello pointed out Moyobamba.

Apparently, the Chavíns were not able to dominate the valley of Cuzco, the Urubamba, and the banks of Lake Titicaca, the Collao lands. Were they repulsed from these lands by another society? Or are their traces there still unrevealed?

Some authors have attempted to establish a link with the history of Tiahuanaco, a society that apparently dominated what are the ruins of Huari (still visible near the colonial city of Ayacucho) and extended its empire as far as the eponymous site in Bolivia, eleven miles south of Lake Titicaca. However, the dates do not agree. Chavín seems to have died out five hundred years before Tiahuanaco assumed its classical form.

Before taking leave of the Chavíns, let us look at their ecology. How and on what did they live? Apparently, the Chavíns were either not able or did not try to achieve great works in irrigation. Was their social organization unsuited to this kind of enterprise? Did they perhaps live without depending much upon the annual floods of the rivers? Did they (like the Melanesians) primarily practice blackland agriculture, an agriculture that used the alluvial marshes in the bottoms of valleys?

In the lower Andes, the lands that can be farmed on the basis of the annual flood and without the help of canals represent only a limited surface. Therefore, the Chavíns perhaps lacked arable lands. This would explain why the sea, always a source of food and protein, seems to have played such an important role for them. All the little fishing villages along the seaboard that were inhabited in that period bear the Chavín stamp. The Chavinoid reoccupation of the site of Las Haldas, which I have spoken of regarding the first wave of corn eaters, was massive. This fact might indicate that this region, abounding with fish, constituted an ecological element of great importance for a society that for centuries governed all the neighboring lower valleys, which were frightfully exposed, as much to violent floods as to episodes of severe drought.

Las Haldas, already densely populated in the time of the preceramic bean eaters and first corn farmers, became a formidable complex in the Chavín period. This complex is still quite visible, despite the effects of the 1925 rains. This storm liquefied the mounds of refuse piled up around the buildings and on the terraces, turning them into a black mud that flowed over most of the buildings. I think I have also found the ceremonial center of the bean eaters, but it is inaccessible, buried under twenty-six feet of debris and embankments heaped up by the people who built the Chavín buildings.

Based on a rock overlooking the ocean in the middle of a long beach, the Chavíns constructed a set of platforms with an east-west orientation. Each was higher than the one before, with the last one overhanging the sea at a height of 130 feet. To reach this height the Chavíns piled up on the rock 83 feet of embankments and brought over rubbish from demolished earlier sites.

Six terraces stretch out from the highest one, which must have been crowned by a temple that has since disappeared. The last and easternmost terrace stands only six feet above the plain. From it one can see, almost seventeen hundred feet away, stone blocks that run along the edge of a road forty-six feet wide that runs in the direction of the Casma Valley.

This central complex, made of enormous stone blocks, measures 1,220 feet long by 260 feet wide. The largest of the Peruvian structures, it covers seven and a half acres.

In contrast to Huantar and Wilkawain, there are no underground galleries here. Everything is aboveground, and if there were covered rooms, which is likely, they must have had walls made of mats and roofs that were thatched or made of leaves.

Building such a complex necessarily demanded serious effort on the part of those who carried it out. Therefore, it is unlikely that Las Haldas did not have at least in part the character of a religious center. The high platform towering over the ocean and facing the setting sun can hardly be conceived other than as the base of a temple.

I suppose, however, that the monument must also have had economic significance. Here I am clearly entering the realm of hypothesis, but every time I see Las Haldas, I cannot help thinking of an enormous crowd of fishermen gathered on the terraces in front of the temple, exchanging sea products for food plants from the neighboring valleys, or delivering their tributes of fish or shellfish to the administrators of the big religious or martial complexes, the ruins of which are still visible in the area.

We have uncovered only a small fraction of the gathering of little buildings and storage bins that surround the ceremonial center, buried under kitchen middens. They must have been inhabited by fishermen as well as by people in the service of a temple. This impression is further strengthened by the number of wide staircases made of stone slabs that link the main building not only to these small ruins of what appear to have been dwelling places, but also to some other large buildings found on top of numerous rectangular mounds. A number of these large buildings are found in close proximity to the main complex, and might also have been intended for ceremonial use.

All these outlying buildings should be seriously studied. Some of them may have belonged to the first wave of corn eaters or to different phases of the Chavinoid occupation, such as the big building with seven platforms representing the final effort, perhaps one that was never completed.

The Chavín occupation of the site apparently did not last more than four to six generations. Las Haldas seems to have been abandoned at the same time as all the other Chavín complexes. Here the latest radiocarbon datings give ages of twenty-five hundred to twenty-four hundred years. After that, there is silence. The site was not reoccupied. A few houses belonging to Tiahuanacoid and, later, Chimu fishermen are found on the terrace overlooking the ocean, but away from the main ruins.

Las Haldas is the only big Chavinoid complex I have discovered at the very edge of the ocean. (Even Tello, who knew Chavín very well, was unaware of this immense complex. He did not associate Chavín with the sea.)

Aside from Las Haldas, I have found only small settlements and little ceremonial units near the sea. Examples of these are Iguanil and the Lurín platform monument, but I cannot describe them here. In order to find other imposing buildings of this period, one must go inside the coastal valleys, to areas where streams coming down from the Andes have already stopped digging their beds and where we find good farmland. Or else we must go straight to the rainy upper cordillera and explore the inter-Andean valleys before crossing over to the eastern slope.

In the lower Andes, the Chavíns must have had a diet centered as much on seafood as on cultivated plants. The marine contributions would have been able to compensate in cases of emergency for losses of vegetable products resulting from violent floods or prolonged droughts.

I have noted, moreover, that the Chavíns dressed in wool as well as cotton, even on the coast. I have found their chestnut-colored *unkus*, or short shirts of guanaco wool, decorated with yellow threads of vicuña wool. It is therefore probable that the Chavíns were also shepherds. Some of their people may have been in charge of herds of llamas that they moved from the upper Andes grasslands to the coastal lomas and vice versa, according to the season.

It is with the Chavíns, also, that *llanque,* or fiber sandals, appear for the first time in Peru.

All signs indicating the presence of the Chavín society disappear abruptly and completely around 400 or 500 B.C. It looks as if a cataclysm occurred then, a real collapse whose causes are unknown and could not have been due solely to human actions. It may have resulted from a climatic crisis that provoked a modification of the microclimatic (local) conditions that prevailed in the majority of Andean valleys and made life possible in regions that at first glance would seem uninhabitable.

Then again, let us recall that the general or eustatic level of the oceans is subject to fluctuations bringing about cycles of rising water and flooding, thus inundating beaches and lowlands, followed by cycles of subsidence (regression) exposing areas that were formerly inundated.

In the course of the period we are now considering, the period from 500 B.C. to about A.D. 700, successive oscillations brought about variations of about twenty to twenty-three feet in the level of the Pacific. One may wonder, therefore, what happened in the course of such fluctuations to the soft-water-bearing sheets that were practically level with the beaches and that moistened the fields through capillary action. Did these sheets remain accessible and usable at all times? They probably did not, and the lands they moistened may have dried up or become salty.

Let us not forget that the pre-Columbians had neither metal tools, explosives, nor cement. It was impossible for them to dig a deep well in rock or sand. When I speak of irrigation in the Andes, then, I have in mind two aspects of the problem: not just the existence of water, but also its accessibility.

One can see evidence of the weakening of Chavín when one walks in their temples, fortresses, and storehouses of the valleys in northern Peru. Pallka, in the Casma Valley, is one of the most typical cases, for the site was not reoccupied. There one sees brown pottery, different from that of Chavín, suddenly pervading the area, superimposed on earlier productions. An analogous situation may be observed in many sites of that time. One wonders if such a situation would not be a sign of a revolt as, for example, by the peasants against their masters the warrior-priests, whose portraits appear, decorated with feathers and armed, on the stelae ornamenting some of the buildings. Or is the existence of this pottery simply an indication of the arrival of new conquerors who would have stormed the Chavín palaces?

THE POLITICAL FRAGMENTATION OF THE CENTRAL ANDES AND THE FORMATION OF REGIONAL SOCIETIES

When the Chavín society came to an end, the big buildings of the period were abandoned, and few of them were ever reoccupied. The central Andes returned to a completely different way of life, one apparently closer to the ancient traditions, especially that of the bean planters. We know this resulted in the phenomenon of political fragmentation of the coastal territory from Lambayeque to Nazca, and it is quite probable that the high Andes of the Chavíns were also stormed and looted, but when this happened has not yet been established. In the Chavinoid buildings of the upper Andes one can detect evidence of the passing through, several centuries later, of groups who were probably plunderers, who brought with them pottery from the lower Marañón Valley.

New societies exhibiting strong personalities were now emerging. How they differed from Chavín is clearly evident when we study the new settlement patterns, architecture, arts, or the decoration of everyday objects. One can also observe the use of new materials and consumption of new plants.

With the use of hammered copper, the Andes timidly entered the Copper Age and moved toward a modernized technology while bringing simultaneously forgotten decorative themes back into fashion.

Furthermore, the location of the new villages seems to indicate a return to agriculture based on floods, an abandonment of bottomlands in favor of sites situated in the middle valleys along stream banks.

It is appropriate to give now a general idea of what the coast could have looked like around 500 B.C. The archaeology of extreme northern Peru beyond the Sechura Desert has not been written about. We know nothing at all about what occurred there.

In the north-central area, from the Lambayeque Basin on, the ancient Chavín coastal domain seems to have become the center of two societies, the Mochica and the Gallinazo. Both left their mark on an area some two hundred forty miles long, ending in the Huarmey Valley.

Regarding the central coast from Huarmey to the Lurín River south of Lima, we also lack information about the period immediately following the Chavín one. Here, in a territory of some twelve hundred square miles, we come up against an archaeological gap of almost a thousand years. Classical authors have simply mentioned the occasional appearance of a cream-colored, slipped pink pottery, Gordon Willey's "white on red," and the so-called Recuay pottery, an Andean ware possibly brought down by shepherds who moved their herds to and from mountain pastures in the upper Santa Valley.

The valleys situated a little farther south, between the Lurín and Cañete valleys, which I have studied in greater depth, seem to have been invaded about 200 B.C. by a tribe that founded the society of the Lapa Lapas.

Still farther south, in what geographers call the Middle South part of Peru, it was the Paracas society that appeared, almost in contact with Chavín in time, or after a short gap at the most.

The Far South has not yet been studied in a more than superficial way.

THE MOCHICAS

The history of the Mochicas has scarcely been outlined, and the little we know of it is confused and contradictory. The classical authors wrote that the

Mochicas had been immigrants who had taken possession of Peru's northern coastal area some twenty-five hundred years ago. Their language was closely related to a dialect that until recently was still being spoken in the Manabí on the cool coast of Ecuador. According to one oral tradition, the Mochicas came on rafts from the north.

Classical authors also affirmed that the Mochicas succeeded several local post-Chavinoid societies, and they placed the Mochica society after that of the Gallinazos of the Viru, to be discussed later. The latest radiocarbon datings, however, have put the Gallinazo society where it belongs, into an earlier period. So apparently the two societies coexisted and fought with each other. This means that the Mochica society would be earlier than was formerly thought. This placement earlier is also confirmed by a radiocarbon dating for the ziggurat known as the Temple of the Sun at Moche—800 B.C.—which seems a little too early to me. It would indicate a coexistence with Chavín that is difficult to accept.

I have obtained another date, 300 B.C., for a fabric found in the village of Vicus in the Piura River Basin. It surrounds a gilded copper disk found in an archaeological stratum that contained items unquestionably Mochican in style. This date supports the idea that the Mochicas followed closely after the Chavíns and were contemporary with the Gallinazos. Duncan Strong having obtained a date of A.D. 100 for a Mochica grave, we thus know that the Mochica society lasted several centuries.

Mochica is especially known to the public for its classical pottery, a term that applies to two groups of objects. One group consists of very realistic vessel portraits of men, some of which are quite handsome, made by modeling the clay while it was still soft. The other group is made up of a pink fired pottery, generally bottles, of varied shapes decorated with mythological or realistic scenes painted in black on a cream-colored background. These are scenes taken from the lives of fishermen or farmers. Demons or chiefs with zoomorphic or demoniacal faces are represented on them engaged in religious or warlike actions such as collecting tribute, carrying off stripped and bound prisoners, or fighting other warriors who are dressed differently.

The prisoners shackled by these Mochica warriors are represented as circumcised men. Now circumcision is a rare practice in the Andes, but as only the prisoners are represented unclothed, we shall never know if the victors were circumcised. The mystery remains complete; are we confronted with two ethnic groups with different customs? In all the ethnographic documents devoted to the Americas, I have found only one allusion to circumcision, regarding a tribe that had lived in the Chaco. Was circumcision brought to South America when Africans landed? If the Mochica cemeteries had not all been looted by an unfortunately well-known pseudoarchaeologist and collector, one could have solved the problem by closely examining the bodies, for the fleshy parts often survive in the hot sands of the Peruvian coastal oases. But such collectors are vandals interested only in gold and marketable items.

The classical pieces have all been removed from graves by looters, but fragments of similar vessels are found in the villages, cemeteries, and on the floors of Mochican buildings from the Lambayeque to the Huarmey valleys. Now many thousands of fragments of another type of pottery that has not yet been the object of serious study—generally brown, sometimes black, and completely different from the classical style—are found on the surfaces of several large Chavín buildings as well as on the floors of Mochican ziggurats. Archaeologists should thus tell us whether or not this brown pottery belonged to a society that destroyed the Chavín one and was itself conquered later by the Mochica warriors whose battles are illustrated on the portrait vessels.

The Mochicas also reproduced much less carefully done portrait vessels in molds. Such pieces would have corresponded to the end of the period, to a phase in which a dense population demanded many pieces from the potters, who could have formed a specialized class of artisans.

In carefully studying the vessels of this type that are assembled in the big private or museum collections, one notes first that the portrait vessels do not represent warriors but men who are generally dressed in white cotton capes and who could have belonged to very different social groups. Some heads are of humble farmers with jolly faces; others represent sick people, prisoners with cut or tied-up noses and lips, and finally, very handsome faces whose eyes seem to look toward the hereafter and are perhaps the portraits of priests, of shamans.

Secondly, some of these portrait vessels were partially covered over with a yellow slip on which were painted the mythological war scenes already described. Perhaps the scenes were added later, after a new invasion.

One then wonders who it actually is that we are calling the Mochicas—the fishermen-farmers, or the warriors seen superimposed on the portraits. In the present state of documentation, we can only formulate hypotheses. The most likely one would be that of a feudality of warriors who took possession of the lower coastal valley that had become the domain of a tribe that destroyed the Chavíns. Obviously, we do not know where these warriors came from and when the invasion took place.

The few stratigraphic excavations I have done on the northern coast lead me to think that the warrior's arrival occurred relatively late. According to radiocarbon datings, the conquest would have taken place around the first century A.D., when a regional society that had probably built the great ziggurats of Moche had already been in existence for at least five or six hundred years. In Site 71 in the Viru Valley, pottery decorated with war scenes appears around A.D. 200, in layers covering the so-called Gallinazo pottery. (See the discussion of Gallinazo, below.)

The discovery about a decade ago in Vicus and in Ayabaca, near the border of Ecuador, of big villages and graves very well stocked with copper, gold, and gilded copper has opened up new horizons in this field. In the Brünning Museum in Lambayeque, one can see several beautiful pieces that the curator managed to snatch away from treasure looters. The Mochicas could have stormed the country, thanks to their copper weapons.

The beautiful Mochican mural paintings that decorated the vast edifice of Peñamarquilla, in the Nepeña Valley, should have been dated before they were destroyed. Fortunately, some years ago Ducio Bonavia copied what remained of them. The authorities have likewise ignored the enormous edifice of Huancaca. Located in the lower Viru Valley, this building is 1,320 feet long with walls 66 feet high. Many crimes have been committed there, perhaps the greatest of which was letting the sites of Vicus and Ayabaca be destroyed before they were explored by professional archaeologists. These sites, which have produced the earliest metal objects known in South America, were practically bulldozed by treasure looters.

The North Coast societies seem to have been fundamentally centered as much on the sea as on the produce of the lower valleys. Their pottery has not yet been found in the cordillera, but solely in the lowlands, below an altitude of about twenty-six hundred feet. The scenes painted on the vessels, such as fishermen on rafts pulling prodigious ears of corn and other vegetables such as manioc and red peppers out of the sea, were plainly inspired by farming in hot climates and by the sea or the seashore. This half-mythological, half-realistic style is completely opposed to the warlike scenes, and the whole North Coast context gives us an inkling of struggles between tribes, of cycles of success alternating with defeats, typical of the life of chiefdoms alternately dominated by a priesthood and by warlike aristocracies.

THE GALLINAZOS OF THE VIRU VALLEY

Gallinazo is the name given to a species of vulture typical of the arid coasts of Peru.

The Viru Valley, which reaches the Pacific three hundred miles north of Lima, is one of the few Andean valleys that has been the subject of a very complete regional study, at least in its coastal section. The fieldwork carried out by Gordon Willey, a pioneer in this area, and the book resulting from it, have served me as a model for other, analogous, studies.

We do not know the boundaries of this society's territory. Some authors have extended it to neighboring valleys. Good archaeological fieldwork is needed here.

In the Viru Valley alone, the Gallinazo territory was made up of some seventy-five hundred acres of land. This was cultivable with the help of small canals making possible the distribution of the waters brought down by the annual flood. The Viru is quite dangerous as a result of its extremely violent floods, which alternate with dry years. Fortunately, the resurgent ground waters available along the shore constituted additional hydrological resources, so inhabitants did not die of thirst while the water level of the river was at its lowest, which often lasted for nine months.

The eponymous site, 71, is made up of a pyramid of unfired bricks—a kind of big ziggurat—more modest than those of the nearby Moche Valley, surrounded by a village typical of the pre-Chavinoid Peruvian tradition. This village is composed of subterranean houses clustered as if in "hives" that were very compact and bound by big, thick walls common to groups of houses. These walls served as walkways and entrances, for there were no doors leading out into the alleys. One went down into the houses by an interior staircase. The whole village covered about twenty-five acres.

The Viru Valley has been occupied since very early times. (Gordon R. Willey's work *Prehistoric Settlement Patterns in the Viru Valley* makes enjoyable and profitable reading in this respect. This pioneering work remains the model for monographs of this kind.) Some preceramic mounds, already containing cultivated plants, are still to be seen at the edge of the beach, where marshes of brackish water permitted fishermen to live all year round. Higher up in the valley, the first wave of corn planters built numerous villages, some of which were fortified.

Apparently, as soon as corn appeared, the struggle to obtain cultivable land and defend it began. We do not know if these struggles (which we may assume occurred, because fortified hilltops existed) resulted from pressure due to population density, or from the arrival of new immigrants. Later, the Chavíns also built several dozen small settlements, seemingly of no great importance, along the center of the Viru Valley.

It was well after the end of the Chavín period that the many great edifices of the Gallinazos appeared. The density of occupation and the size of their monuments lead me to suppose that the Viru underwent more substantial floods at that time than it does today and that small lateral canals running parallel to its banks facilitated the use of its waters. The lower valley was, moreover, wooded— covered with a savannah of acacias and mimosas—and intersected by marshes and ponds where the water sheet was level with the surface. Thus, the territory could have constituted an ecologically important complex.

The position of the village, agglutinated in a compact fashion on little hills and dunes, is explained by the violence of the Viru's floods. In some years, these floods reach the beach along several miles of its length and wash over the whole lower valley.

The V-71 ziggurat, eighty-two feet high, clearly must have been connected with religious activities. I see it as one element of a complex that included not only the temple but also the village, the palace, and storehouses for corn. Once again, I think here of predynastic Egypt.

Stratigraphic excavations show that the Mochica pottery in the warrior style is found at V-71 over the Gallinazo pottery. This seems to indicate that the Mochica warriors had to wait some centuries before they were able to conquer the Viru Valley and storm the huge palace of the Huancacas, the ruins of which still form an extraordinary sight in the now sand-covered area of the river's south bank.

Prehistorians will find it very hard to reestablish the lost thread of this story. All the sites in northern Peru have been systematically looted for nearly a hundred years, because they contained gold objects. There is hardly an undisturbed site still in existence where one may find intact archaeological strata valid for solving problems of chronology.

THE MARANGAS OF THE RÍMAC, LURÍN, AND CHILLON BASINS

In the heart of the central coast of Peru, the archaeological situation is worse still: researchers have not filled the extremely long gap between the end of the Chavín society and the next cultural manifestation of any importance, known by the name of Early Lima. I myself call it the Maranga society, after the name of the large hacienda where a number of ziggurats were still visible some twenty years ago. These emerged from marshes fed by resurging underground waters. All these ruins have since been eradicated, and the area now forms part of the city of Lima.

The pottery used by this society was formerly called the "interlocking" style by English-speaking researchers because two inverted fish heads formed one of its main decorative patterns.

Several radiocarbon datings indicate that the Maranga society did not begin making rapid strides until around A.D. 450 and that it apparently did not survive long. This leaves us with only embryonic information for a period of nearly a thousand years.

The Marangas appear to me to be a good example of the coastal societies of this period of fragmentation, of the rise of chiefdoms dominating a region. The Marangas left indications of having been a homogeneous society centered on the exploitation of vast resurgent water sheets and springs that fed the lower plains of the Chancay, Chillon, Rímac, and Lurín basins, and of the lomas of this region. At the mouth of the Lurín River, Maranga pottery is found in the deep strata of the big town of Pachacamac, above which the Incas built a temple of the sun. Along the Rímac we find it deep down in the city of Cajamarquilla. One also finds vestiges of Maranga edifices a little farther north, in the Chancay Basin, and even around Huaral, at the edge of the archaeological no-man's-land that extends as far as the Mochicas' domain, where these buildings might have been outposts. The real Maranga territory seems to have stretched from the Chillon to the Lurín.

It is probable that the Marangas also used river waters, with the help of lateral canals, in order to irrigate good land for farming. In general, however, judging from where they lived, the ecology of the Marangas seems to have been based on the exploitation of the black bottomlands, the marshes of the lower valleys, with the sea contributing its usual food complement, of course.

In addition to the Maranga hillocks emerging from the marshes of the lower valleys, there were still about seventy-five of their great pyramidal mound dwellings in and around Lima at the beginning of the twentieth century. Nearly all these complexes have now disappeared, and the study of the little that has escaped destruction is made difficult by severe overpopulation in the capital.

Fortunately, one of the big temple-storehouses of the Marangas has survived in fairly good condition in the lower Chillon Valley in the place called Culebras. Here one may observe the ruins of a vast rectangular enclosure seven hundred feet long. It was made of trapezoidal clay blocks each weighing several hundred pounds. The enclosed area was subdivided into terraces at both ends, with a large

The principal motif painted on a fifteen-hundred-foot-long decorated wall surrounding the Huaca Culebras temple in the Chillon Valley on the central coast of Peru. In use A.D. 450.

central plaza occupied by a great number of rooms and halls. Polychrome mural paintings decorated the upper parts of the high walls.

The basic Maranga decorative theme, both on the walls of their ceremonial or community buildings and on their pottery, was a pattern of two inverted and interlocking triangular heads of a serpent or fish. I have also discovered an anthropomorphic figure, possibly of a god, along one wall at Huaca Culebras. The big jars I found in the temple-storehouse and the surrounding debris of the period had been filled with corn and shellfish.

Archaeologists have not yet succeeded in determining the role played by the big, high, straight walls, several miles long, with which the Marangas laid out in squares the lower plains of the valleys that made up their domain. Several long sections of these walls have survived down to our times. One might have expected such walls to run perpendicular to the riverbanks or the beach, but they in fact ran obliquely; that is, perpendicular to the direction of the subterranean water flow. One may therefore suppose that they delimited gardens and could have permitted the regulation of irrigation rights while also facilitating traffic from one occupied site to another.

Once again, we are dealing with the Marangas, with an eminently coastal society, of which no traces are found more than twenty-four miles from the sea, and are dealing with the vestiges of a society that appears abruptly and, as one might say, out of nowhere. The society seems to have prospered for only a few centuries, until other invaders, of whom I shall speak again, came and settled in their area.

THE LAPA LAPAS

South of Pachacamac, past the Lurín River, we are on a high coastal terrace that has no accessible water source. The next inhabited area was the big Chavín fishing villages at Curayacu and Santa Maria. After crossing another desert spur of the Andes, one then enters the Chilca Plain.

Curayacu, meaning "green waters," was a fishing village three to five acres in area, superimposed on a preceramic village. The site, which is excellent for fishing, was reinhabited much later, in the fifteenth century. Today a seaside resort covers the archaeological strata, and excavating has become impossible. I had to interrupt our work by order of the mayor, who came wearing white gloves to give us formal notice that we had to "stop poisoning the place by stirring up pestilential dust." But if his gloves were white, our faces were coal black; digging into twenty-six feet of ashy refuse is no fun.

The Chilca Basin is about five hundred square miles. It forms in the upper cordillera at an approximate altitude of thirteen thousand feet and ends up in the ocean forty-two miles south of Lima. It is an extremely dry basin comprising several narrow, parallel, totally deserted gorges, only two of which receive a thin trickle of water a few days a year. Rain occurs only in the upper section.

When planning to examine Chilca, I had counted upon finding a territory that must have remained deserted, but was mistaken. A systematic exploration of each square mile of land has, on the contrary, permitted me to locate more than a thousand pre-Columbian sites stretching out in time from the end of the last ice age up until Hispanicization. Therefore, this territory has undergone practically all the successive occupations typical of the lower central Andes. There each society chose an altitude floor and environment suited to its way of life and agricultural techniques.

I shall not bring up again the distant past, which left at Chilca the same types of remains as those described in preceding chapters. Instead, let us jump in time to the post-Chavinoid period.

About 200 or 300 B.C., a tribe that must have been numerous arrived in the Chilca Basin. We do not know where it came from, but its homogeneous character is attested to by several traits found in all the villages of the society: the same architecture, pottery, panpipes, decorative themes, and so on.

I named the Lapa Lapas after the hill on which I rediscovered their temple, their storehouse-fortress, and the main cluster of dwellings, a complex that could have been their metropolis. They appear to have settled first in the lower plains, where I found their little houses made of hand-molded conical clay blocks, and on the hill around the fortress, where I found a large village extending over some twenty-five acres.

The temple was built the same way. It resembles a Polynesian *maráe*, a horizontal platform surmounting a truncated pyramid, which one reached first by way of a terrace, then by flights of stairs.

Building with conical adobes has never been described properly. Here is what I have observed. One begins by laying down pairs of unfired conical bricks in alternate rows, point to point and base to base. This continues until the desired length of the wall is reached. Then one builds a second row on top of the first and so on to the desired height. This system also allows building thick, double walls by adding a second double row of bricks flush against the first. When the wall is completed, it may be plastered, then painted.

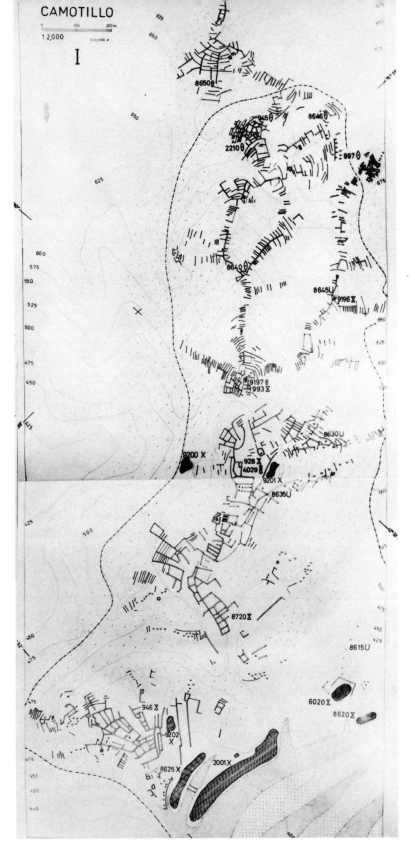

Ground plan of the Camotillo agricultural complex in the Chilca Basin on the central coast of Peru. The numbers refer to villages. The symbols following the numbers indicate the age of each settlement: prefarming, preceramic farming, early corn-eaters, Chavín, and late pre-Columbian occupancy. Today no surface water is visible, but pre-Columbian wells had been dug along the dry bed of the main canyon.

The reed huts were set on stone-lined terraces to make up for the steepness of the sand-covered slopes. Apparently it was in the lower plains, moistened by resurgent fresh waters, that the Lapa Lapas first grew corn. Furthermore, the soil of the plain is fertilized from time to time by one of the brief, heavy floods of the Chilca wadi, which then carries a thick silt as far as the dunes bordering the beach.

These little houses found around the cornfields may have been those of the crop keepers, peasants engaged in tending and watering the plants.

The hill surrounded by the main village reaches an altitude of eleven hundred feet. All winter the village is in a heavy mist, but nothing grows there, the altitude being insufficient to allow fog to condense.

On the summit I found a fortified granary made of strong stone walls and defended by a parapet. The steep, sand-covered slope also contributed to defense —climbing up over these dunes was a slow, painful process.

After brushing away the sand, I found low terracing walls to hold back the sand, and the bases of most of the posts that had supported enclosing walls (made of mats), as well as the roofs of the houses.

In fact, one was supposed to reach the village from the north side, by a road that came from the beach and wound among the rocks. It ended in a big gateway with a frame of monolithic stones giving access to the heart of the settlement.

The temple was a little to the south, overlooking both the plain and the sea. It consisted of a trapezoidal mound with various platforms built of two rows of conical blocks made of crude clay. This building was buried under a heap of earth and shells and seems to have been purposely hidden when the inhabitants departed.

Assuming that an Andean family normally consisted of five persons, I would say, after counting the houses that have survived in Lapa Lapa, that the settlement could have contained about twenty-five hundred persons, if not more, for many houses must have disappeared in the meantime.

What, then, did the inhabitants live on? On seafood, of course, and corn sown in the plain—the kitchen middens of the metropolis are full of ears of corn. But in sifting the refuse surrounding the big walls of the fortress, we also found potatoes. This was quite a surprise, as this tuber used to be described as having been spread through Peru by the Incas, and because the samples already found on the floors of ten-thousand-year-old huts did not belong to cultivated species.

Lapa Lapa potatoes were a very interesting element, since they were the earliest remains belonging to a cultivated species that had so far been observed in Peru. Could they have grown in the sands of the lowlands? One may wonder, but the answer of eminent botanists is no. So I thought of searching further and decided to enter the dry, narrow gorges that start out from Chilca and go through the lower Andes. There I discovered a completely new aspect of the life of the pre-Columbians. I have now established that in such gorges, now totally dry, untimbered, and abandoned, the pre-Hispanic settlers built vast villages surrounded by terraced gardens; and how astonished I was to see wild potatoes in full growth in these areas!

Transplanted to my garden in Lima, these potatoes yielded little tubers; not very tasty, but edible. According to a colleague, this potato belonged to the solanum family but was of a species different from the potatoes we eat today and was a wild species that must have invaded the pre-Columbian terraces after they had been abandoned. According to this authority, the terraces of the lomas, moistened only by fog condensation, would not have been able to yield crops of cultivated potatoes. The mystery of what the pre-Columbians were harvesting on these terraces remains unsolved.

Now of course such villages are found only in gorges that give life to a loma, or fog oasis, vegetation. This means that such complexes of dwelling, planting, and herding systems will be found only in very specific areas; that is, only between 660 and 2,640 feet in altitude. Trees can grow in these oases, and their existence then increases the supply of underground water. This becomes accessible to man either as a result of a natural fault or when a well has been dug.

Once the eye and mind are ready for this kind of research, it is easy to find one or several wells in each village. Bordered with stone walls, generally rectangular, and about seven feet deep, these wells were furnished with a spiral staircase.

I have found only a few such wells still working. The almost total deforestation has now dried out the region. Ground water is still visible in a few natural faults, where one can photograph it between two slabs of rock, greenish and not very tempting. The earliest wells I know of are those of the Lapa Lapas. I have not yet found the springs that fed the enormous preagricultural villages I have discovered in various oases, usually not far from the establishments of people using pottery that developed several millennia later.

I took some geographers to visit these canyons and showed them the heaps of stones piled up there. Their reaction was unanimous: these piles could not be the work of men but must instead be rocks brought together by earthquakes or erosion. Once the fallen stones had been withdrawn, however, and the intact bases of walls had appeared, my colleagues could no longer deny human intervention. They then declared that the walls had served as fog condensers by facilitating the fall of a fine rain through accentuating the contrast between the cool marine air and the still cooler stones chilled during the night.

A little archaeology had fortunately permitted me to solve the problem and to establish that these piles of stones were simply collapsed walls covering complex assemblies of diverse elements: dwellings, planting terraces, a large number of storage bins, and corrals for llamas. I have called such assemblies *systems* for lack of a better word. Such systems are still in existence in all the places inhabited by the Lapa Lapas. Although these systems were reoccupied during the final pre-Hispanic centuries, I have not found them outside the gorges on the central coast from Chancay to Chilca.

Digging out these walls meant some very hard work, incidentally; tons and tons of stone blocks had to be lifted before the surviving bases of the walls were again visible. The upper parts had probably collapsed as a result of the earthquakes that are so frequent in the Andes and of erosion that eliminated the clay mortar binding the stones. Once these heaps of stones are removed, the terraces, walls of houses, silos, and wells all reappear.

Going into technological details, let me add that the structures are composed essentially of heavy walls, some of which are as much as thirteen feet thick. The lower portions are generally still standing, up to one or two yards. These walls are placed in such a way as to create level zones in the bottoms of the gorges. Their alignment is not regular, therefore, but depends on the topography. In canyons with steep slopes, they are perpendicular to the gradient and form a series of tiers and terraces. Where the slopes are more gradual, ground is gained by elongating the walls and placing them diagonally. Oval, walled enclosures that look like the corrals of late pre-Columbian days are often found next to the walls, but the humidity there has destroyed the organic materials. So I cannot prove that the Lapa Lapas already kept domesticated alpacas or llamas, though it is quite likely they did.

Cylindrical or conical piles of stones are found on whatever pieces of land could be used for planting. Similar heaps are found in Western Europe, Britain, and Ireland. Treasure looters destroy them, thinking they are hiding graves. Instead, it seems that they were heaped up in the form of towers in order to clear the land for planting. (Such towers are called *melgas* in Cuzco today.)

How do we distinguish a house from a silo? At present, we do not know. Provisionally, I have called anything over a certain size and height a house. By this definition, houses are at least six feet in height, high enough for a man to stand up in, with a floor space seven feet by eight and a half feet, big enough to accommodate an Andean family, which generally slept in a sitting position.

Houses and silos were built at least partly underground. An air space was left inside one section of a very thick wall. The flat sides of stone blocks were laid evenly to form smooth surfaces that had probably been plastered with clay. The roof was made of stone slabs forming a corbeled arch or false vault. To build such a roof, long, flat slabs were first placed in a circle around the opening on top of the walls and perpendicular to them. Once securely held in place by heavy blocks set behind them, these flagstones served as supports for another series of flat stones laid parallel to the walls. These were balanced if necessary by counterweights. Finally, one central stone held in place by the others closed the top. Earth was poured over the roof to make it watertight.

One entered the house through a square side opening hardly wide enough to squeeze through. This opening extended to the roof line, with no wall across the top of it.

All this was very uncomfortable, and every time I see such a house I still wonder if such structures could really have been houses. At times I have counted up to fifty of these underground structures with corbeled roofs—circular, roofed holes dug into massive stone platforms built in tiers along the thalweg (a line following the lowest part of a valley) of a very steep gorge completely covered by vegetation. Clearly, these may have been silos for storing grain. But was so much effort, involving such massive walls, indispensable for garnering crops? According to its size, each structure could have sheltered one family. In one gorge I drew a ground plan of the entire system and realized that I had uncovered over a thousand or fifteen hundred of such round-roofed underground bins inside a system of walls extending about two miles in length.

In any case, it is an unquestionable fact that these systems must have been inhabited. One does not see why farmers who lived in the coastal plain would have gone up to the gorge every day, sometimes walking twelve miles in sand or rocks, while carrying up the tons of marine mollusks whose shells we find at these sites. It seems that the Lapa Lapas really lived in these gorges, at least for a part of the year.

In some villages I have found a building that seems to have served communal and perhaps ceremonial purposes. However, the location of such buildings at the top of an easily defensible crest also indicates they played a strategic role. Perhaps they were built at the end of the period, when the Lapa Lapas were being attacked by new immigrants.

Seven Lapa Lapa systems seem to have existed in the canyons of the lower Chilca Basin alone, and I have marked some ten thousand structures on the maps I have prepared for each system. In summary, most of them must have been silos and some dwellings, but building such enormous complexes of very heavy stone blocks must have meant a great deal of labor on the part of the Lapa Lapas.

My experience in restoring buildings has taught me that a three-person team, a *pircador* (a kind of foreman very experienced in placing stones held together by gravel in the chinks) and two assistants, can hardly put up more than one hundred cubic feet of wall in an eight-hour working day. And this only holds true once the stones have been brought to the site, selected, and sorted, with water and clay for the mortar likewise being available.

Of course, a small amount of manpower would have been enough to build such enormous systems over a period of time, but the mobilization of a large group of men would certainly have been necessary to finish the work in one winter, the least-hot season. Building one system during the summer months would have been unthinkable; because of the lack of any breeze, the gorges become furnaces from January to April.

We thus find ourselves confronted with the results of a massive effort toward colonizing the fog oases, which could indicate either a lack of sufficient arable lands in the lower plain because of population increase or a famine resulting from adverse climatic conditions.

During the last pre-Hispanic centuries, the pre-Columbians succeeded in putting some three thousand acres of the lower Chilca Plain into cultivation. Since they could harvest two crops a year, farming this surface could have given them enough to feed several thousand people, perhaps as many as ten thousand. This figure of three thousand acres results from studying the land against an aerial map. It corresponds to the fifteenth century A.D., to the last pre-Hispanic centuries. The Lapa Lapas, on the other hand, lived in Chilca two thousand years ago, and apparently did not yet exploit such a large area.

Colonization of the lomas could thus have been an urgent necessity for the Lapa Lapas. But apparently this achievement, impressive even in its ruins, did not alone solve all their problems. What actually happened will probably never be known, but in about A.D. 200, the Lapa Lapas left, leaving the territory between the Lurín and Omas valleys empty for some five hundred years. To this day we have not found their traces.

Certain decorative themes of the Lapa Lapas have survived in the Omas River Basin, two valleys farther south. In the intermediate basin of the powerful Mala River their traces have been lost, perhaps because of the massive reoccupation of the land that took place there during the last pre-Hispanic centuries. In the Omas Valley the decorative themes of the Lapa Lapas had been painted on pottery before firing it, whereas in Chilca they were painted on after firing. The latter denotes a less-developed technique. Perhaps the Lapa Lapas had to move out of Chilca and survived in the Omas Valley, where they learned to paint their pots before baking them.

In Chilca, several traits may be noted among the Lapa Lapas that were typical of the Nazcas, their contemporaries who lived farther south, in the Chincha, Pisco, Ica, and Nazca river basins: panpipes with ten holes, triangular obsidian projectile points, dishes in which manioc or dried fish were ground, use of the same colors in painting vessels, and bottles with two pointed spouts joined by a handle.

THE SOUTH-CENTRAL COAST: PARACAS AND NAZCA

Paracas and Nazca are two names familiar to collectors, for grave looters have brought back very beautiful fabrics and strange vessels from the Middle South desert. Unfortunately, practically all the southern pre-Columbian sites were disturbed before proper archaeological work could be completed.

Moreover, foreign archaeological expeditions that went there were preoccupied essentially with completing the collections in their museums and did not carry out any serious fieldwork. Fifteen years ago, the situation was deplorable, with few expecting really to work and excavate scientifically. So-called archaeologists felt content just to walk around picking up pottery shards and to publish apparently serious books that were supposed to re-create history on the basis of evolving styles in pottery decoration. I tried to restore some order, deliberately taking a course opposite to what had been done until then, especially in the systematic pillaging of sites. I also founded a museum to display all the beautiful and interesting objects gathered during my excavations and explorations. This museum, now nationally owned and operated, is on the very site of the pre-Columbian village of Paracas. I have given this museum to the Peruvian government, which is now responsible for its maintenance. It has many visitors, tourists from all over the world, and especially Peruvian schoolchildren and young people coming to learn something about their past. It is called the J. C. Tello Museum in homage to the Peruvian founder of central-Andean archaeology, and contains a unique collection of fabrics revealing the most diverse techniques, used in Paracas from nine thousand years ago until Hispanicization.

The Peruvian Middle and Far South are two distinct geographical and cultural entities. Both regions are very important in the history of the south-central Andes, for they witnessed migrations of the most diverse populations. Tribes or groups of unknown origin appeared there, bringing with them cultural traits that were not at all typical of the Peruvian coast. Some evidently showed distant influences from east of the Andes—perhaps Atacamanians or Diaguites from Chile, or even groups from the Chaco, or Arawaks. Contacts with forest societies are evident, such as, for example, the long spear made of *chonta,* or hardwood palm, with the point carved in the shape of a human face, which I found in a tomb from the second period of Paracas.

The Middle South is a territory made up of eight narrow river basins stretching through a desert two hundred miles long, from the southern bank of the Pisco to the Acari River. It follows the piedmonts of the cordillera, but at unequal altitudes. Thus, the lowlands of the Jaguay, Chincha, and Pisco basins lie at an altitude varying from 16 to 165 feet, whereas the Ica and Nazca rivers flow through a plain that is 600 feet above sea level. The latter disappear while crossing the mountain ranges that separate this plain and the ocean.

Except when the land is crossed by watercourses that provide an extremely irregular annual flood and permit the irrigation of a hundred or so square miles, the area is largely covered by rock and salt-laden sand blown up from beaches by strong winds. In short, the whole area constitutes one of the least propitious territories for the development of a society.

It is true that the aridity and sandiness have been greatly increased by the accelerated deforestation of recent years. Some twenty years ago, the lower Ica Valley was still covered by an acacia savannah, whereas today it is a desert. But in any case, the Middle South must never have been a very prosperous territory. Except for the large complex of Cahuachi, in the Rio Grande Valley, the only important buildings surviving there (the big Inca storehouse of Tambo Colorado, the complex of Tambo de Mora, Paredones in Nazca, and a few other big tells in the lower Chincha Basin) are of relatively recent date. They belong to the last prehistoric centuries, to an age of intensive agriculture based on canals. They are all found in the Chincha and Pisco basins—Ica and Nazca seem never to have been favored with development. The Middle South has been exploited by man—not continuously, but throughout the course of the last ten thousand years at different intervals.

In the Paracas Desert I found one of the earliest coastal villages, described above as Village 96.

Later, bean eaters who wore cotton garments settled there, to be followed by the Chavíns. Similar villages are found all along the coast between fifteen and thirty miles from any river. This means they could rely only upon underground filtration coming from the Andes.

In the middle valleys, where the water sheet runs so deep as to be inaccessible to the pre-Columbians, who could not drill deep wells, inhabited sites are found only along the edges of rivers.

Upon arriving in Peru some twenty years ago, I observed how workers in the shipyards on the northern shore of Paracas Bay practiced horticulture around their little houses. They grew food plants such as corn, beans, and red peppers at the very edge of the beach in the sand, with only the help of ground water that reappeared at the surface. So I concluded that the Chavinoid villages, whose remains still extend several miles along the terrace overlooking this same beach, would all have been able to feed themselves with the products of gardens comparable to those of the present inhabitants.

The idea of fish-salt-corn bartering is of course a valid explanation of how the fishermen could have lived without providing their own vegetables. Nevertheless, we cannot discard the idea that they obtained sufficient crops locally when we see the voluminous flow of fresh water that still emerges there today.

In the Middle South, archaeologists have succeeded in narrowing the gap notable everywhere else between the end of the Chavín period and the birth of subsequent societies. In almost all the places it existed, the Chavín society died out twenty-four hundred years ago at the latest. Twenty-three hundred years ago is the age indicated by radiocarbon datings for the first post-Chavinoid villages of the Middle South. The objects found in villages are decorated with motifs belonging to what archaeologists have called the Paracas-Cavernas style.

Tello invented these names, calling the first period of Paracas the Cave period and the second the Necropolis period. Actually, the "caves" were bottle-shaped silos hollowed out of soft sandstone and used as buildings during the second period. A "necropolis" was a big Nazca village or, in other words, a village of the third period. Countless bodies have been found buried in the houses of this village, whence comes the erroneous notion of a necropolis.

Chavinoid traits surviving in the Paracas-Cavernas style may be seen in the decoration of pottery, gourds, wood, painted cotton fabrics, and even in the decorations of some walls made of unfired clay. These walls were sometimes ornamented with polychrome paintings that could well have been transposed from the Chavinoid sites in the northern valleys.

However, various differences show that we are no longer dealing with the same society. First of all, the settlements were now located along the rivers—in the lower parts of the valleys, to be sure, but far from the beaches. What has survived near the ocean gives more the impression of fishermen's camps. What the grave looters have brought to light farther up in the valleys must have been from large villages. Some good examples are Teojate, Cerillos, Callango, and Tambo Colorado in the middle Ica and middle Pisco basins.

Secondly, pottery and clothing were no longer the same. Certain aspects of the Chavinoid style, such as a mouth with feline teeth, survived in the decorative themes, but pottery was now painted in several colors after firing, whereas Chavín pottery had been generally monochrome. Let us remember, however, that the Chavíns also practiced the technique of negative decoration, which survived in Paracas and in most coastal societies until around A.D. 200.

The Chavíns dressed primarily in wool shirts and wore sandals as well as baskets on their heads. The Paracas, on the contrary, dressed in white cotton, in fabrics ornamented with little embroidered strips of black, green, yellow, or red threads. In a fisherman's house I found a piece of white cotton fabric ornamented with a picture of four people dancing—two men and two women holding each other's hands. The men were embroidered in golden yellow thread and wore short hair; the women were embroidered with red and wore their hair in two braids.

The homes of these people seem to have been of the most modest sort, little huts probably of mats bordered by low stone walls. The absence of monumental or communal buildings seems to have been characteristic of both the period and the region.

Objects of hammered gold had disappeared, to reappear during later periods. Weaponry consisted only of slings, staffs, and spear throwers. The latter were used to shoot detachable spears that separated into two parts. The part with the obsidian tip remained in the flesh of the game or enemy. The projectile points were triangular, with pointed edges reshaped by pressure. I found one of them deep in the arm muscles of a body of the period.

This society is usually called Paracas I, because it was first recognized along the bay by this name. In fact, this society extended its influence over a rather large area, including the Jaguay, Chincha, Pisco, Ica, and Nazca basins. Its traces can be found 75 to 350 miles south of Lima; that is, on a strip 240 miles long. This fact prevents us from classifying the Paracas as a tiny group of immigrants. The rise of this society must instead have been the consequence of the arrival of a large tribe.

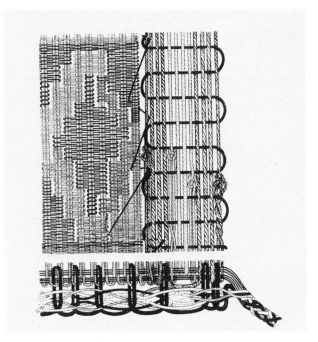

An analytical drawing of Chavín and Paracas fabrics showing the complexity of structure.

However, we must not delude ourselves as to the size of these groups. Their villages were small, giving shelter to perhaps one to two hundred families, meaning from five hundred to one thousand people. Such villages are found far apart, as they were dependent on spots where water was accessible.

Paracas I was not a high-Andean society. Its remains are not found above an altitude of twenty-six hundred feet, which is to say it was basically a coastal society.

How long did these settlers, whose origin remains unknown, live undisturbed by newcomers? Hardly more than one to two hundred years, I would say, for in about 200 B.C., the kitchen middens of Paracas I were covered by debris left by other people. These contained objects showing that a new society had settled in the area. I call this group the second regional society of the Middle South, or Paracas II, instead of its obsolete name, Necropolis.

The legends are so strongly rooted that many Peruvians still think that Paracas was a vast necropolis where populations from all the farthest parts of the Andes brought their dead to bury them, dressed in their finest attire.

The formation of this new society, which had very few traits in common with the first one, could well have resulted from the arrival of a new wave of immigrants. To be sure, Paracas II occupied the same territory as Paracas I. The Paracas II society seems to have lived in the same way, along streams and near springs and ponds, practicing both agriculture and fishing; and they also were a coastal society rather than a cordillera one. But in other respects, practically everything was different. Only the pottery decoration indicated a certain relationship—earlier geometric motifs were still being copied, and paint was still being applied after firing. But new naturalistic forms had appeared—birds, frogs, and parrots were now being modeled—and the whistling vase typical of Ecuador and little ceramic whistles were in use.

Architecture was still limited. People lived in small, square wattle-and-daub huts. The discovery of a dismantled but intact house buried with all its component parts—posts, trusses, mats, ropes, and pegs—has permitted us to reconstitute a complete, authentic example of these fishermen's dwellings in the Paracas museum. Their houses resemble those built nowadays by Andean peasants who come down from the highlands in groups and settle, usually by force, in lands they invade on the coast.

Copper had made a cautious appearance (for spear-thrower hooks or tweezers), and gold had again come into use.

But on the other hand, the art of weaving had reached a very advanced stage of development. The skeletons I found were all dressed in countless pieces of clothing: turbans, loincloths, shirts, cloaks, immense shawls, G-strings, fillets, and hairnets. I discovered some very well preserved bodies wrapped in as many as twenty pieces of clothing and accompanied by up to twenty diverse objects that were either wrapped up with the corpse or just dropped into the grave. This would apparently indicate that the deceased had been buried along with all his personal belongings, as well as with offerings by his close relatives and friends.

The multicolored turbans were very long, extremely beautiful, and were wound around the head several times. The shirts and loincloths were made of cotton. And I found long, gauzelike shawls decorated with interlocking fish heads and dyed sometimes a wine color, sometimes a shade of green. Most shirts were of cotton, dyed wine red and decorated with sewn-on polychrome motifs. Other shirts and cloaks were woolen. The decorative motifs were now woven, no longer just embroidered. I also found shirts made of vicuña hair, large cotton fabrics like bed sheets with painted motifs, and cloaks decorated with multicolored feathers.

The decorative themes of the period, made up essentially of zoomorphic and demoniacal motifs of monstrous animals vomiting trophy heads, were entirely original and were in no way connected with decorative themes formerly used either in this area or anywhere else on the central or northern coast.

Most bodies were sewn into two or three big bed sheets of cotton cloth and formed into a cone-shaped mummy bundle. The corpse was seated in a fetal position with the hands placed either over the face or over the pelvis. A false head, made of a gourd or bundle of fabric, often created an illusion of a pear-shaped head emerging above the bundle.

There may have been rites corresponding to matters of sex, but the condition of the bodies did not permit me to state positively the original position of the arms at the time the funerary bundle was prepared. Hands crossed in front of the face could have fallen as a result of the arms' decomposition. It seems, however, that hands over the face relate to female traits and hands over the lower part of the abdomen relate to male traits.

The so-called Paracas mummies have been much talked about. Tello, the first Peruvian scientist to see them, was a physician, so I do not wish to challenge his observations. Nevertheless, though I admit that the viscera of the deceased may have been extracted, I wonder if actual mummification was practiced. Perhaps the corpses had simply been dried near a fire or in the sun. These corpses always reach us full of dead worms and with the bodies' hair covered with lice, the eyes sometimes intact in the sockets, the sexual organs often visible, and the skin painted with a green oxide but without tattoo marks. Perhaps the tattoos are hard to see as a result of carbonization of the flesh, which gives it a uniform dark brown color. The fingers were generally bound together with fine threads.

Almost all corpses were accompanied by gold objects such as tweezers, nose or ear ornaments, and little star-shaped pendants. Amulets or small figures carved in shells, and pendants, rings, and necklaces completed the array of jewelry.

Numerous gourds cut in the shapes of bottles, cups, and plates were used to place the most diverse foods in the grave. Some gourds were ornamented with beautiful fire-engraved decorations representing naturalistic or animistic scenes.

Fans made of feathers were also abundant, as were the *coladores*, or little sieves with handles, with a grating so fine and well decorated as to remind one of a spider web. Such objects constitute some of the curiosities of this period. The way in which these *coladores* were used is unknown. For the time being, they remain objects unique in the world. No one seems to have seen their like anywhere else, and Peruvian tradition is silent on this point.

The bodies were those of stout, muscular individuals who seem to have died in perfect health, as well as those of emaciated old people and very young children. All the skulls were exaggeratedly deformed, some to the point of being pear-shaped as a result. Trepanning was widely practiced and usually successful, which is indicated by the bone's being regenerated.

The graves were generally modest, merely a hole in the sand bordered by a few stone blocks. Up to eight individuals were buried in one grave, possibly an entire family. Big dolls made of cloth and straw and adorned with turbans and jewels were buried with the children.

The complex from the Paracas II period was thus entirely different from that of Paracas I. It is marked by some elements found in the eastern Andes of Argentina and the Chaco, which could indicate an early migration from the Atlantic slopes of the cordillera that would have reached the Peruvian coast by coming up from Chile.

The food remains indicate a dietary prosperity. Seafood as well as manioc, corn, sweet potatoes, and peanuts, mixed with all kinds of fruits, abound in the kitchen middens. The population was also more concentrated. For example, the ruins of a village such as Monte Fertil, located farther to the northeast, on the southern bank of the Pisco River, extend over almost a mile.

Despite the visible economic prosperity of Paracas II, living conditions on the whole seem to have been different, in the sense of being far from peaceful. Never in my excavations have I found graves containing so many weapons surrounding each corpse. A terrifying throwing weapon, the hafted stone mace typical of Chavín, had reappeared. So had the *celt*, or hafted, polished-stone axe. The sling was present, of course. I found spears made from the magical *chonta* or hardwood palm tree together with big obsidian knives, clubs, or staffs, long daggers made of bone, and spear throwers to shoot spears with obsidian points. All

A mace on a shaft. Paracas, two thousand years old.

A drawing of a Paracas reed hut, found intact in the sand and moved to a local museum. It is eight feet square.

this seems to constitute what must have been terrifying weaponry. Around a certain grave that had been looted, most skulls of adult men bear a circular hole produced by a stone mace being thrown at them.

Battles must thus have been violent and constant. But were they perhaps intergroup struggles of a sportive or magical character rather than wars to defend a rich fishing territory? I hold the first hypothesis, since trophy heads, which seem to have entered into Andean iconography along with Chavín, were abundantly represented in fabrics at Paracas II.

The lower and upper parts of a subterranean granary in the Bay of Paracas, Peru. One of the rare instances where the roof is still intact.

A light beige woven-vicuña shirt. From Paracas.

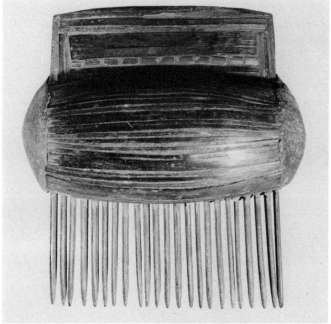

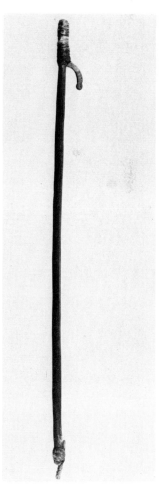

A reed-decorated comb made of mimosa spines held together in clay. From Paracas, two thousand years ago.

This two-thousand-year-old spear thrower from Paracas with copper hooks is an extremely unusual object because copper is rarely found on the Peruvian south coast before the fourteenth century A.D.

156

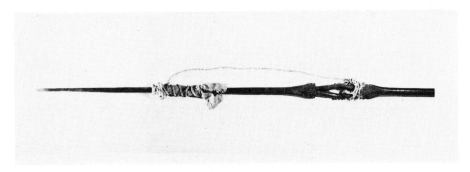

The upper end of a Paracas spear of hard palm-tree wood. The carved area shows the head of a warrior.

In order to portray this Paracas society, I usually make analogy with New Guinea, to groups of fishermen-farmers engaged in tribal struggles. They were artists and produced beautiful objects, were very preoccupied with the idea of death, and, as in Paracas, they lived in villages surrounded by gardens.

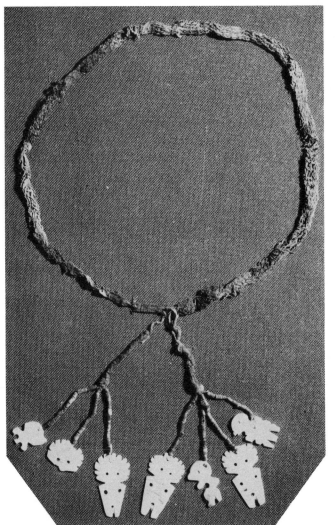

A necklace with small anthropomorphic figures carved from shells. From Paracas, south coast of Peru.

A typical Paracas II motif. The pattern is produced by leaving the design area bare of embroidery.

As an anthropologist and historian I must report facts, but naturally my comparison does not appeal to Peruvians, who have imagined Paracas as a highly developed society that was technologically more advanced and sociopolitically more important than it actually was.

Paracas II seems to have lasted about two centuries. After that, the Middle South was taken over by what I call the third regional society, known as Nazca. With Nazca we can observe obvious modifications in social structure; indications of some stratification appear.

One might imagine the Nazcas as direct successors of the Paracas. Indeed, they inhabited the same territories as the preceding societies. The Nazcas, like the Paracas, remained a coastal tribe; one does not find either in the upper cordillera. The ruins of Nazca farming systems can be seen in the Far South of Peru as far down as the north bank of the Camana River.

Regarding social structure, however, Nazca organization seems to have differed greatly from that of their predecessors, who were living like socially unstratified groups in villages of isolated and poorly arranged houses. Also in the earlier society, each adult male was armed for fighting.

The Nazcas, on the contrary, lived in villages made of stone units, each containing several houses grouped around a vast central patio. These houses were well designed and were built according to a preestablished plan, with staggered doorways, underground silos dug into patios next to hearths, sleeping platforms and stone benches, tree trunks to support the roofs of houses and porches, and so on.

The villages were generally located along the banks of streams where the inhabitants could practice agriculture on land soaked by the annual flood. But the Nazcas also sustained themselves in specialized fishing villages. Paracas is the largest of those that have survived, but I have rediscovered numerous similar villages stretched along the whole desert coast as far as the Acari Valley.

Monte Fertil, on the southern bank of the Pisco, already a big village during the second regional period, was reoccupied by the Nazcas, who built a settlement comparable to that of Paracas but on a much larger scale. Monte Fertil is located just before the offtakes of the modern irrigation canals bringing water from the Pisco River to the lower valley. Is this a coincidence? Had the Nazcas built similar offtakes that were too weakly constructed, so that they were carried away by a flood? Monte Fertil suddenly came to an end some eighteen hundred years ago and was not reoccupied until modern times.

Apparently, the Nazcas did not build large structures. The only monument of imposing size that archaeologists attribute to them is Cahuachi, located in the Rio Grande Basin. It seems to have been a command and ceremonial center. But because the site was subsequently reoccupied on various occasions, and because of poor archaeological work carried out at this site, we shall never know what should be attributed to the Nazcas and what to others, possibly the Incas.

The Cahuachi ceremonial center is near a vast plain located at an altitude of sixteen hundred feet, where what tourists call the Nazca lines can still be seen. Comparable lines existed in several places in Peru; in the Lima area, for example. Unfortunately, only those of Nazca survived, and they are very much threatened by the truck traffic now going through the plain.

In approaching the modern city of Nazca, the traveler must not fail to climb up on one of the hills emerging from the pampa. Then he will observe first a vast network several miles long of extremely straight lines that seem either to meet at infinity or at acute angles. These lines are made of low stone walls. Then he will see groups of zoomorphic figures also formed by the dry stone walls. These represent monkeys, spiders, birds, and other animals, and are from six to thirty-three feet long.

The Nazca lines obviously constitute a highly interesting complex, around which polemics arise periodically. Maria Reische has tried to show by calculations that a Venusian calendar was involved here, but other mathematicians have maintained that no such calendar existed. I am rather inclined to look for a cabalistic, religious meaning in the lines. In my opinion, their existence is one of the most important clues regarding the history of the Andes. The lines could provide suggestions relating to the sociopolitical organization of the Nazcas, insofar as they really were the creators of this complex, or of an earlier society. In order to choose the best location for creating this system of lines, it would have been necessary to command autocratically a vast territory. Such a requirement would mean that the Nazcas had been ruled by an authoritarian power and had not lived like fishermen and the earlier Paracas, who were farmers still living as tribes of headhunters.

If we are misjudging the Nazcas, grave looters are to blame, for they destroyed everything before archaeologists were able to study the villages. If I had not mapped out the architectural units of Paracas and restored one of them, no one would know what a Nazca village looked like.

The very beautiful cloaks known as Paracas mantles were woven actually by

A ceramic head of a Nazca girl with a polychrome headband.

women contemporary with the Nazca period. These large rectangular mantles were woven of very fine cotton cloth. Strips as big as large oriental rugs and entirely embroidered with mythological motifs were sewn along the four edges. The predominant theme is a masked human figure who appears to be floating in the air, armed with a spear thrower and spears and holding a trophy head in his hand. The colors are quite varied and extremely beautiful—various reds, greens, blues, oranges, and yellows on a black or wine-colored background. The Nazca society also produced fabrics embroidered with naturalistic and realistic decorations such as birds, flowers, and insects.

The art of textile making, already highly developed in the second Paracas period, now attained a florescence that would never be equaled elsewhere in Peru. The most beautiful pre-Hispanic fabrics and, technologically speaking, the most complex and most interesting fine garments made in the whole premechanized world were made by the Nazcas.

Treasure looters have found several hundred of these Nazca cloaks, very well preserved, but in houses and silos, not graves. So the question arises whether these garments were used to dress the men of the village during ceremonies or were used for bartering. The latter hypothesis is not to be brushed aside, for in one of the Nazca houses of the village of Paracas I found two fragments of cloaks in the process of being made, still placed on a small portable loom such as a wife could have used while sitting by the hearth weaving while the soup was cooking.

Whereas during the Paracas I and II periods everyone was buried in his best-decorated clothing, the bodies in Nazca graves are to be found wrapped in a simple cotton sheet and in several pieces of plain cotton fabric looking more like rags than cloths. Sometimes a sling was wound around the skull and a dagger laid next to it, but the heavy armament found in pre-Nazca times had disappeared. In the course of my excavations, I have not been lucky enough to find a single tomb of this period containing a set of valuable funerary furnishings, which I needed not for their material value but to establish a better cultural chronology. What I found was skeletons of fishermen or farmers so poor, or so apathetic toward material goods, as not even to own a nice handkerchief or colored belt. It is only from hearsay, from the indiscretions of grave looters, that we know that gold masks and other gold ornaments as well as beautiful cloaks have been found in these Nazca houses.

It is clear that this history of the Nazcas should be placed in a more precise chronological and cultural framework. Unfortunately, such a task will be difficult, for the Paracas village as well as all the settlements that had existed in the middle Chincha, Pisco, Ica, and Nazca valleys have all been plundered by treasure looters or destroyed by farmers. The latter will bulldoze an entire village in order to gain a few hundred square yards of arable land, with no one having any consideration for their gentilic pre-Columbian ancestors.

The Nazca society has attracted the attention of collectors, and archaeologists have attached great importance to it because of its success in decorating polychrome pottery and embroidery fabrics. But in other respects, the Nazca society must never have evolved beyond the level of a chiefdom that ruled small groups of people who lived scattered throughout a vast and extremely poor territory. In fact, their land was so poor that the Nazcas survived for centuries without anyone coming to drive them out of their arid and unattractive lower valleys. According to archaeologists, the Nazca society, which seems to have taken shape around 200 B.C., was still in existence in about A.D. 700. What an example of stagnation! Were these nine centuries devoid of history, or have archaeologists simply been unable to reconstruct the past? Time will tell.

Pottery with Nazca decorations fell into decadence, and the ruined villages yield only undecorated vessels. But must we automatically conclude from this a decadence in the economic as well as artistic sphere? Isn't it possible that the disappearance of a skilled pottery craft was caused by population pressures? In order to meet the demands of many more customers, craftsmen would have had to resort to mass production and thus to producing undecorated vessels.

On the basis of presently available information, one may suppose that the Middle South could have developed along the following lines.

The Preagricultural Period

Fishing camps or perhaps villages were established in acacia savannahs or along the sea, wherever water was accessible.

The Beginnings of Agriculture

Some fishing villages were still located along the sea but near wooded areas.

Cotton and beans were now present, which may indicate control of secondary territories along rivers.

The Bean Farmers

Some villages could have existed in the central valleys and could have been destroyed by later farmers. Only small camps, few and far between, have survived all along the coastal desert. A poor period.

The First Corn-growing Period

Fishermen's villages of the period from thirty-five hundred to three thousand years ago have not yet been found. Such sites must have existed in the middle valleys, however, since radiocarbon datings showing ages of thirty-three hundred years have been obtained there, as in the Acari Basin. After 800 B.C., pre-Chavin corn eaters were living in villages around Paracas Bay at Puerto Nuevo, Disco Verde, and so on. They used pottery similar to that found by Ramiro Matos high in the Pisco watershed on the shores of San Francisco Lake.

The Second Corn-growing Period (Chavín)

Heavily populated villages are found not only at Paracas, on a strip several miles long, along the shore, but also far away, down to the middle of desert areas. For example, the village of Carhua is located thirty miles from the nearest surface water system. Objects of hammered gold leaf and beautiful painted fabrics depicting Chavin themes have been found in abundance there.

Paracas I or Regional I

This period corresponds to the formation of a regional society of farmers practicing river flood farming. The society was homogeneous over an area of some eight hundred square miles. (This figure is advanced as only a working hypothesis. It is obtained by multiplying the maximum length [240 miles] by a mean depth of 3 miles, then applying the usual coefficients to arrive at a figure that represents 50,000 cultivable acres, or a territory large enough to feed 65,000 inhabitants.) Paracas was only one of a number of villages, most being located along riverbanks.

Paracas II or Regional II

New cultural traits seem to indicate that there was an invasion of the area inhabited by Paracas I. Paracas was still a little village at this time. But large villages, all made up of farmers, are to be found in the Ica and Pisco valleys. Some such villages are Tambo Colorado, Monte Fertil, Ocucaje, and Callango. An unsettled period—skulls from this time are found crushed; everybody was armed.

Nazca or Regional III

We know very little of what could have happened during this time except that the population must have increased. Nazca villages are found all along the riverbanks from Jaguay to the Acari. A colonization of the Far South could have been attempted. The large planting terraces still visible around Chala and down to Camana have yielded classical Nazca pottery. For more detailed information we must go back to Paracas and to my own study of this small area.

Phase 1.   A new pattern of social organization is visible at first sight. By now Paracas had become a settlement of about twenty stone architectural units with up to eight houses and with underground silos grouped around a central patio. Individual weaponry had disappeared. Pottery was no longer polychrome or painted. The shapes of plates, cups, and jugs were completely different from before. Monochrome red paint was applied after firing. Fabrics were very poor and were rarely decorated.

Phase 2.   The village was consolidated, perhaps after an earthquake. Pottery with polychrome motifs painted on before firing made its appearance. Themes were realistic—fish, birds, toads, parrots, felines, and sea mammals—but there were no scenes representing navigation.

Phase 3.   Decline. The village was partly covered by sand. Hundreds of skeletons shabbily wrapped in rags have been found in its houses. Pottery retained Nazca shapes but was now decorated only occasionally and poorly.

Phase 4.   The village was rebuilt and enlarged on top of the sand that had accumulated during Phase 3. Pottery became polychrome once again. This phase was contemporary with the so-called classical Nazca art. This was the period of beautiful cloaks and probably also of gold masks that have all been stolen by treasure looters.

Phase 5.   All life stopped in the village, which was abandoned and never reinhabited. The houses are now to be found covered by up to six feet of sand.

Paracas was permanently abandoned in the second or third centuries A.D. Perhaps the bay was struck at that time by a tidal wave similar to the one it experienced in 1960, in the course of which the ocean rose ten feet, after the bay had entirely emptied, flooding all the freshwater wells still existing at the edge of the beach. The tidal wave began in Valdivia, in southern Chile, went to Japan, and struck back right into Paracas Bay. Up to a few years ago, the bay still abounded in fish and shellfish. This may explain the tenacity of fishermen in living in this harsh climate, where violent winds raising sand clouds sometimes prevented them from leaving their houses for several days at a time. No lack of seafood caused them to emigrate. And although Paracas was abandoned, other Nazca villages survived for centuries, a fact that suggests some sort of catastrophe at Paracas.

For those who love nature and the desert, the region was still very beautiful a few years ago. The water in the bay takes on shades of pale turquoise, and pink volcanic stones form a background that contrasts strongly with the yellow soil of the continental terrace. To the west, the summit of the coastal range sheerly overhangs the ocean from an altitude of sixteen hundred feet. From that height

A heavy stone pick or spade from a
Nazca village. It dates from about two
thousand years ago.

one can see Sangallán Island, the terror of early seamen, where whirlwinds broke
the masts of sailing ships.

Moreover, hundreds of thousands of birds used to invade the bay periodically, and dolphins used to come there to play, while a little farther away, at the foot
of the cliffs, sea lions fought to defend their harems. Ten years ago it was still impossible to be bored for a single minute in Paracas.

Today all the wildlife is gone, destroyed by poorly planned industrialization.
The bay is polluted now. A harbor and shantytowns have been built in a unique
landscape that clearly would have attracted many tourists and could have become
one of the most attractive zoological, archaeological, and natural parks in the
Andes.

In addition, the road leading to the harbor was built right on top of the earliest village (nine thousand years old), and bulldozers destroyed all the skeletons
that I had left in place for future research. Now the Paracas of former times has
finally disappeared.

I know people who would even willingly raze all the ruins, to destroy all
traces of a past they abhor. All our efforts to save the Paracas archaeological area
have been in vain, and the protocol on the subject drawn up between various
government bodies remains a dead letter. Today a brave group of Peruvians is
trying to save the environment by creating a national wildlife reserve there. I
pray for its success, simply recalling how, during the presidency of Don Manuel

Prado, I secured a decree stating that the whole department of Ica would be considered a protected archaeological territory.

THE FAR-SOUTH COASTAL AREA OF PERU

After crossing the desert that extends as far as San Nicolás Bay and the lomas of Marcona, we meet the Acari River, the boundary of what geographers call the Peruvian Far South, a very arid and mountainous zone stretching as far as the twenty-seventh degree of south latitude at the end of Chile. Although the modern political boundary between Peru and Chile is seemingly artificial, it actually corresponds to the real pre-Columbian situation and would have to be only slightly readjusted to match the cultural history. The boundary should be shifted north to a point some one hundred fifty miles south of Camana. North of Camana the territory typically was Peruvian; to the south it was Atacamanian or Diaguite.

The Peruvian Far South is four hundred twenty miles long and is hard to reach by land, for the Andes, intersected by deep gorges, plunge into the ocean down there. Consequently, the area has been neglected by archaeologists. Flat areas are limited to river deltas. Some large, powerful, and dangerous rivers with a continual flow run through some valleys.

At first glance, the Far South does not seem to have played an important part in pre-Columbian times. Nevertheless, some coastal stretches have been heavily populated and the scenes of active existences. The ruins of various large pre-Hispanic settlements, some having been fortified, may still be seen there along Chaparral Wadi and from Tanaka to Chala. It is quite unfortunate that archaeologists have not yet taken the trouble to study this territory as thoroughly as it should be, for it formed a natural gateway between Chile, the Argentine Andes, the high Bolivian plateaus, and Peru, and must have played an important role in the history of the migrations that influenced the continent in highly diverse ways.

The main valleys, the ones with large rivers running through them, do not seem to have been equipped with side canals. The agriculture practiced there must have remained technologically primitive.

In addition to the valleys, however, the pre-Columbians exploited the fog oases on a large scale. Up to now, in the Peruvian Far South alone I have mapped out some 175,000 acres of lands that were cultivated in pre-Hispanic times. Today such lands are completely deserted and are little by little being covered by sand.

Around Chala one can still observe stone-lined terraces extending for miles. It is difficult to understand how they were built, without the aid of surveying, for they follow the contours of the land perfectly. These terraces are intersected by small canals running perpendicularly down the slopes. We still do not know if these canals were used for irrigation or for draining off the water in case of heavy rains.

Today rain does not fall anymore in the Far South. The surviving vegetation is that of the fog oases. However, now one still sees practically everywhere the dry springs that in the past must have provided at least modest irrigation for the fields.

Archaeologists used to teach us that the Far South had not been inhabited prior to the last prehistoric centuries, when it probably had been invaded by Atacamanians. But, thanks to the pottery fragments I dug out from several heaps of rubble, I now know that the Nazcas must have tried to colonize these lomas and apparently must have built the terraces surviving there.

THE TIAHUANACO PERIOD

The name *Tiahuanaco* evokes one of the largest architectural complexes in South America, one that has even inspired fiction and science-fiction writers. Some authors have seen Tiahuanaco as a complex built by Martians, by giants who lived there ten thousand years ago, or by technologically advanced men using bronze in the Stone Age.

Of course I reject such fanciful notions, but I must admit that many aspects of Tiahuanaco remain unexplained. The complex is located at an altitude of nearly thirteen thousand feet in a marshy region about eleven miles south of Lake Titicaca. It was known by the Incas, rediscovered at the beginning of the Spanish Conquest, and mentioned by the chroniclers. Then it went into oblivion and was badly damaged during the building of a Hispanic village and churches nearby.

Max Uhle studied the site at the end of the nineteenth century and published remarkable ground plans and drawings of what remained of the buildings. He was struck by several original technological characteristics. Building materials had been treated here very differently from the manner usually found in the Andes. In Tiahuanaco, the monolithic blocks used in the walls weighed a hundred tons and were cut with great geometric precision. These blocks show mortised joints and recesses in which to install metal hinges intended to support monumental doors.

It is now impossible to have any idea about the original shapes of the buildings, because of the destruction over the centuries. Tiahuanaco had probably already been plundered even in pre-Columbian times, and some of the geometrically cut stones must have been used to build Inca buildings. Even so, one can still observe that the site had grouped at least three big temples and may have contained as many as four high and imposing buildings, all rectangular, plus one that was half underground. One was the Pumapunko, measuring five hundred feet in length; another, the Akapana.

The monumental door called the Gateway of the Sun stands on the Akapana, now a large mound bordered by raised flat stones and covered with debris and earth. The door is decorated with motifs sculptured in high relief that are so characteristic that the so-called Tiahuanacoid style was named after them.

The function of the Gateway of the Sun is poorly understood. If it was not moved and really stands in its original position, we must consider it as having been surrounded originally by a building that has since disappeared. The debris of several similar gateways was found in the vicinity by Uhle, who sketched them.

As in Chavín, great monolithic statues representing mythological beings were unearthed around the buildings. The style of their decoration is the same as that appearing on the Gateway of the Sun.

The carved stones of Tiahuanaco are not the only ones found in the Andes. We know the statues of San Agustín, Bogotá, and Tierradentro in Colombia; those of the upper Santa Valley in Peru; and those found in the Collao area around Lake Titicaca, as in Mocachi and the Lake Poopó area. But we fail when we try to compare these works of art with what is visible in Tiahuanaco. The completely original character of the decoration and the cutting techniques of the Tiahuanacoid monoliths and statues is beyond comparison.

A statue typical of Tiahuanaco. Note the unique double circle around the mouth.

Straight noses and deep-set eyes are characteristic of Tiahuanaco's sculptures.

The straight noses and deep-set eyes are quite different from the round Chavín eyes and the deer-shaped ones at Mochica. Another difference, and one that is unique in the Americas, is the mouths surrounded by a double circle. Also, the Mocachi sculptures often represent *soutchés*, or large, moustached fish. I have not seen representations of *soutchés* in Tiahuanaco, but they do appear on the carved stones of Pucara. Finely sculptured stones are in fact found only during the Chavín and Tiahuanaco periods. All other statues are roughly treated, in a manner that calls to mind the ones at Easter Island.

It is most annoying that the Bolivian government has reserved all excavation privileges at Tiahuanaco and Mocachi for itself. This would not be so bad if

A sculptured monolith typical of the Tiahuanaco period.

local archaeologists were working in the field, for it is necessary to try to place such diverse styles in a chronological framework.

At one point, Tiahuanaco reproduced a theme typical of Chavín art, that of serpentlike animals protruding from the body of an armed figure. Here, however, the head of the animal clearly represents sometimes a feline with a prominent nose, sometimes an eagle. Whether the Chavín mythical animal is a llama, a crocodile, or an elephant is the subject of heated discussions.

The weapon the Tiahuanaco gods carry is usually the spear thrower, but the bow also made its appearance and makes one think of the hot forest. Let us remember that one of the territories where the greatest number of Tiahuanacoid sculptured stones have been found is called the province of Mojo, on the eastern shores of Lake Titicaca. Mojo is also the name of a tribe that lived in the tropical Bolivian Chaco. Another typical hotland item, the feathered shield, is also represented at Tiahuanaco.

Significant details are also visible to the collector of pottery. On the painted vessels found in the upper Andes, the Tiahuanacoid eye is divided in two vertically. It is half black and half white, with the white generally on the left. But on pottery belonging to the Tiahuanacoid period and found on the coast, the eye becomes Nazcoid or almond shaped. Sometimes, however, both types can be found on a single piece, showing the hybridization of the two cultures.

Trophy heads, trumpets, and the *chuyo* or cap appear on the majority of statues. On fabrics the god is often depicted with a painted face.

Right in the vicinity of the Tiahuanaco monuments, on the ground and in the earth, one can find fragments of a pottery that is remarkable in its workmanship and very fine polychrome decoration. Red, orange, wine, black, and white are the usual colors here. The motifs are the same as those decorating the carved monoliths, with a stylized feline or bird of prey as a leading theme.

Wendell C. Bennett, the archaeologist who with Alfred Kidder II and Ponce Sanguines previously did the most excavating at Tiahuanaco, noted a three-phase evolution in pottery decoration. The first and classical phase was one of well-decorated vessels, whereas the objects of the second phase indicated a decline in decoration. This decadence was very marked in the third phase, during which the motifs were lost, surviving only as fragments that served to fill empty spaces on the surfaces of the vessels to be decorated.

A stone statuette of a typical Tiahuanaco deity.

A vase from coastal Tiahuanaco. Note the typical harpy motif, with feathers, beak, and claws.

Tiahuanaco produced very small microlithic projectile points of obsidian, quartz, or flint, less than half an inch long, delicately shaped by pressure. They were triangular, with a stem and two pointed barbs. When I was at Tiahuanaco, the ground was still littered with these points, but now the native children imitate them quite well to sell to tourists.

Bolas are also typical of the Tiahuanaco area. These are small stones filed down into spheres or cones and tied to the end of a long, thin cord by leather tongues. Bolas are hunting devices used in prefarming times and after to catch camelids such as vicuñas or guanacos by throwing them around the legs of the hunted animals, which then fell as they ran.

The same technique was used much later by the Puelches and Tehuelches, in order to hunt on horseback European cattle in the pampas of Patagonia. It was from the ancient customs of these natives that the gaucho tradition of the Argentine plains originated.

The jewels of Tiahuanaco were very fine. Practically everything made of gold has been melted down and lost, but necklace beads, small pendants, and small anthropomorphic statuettes can still be found. The latter were made of green stone, and delicately portrayed men with hard faces and large aquiline noses. This detail attracts attention, because the winged god of the Gateway of the Sun has a nose so straight and pointed that it looks like a triangle drawn with a ruler and is comparable to the noses of gods on Easter Island.

In no museum have I seen copper objects clearly associated with a Tiahuanacoid stratum. However, the notches observable in the monolithic blocks that make up the walls of the temples must have been intended to hold metal hinges and hooks—otherwise, how could such heavy doors have been opened and closed? It is possible that all the metal to be found in these temples was later removed by the Incas.

In dry regions where fabrics have survived, the Tiahuanacoid period reveals very beautiful garments with polychrome decorations reproducing the same design themes as those found on the sculptures. The evolution of the decoration (from the classical to the decadent) is similar to that of pottery, the only difference being that the decline goes further. During the last phase, only occasional Tiahuanacoid elements are recognizable, mingled with decorations typical of other societies.

With respect to clothing, *unkus*, or shirts with neck openings and short sleeves, have been found, as well as mantles and the *chuyos* already mentioned—caps shaped like a truncated pyramid, like the ones a few men in Collao were still wearing just a few years ago.

Nothing is known regarding the origins of the Tiahuanaco society. Radiocarbon datings obtained for the deepest strata of the eponymous site indicate an age of two thousand years. These layers already contained pottery fragments decorated in the high classical Tiahuanaco style.

The Bolivian archaeological school also attributes to Tiahuanaco objects that are decorated in a different style. These pieces, on display in the little museum that has been opened at the site, are said to have been recovered from strata that are deeper than the ones containing classical Tiahuanaco. Thus, they may constitute traces of an earlier, formative phase, which could possibly be linked with the Chiripa style. Such a situation, characterized by the sudden appearance of a fully matured classical style whose antecedents remain unknown, is typical of the Andes.

The map of the political domain of the Tiahuanacos has not been established either. Numerous upper-Andean sites are strewn with Tiahuanacoid pottery. Thus, the eponymous site was perhaps only one center of this society. Other complexes, such as the large grouping of structures at Huari (located near the Peruvian colonial city of Ayacucho, which replaced pre-Columbian Huamanga) must have played an important role in this period.

Tiahuanacoid remains are also found over an area extending as far as the entrance to the forest in eastern Bolivia, and found in especially great quantity on the eastern shores of Lake Titicaca.

In the beginning of the twentieth century, grave looters started selling pottery and fabrics decorated with themes that appear on the Gateway of the Sun and that were similar in style to the pottery to be found in Tiahuanaco itself. The looters admitted that the objects had been found in different places along the central coast of Peru. Nothing more was needed for archaeologists to formulate a theory of a conquest, of an invasion of the lower Andes by armies serving an upper-Andean empire of Tiahuanaco. For several decades thereafter, archaeologists taught that Peru had known a Tiahuanacoid horizon just as it had a Chavín horizon.

Around 1950, some specialists in American prehistory attempted with much goodwill and in a very useful way to place into a slightly less incoherent framework the few concrete facts then known. They even suggested that the entire central Andes had experienced an era of great fusion in which Tiahuanaco consolidated a territory that had been fragmented since the end of Chavín. This may have been true. However, in our present state of knowledge, such statements are no more than hypotheses and ultimately constitute only subject matter for entertaining novels.

It is true that Tiahuanacoid objects that seem to have been made in the upper Andes appeared at various places in the lower-central Andes around a date that most authors set at about A.D. 750. But we do not yet have proof that political domination of the coastal lands materialized at that time. What could have happened is immigrations from the highlands by small groups of warriors. Such movements certainly had an impact on specific rich and strategically important points in the lower Andes, as for instance large settlements attractive to plunderers or strongholds that were useful for protection. Perhaps this impact even resulted in establishing the small, isolated Tiahuanacoid chiefdoms that exercised their power in the lower valleys for some generations.

However, from admitting this to speaking of the political domination of all Peru is a big step that I am not ready to take. To me the impact of Tiahuanaco seems instead an example of a warrior group moving down to plunder the rich lowlands, as so frequently happened in the Andes. But of course I cannot rule out the hypothesis of religion, as represented by gods in birdlike and feline forms.

In any case, whatever the nature of the Tiahuanacoid influence, it apparently did not have long-lasting effects. It was not long before the highland themes fell into decadence and disappeared. By around A.D. 1000 (even earlier in some places), everything again agreed with coastal traditions. The coastal populations had eliminated foreign influences, and all objects were again decorated with the usual motifs. The invaders—if there had been any—had blended into the local populations.

Today a massive migration by inhabitants of the upper Andes is taking place on a large scale in Peru. Starving and idle on their tiny, impoverished pieces of land, the highland peasants leave their villages to go down to the coast, mainly to Lima, in search of work. As they progress they form communities and invade areas they consider vacant, poorly occupied, or insufficiently farmed. One might imagine a similar Tiahuanacoid migration caused either by overpopulation, by a succession of bad years in the upper Andes, or by a need to escape a territory that had been overcome by an enemy.

Other authors have imagined that the pre-Columbian coastal populations could have carried out raids on the upper Andean towns, from which they would have brought back the objects typical of Tiahuanaco that have been unearthed along the Pacific. Although this hypothesis is not warmly received, this does not alter the fact that the more we excavate the more we find indications of migrations not only from the upper Andes to the lowlands but also from lowlands to highlands, a possible sign of withdrawal toward less-arid lands. And one cannot fail to note the use, in classical Nazca pottery (contemporaneous with that of Tiahuanaco) of interchangeable clays and pigments. Contact seems to have existed between the Nazca and Huari peoples. The two areas are only 120 miles apart.

But would a society that was driven out of its home territory and dispersed have had the strength to seize the strongholds of all the lower coastal valleys of central Peru? Objects showing the influence of Tiahuanaco and still decorated in the classical style have been found from the Nazca area to the Lambayeque Basin. How many men would have been necessary to conquer and militarily occupy a territory over 840 miles long? This history is still incomplete. For such an adventure to have succeeded, the coastal societies must have been in utter decay, and the people of the upper Andes must have had greatly superior weapons, perhaps bronze axes.

According to radiocarbon datings, Tiahuanaco produced nothing of any value either on the shores of Lake Titicaca or on the coast, after A.D. 1000. Something serious must have occurred such as caused the demise of Chavín. The beautiful pottery and fabrics disappeared and were replaced by new ware with decorative motifs typical of Collao. But we are again unable to affirm that there was a cause-and-effect relationship and that there was an immediate reoccupation of the

Tiahuanacos' territory. A long hiatus may have separated these two distinct sociopolitical systems.

It is a real shame that no archaeological team has drawn up the ground plan of a settlement from this period, such as Huari. Tiahuanaco, the eponymous site, was obviously a ceremonial center, but the excavation trenches that I saw all around the temples revealed drainage canals and the bases of rectangular stone walls that are probably the ruins of dwellings. Some archaeologists, such as Alfred Kidder II, maintain that a large city surrounded these temples, and I quite agree.

The most complete document available in this regard is the one drawn by Emilio Harth-Terré in Piquillacta, a large rectangular settlement surrounded by high defensive walls and irrigated by an aqueduct at the edge of the Cuzco highway near the Raya Pass, before the entrance to the Collao puna. The bad excavating done there at the beginning of this century revealed some typically Tiahuanacoid statuettes. These seem to date the complex, though parts of it were reoccupied by the Incas, who left us big houses with two-sided roofs. However, there is nothing Inca about the original settlement.

THE GOLDEN AGE

If we agree to face the facts, we must admit that we know practically nothing about what happened in the upper Andes up until the Inca period, immediately preceding the Spanish Conquest. About ten millennia of apparently intense life have left us cities, monuments, countless villages that are now in ruins, and extensive agricultural systems. With a few exceptions, the existence of large monuments had already been revealed by nineteenth-century travelers but had not attracted archaeologists. Aside from at Chavín and Tiahuanaco, prehistorians have done practically no scientific and systematic fieldwork in the cordillera.

Our great ignorance is not surprising, since not even the most basic documents have yet been established. Julio C. Tello has drawn a valid but elementary map of places influenced by Chavín. Archaeologists formulate clever hypotheses regarding the successive existence of the two large centers, Tiahuanaco in Bolivia and Huari in the department of Ayacucho. But what we really know about the Tiahuanaco period comprises stories fit only for novels, with no serious foundations.

We are a little better informed with regard to the lowlands of the Pacific slope. Because the vast ruins and hot sands of the desert are easy to excavate and often yield treasures, they have attracted archaeologists, whereas excavating in the rainy upper Andes requires hard work and much harsher living conditions. But even our basic documentation of the lowlands is not what it should be, and I say "a little better informed" only so as not to seem too pessimistic.

A primary index of the economic and social situation that must have prevailed in the lowlands around A.D. 750 is provided by the fact that Tiahuanacoid groups were apparently able to establish themselves easily in many of the rich coastal sites between the Lambayeque Valley in the north and the Nazca Basin in the Middle South. Even if we consider the Tiahuanaco influence to have been of only a spiritual and religious nature, it is hard to see how these groups could have been able to obtain such immediate results if the coastal chiefdoms had not already been quite weak. These results are proven by the appearance of Tiahuanacoid motifs in most strongholds in the lower coastal valleys. These motifs appeared simultaneously with the disappearance of Mochica motifs in the north, Maranga ones in the Lima region, and Nazca themes farther south, at dates ranging from A.D. 750 to 850. Thus, the Tiahuanacos seem to me to have been plundering invaders who brought their gods to societies whose leading caste had been weakened so much that the society no longer knew which way to turn.

Does the fact that production of the elegant, carefully decorated pottery ceased necessarily indicate a social crisis? Even if population pressures and social stratification led to the formation of a body of artisans forced to mass-produce the pots, plates, and cups required by the large population, if a ruling class had survived, wouldn't it have maintained a class of craftsmen capable of producing nicer vessels? But for about four centuries the Nazcas no longer used any but the plainest vessels for cooking and eating. Basing his thinking on such facts, Steward suggested that this type of decadence that affects artistic activities denotes a rupture of the social framework and a weakening of the ruling elements.

Until we are better informed, let us theorize that there was a general crisis along the Peruvian coast over an area at least six hundred miles long, but let us keep in mind that what happened during that time in the upper Andes remains completely unknown.

According to classical archaeologists, the appearance of the decorated pottery called Marañón ware, in the northern upper Andes around Cajamarca, and even in the upper Santa Valley, was related to the phenomenon of Tiahuanaco. I see it rather as proof of the ascent of tribes from the Amazonian lowlands in the east, attracted by the wealth of declining societies. Decorative themes typical of the hot lands are found in this Marañón pottery.

Let us also keep in mind that the influence of Tiahuanaco lasted not more than two to three centuries. But we have no idea who then took control of the coastal societies. In the north it was supposedly the Chimu princes, who built their capital near the sea at Chan Chan, at the gates of what later became the colonial city of Trujillo. But there is still a long gap of about four centuries to be filled. The Chimu princes were apparently subjugated by Inca generals in the fifteenth century, so we must find out what happened in these rich northern valleys during the preceding four hundred years, which is quite a long period not to have had any history.

Fortunately, a team of archaeologists from the Peabody Museum and Harvard University is currently working at Chan Chan. I am counting on it to set matters straight. At present we do not even know when Chan Chan was built, but it is one of the largest settlements in coastal Peru.

In Chan Chan one can still admire buildings of various sizes, some of which are very large and seem to date from different periods. The earliest ones, such as the Temple of the Dragon, used to be attributed to Tiahuanaco invaders. However, I share the opinion of archaeologists such as Richard Schaedel, who thinks these buildings were the work of invaders from the north who came about A.D. 1200, perhaps from the Piura Basin or even farther away, from Ecuador. Here is an enormous field still open for research.

The end of Tiahuanacoid influence and the resurgence of typically coastal societies during a chronologically ill-defined period that I place between the eleventh and fourteenth centuries A.D. coincides with profound changes in social and economic organization. This period must have been one of developing kingdoms, or at least more-powerful chiefdoms, that were able to effect vital transformations in agriculture.

Up until the time under discussion, Peruvians practiced an agriculture that was already technologically advanced, to be sure, but was still archaic in that it exploited the resources offered by the environment but did not try to increase them by building great irrigation works. Before around A.D. 1000 or 1200, it was not the great, powerful, and torrential rivers, with waters collected from many springs and tributaries and usually with a continuous flow, that helped the coastal societies the most. Smaller rivers were apparently better suited to their technological possibilities, so the ruins of early societies are concentrated around the secondary or even tertiary valleys: the Moche, Viru, Chao, Casma, Sechin, Huarmey, Chillon, Lurín, Chilca, Omas, Ica, and Nazca valleys. Moché, the capital of the Mochicas, was built on the banks of the little secondary river of the same name, on the edges of vast marshes far from the sea. The Viru Valley, a completely mediocre area in which no more than seventy-five hundred acres could be cultivated, played a role in the early agricultural history of Peru that was completely out of proportion to its size.

But with the Chimus we witness an entirely new phenomenon. The Chimus, who succeeded the Mochicas after several centuries, did not reoccupy Moche. Instead, they established their capital at Chan Chan, where the nearby waters of the powerful Chicama River could be brought by a long canal that transformed a formerly desert zone into a huge cultivable and prosperous area.

In the Middle South, the Chincha Basin, which previously was mostly desert, was also developed on a large scale. The cultivated land extended over about twelve miles on the formerly sterile terraces that extend along the seacoast. Thus, the Chincha Valley became active, whereas the Ica and Nazca basins became quiet and remained so until the Incas' arrival.

The Chincha Valley must have become very important in the Inca economy. The chronicles say that the princes of Cuzco considered that region to be their richest coastal province and they did not hesitate to marry the sisters of the local *caciques* (chiefs).

In the Cañete Basin, some thirty-seven thousand acres of land were developed, whereas previously, barely thirty-seven *hundred* acres were cultivable in this valley. As a result, the Cañete and Chincha basins, at first politically

Pre-Columbian navigation: fishermen on a reed
raft. From Chimu, north coast of Peru.

A Chimu warrior carved in wood and adorned
with stone and shell inlay.

unimportant, began to play a leading role in the struggle against Inca invaders.

To increase ten times the productivity of a single valley in a country where
it never rains is obviously an astonishing success. This resulted from constructing
lateral canals twenty-four to thirty-six miles long along one or both riverbanks.
The offtakes from these canals were several hundred yards above sea level, so they
could carry water away from the river even in periods of near drought and distribute it to the high terraces on both sides of the deeply cut riverbed. Without the
help of pumps or *shadoofs* used in the Near East, big rivers such as these between
high vertical banks were of no use to the pre-Columbians before they could build
canals.

Let us remember that these people, unlike those of the Near East, had no
device for raising water—not even the *shadoof,* a counterweighted sweep that
allows one to water any garden above a river or canal. Neither did they have
water-resistant mortar with which to construct big dams and thus accumulate
large water reserves during periods of flooding.

Modern canals sometimes still follow the routes of the pre-Columbian ones,
as, for example, from the offtakes of the Cañete River's modern canals at Pacaran, a native community that has survived in the central part of the valley.
There one may still see the little palace with square columns that once belonged
to the *cacique* of the Puerto Viejo society. He would have controlled the distribution of water before the arrival of the Incas.

One may still find sections of similar canals in numerous valleys in the
lower central Andes. Those in the Mala, Lambayeque, and Huara valleys are
the best preserved.

The ability to irrigate the Chincha and Cañete basins is a good example of
the changes that took place after the coastal chiefdoms were flourishing again. Up
until the development of the large valleys, the centers of cultural influence in the

Middle South remained the poor, sandy, and exposed territories like those of the Ica and Nazca basins. Once Chincha and Cañete became rich provinces, the ancient chiefdoms, which remained poor in resources, lost their standing and were subjugated. This might have been when Nazca could have lost its influence, perhaps because it was too arid and too difficult to irrigate. But tradition holds that canals were still operating in the Ica Basin when the Incas arrived on the coast, and in addition, Chincha-style pottery abounds in the area. Therefore, one may suppose that the people of Chincha could have extended their influence southward and been developing conquered lands when the new rulers arrived from Cuzco.

Coastal Peru had thus entered a period of extensive and intensive agriculture of a kind completely different from that practiced in preceding centuries. In the period of what I call archaic farming but farming with implements, the only lands that could be developed were in the lower coastal section that had valleys irrigated by intermittent streams that flooded annually. At most, the water of such streams was usable only in the immediately adjacent lowlands, which could be irrigated with the help of light dams. Only one crop could be obtained per year, for it was necessary to wait some nine months for the next flood before sowing again.

Big canals permitted not only the irrigation and colonization of immense lands that were formerly unusable but also made possible (thanks to big rivers with a permanent flow) two and sometimes three crops per year. (There is no winter in our sense of the word along the Pacific. Cieza de León tells us that Colombian peasants obtained up to three crops of corn a year. Here everything depended on water.)

The use of supplementary and more-stable water resources may have been the factor that favored the setting up of new political regimes like the Chimu kingdom. (Apparently, the Chimus were formerly called Chimors. The Asiatic sound of this name calls to mind Timor in the East Indies.) The rulers of Chan Chan seem to have been able to control a domain that covered some twelve valleys in the north and had some 125,000 cultivable acres.

Tradition holds that the southern border of their kingdom was defended on one bank of the Pativilca River by the beautiful Paramonga "fortress," which has survived almost intact there. Paramonga is an edifice made of stones embedded in clay, with a polyhedral floor plan and high surrounding walls that rise in tiers on four levels to form a fortress comparable to some medieval structures. But archaeologists now maintain that the Chimu kingdom's frontier was not the Pativilca and that Paramonga was a religious center and never a fortress.

South of the Pativilca Basin one finds Chimu pottery only rarely, as isolated pieces that came to be there possibly as the result of exchanges, visits to friends, or journeys.

To the north, the Chimus do not seem to have imposed their rule beyond the boundaries of the Sechura Desert. In the Chira Basin in Piura, one finds traces of a distinct society that has unfortunately not been studied but which produced an original black pottery.

On the other hand, the villages of Vicus and Ayabaca, which yielded so many gold objects, seem to have been marked by the Chimu presence. From these sites treasure looters have taken objects decorated in the purest Chan Chan style that were found in strata superimposed on layers containing Mochica-style objects. Beautiful copper disks covered with gold leaf and pierced by a central hole have appeared there. These pieces, so out of keeping with the Americas' traditions, are called sun disks by archaeologists. Who says that the inhabitants of Vicus and Ayabaca were not specialized metallurgists, producing the objects in fashion at Chan Chan?

By dominating a dozen valleys and some 125,000 to 250,000 acres of cultivable lands, the princes of Chan Chan were able to feed the population of a kingdom of up to a quarter of a million inhabitants.

While the new valleys were assuming importance, a good number of those that were formerly of consequence were forgotten. A shifting of forces and manpower could have followed and provoked social upheavals.

Some writers think that the Tiahuanaco bands that had come from the highlands were the creators of the social and economic revolution that seems to have ended with the development of extensive and intensive farming, but I do not agree with this hypothesis. First, I have found no more Tiahuanacoid fragments in villages bordering the big canals of the Chimus or Huaras or in the villages of the people of the Cañete and Puerto Viejo than in the formerly deserted plains that were now settled.

In addition, the impact of Tiahuanaco took place around A.D. 750, whereas the sociocultural revolution in question was not achieved until several centuries later, when the Tiahuanacoid contributions had already been assimilated.

Moreover, the system of big canals constructed in this epoch would not have been built if the coastal valleys had not experienced a period of peace and even prosperity, and had not been governed by firmly established authorities.

Therefore, I think that after a period of crisis which Tiahuanacoid bands took advantage of, the lowlands experienced a golden age, an age even of happiness for the inhabitants. (Pornographic vases abound in this period. Isn't this kind of amusement typical of happy people?) The Peruvian coast also seems to have entered a period of urban life at that time.

Before then there were no real cities, at least not in the lowlands in the sense used by anthropologists, who define a city as "a planned agglomeration in which one moves about between groups of dwellings separated by streets, and in which most, if not all, the temples, princely buildings, and other buildings for communal use are concentrated."

Earlier, the inhabitants of the lower Andes had constructed only large buildings or architectural complexes that were probably half ceremonial, half utilitarian or defensive. These were surrounded by villages formed either by little clusters of houses or by dwellings scattered throughout the countryside. Cities in the strict sense of the word did not exist on the coast.

Now very big cities developed. Pacatnamu, on the northern coast, measured

The city of Pacatnamu, on the north coast of Peru, was one and a half square miles in area. Late pre-Columbian Chimu period.

one and a half square miles. Chan Chan measured three and a half square miles. Cajamarquilla and Pachacamac, located respectively six and eighteen miles from Lima, covered an area of just under one square mile each. These settlements were real cities, no longer just villages, and were filled with houses joined into units forming districts delimited by avenues. Such units were composed of houses, granaries, and silos. Big temples were built at several points in each city.

In Chan Chan, the norms appear to have been different. Here there were rectangular units bordered by very high and solid walls, some of which included a building for ceremonial use. The people's houses were outside these units. Here again I am reminded of the storehouse-palace-temples of the Near Eastern princes of the last preliterate period in Egypt.

With a few exceptions, these cities were much bigger than European cities such as Rome, Byzantium, and Alexandria. Athens was small, and in 1500 Paris covered only a few acres. The insecurity of the times obliged Europeans to crowd together behind high defensive walls in dark houses separated by narrow alleys. The cities of Peru and Mexico were more like Mohenjo-Daro and Harappa in Pakistan, which seem to have accommodated about a quarter of a million persons. Madrid and Rome were nowhere near that size during the Renaissance.

In order to feed the inhabitants of these big centers, much more food was needed than could have been supplied by the valleys constituting the domain of the coastal princes in earlier periods. Once more, then, we are confronted with the philosophical problem of what and why. Was the creation of large urban centers the result of an increase in population, itself the result of a policy of developing new lands that made it possible to feed more people? Or did urban expansion lead to famine and the necessity of colonizing new lands in order to survive?

My fieldwork inclines me to accept the idea of a large increase in population, an overpopulation that obliged the inhabitants of the coast to find new lands to exploit no matter what the cost. Indeed, there is evidence dating from the last pre-Hispanic centuries not only for a colonization of the desert lowlands but also for a systematic development of the whole Andean area. One need only go about on foot or by mule in order to discover (almost everywhere in the cordillera) traces of works indicating the development of every tiny plot of usable land for either cultivation or grazing.

One day, upon leaving Jauja, in the upper Mantaro Valley, out of curiosity I followed a path leading into the puna. At the edge of some modern potato fields I discovered some pre-Columbian villages in which I counted over a thousand houses. This is only one example of a hundred similar situations I have encountered. Such phenomena may be observed everywhere between the altitudes of six thousand and eleven thousand or more feet where springs flow, where one may cultivate on terraces without suffering from the cold, and where one is already within reach of vast, bushy fields where camelids (specifically llamas and alpacas) used to graze. The other two species, guanacos and vicuñas, remained wild.

Apparently, in those days the peasants were very skillful in locating barely visible water resources and in developing lands that today seem unusable. I was particularly struck by their search for an ecological equilibrium, as shown by the complexes created by farmer-shepherds located at junctions of three complementary zones: the highlands (which permitted potato cultivation and supplied pastures), the lower valleys, and in the background the sea, which furnished the proteins so badly needed by Andean populations.

It matters little whether the efforts of the coastal princes ended in success or failure. Although those who insist on attributing all progress in the Andes to the princes of Cuzco may grieve, I am now able to affirm on the basis of concrete archaeological evidence that well-organized principalities and kingdoms, equipped with cities, roads, vast water systems, and maybe even standing armies, existed in the central Andes well before the imperial attempt of the Incas. From north to east—from Pacatnamu on the coast to the Marañón on the eastern slope of the Andes—and in the south around Lake Titicaca, we find the ruins of cities. Although the numbers of the inhabitants and the exact purposes of these settlements are still being discussed, one must admit that the face of the central Andes had changed and that the Andes were coming out of the past into modern times just when the Incas were about to take possession of them.

DISTURBANCES, FRAGMENTATION, AND FEUDALITIES

If the Peruvian lowlands experienced a golden age, it must not have lasted very long. How could the Incas have seized the coastal principalities easily (except for the principality of Huarcu, now called Cañete, whose conquest I shall discuss later), if the latter had not undergone a new period of crisis?

Some geologists theorize that the efforts made by pre-Columbians to keep on farming their lands threatened by aridity may be associated with the climatic crisis called the long drought, which affected North America in the thirteenth century. It is quite possible that future research will reveal that a comparable climatic crisis occurred in the Andes and produced dramatic results in arid lands where the slightest loss of water can become fatal and render a territory sterile. The need to construct big canals and irrigate desert lands may thus have corresponded to unfavorable climatic conditions, to a progressive drying out of the little valleys.

Let us not forget that the South American pre-Columbians in the course of their last five centuries of autonomy were not the only ones to undertake the construction of vast hydraulic works. The natives who lived in what are now the states of Colorado, Arizona, and New Mexico were responsible for the greatest achievements of this sort in the New World. The great Snaketown canal was 480 miles long.

Major hydraulic works were probably begun in the southern United States before the big Peruvian canals were built. Specialists place the beginning of irrigated agriculture in Arizona at around A.D. 800.

When I wonder what could have destroyed the Chimu kingdom, I am reminded of Egypt, where a historically known phenomenon occurred—new farmland that had been overirrigated or insufficiently drained became salinized. I wonder if it was not the efforts of the coastal princes to increase their irrigated acreage that brought ruin to their domains. The lowlands of coastal Peru are saturated with salt, so one must not irrigate and plant them without first washing them out thoroughly. This requires ensuring excellent drainage as well as flushing the salty water into the sea until the earth becomes fresh.

The pre-Columbians certainly did not realize the dangers that would arise from the construction of big canals. Even today, something similar is happening in Peru, endangering up to 30 percent of the coastal farmland.

Furthermore, in earlier times the fields were fertilized by the silt brought by the yearly flood. When the new fields were watered by larger rivers and forced to produce more than one crop per year, they could have lost their fertility.

Archaeology teaches us that during this period the pre-Columbians exploited the layers of guano, the dung of sea birds, which is an excellent fertilizer. Portrait statues representing prisoners from the time of the Chimu princes have been found on the islands just off the coast where the birds used to nest. Apparently, the princes used to get rid of people by sending them to work on the guano islands as the Chinese do today by sending men who challenge the political system to farms where they have to make human excrement into fertilizer balls for the fields. When no guano was available, pre-Columbian farmers used to fertilize each maize plant with an anchovy, a kind of sardine, or with human feces. In pre-Columbian villages one finds what Andeans call the *tonel Chino*, the Chinese barrel. Excrement was accumulated in it in order to make fertilizer pellets.

All these indications of a need to renew the land's resources are relatively recent in the history of coastal Peru. In the little valleys watered by the yearly flood, the torrential waters brought approximately half an inch of fertile alluvium each year. After three years of well-conducted irrigation, farmers could plant cotton on a terrace of pebbles irrigated by a muddy stream, as I have witnessed. In such circumstances they needed neither sardines nor guano.

The fifteenth century A.D., though so close to us, has remained an obscure period in Andean history. Radiocarbon datings are not very helpful for dates within a given century. With results that are accurate to within 5 percent, an age of 500 years counted from 1950, for example, would leave 50 years of uncertainty. Thus, the date could be anywhere between A.D. 1425 and 1475, so it would be useless. And the oral tradition, like the chroniclers' texts, becomes completely uncertain about events that would have occurred three generations before that of the last Inca.

For a long time, specialists in American studies imagined they could neglect archaeological fieldwork when it came to investigating protohistory and were content to repeat what the Spaniards had told us. This shirking of responsibility has created a situation in which we know almost nothing about the sociopolitical state of the fourteenth-century upper Andes, when the epic of the rulers of Cuzco was beginning.

In the north-central Andes, archaeologists had noticed the diffusion of a pottery made of white or cream-colored kaolin clay and decorated with red or black lines. This so-called Cajamarca style showed a decoration that was sometimes well made, sometimes decadent. Thus, it seems clear that a society of some duration would have dominated the high Santa and Marañón valleys. However, archaeologists ignored the question of when the society was established, what territory it controlled, and who destroyed it.

Archaeology also teaches us that these Cajamarcas visited and looted the Chavín monuments. We have found their pottery at La Copa, Huantar, and Wilkawain. But this happened relatively late. The Chavín society could not have been destroyed by the Cajamarcas but must have been demolished much earlier by a group of tribes that revolted. Huantar could have been one of their final redoubts.

In the south, excavations in Collao have not even begun. Not a single study has been done on the poor-quality ware that replaced the Tiahuanacoid pottery. This pottery is literally strewn over the surface of all the inhabited sites, but I doubt that it can be associated with the great carved monoliths, very different from those of the Gateway of the Sun, that one found all around the lake. The verb is in the past tense, for treasure looters have stolen almost all the statues of any portability. The ones near Jésus de Menchaca, in Bolivia, half buried in burial mounds, are fortunately too heavy to be clandestinely carried off.

Apparently, the *chulpas,* or big funerary towers that abound in Collao, postdate Tiahuanaco and would have been erected little by little after the fall of Huari. These chulpas demonstrate styles representative of different periods. In the vast agglomeration of Sillustani, surrounded by defensive walls, some chulpas appear to be Inca, particularly the ones ornamented with several stones decorated with a feline or serpent carved in high relief. Others were built by reemploying the finely cut blocks of Tiahuanaco.

It is unfortunate that no architect has made a serious study of these chulpas. Some are round; others, square; others, shaped like mushrooms, covered by an overhanging roof made of flat tiles. The most modest ones, cone shaped and daubed with mud, are probably also the latest ones. One of them has yielded a radiocarbon date of 1535 plus or minus one hundred years. Today these daubed chulpas are still used as dwellings by shepherds in the puna.

The whole region surrounding the rich valley of Arequipa has also remained archaeologically unknown. A site near Arequipa gave its name to the so-called Churajon pottery, but Augusto Malaja, the director of the university museum there, says that there is no such site in the area. Writers on the subject have told us very little, and it is meager information for a territory of about eight thousand square miles, connecting Titicaca to the coast.

I have found Churajon pottery in the fortified settlements I have discovered on the coast of the Far South, in the vicinity of Chala and Aquipa. Aquipa, Atiquipa, Quipa, and Arequipa are place names that recur frequently, and it would be interesting to draw up a map of all the places bearing such phonetically similar names. For instance, among the Quimbayas of Colombia, Juan Friede cites the existence of a cacique named Arisquipa, a name comparable to *capac*, or chief, of the Incas.

Classic authors state that the Far South was colonized by the Tiahuanacos. My feeling is that the southern Peruvian lowlands and northern coastal Chile had in effect been developed by men coming down from the altiplano, but the migrations might have happened after the fall of Tiahuanaco.

The chroniclers wrote a great deal about the difficult campaigns the Incas had to conduct against the peoples who separated them from the sea to the southwest, but everything the historians tell us in this regard is in fact legendary. I prefer to forget it and wait until archaeologists finally start doing fieldwork there. (Glottochronology has already yielded some interesting results in this regard. For further information on this subject, see the works of Alfredo Torero.)

Let us turn again to the lowlands, about which we are better informed.

In the Far North, the Piura Basin apparently remained autonomous until the Incas crossed it to take possession of Tumbes, which seems to have been a settlement of the Ecuadorian Cañaris.

Here again it is most unfortunate that the immense monuments of unbaked cone-shaped bricks that could still be seen twenty years ago near Sullana and in the lower Chira Valley were not studied before overpopulation destroyed them all. I knew Sullana when it had eight hundred inhabitants. Now twenty-four thousand people live there.

This region must have been extremely rich, with verdant pastureland expanding below acacia savannahs during rainy winters. Today these savannahs have been destroyed for domestic fuel and as a result of introducing cattle, and all the land that has not been irrigated is turning into desert.

As one goes northward, the descending cordillera allows the Atlantic rains to cross the Andes more easily. The rains often affect the coast, where occasional displacements of the equatorial countercurrent also create disturbances.

It was in these savannahs that I experienced my strangest sensations as an archaeologist. While walking through vast acacia forests that have since become deserts, I would suddenly find myself before a dead city or a ziggurat, with the debris of gold jewels glittering virtually everywhere in the sand.

Nor is anything definite known about the state of crisis in which the Incas are thought to have found the Chimu kingdom. According to one legend, the princes of Chan Chan were defeated by the generals of Cuzco, but other legends say that the Chimus had already lost all their power by then, for some people had come down from the upper Andes to take possession of all the water catchments that fed the canals serving the lower plain, and had thus starved the populations. I have already expressed my distrust of sources of this kind. In this particular case, however, the geographical framework undeniably encourages one to accept a hypothesis like the one proposed by folklore.

The fragility of "hydraulic societies," of societies in arid lands whose existence is completely dependent on irrigation, is well known. (Steward coined this term. This problem has been brilliantly studied by such specialists as K. A. Wittvogel and Angel Palerm.) In such societies, control of the water resources becomes a source of political power for the prince. There are numerous historical examples of this in the Near East, notably in Iran. But concentrating control of the irrigation systems in a single hand also becomes a weapon for nomads or other rebels, who soon find out that all they have to do to starve a kingdom is to take possession of the water catchments or destroy the main canal.

I have not had opportunity to work in the Trujillo region. The most important valley in the central Andes, the Santa, which is filled with enormous edifices, has unfortunately never been the subject of any archaeological study or published work. Now the middle Santa, or Huaylas, gorge establishes communication between the coast and the inter-Andean valley of the upper Santa, in which Wilkawain and Recuay, two formerly active centers, are located. And Huantar and then the Marañón Basin are also reached by way of the Huaylas. It would be surprising if such a communication route had not permitted various pressures to be exercised on the rich lower part of the basin and facilitated violent or peaceful migrations.

Problems are also presented in the big Huara Valley, located south of the Paramonga fortress. In this valley one sees the ruins of numerous large agglomerations and enormous buildings, and the ground there is strewn with pottery. However, it is not Chimu pottery. Who, then, dominated this valley?

In cases of this kind, archaeologists hide their ignorance by speaking of formative, intermediate, middle, or late horizons. This concept of horizons has played a pernicious role in Andean archaeology. By means of horizons, long

spans of time have been created that obliterate the local and regional events oc-
curring during the centuries in question. For example, when one asks a Peruvian
archaeologist what happened in a certain era in a particular valley, he replies
that the valley was living in the "middle intermediate horizon" at that time. This
answer really tells us a lot! Eliminating such terminology would at least help to
highlight the main problems that must be solved, rather than to conceal them, the
way Molière's doctors concealed their ignorance by using fantastic names.

A little farther south we enter the Chancay Basin, another living example of
false ideas that become established following premature generalizations. For example, we are still being told that the Chancay civilization prospered in the Lima
region and dominated a territory extending from the Chancay to the Lurín
basins, or from fifty-four miles north of the modern capital of Peru to eighteen
miles south of it. I confess that I fell into this trap myself and reproduced this
theory without criticizing it in my first general works.

But if one is willing to go study the land, one will find that, though the so-
called Chancay pottery, which is made of a pink paste coated with a cream-
colored slip and decorated with black motifs, appears in many sites in the Chancay and Chillon basins, it hardly ever reaches the basin of the Rímac, the river
that waters Lima. Only occasional Chancay vessels, trade pieces, are found in the
Rímac Basin. They probably ended up there as a result of barter or trips.

One will discover that Chancay pottery is also found along the Andean
ridges that close the Chancay Basin on its north side, but there the ware is superimposed on a brown pottery known as Teatino. On the other hand, as soon as

A typical Chancay ceramic grave
figure. Late pre-Columbian, Peru.

one enters the Rímac Basin to the south, guarded by the large oval fortress of Collique, which is surrounded by several high, concentric, defensive walls, one sees that Chancay pottery is replaced by vessels related to those to be found south of Lima.

To me, the Chancay so-called civilization appears simply to correspond to the migration of a tribe that would have dominated a restricted area and whose yellow-slipped jars remind me of upper-Andean products made of mixtures of kaolin and other clays. The Chancays may have acted like a wedge between the society that dominated the Huaura Basin to the north and the one dominating the Rímac Basin to the south. Moreover, the Chancay civilization is very late. I found glass trinkets from the Mediterranean in a tomb containing pottery painted black on a yellow slip, and a *cuchimil,* a ceramic doll typical of the last pre-Columbian century.

The Collique fortress may very well have marked the border of a territory controlled by the powerful feudality of the Puerto Viejo tribe. This name was given to a pottery that was found in Chilca by Ducio Bonavia, who studied it for the first time. Puerto Viejo pottery was identified as early as the 1940s by Strong, in the big city of Pachacamac, located eighteen miles south of Lima at the mouth of the Lurín River. William D. Strong called it Inca associated because he found fragments of it mixed with pottery from Cuzco, and I feel he was quite right.

The attempt to describe the outer limits of the society that used this Puerto Viejo ceramic is far from complete, but we already know that the Puerto Viejos controlled a large territory that reached Huarochiri in the high cordillera to the east. I have also found their traces in the community of Pacaran in the Cañete Valley, ninety miles farther south. To the north, the Puerto Viejos may have protected their borders with the Collique fortress.

We also know where to place the Puerto Viejos in time, as a result of the regional study I carried out in the Chilca Basin. In Chilca, I noted that immigrants who lived there briefly were still using completely classical Tiahuanacoid vessels that dated back to the ninth century A.D. After that, the era may have known a period of inactivity. Around the fourteenth century, or perhaps a little earlier, the Chilca Basin was occupied by farmers and herders that I call the Cuculi ("little dove" in Quechua), after the village where I carried out my first stratigraphic cut in the kitchen midden of one of their houses. After that, Puerto Viejo pottery pervades the basin, and when superimposed archaeological strata have survived, they show us Puerto Viejo ware mixed with Cuzco pottery in the youngest levels.

Tradition concurs here with archaeology, since the chroniclers tell how the lords of Huarcu and Lunahuaná, who controlled the coastal valleys from the Mala to the Cañete, in alliance with the people of Chincha, were able to assemble thirty thousand warriors, with whom they opposed the Inca troops. It is thus quite possible that the big stronghold of Bandurria, built by the Puerto Viejos in Chilca, would have been demolished by the Inca's men.

The alliance between the peoples of Chincha and Cañete apparently did not last long. The chroniclers write that, though the princes of Cañete remained un-conquerable, the princes of Chincha put up very well with the Incas and made agreements with them. And although the territories of Chincha and Cañete were very close to each other, each society apparently retained its own personality. For example, the Chinchas produced a pottery that was original in its shapes and dec-orations, ugly compared to others, but well made, of a pink paste. Apparently they still had at their disposal the raw materials the Nazcas had made use of dur-ing their artistic golden age.

The classical ceramicware called Chincha has not yet been dated. Archae-ologists consider it to be post-Tiahuanacoid and close in time to the Incas. Nazca pottery became decadent very early, perhaps as early as the fifth century A.D., and the Tiahuanaco period was brief, from about A.D. 750 to 900, according to radiocarbon dating. Thus, a gap of about five hundred years remains to be filled. In order to fill it, it is not enough to appeal to the so-called Chincha pottery, with its very stylized shapes. A pottery of such an assertive style would hardly have been made for longer than a hundred years.

The Chinchas were also metallurgists and worked in silver. In early times, the Chincha territory did not lend itself well to agriculture. The middle valley is separated from the coast by a high mountain barrier across which the river has with difficulty dug a passage for itself, and the lower plain forms a half cone that slopes toward the sea. Only after the river was channeled did it become possible to develop the whole delta, made of pebble terraces. Only then were the Chinchas able to create a rich and powerful society.

The enormous buildings that survived until some years ago in the coastal plain (which is twelve miles long) abundantly prove the wealth of this period. Near the sea stood the magnificent ruins of the beautiful unfired-brick complex of Tambo de Mora.

The southern part of the Middle South—in other words, the Ica and Nazca basins—apparently was not very active after the decline of its archaic society. Cahuachi, the big Nazca communal center in the Rio Grande Basin, apparently was not plundered by the Tiahuanacos. Thus, I think that it was already aban-doned, and maybe covered by sand, by around A.D. 750. No traces of the Chin-chas have been found there either; the site was revisited only by the Incas.

Paredones, a settlement located at the entrance to the Orcona Valley in the Nazca Basin, could have been built for Chincha rulers. In any case, it has nothing to do with the classical Nazcas, who apparently built only little villages.

In order to reach the Pacific shore after leaving the middle and Nazca valleys, where the rivers flow at an altitude of sixteen hundred feet and are sepa-rated from the ocean by a high coastal range, we must cross once more the impressive desert that extends from Paracas to Marcona. We then reach the Far South coast, which is intersected by a number of big rivers: the Acari, Yauca, Ocoña, Majes, Victor, Tambo, Moquegua, Locumba, and Saña. This is the lower-central Andean area best irrigated by streams. Nevertheless, I have now observed that if some areas had been densely populated during the last pre-

Columbian centuries, such areas were not the irrigated ones. Large villages and even fortified settlements are found at the bases of the fog oases. These complexes, with the Arequipa pottery style predominating in them, are made up of houses and quite numerous storage bins.

Some agglomerations are paired with others, perhaps refuge cities, which I have found in strategic positions on high, rocky crests, where springs would have sustained life. This type of settlement calls to mind the pucaras discussed earlier, the fortified agglomerations of the Diaguites in Argentina or Chile. The existence of solid fortifications may indicate a period of insecurity. In Quebrada de Vaca, near Chala, Inca pottery is mixed with Arequipa pottery. The Incas left their traces, such as star-shaped stone maces, throughout the settlement. But the little fort and the long defensive wall could have been built to protect the settlement against armies from Cuzco, because the Incas' detritus is found inside a new settlement that had been built outside the defensive wall.

PEASANT LIFE IN ARID LANDS

I have already discussed peasant life in arid lands apropos of the occupation of coastal lomas by the Lapa Lapas, and the hydraulic works of the Chimus and their brothers in the other big valleys of the north coast.

The cultivation of potatoes on terraces and of corn on irrigated plains with the help of canal networks constituted only one farming method used by the highly skilled farmers that the pre-Columbians became. They also knew how to utilize ground water.

Several years ago, there were still marshes and ponds at several points on the Pacific shore. The water in them was brackish as a result of its entering the salty sea sands. However, this water actually came from the upper Andes, from the piedmonts of the cordillera, whence it traveled underground, sheltered from evaporation and maintained at a certain level by an impermeable layer in the ground beneath it. According to the level of this layer, the underground water table either was accessible or was too deep to be utilized by people. At the edge of the sea, when fresh water could not flow into the ocean because the denser salt water acted as a barrier, either a water-bearing bed or a pond was formed, according to the topography of the land.

Today almost all these ponds have dried up, but we have already studied a great many of them. When the water level remained underground but near the surface, its presence was indicated along desert beaches by tufts and bunches of purslane, a succulent plant with fleshy leaves full of moisture. The existence of a bunch of purslane so clearly indicated the accessibility of drinkable ground water that I got into the habit of locating pre-Columbian villages and camps in coastal deserts by searching for the green spots of vegetation. And the reverse was equally true. Thus, the presence of a chain of these camps permitted me to follow the seepage of fresh water dripping under rocks all the way out to the tips of rocky peninsulas that penetrate deep into the ocean.

The volumes of the underground rivers, whose importance is now recognized by well-known geographers and geologists, evidently varied according to unknown, probably climatic, factors. However, the present drying out seems to me to be the result of deforestation and excessive pumping practiced by the farmers.

When a water-bearing bed was large, it sustained a savannah, which generally consisted of acacias or mimosas. These savannahs died during a drier climatic cycle, but one finds them fossilized beneath the sand, and in searching for them finds the spots that were formerly inhabited. Thus, I discovered villages in the Paracas Desert in an environment so dry that nothing about its present state explains why the inhabitants chose to settle there. It is even possible that camelids lived in these savannahs and that the pre-Columbians hunted them there. All the dead in the Paracas ossuary were dressed in vicuña skins, and a year ago I came across a stray alpaca as well as a deer in the lomas of the Far South.

Sometimes the water near the beach is so pure that one may water gardens with it. In Paracas, I was able to observe this ancient practice reenacted by workers in a boat-repair shop. Then I understood how people had lived in the vast pre-Columbian villages whose presence in this vicinity was indicated by Tello.

While studying the Cuculi and Puerto Viejo societies, I discovered their techniques, which had been lost for centuries. The Cuculis were settled in the middle Chilca Valley. There, vegetation in the form of willows, pepper plants, acacias, and other bushes led me to suspect the presence of a rather large underground system that was not too deep. In areas with underground water that was accessible because of its shallow depth and was in enough abundance to search out, the pre-Columbians proceeded to use the water sheet as if it were a river.

Today, small farmers proceed as their pre-Hispanic ancestors did. They dig wells that fill slowly in twenty-four hours. Every day, at the end of the afternoon when evaporation occurs most slowly, each farmer opens a sluice and lets the water flow from the well into his garden through a network of little canals.

These small farmers are trying to redevelop dry central valley lands in the western Andes, using little motor-driven pumps. But their attempts are hardly successful. Due to deforestation, the water sheet is not being replenished and is steadily diminishing. Furthermore, without the cover of a savannah, evaporation is too rapid and plants cannot survive.

Often the water sheet is level with the surface and forms ponds in the upper-Andes piedmonts. In such cases, by means of canals the pre-Columbians brought the water to their villages and gardens, which were located farther down the valley.

Thus, these astute peasants utilized various resources in combination, since no one resource was sufficient in itself. They made use of ponds, underground water systems, and a small yearly flood or a surface brook if there was one. As a result of their skill in making plants grow with practically no water, the Cuculis succeeded in feeding about a hundred villages, each of which was inhabited by fifty to a hundred families, or sometimes by as many as five hundred people. They did this in a region where one cannot even find a lizard today; at most, one finds some scorpions.

However, the Cuculis did not live only on edible plants. They dressed in wool and therefore must have been herdsmen. Besides, there are numerous camelid remains in the cemeteries they have left us in the lower plains, where their tombs were made of rectangular underground chambers dug in dry sand and covered with mat roofs supported by thick sticks. Looters found rows of skeletons seated in forced bent positions, wrapped in a great many garments and surrounded by the most varied objects. Llamas and alpacas had been buried outside the human graves.

Cuculi pottery is rarely pleasant to look at. On the other hand, their fabrics with multicolored decorations are cheerful. The frenzy with which looters tore Cuculi funerary bundles to pieces leads one to think that their tombs also contained gold jewels. In any case, we know that the Cuculis used copper, if not as tools then at least as units of exchange. We found chisels, *tumis* (pins), and hatchets made of red copper in tombs in several of their villages.

Beam scales, which were thought to be a product of European contact, were already employed by the Cuculis. These scales are therefore undoubtedly pre-Columbian. Otherwise, they might have been copied from Portuguese scales acquired by the Guaranis, who might have exchanged them for other products of the upper Andes. However, the dates do not coincide. The Cuculis and Puerto Viejos apparently lived in the fourteenth and fifteenth centuries, whereas scales of European origin could not date back any earlier than the very end of the fifteenth or beginning of the sixteenth century. Here is an interesting little problem clearly illustrating the confused type of situation prehistorians must clarify.

It is possible that castes of specialized artisans such as potters already existed among the Cuculis. It was in the village of Chichacara that I observed for the first time the existence of a community that could devote itself entirely to pottery manufacturing. This village is located in a narrow gorge at an altitude of six thousand feet. Its wealth, an enormous vein of superior-quality clay, was prudently hidden behind a high terrace. The Cuculis had settled next to this inexhaustible source of objects for barter and had constructed an elegant, planned cluster of buildings embellished with a central square and paved roads leading to it. Four roads left the village in the directions of the cardinal compass points. These roads, as well as enclosures for llamas and grass fields extending into the surroundings, bear witness to a pottery business and the transport, on the backs of camelids, of products manufactured in the village. In exchange for these products, corn and seafood were obtained, and perhaps copper tools as well. The majority of the Cuculis I found buried in this village were accompanied by metal objects.

Every house in the village of Chichacara had an open patio whose roof was supported by square columns. The bins tiled with stones, where clay was put to mature, are still visible beneath these roofs. Hearths may still be seen on the patios or porches such as were used to fire pots and shards of items that either

Women firing pottery at Chichacara in the Peruvian lower Andes.

The Chichacara pre-Columbian village, inhabited six hundred years ago, was a potters' village built near a huge bed of clay.

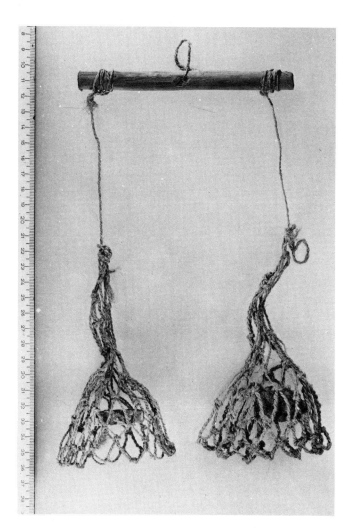

A Chichacara weighing scale. Late pre-Columbian.

broke during firing or were defective. The pre-Columbians fired their pottery in the open air. Kilns seem to have been used only to reduce ores or melt down metals.

The exchanges that the Cuculis must have made in their roles as traveling merchants are also indicated by the existence, in absolutely desert areas of the dry Andes, of their *tambos*, or stopping places. (These *tambos* must have had wells, which I have not been able to find.) Here the floors of big stone enclosures were strewn with camelid dung, and one can still see closetlike niches and silos there that could have been used to store merchandise.

Pottery manufacturing has remained a tradition in the Chilca Valley, where several families still fire big jars and cooking dishes to be sold in the market in Lima. I saw these big jars being sold for three soles, or about ten cents. The inhabitants of the village must have been very attached to their traditions not to have abandoned such an unprofitable activity!

Usually the women make these jars, the men being content to fire them. The tradition of decorated pottery has been lost in Chilca—now only plain, chocolate brown pieces are made. When broken, these items yield fragments that are interchangeable with ones left by the ancestors of the present inhabitants, who lived in these villages four or five hundred years ago. Only a few women still know how to make beautiful pieces, so when they die, their art will be lost. The potters of Chilca refused to tell me where they extract clay, but I suspect they go to Chichacara for it.

The big problem in these dry gulleys is to procure fuel. The poor potters no longer have wood, and they must sometimes travel as far as eighteen miles to bring back cactus trunks to feed their fires. Their ancestors used to burn camelid dung, but these animals have now disappeared from the western slopes.

Firing is done outdoors between houses. The temperature obtained barely exceeds eleven hundred degrees Fahrenheit. The result is not a well-oxidized paste, but rather a kind of brown biscuit with a core that has remained gray.

The potter's wheel has not yet been introduced into the region. Women continue to make their pieces in the old way, on a flat stone that they turn a little at a time while the sides rise as the women pinch them. When the piece is finished, it is left to harden before its neck and handles are attached. After this, two or three days of drying are all that are needed before it may be fired. Then all the pottery is loaded onto the donkeys that have replaced llamas.

The Puerto Viejos, successors of the Cuculis in Chilca, offer an excellent example of the advanced agricultural techniques that the pre-Columbians developed. In Chilca the Puerto Viejos settled in the lowlands, but without returning to the Lapa Lapas' metropolis of two thousand years ago, a city that in the meantime had become a cemetery for the Tiahuanacos.

We have unearthed two Puerto Viejo villages. They are strategically located —one at the southern tip of Chilca, where the Andes enter the ocean and cut off the beach—the other at the northern tip, where Mount Bandurria plays a similar role.

These villages were unpleasant, covered with blackish ashes and debris formed into compact clusters, and half underground in the sense that the houses were partially dug into debris accumulated by earlier settlers. This return to the half-underground house, a type that disappeared on the Peruvian coast more than three thousand years ago, indicates a different tradition, perhaps the arrival of immigrants. Such houses have been found among the Diaguites on the Argentine slope of the Andes.

The low walls of these houses were barely higher than the passages between the clusters. Therefore, the walls must have been heightened by branches, for otherwise the houses would have been too low for people to live in. The two villages each covered just under half an acre, and each must have provided shelter for several hundred people.

The Puerto Viejos also inhabited numerous other places all over the plain of Chilca. One finds their silos, ashes from their hearths, and all the signs of human life scattered between gardens. These are probably the remains of huts of farmers who cared for the crops.

When they were not busy farming, the Puerto Viejos built temples and palaces. The ruins of one of their palaces have survived on the cliff. It was a large building of about thirty-six hundred square yards and made of adobe—big, rectangular slabs of unbaked clay. This many-roomed palace was probably used as a fortress as well as storehouse.

The temple was erected in the plain, at the foot of the palace. It was a rectangular building 330 feet long and 33 feet high, with a stairway leading up to it. All around the temple, one still sees small buildings that were probably storehouses.

The Puerto Viejos seem to have reoccupied neither the middle valley nor lomas, in which one finds only traces of camps and enclosures for cattle, which correspond to this period. Camelids must have been taken to graze here.

In addition to what may be found in these areas, small fortified villages I discovered in the central Andes, between the altitudes of thirty-three hundred and ten thousand feet, also contained Puerto Viejo pottery.

The farm system of the Puerto Viejos of Chilca makes up one of the most complete ones to have survived. It can be seen almost intact in the plain. An aerial photograph taken about twenty years ago shows that the cultivated lands between the two Puerto Viejo villages to the south and Bandurria to the north covered three thousand acres. They were probably sown with corn, judging by the quantity of cornstalks one finds mixed with ashes and debris in the mounds separating the gardens.

This cultivation of corn without the aid of surface water or rain won the admiration of the Spaniards who first crossed the plain of Chilca, then the plain of Villacuri.

Villacuri, stretching between the Pisco and Ica valleys, is nearly seventeen hundred feet above sea level. The pre-Columbians also farmed there with the help of the underground water sheets.

The chroniclers described how careful the natives were in removing the salt that had covered their gardens and in fertilizing their gardens with anchovies. These texts seem to confirm that the Incas found the coast to be in a critical state. In 1532, the natives were removing sheets of salt in order to put their gardens in shape to cultivate again; a period of abandonment must have preceded the reestablishment of a traditional economy.

Since the water sheet was underground in Chilca, the pre-Columbians had to dig to reach a moist layer. Consequently, they created what we call depressed gardens, whose surface is below the level of the surrounding plain. They dug rectangles that varied in size according to the terrain and were just deep enough to reach the moist earth. Some gardens were at least 160 feet long, though others were no longer than 66 feet.

At first glance, the process appears to be simple and the problem to be resolved. However, archaeologists have a mania for digging, and in going beneath the surface of the gardens I noticed that the bottoms of these gardens were made of a bed of river silt, under which were sea sand and shells from the beach. In other words, not only did the Puerto Viejos have to dig to reach a moist layer, but they also had to create a layer of fertile silt to isolate the plants from the sterile and salty subsoil. Fortunately, while I was doing this fieldwork, the Chilca wadi experienced a year of exceptional flooding, as it does every five or ten years, and I saw it wash down large quantities of fertilizing deposits as far as the beach. Studying the topography in greater depth, I finally found two channels made by the pre-Columbians that allowed these muddy waters to reach the gardens. They dug, then, in order to reach a moist layer, but also to maintain a gentle slope to the end of each channel.

Assuming that the inhabitants of the region were able to obtain two crops a year, and remembering that an Andean family of five persons consumed on an average the annual production of almost four acres planted with corn, one can calculate that Chilca's three thousand acres could have fed eight hundred families, or about four thousand people.

At first sight this figure seems normal if we compare it with the thirty-five hundred inhabitants in the modern settlement at Chilca and bear in mind the enormous church the Jesuits built there. But then where did the inhabitants live?

If the villages of Puerto Viejo and Bandurria lodged eight hundred families, each family would have had to be content with a house of one hundred square feet. This figure does not surprise me, for living spaces of this size have been reported for the pit dwellers of the pueblos in the southwestern United States. Furthermore, other villages may have disappeared. The Puerto Viejos could have lived also in straw huts made of four willow posts supporting mats, the type of mats the Peruvians still use today.

But one can also imagine that agricultural production far exceeded the needs of the region's inhabitants. If so, the surpluses, which were first deposited in the "castle" at Bandurria, were finally sent to the princes of Huarcu and Lunahuaná, in the Cañete Basin, since the Puerto Viejos of Chilca were probably under their domination.

Using one's imagination is not forbidden, and all conjectures are permissible here, on condition that they be formulated as working hypotheses and that we do not create novels with the help of pseudohistorical facts that have not been confirmed.

THE INCAS

The history of the Incas was recounted in a masterly work by William H. Prescott in 1850. After that, our knowledge of this subject progressed hardly at all until John Hemming produced a very fine work giving a detailed description of the Spanish Conquest and destruction of the royal line of Cuzco.

For the bibliography and details of this history, consult Julian Steward's *Handbook of American Indians,* a work that completely outlines the subject. Since it was written, Alfred Metraux has produced a useful work in which he places Inca history in a less sociopolitical framework than Louis Baudin did

before him in a book that has become a classic. Baudin's text, though much fic-
tionalized, remains useful in that it clarifies certain aspects of the economic life of
Andean peoples that had not been dealt with previously, notably those relating to
the use of water in very arid lands. Baudin was the first to make us understand
that the Incas were trying to create a "hydraulic civilization," as this type of society has since been called.

However, we know no more than in 1850 regarding the actual history of
the dynasty, its origins, and the sudden changes of fortune that transformed the
petty chieftains of a mediocre valley in the upper Andes into the masters of a territory that covered some half a billion acres and was over eighteen hundred miles
long. It is odd that this period has not found its deserved place in history text-
books or caused more enthusiasm among researchers. As the only known example
of a genuine preliterate and Neolithic empire, the Cuzco monarchy should have
fascinated prehistorians.

This lack of interest for such an important subject derives in part perhaps
from the fact that we think we are better informed than we really are—we think
there is nothing left to delve into and the subject is exhausted.

However, if we relegate everything that is in the field of legend rather than
history to the background, in order to keep in mind only what is fairly verifiable,
we see that we are really very ignorant.

We are told that the princes the Spaniards found were the heirs of a dynasty
of eleven sovereigns who had been reigning since the thirteenth century A.D. According to tradition, their names were Manco Capac, Sinchi Roca, Lloque Yupanqui, Mayita Capac, Capac Yupanqui, Inca Roca, Yahuar Huacac, Viracocha,
Pachacuti, Topa Yupanqui, Huayna Capac, Huascar, and Atahualpa. The story
I am about to tell begins with the successors of Huayna Capac—Huascar and
Atahualpa. This is all in the realm of poetry, like the Trojan War and the *Odys-
sey* of Homer. The legend of the Ayar brothers, ancestors of the Incas who are
supposed to have come out of a cave, calls to mind the hero cult of ancient
Greece.

Once the dynasty had been destroyed, it was natural for its admirers, sup-
porters, and descendants to try to glorify the lost cause, exaggerate its duration,
and create an apparently genuine genealogy. The chronicler Garcilazo de la
Vega, who was related to the royal family of Cuzco, occupied himself in openly
doing just this. But as historians we must distinguish between traditions that were
reinvented and rewritten by sixteenth-century chroniclers, and popular tradition,
which was less distorted and which one could still collect in its original form in
the Andes proper during the years immediately following the Spanish Conquest.
Unfortunately, this kind of tradition never continues very far in time; it generally
relates only the events experienced by the last three or four generations.

This is apparently what happened to the traditions regarding the Inca
regimes. In studying this matter more thoroughly, I shall note that only beginning with the reign of Prince Pachacuti, who mounted the throne in about A.D.
1438, does the information transmitted to us by tradition become in any way re-

liable. Everything prior to that reign is summed up in a series of names to which one cannot attach any value. Practically, this is of little importance, for in the time of Viracocha, Pachacuti's predecessor, the so-called empire was still restricted to the narrow Cuzco Valley, to a territory of a few thousand acres located between the altitudes of ten thousand and thirteen thousand feet and surrounded with restless, powerful, and dangerous neighbors. A detailed history of this territory would be of little interest.

Moreover, shortening the period of these princes' rule in no way diminishes its value. My intention is not to denigrate their achievement, but quite the contrary, since I began this discussion by stressing the attention the period deserves. It is equally useful, however, to place it in its true perspective, to see it as it really was, a feat as sudden and brilliant as lightning, comparable to the conquests of Alexander of Macedonia or the campaigns conducted by the sovereigns of Iran or predynastic Egypt.

In the Andes we face a situation very different from that which historians face in Mexico, where embryonic writing existed and where order has reigned since the end of the Conquest. In Peru, a civil war lasting thirty years followed the taking of Cuzco by the Spaniards. By the time peace had been reestablished and the chroniclers were able to start working, nothing much was left of the former society.

Now let us see what can be learned from popular tradition regarding the last pre-Columbian century, that part of tradition that historians accept as valid.

It seems that it was only with Pachacuti that the dynasty was able to extend its territory sufficiently and to have at its disposal the necessary men and resources to dream of becoming a nation.

Who were the Incas, where had they come from, and how did these petty chieftains of a few hundred groups of families succeed in assuming leadership over neighbors who were apparently better equipped than they to create Andean kingdoms? There are no answers to these questions, and we will probably never know for sure. Even the exact meaning of the term *Inca* is unknown. Was it the name of a tribe, or only the name of a leading family?

To use the term *Inca* to describe populations or a race is absurd. The word should be reserved to describe the members of the Cuzco dynasty of princes, what belonged directly to the dynasty, or, finally, the system these princes created. Some clans were "Incanized," but they were never composed of Incas. Given the short duration of this period, it is better to speak of an attempt to establish, organize, and consolidate an imperial system, rather than speak of an Inca empire. I leave that work to the faithful partisans of the old Peruvian school, that of Luis Valcarcel, a now-retired teacher I hold in the highest esteem. For Valcarcel's school, all of pre-Columbian history is summed up in the history of the Incas and their empire, whose splendors compensate for the less-brilliant aspects of prehistoric times. Let me recall that the imperial expansion lasted one hundred years, whereas Andean history began more than ten thousand years ago. The restricted position that, for psychological reasons, is held whenever Andean history is dealt with has hindered its progress. This is normal; every great people has looked for poets to sing its mythology.

It is equally fitting to forget the notion of an Inca empire that sought to administer its territory for the good of the conquered populations. The notion of a welfare state, formulated by Louis Baudin, does not seem to me to correspond to reality. One hardly sees how petty chiefs of bands engaged in a savage struggle, first to defend their domain, then to enlarge it, would have had time to think of the well-being of the people under their jurisdiction. Then, psychologically speaking, one feels a false note—the welfare state is a political concept that hardly agrees with what we know of the thought and institutions of the Andean peoples.

And finally, how long did the empire last? Within seventy years, a territory that was four times as large as that of the Gauls was conquered, lost again, and finally recaptured by Europeans. If the Inca devoted time to the administration of subjugated provinces, as tradition would have us believe, it must have been above all in order to ensure for himself, his relatives, and dependents the resources they needed, resources they could obtain only from territories in which social life was well organized.

I am in no way depreciating the Incas' achievements by seeing events from this point of view. On the contrary, the fact of their having risen above their neighbors, their having organized conquered territories instead of being content with the customary looting operations, indicates that these princes had a political maturity unusual among pre-Columbian tribal chieftains.

However, let us not fall into an excess of sentimentality. Alfred Metraux reminds us that Pachacuti had to drive out all the inhabitants within a radius of five leagues around the Cuzco Valley in order to distribute lands to members of his family. This is how the dynasty began. Subsequently, each territorial expansion corresponded to the expulsion of populations that had become rebellious. The big royal domains were bestowed personally upon the Incas "for the service of the mummies of their ancestors." The great herds of the puna, hunting rights— everything—belonged to them. In order to exploit the royal domains and pay the costs of war, kings subjected their vanquished populations to payment of tribute.

If the Spaniards had not come out the victors in the battles of conquest, vast domains—baronies—would have been created. Feudal bonds would have developed between protectors and dependents, and the latter would have been enslaved.

Metraux also compared the Inca empire to the kingdom of Dahomey, with which he found numerous points of similarity. Both were preliterate, had a bureaucratic administration, levied taxes, sent circuit judges, generals, and inspectors out into the provinces, and so on.

If the Andes had not undergone the horrors of the Spanish Conquest, no one would have boasted of its being a welfare state or of aid to the aged and sick and the Pax Incaica. Mutual aid is an innate practice among Andeans. One sees it every day in humble families, where at times some people work their whole lives for other members of the community.

In reality, the Incas were absolute despots. They were tolerant only of the social and political order of the conquered peoples, and this much only so as to be able to exercise the emperor's will through the local chiefs. More than gold, the Inca needed workers in order to feed the people of his house, his administrators, generals, and armies. The prince took two-thirds of each harvest: a third for himself and a third for the sun, to serve the divinity. The producer kept only a third, but he did not pay any taxes. By way of example, let me cite the case of the rich coastal province of Chincha where, if we believe the chroniclers, each group of a thousand houses had to deliver sixteen bushels of grain per harvest. Heinrich Cunow analyzed the situation well in saying that "the Inca empire could not have been socialist, since its economic and social structure derived only from that of the 'Ayllu,' small peasant communities composed of endogamous lineages, each of which possessed a common soil."

Let us now return to the facts historians consider reasonably admissible regarding the formation of the empire.

Between A.D. 1463 and 1471, Topa Inca, Pachacuti's son, reached northward to conquer the central Andes and Mantaro Valley as far as Lake Junín. Next to the modern city of Tarma one finds the Inca site of Tarmatambo, superimposed on a vast agglomeration built by the earlier inhabitants of the country. It is strange that in connection with this conquest no one has mentioned the big complex called Huari, a third of the way from the town of Huari to Cuzco. It is likely that the Tiahuanacos, to whom this city is attributed, had long since disappeared.

In the south, Topa advanced as far as the northern shores of Lake Titicaca, whose other shores still remained under the control of other chiefdoms, Mojos or Collaos.

Finally, Pachacuti seems to have been the Inca who seized possession of the upper Urubamba Valley and extended his territory as far as Machu Picchu, at the very edge of the forest, or at the very least as far as Ollantaytambo, at the edge of the flat middle Urubamba Valley, which was rich in cultivated lands. This central part, with its milder climate and extremely fertile lands located between the altitudes of seventy-five hundred and ten thousand feet, must have played a vital part in supplying Cuzco, which was surrounded by high, poor land. (Cuzco is 10,890 feet above sea level. To reach it, one must cross mountains that are 11,880 feet above sea level.) One can easily see how the conquest and development of this region permitted provisioning the armies that then conquered other territories.

However, all this did not occur without trouble. Chroniclers tell us that in the face of the danger represented by the power of Collao (the territory located southwest of the narrow Cuzco Valley, from the shores of Titicaca to Arequipa), the Incas had to support the Lupacas in their struggle against the Chancas before Pachacuti could return to an expansionist policy. Only after absorbing the heart of the central Andes did Pachacuti, aided by his son Topa Yupanqui, attack the Far North and build fortresses as far as Ecuador—in Ingapirca, for example, near the Hispanic city of Cuenca, and what was later to become Quito. During these campaigns the Inca led raids on the rich Ecuadorian coasts of Manabí, Manta, and perhaps even Esmeraldas. Tradition has it that he even navigated the Pacific and visited La Plata Island.

In the south, Pachacuti and Topa Yupanqui had to wage difficult campaigns against the Collaos, campaigns that could explain the destruction of the big settlement of Hatuncolla and the "necropolis" of Sillustani, on the southwest shore of the lake. I recommend a visit also to Tanka Tankani, which is surrounded by cyclopean walls. This notable complex is west of the lake, in the puna on the track leading to the coast by way of Tacna.

Collao, the Collasuyo of the Incas, must have been one of the most densely populated regions of the Andes. Today this territory is poverty-stricken, though it is still densely occupied by some two million inhabitants. At present, peasants exploit it by practicing only a dry subsistence agriculture in soils that are exhausted and washed away by rains. Puno, at the edge of Lake Titicaca, receives only twenty-four inches of poorly distributed rain annually and suffers the southern hemisphere's winter frosts from May to October. (One should remember that the winter months in the United States correspond to summer in this area and that the dry winter season in the Andes contrasts with the humid coastal winter.)

All things considered, Collao must formerly have had a great deal of economic power by the standards of the time. One still sees there vast systems of farming terraces, traces of irrigated fields, gardens bordering Lake Titicaca—in brief, a multitude of works indicating that the pre-Columbians practiced a technologically advanced agriculture there. By plowing in the direction of the slope, today's peasants are accelerating the soil erosion. In addition, the total deforestation of the upper Andes prevents a regeneration of humus and contributes further to erosion. The Collao landscape must have looked very different to the fourteenth-century princes of Cuzco from the way it looks today. These rulers must have known a territory still covered with trees, lands capable of yielding good crops, and a puna abounding with camelids.

The conquest of Collao also opened the way to the eastern slopes of the Andes and hot Bolivia, where the Inca outposts succeeded those of the Tiahuanacos and where the forest began.

In order to be persuaded that Collao must have been an important economic addition to the empire, one need only walk about in the ruins of the enormous complex of buildings and silos that have survived next to a high building called the Temple of Viracocha at Rach-tché, next to San Pedro in the bottom of the narrow valley facing the Raya Pass. At Rach-tché there are still about two hundred stone silos, each capable of containing several tons of grain. The whole complex, now partially destroyed, must formerly have stored enough crops to feed several thousand people for a year. Moreover, the site is surrounded by a vast cluster of stone houses that are now in ruins. The so-called Temple of Viracocha, a three-story building, could have served as a storehouse for precious products such as metals, salts, coca, dyes, and other media of exchange. By saying so-called I do not mean, of course, that the Incas did not build temples, but rather that the high, rectangular edifice at Rach-tché could have been intended for other, more secular, purposes.

Once the Collaos weakened, there was nothing to stop Topa Yupanqui from exacting tribute from all the populations on the two slopes of the dry southern Andes, in the Argentine cordillera, on the Peruvian coast, and in the Atacama Desert. He even subdued the Diaguites of Chile. It is said that, discouraged by the forests and rains, he did not push farther but established his borders at the Maule River, around the thirty-fifth parallel, at the edge of the Araucanians' territory.

My studies show that once the conquest of what was to be the heart of the empire was completed, the princes of Cuzco must have possessed a territory of some 6,100,000 acres, of which about one-tenth was available for farming and herding. Here are the figures:

Territory or Zone	Total Area (in acres)	Area Usable for Farming or Herding (in acres)
Cuzco Valley	571,250	180,000
Upper Urumbamba Valley (as far as Machu Picchu)	181,250	87,500
La Convención Valley and its approaches	441,250	112,500
Apurimac	145,000	17,500
Vilcanota Valley, from Rumicolca to the Raya Pass	455,000	196,250
Rocky zones, glaciers	4,306,250	0
	6,100,000	593,750

Huayna Capac, who succeeded Topa in about 1493, extended the northern frontier of the empire so it now stretched along the Ancasmayo River, where the first Colombian tribe, the Pastos, lived. Huayna Capac is also thought to have liberated Cajamarca from the danger represented by the Chachapoyas of the lower Marañón. The highlands Andeans had unpleasant memories of the forest tribes, and Inca tradition mentions the highlanders' fear of new incursions by forest tribes. Probably the tribes of the hot lands, like those from the Mojo, had already gotten into the habit of sending looting expeditions against the societies of the cold Andes.

One can still see the ruins of strongholds built by the Incas along the *limes*, the border separating the upper Andean society from the forest societies of the Amazonas. I visited a few of them. They are found on the other side of the eastern cordillera and behind the glacial Veronica Massif; that is to say, east of Machu Picchu.

Quillabamba, in the lower Urubamba Valley, seems, on the other hand, to have been only a market, a trading place where people from lowlands and highlands came to barter their products.

Access to the Bolivian hot lands was likewise guarded by analogous buildings, *tambos* that were simultaneously used as storehouses and fortresses.

Let me add here a detail that, though not historical, is interesting. According to tradition, the Incas seized the Chimu kingdom in the north, upon the Chimus' return from an expedition to Ecuador, and obliged the princes of Chan Chan to become their vassals. The fortress of Paramonga, which defended this kingdom to the south, would thus have been taken without a fight.

The empire was, then, practically formed in 1493, extending over thirty-seven degrees of latitude. The few additions made by Huayna Capac during his reign (1493-1527) produced but few changes. Thus, the system existed in its complete form for only forty years or so, this period being that which Huayna Capac, traditionally considered to have been an excellent ruler, devoted entirely to the administrative and social organization of the conquered territories.

Most unfortunately, Huayna died in 1527, when Pizarro was already looking for Peru. If he had had to confront a respected Inca dominating the whole empire, would the conqueror have triumphed? Moreover, the Europeans may have been indirectly responsible for the prince's death, which resulted from an epidemic illness believed by classical authors to have been either smallpox or malaria.

When smallpox was brought to the West Indies in 1519, it completely destroyed the native population. From there it must have gone to the continent, and then from tribe to tribe to Colombia and Peru, for this disease is transmitted by direct contact between persons instead of being carried by a parasite. Smallpox could also have penetrated by other routes. In 1521 the Portuguese began building strongholds in Brazil and trying, as rivals of Cabot and the French, to reach the empire of gold from the east, across the Chaco. The Guaranis organized these westward expeditions, used as they already were to pillaging the rich Incanized slopes of the eastern Andes. When the Spaniard Martinez de Irala, aided by the Guaranis, finally succeeded in reaching the upper Andes in 1548. it was too late; Peru and Bolivia were already in the process of Hispanicization.

Huayna's death marks the beginning of the empire's collapse. He left two of his eleven children in charge of the territory: Huascar held Cuzco, and Atahualpa was in Quito, with the best troops and generals.

How many men did the Inca command? Hemming mentions armies of thirty-five to fifty thousand men under the command of a single general. These figures seem quite exaggerated if checked against the logistic possibilities of the time. How would they have fed such an army—by laying a heavy burden of tribute on the inhabitants? The need to collect food, and sometimes to wait for harvests, may explain the slowness with which armies moved.

After Huayna's death, a fierce civil war resulted that lasted five years and ended only with the assassination of Huascar in 1532 by Atahualpa's generals, just as the Spaniards were meeting Atahualpa, the surviving Inca, in Cajamarca.

(Pizarro indirectly avenged Huascar by assassinating first Quisquis, then Chal-cuchima, the two generals in question.) Pizarro thus found himself facing a single Inca, but also an empire that was divided into two factions, a territory where hatred and discord prevailed. The subject tribes were revolting against the Inca system, Huascar's faction was seeking vengeance, provisioning was disorderly, and there were famines. Such an environment permitted the Spaniard to exercise his talents as a diplomat and apply what he had learned from Machiavelli, his contemporary.

To start with, Pizarro gave himself over to an act of extraordinary audacity. Atahualpa, who had been aware of the arrival of white men but had taken no action to have them suppressed, was seized without warning and executed. After that, Pizarro rushed to conquer Cuzco, the real capital, where the treasures were accumulated. These "treasures" do not seem to have had greater commercial value for the Andeans than any other products they used as media of exchange. The Incas needed feathers for their headdresses, wool for their cloaks, dyes, Andean and Amazonian drugs, coca, and so on, but most especially corn to feed their people, which they needed as much as or more than gold.

In Cuzco, the conqueror placed a puppet Inca on the throne—one of Ata-hualpa's younger brothers, Tupac Hualpa—but he did not last long. That same year, the Spaniards had to crown his brother Manco, who was murdered in 1544.

The period that followed (aside from the dramatic siege of Cuzco, to which I shall return) could have been one of pacification and acculturation. Once the two distinguished Inca generals had been put to death, native resistance was very much weakened, and Spanish reinforcements were arriving continually.

But instead the opposite occurred, during the period from 1533 (the year of Atahualpa's execution) to 1572, when Tupac Amaru was executed. (Tupac Amaru should not be confused with the man of the same name, a descendant of his daughter, who was executed in Cuzco in 1781, after leading the last Indian revolt in colonial Peru.) This represents the end of resistance to the Conquest. These years witness only a succession of bloody episodes during which the prince-ly dynasty was decimated while the conquerors cut each other's throats.

The young Cuyuchi, another son of Huayna Capac, had died of an illness as early as 1525. Tupac Hualpa died in 1533, the same year he was crowned, perhaps poisoned by the faction of the conqueror, Almagro. Of Manco's three sons, Sayri Tupac was never crowned, and died of illness in 1560. Manco's half-brother, Titu Cusi, was crowned, but died by 1571. He was succeeded by the last son, Tupac Amaru, who took refuge in the Cordillera Vilcabamba, was finally captured, and was executed in 1572. Only Huayna Capac's last brother, Paullu, died a natural death, in 1549, after having served for some time as a puppet Inca in the hands of the Europeans. All five of Atahualpa's daughters having married high-ranking Spaniards, the dynasty was eliminated. The last male members of the family—Carlos, Quispel Titu, Alonso Atahualpa, and Melchor—all disap-peared between 1572 and 1610.

But things went hardly any better for the conquerors. Francisco Pizarro, the leader of the expedition, was assassinated by his own men in Lima in 1541. His brother Hernando, the governor of Cuzco, was imprisoned and died in Spain. His brother Jean had been killed in 1536 in the assault on the Sacsahuaman fortress during the siege of Cuzco. His other brother, Gonzalo, the governor of Peru, was executed in 1548 by the Spanish king's representative, Pedro de la Gasca.

Without going into details let me simply add that all the members of Pizarro's expedition met their ends in similar fashion, either having their heads cut off by the king's executioner, or dying in the course of brawls, or falling from the resistance of the Mapuches or other Andean natives. The first bishop of Cuzco, Vincente de Valverde, was eaten by the inhabitants of Puná Island while he was trying to flee to Spain. Undoubtedly, the natives allowed themselves this pleasure in order to acquire the virtues of this holy man by gnawing his bones, much more than to have a good meal.

Before passing judgment on these tragic events, let us remember how sixteenth-century Europe was torn by military campaigns and religious wars. The conquest of the Indies took place in a century of fanaticism and cruelty, and it must be placed in its true perspective.

Now let me try to isolate the positive aspects of the work of the Cuzco princes who reigned between 1438 and 1533. In the field of political, administrative, and social organization, the little we know has been said and repeated by W. H. Prescott, Luis E. Valcarcel, Louis Baudin, Alfred Metraux, and many others. It is not my concern here to summarize these scholarly works. I refer readers to them, reminding them to be cautious and to remember that some information in them is either fictitious or is based on traditions that are not historical.

It is very difficult to distinguish what was organized and imposed by the Incas from what already existed when they made their conquests. For example, we know that the poor, less-sophisticated populations in the Atacama Desert of Chile had made trails through their territory so as to be able to cross it easily, for these people traded a great deal. The Incas must certainly have improved the system of communicating routes in the Andes, but the roads were already in existence before they came to power. I think the same was true of bridges.

On the other hand, the network of fortresses and storehouses along the whole length of the empire seems positively Inca. One still sees ruins of several of these complexes at points as far from the center of the empire as Santa Cruz in Bolivia and Ingapirca near Cuenca in Ecuador, not to mention the ones that have survived on the Peruvian coast.

In order to obtain crops to feed big armies, it was obviously necessary to organize the farmers' labor. When farmers did not submit to the desires of Cuzco administrators, populations were displaced and unruly groups settled among peaceful ones.

On the other hand, there was incredible military weakness. It is astonishing that even when they had overcome their terror of the Spanish cavalry's charging with swords, the Andean troops were practically never able to kill more than a few dozen invaders, even in the bloodiest battles. And it is almost incomprehensible that twenty thousand warriors did in fact surround Pizarro and his one hundred fifty men in Cajamarca, and then an army of thirty thousand men besieged him in Cuzco for three months. Clearly, if they had driven home just one attack without breaking off the fight, they could have annihilated the invaders. Moreover, the Andeans could easily have crushed the little troop of Spaniards as it filed along the bottoms of narrow canyons. Nothing of the kind ever succeeded, however, and such fights usually remained skirmishes. As a result, famines, privations, and especially internal quarrels claimed more Spanish victims than wars did.

The disproportion between the forces facing each other was such that one starts to imagine a sort of psychological conflict, almost a case of collective masochism, to explain the breakdown of the Andeans. They felt they were in an inferior position. Perhaps their fear of incidents resulting from magic was also involved —did they feel a spell had been cast?

As Jacques Soustelle says with regard to the Mexicans, the American peoples did not understand that they faced a war of conquest and extermination and that it was necessary to eradicate the evil at its very outset. Sometimes a parallel is drawn between the Conquest of the Americas and the Gauls' struggles against the Romans. True, there were certain similarities; anarchy, individualism, unorganized resistance, hesitation, and, above all, lack of a coordinated plan. But Caesar had legions, whereas Pizarro led his campaign with 150 men.

When one realizes how hard it is to understand even historical events with written testimonies that have survived, one becomes more and more cautious about everything prehistorical, everything relating to the existence of the four Incanized generations, only the last of which was confronted with the Spaniards. As always when we enter the field of prehistory, only archaeology can inform us with some reliability and enable us to confirm or invalidate specific statements made by the chroniclers. Archaeology, for example, permits us to confirm the Inca presence in this or that region.

Pottery is our most valuable guide in this respect, for it survives the elements and often bears a decoration done in a style characteristic of a period or sometimes even a phase in the life of most Andean societies. Thus, in sites where layers of debris have survived undisturbed, we can date the arrival of Inca elements and evaluate the duration of their presence by determining the local society with which the pieces having Cuzco decorations are mixed. All this is difficult, of course, because the period in question lasted only a short time, and what are fifty or even one hundred years in prehistory?

Although Inca pottery was well made, it hardly expressed artistic talent. Vases were decorated with geometric figures or naturalistic scenes representing ferns, for example (plants with magical and medicinal powers), or ornamented with animal heads modeled in clay. Checkerboard patterns played a big role here, as did grids, but without stylized motifs.

This pottery was very fine in texture and quite glossy. It was fired until it turned pink, and before firing was painted with colors similar to those the Nazcas and Tiahuanacos had used. The usual dyes in Peru were white, gray, beige, black, dark red, yellowish red, yellow ocher, and maroon. Apparently the Incas had access to the same veins of raw materials as did their ancestors. Typical shapes were the aryballos, dishes with handles, vessels with stands, and cooking dishes with handles shaped like animal heads. By an odd coincidence, one can see aryballoses, Inca-style jars with black-on-cream decorations and lines forming grids, at the Musée de l'Homme in Paris. These aryballoses were made by the North African Berbers. Do they indicate a multilineal evolution?

In all this, Inca pottery differed from the pottery previously made in Peru. And the differences are so typical that when nothing else has survived, archaeologists use Inca pottery to prove the passage of the Incas through this or that part of the Andes. Here archaeology confirms tradition. Fragments with decorations typical of Cuzco have been found from the Cauca Valley in Colombia to the Maule River in Chile and even in the Argentine Andes.

Certain pieces of pottery found in the Inca-occupied territories are so perfect that they appear to have been made in Cuzco itself. They were apparently carried in the baggage of the conquerors. One also finds pottery pieces of lesser quality almost everywhere that were probably made by local potters who copied the decorations as well as shapes of the original models, with greater or lesser skill. The first pottery category is what Peruvians call "imperial Inca," in contrast to the second type, provincial Inca, which was produced by the subject peoples once the Cuzco style had been adopted in the conquered territories.

Even in the narrow Cuzco Valley, in the heart of the empire, when one finds a shard in a heap of debris, the Inca pottery appears either on virgin soil or above fragments of a different style—it does not have antecedents. The question that always recurs regarding such a find in the Andes is then asked: Where did the Incas come from? Where did their pottery decoration develop? One then thinks of the migration of a group (from the hot lands, for example) who became established in the Cuzco Valley and made local artisans paint and weave the decorative themes that had traditionally ornamented the cookware and clothing the group had used prior to its migration.

No pottery earlier than that of the Incas has been found, either in Machu Picchu, in Ollantaytambo, or in Chinchero near Cuzco, one of the most imposing complexes built by the princes of Cuzco. All these sites seem likely to have been built shortly before the Spanish invasion. At Chinchero, moreover, the upper layers of debris contain a mixture of imperial and European pottery.

In other places, such as the outskirts of Cuzco, for example, contact with a different period is established from lower levels of debris. Under the layers of Inca pottery one finds layers containing the so-called Killki pottery. Desirous of prolonging the duration of the Inca period, some specialists in Peruvian studies have called this substratum "early Inca." However, I do not see what connection Killki can possibly have with Inca themes.

The *keros,* or hardwood flaring vessels with flat bottoms and polychrome decorations, are supposedly associated with Inca times. There are astonishing collections of them, and it is really regrettable that almost nothing has been published regarding these archaeological treasures. The shape of the keros is clearly Tiahuanacoid, however, and the many-colored decorations ornamenting them indicate that many of them, if not all, belong to the period of protohistorical transition. Flowers, European costumes, or African faces are depicted on them. I do not think these keros constitute an element very typical of the final pre-Columbian period.

What *is* very typical of this period is Inca architecture. Like the pottery, it rises from obscurity and appears in the Cuzco Valley fully realized, without there being any known antecedents on the site.

This architecture is easily recognizable. On the ground floor, the walls are made of slightly slanting stone blocks, of which the visible sides have been flaked off to form concave surfaces. Niches or doorways are trapezoidal in shape. Some of these blocks were squared off so perfectly that they could be assembled without mortar—by simply adjusting them, the flanges on the sides of one block fitted exactly into slots prepared on the sides of the next block. Thus, in extreme cases we can observe blocks with as many as fourteen sides. These blocks were always big and were sometimes very heavy, occasionally weighing up to several tons.

One or two additional stories usually had been added above the ground floor. According to the climate and the materials available nearby, these levels were constructed either with pebbles brought over from a river and cemented by crude clay, or with bricks of unfired clay. The roof was high and sloped at a more-than-forty-five-degree angle. (I do not know of any two-sided roofs in Peru prior to the influence of Cuzco.) It was supported by hardwood beams attached to stone tenons fixed in the walls. Most of the roofs themselves have not survived, but some of the beams are still visible in Ollantaytambo. The chroniclers drew and

A colonial house built on top of an Inca palace made of cut-stone blocks. Central Andes.

described the roofs as being covered with straw, like the roofs of houses that are still constructed today by natives in extremely varied Andean regions. In Colombia, for example, one recognizes the natives' houses because of the smoke going out through the thatched roof, whereas the European-style houses have chimneys.

In most cases, only the ground floors of these buildings have survived. Uninformed people consequently see these Inca buildings as one-story constructions, but if this were so, they would have lacked architectural proportion, being too low relative to their length. This is clearly a mistake. The height and correct proportions of big Inca buildings may still be appreciated in Rach-tché, the storehouse city with two hundred stone silos where a building thirty feet high has survived, and in Ollantaytambo, where houses with their original roof beams have remained intact. Ruins of Inca buildings constructed on the model of a rectangular house with a two-sided roof may also be seen on the Peruvian coast and at several points in the inter-Andean valleys.

The construction technique of using enormous polyhedral blocks that hold together without mortar appears abruptly in the Andes during the fifteenth century, and I do not know any local antecedents for it. Only far away in Polynesia can one observe a comparable architecture, notably in the Marquesas Islands. The Tiahuanacos also had cut stone blocks (and in a much more refined way), but not in polyhedral units. Unlike the Incas, they built by binding together elongated rectangular blocks with metal spikes and mortar. Moreover, the Incas seem to have reused blocks after reclaiming them from Tiahuanacoid temples. Or had they started to copy Tiahuanaco's techniques? In the Temple of the Sun, the Coricancha temple of Cuzco, one may note elements that appear to be heterogeneous. Tiahuanacoid blocks seem to have been incorporated into the building.

The ground floors and outer walls of the Inca palaces that have survived in Cuzco are always covered with beautifully fitted granite blocks. The temple of Coricancha even includes a hemispherical wall, a kind of apse. Terraces with trapezoidal niches and doorways have survived in the palace of Colcampata.

All the carefully built structures that have survived in the heart of the empire show us a well-established, homogeneous architectural style. This style was achieved probably by teams that had come out of a school open to foremen and craftsmen.

Unfortunately, many Inca buildings have been destroyed, either so the materials could be reused or because they symbolized a dangerous paganism. Any description of what remains deserves an entire book. In going to Cuzco and Machu Picchu, the reader will feel the full force of first encountering an Inca architectural complex. Europeans experienced something similar in the sixteenth century. Upon entering Cuzco, the first conquerors described it as a very beautiful city, the finest they had seen in the Andes, and as pretty and well-constructed as many Spanish towns.

According to the chroniclers, Cuzco was a planned urban center with public monuments and inhabited by people of all classes, engaged in the most diverse occupations. In short, Cuzco was a real city. The chroniclers add that they had counted three or four thousand houses in the city itself, plus nineteen to twenty thousand in the suburbs. These figures, which would indicate a population of more than one hundred thousand, seem exaggerated. They indicate, however, that Cuzco was much larger than Quito or other complexes such as Huanuco Viajo. Cuzco may even have been larger than the big coastal cities.

Further study is needed here. The plan showing the ruins of Cuzco, as I have been able to establish it, is very rudimentary, unfortunately, because of the severe destruction the site has suffered since its Hispanicization and the siege of 1535. (My maps of Cuzco and the Inca domain, made for the Anthropological Institute of the National Agrarian University of Peru, were finally incorporated, for lack of anything better, into the general atlas published in 1969 by the Peruvian government and edited by Carlos Peñaherrera.)

This plan, however, gives a glimpse of the cluster as a complex of palaces, princely residences, and villas in the Roman sense, surrounded by temples, storehouses, and everything that could constitute a cultural complex that was then entering the Copper Age but was still preliterate, like the complexes of predynastic Egypt. (It has been said that Andean urban planning in the sixteenth century was superior to that of Renaissance Europe. It seems to me that we should map out Andean settlements more thoroughly before indulging in comparisons.) It is difficult to recognize here the ruins of a city like Pachacamac or of Cajamarquilla on the coast, which were compact cities with houses forming unitary blocks of dwellings.

A few years ago, vast, thick expanses of pre-Columbian detritus still existed around areas where palaces had survived, and specialists in Peruvian studies explained to me that the dwellings of common people had formerly existed there. Today, very unfortunately, only traces remain of what may have been suburbs. These traces do not contain debris from houses of wood, which was a rare material in the upper Andes, but rather from buildings with low walls of stones and pebbles, thirty-nine inches to seventy-one inches high, like the ones that may be seen everywhere in the Andes, with walls topped with cone-shaped thatched roofs.

Investigations in the capital's suburbs have revealed, under the present surface of the soil, layers that contain a smoky black pottery called Marcavalle (*Marca* means agglomeration in Quechua). Marcavalle, however, has yielded radiocarbon dates that place these pieces well before the Christian era. Marcavalle has nothing to do with Inca Cuzco; instead, these layers show that the valley was inhabited at several different times and perhaps even continuously since bands of farmers first entered the upper Andes, which they seem to have done some thirty-five hundred years ago. To the north of the city, on the Santa Ana slope, the ruins of the little village of Chanapata could still be seen a few years ago. I obtained a radiocarbon date of 1300 B.C. for this village.

The topographical position of Cuzco adds to the charm of the city. One reaches it by the Anta Plain, and only after cresting a circle of hills, at an altitude of about 11,900 feet, does one catch sight of the city spread out, a thousand feet below, in a small valley watered by the Huatanay River. The whole city is very pleasant, but today it is clearly more Spanish than Andean.

In order to have a comprehensive view of an unchanged Inca complex that has been sheltered from European influences, one must go to Machu Picchu. It is located in the hot forest at an altitude of sixty-six hundred feet. The cluster of buildings overhangs the valley of the Urubamba, one of the Amazon's tributaries. It is quite worthwhile taking a trip to Machu Picchu. Many comparable sites have survived in the Andes, but here the forest has been removed and restorations have been made fairly successfully. Here the traveler may have the distinct impression of entering a place that was abandoned recently. As in Paestum or Venice, walking around in Machu Picchu is rather like physically entering the past.

Machu Picchu includes some beautiful buildings of cut stone with perfectly inserted blocks, some of which were probably used as temples. There are several hundred buildings that are either dwellings or storehouses. The second stories of these buildings were made of cobblestones from the river, cemented with unfired clay. The buildings were surrounded by a beautiful complex of terraces that were undoubtedly intended for farming, since they were watered and drained by a system of fountains and canals that brought water from the piedmonts of the high Cordillera Vilcabamba and the Salkantay Glacier. The surface of these terraces, which does not amount to more than seven and a half acres, was too small to feed a community the size of Machu Picchu. Therefore, I think that provisions and food must have been brought from the surrounding area and stored in granaries. The terraces permitted either additional cultivation or specialized hot-land farming like coca growing. Paved roads led out of the site in different directions. The one leading toward the southwest could be blocked by two gates. For lack of hinges, boards were tied across the gateway. The stone tenons around which ropes were wound can still be seen. By this road, which went through the puna, one could reach Cuzco in three days.

Today one reaches Machu Picchu by a train up the Urubamba Valley. From the station one takes a bus up a winding road to the hotel and, alas, to the first visible building, the sanitary facilities intended for tourists. It would have been better to go on using the former Inca route, which passed through the puna, because by going through Chinchero and Maray, sites of the greatest interest, one gets a comprehensive view of the Salkantay Glacier. One can reach Machu Picchu in three or four days, and this is a magnificent hike.

Another road winds around the mountain to the northwest. It was cut out of the rock and in places is so narrow that passage is almost impossible. The tourist finds himself clinging to the wall on a path one foot wide, with a drop of several hundred yards in front. A reckless tourist recently met his end there. He was too adventurous and fell down, probably while trying to turn back.

Machu Picchu, which has been known for quite a while, was found and restored to admirers of the Incas by Hiram Bingham in the early twentieth century. He saw it as the refuge of the last princes of Cuzco, but more-recent investigations contradict this hypothesis. The last Inca, Tupac Amaru, was captured in 1572 not at Machu Picchu, but in the Vilcabamba massif nearly sixty miles northwest, at the source of the Coribeni, a tributary of the Urubamba.

Several other complexes of storehouses, houses, and terraces have survived around the Machu Picchu agglomeration, some above and some below the main grouping of buildings. These complexes must have been part of a single system. Today they are little by little being swallowed up by the forest, which the North American scientific expedition that uncovered the foundations took great pains to clear away. The best-known complexes are Llacta Pata, Intipata, Phuyu Putu Marca, and Runca Raccay. After visiting Machu Picchu, the tourist need not make the effort to visit them, unless he wants to get lost in the forest.

But on the other hand, tourists able to spend a few weeks visiting the central Andes will be interested in traveling to Cuzco by land. They should choose the most instructive itinerary, the one through the coastal deserts and over Nazca. Eighteen miles from Lima, the traveler can visit the big city of Pachacamac, dominated by the temple dedicated by the Incas to the sun. When I saw this temple twenty years ago, naturalistic designs in red, ocher, black, and yellow were painted on it, but by now these have disappeared from wind erosion. After leaving Pachacamac, the tourist should stop next in the Pisco Valley to admire the ruins of the Inca palace of Tambo Colorado. Here, for lack either of stones or time, coastal artisans copied in unfired bricks the blind trapezoidal niches and windows typical of the upper Andes. The whole complex is very imposing, and was painted in yellow and red.

Farther up in the Pisco Valley, and hard to get to, the temple of Huaytara has survived. It is one of the rare cut-stone buildings that has been found outside the upper Andes.

I have found only two of these buildings on the coast, the Huaytara one and another in Cajur in the Casma Valley. Huaytara is of major interest, moreover, on account of its trapezoidal rather than rectangular ground plan and its many triangular niches. Above Huaytara, located at the entrance to the puna and its pastures, the ruins of the large site of Incahuasi have survived.

Nazca has not retained any interesting ruins. The big ceremonial center of Cahuachi, on the Rio Grande, has not been restored, and what remains of it is buried in sand.

From Nazca one climbs up to the Galeras Pampa, now a camelid reserve, where vicuñas still abound. One reaches the puna by passing next to a fossil sand dune that reaches an altitude of sixty-six hundred feet. The road then threads around lakes and glaciers, then descends some thirteen thousand feet to cross the Apurímac River.

A visit to the marvelous site of Choquequirau, which overhangs the river, presents too many difficulties for the tourist who is only passing through. However, he could easily visit the Inca site of Saywite, where a big boulder rolled down by the waterside and some eight feet in diameter has survived. This stone is entirely carved with motifs of fountains and canals. It may have been simultaneously a *huaca*—a magical object—and an irrigation system model.

After this, one arrives at the Inca palace of Tarahuasi, whose ruins serve as the foundations of a pretty colonial villa. From there the road climbs over the hills before redescending into the valley of Cuzco.

Cuzco is worth a visit of several days, for many colonial monuments have survived earthquakes and the ravages of modernism. Here I shall speak only of Cuzco's Inca ruins. Overlooking the city from the northwest is the immense fortress of Sacsahuaman, surrounded by high defensive walls of granite monoliths. These stones fit into each other to form a perfect uncemented wall, and were cut in such a way as to throw the face of each block into relief like a well-set precious stone. From this fortress the Incas besieged the city in which Pizarro found himself, and the conqueror's brother died while attacking it.

In the Cuzco Valley one should visit Tipon, an agricultural complex including terraces, contiguous fountains, houses, and a palace.

Farther along, on the way to Lake Titicaca, one passes by the beautiful monolithic door called the Portada de Rumicola, which blocks the Raya Pass. By way of this gateway one enters the puna of Collao.

Not far from Cuzco one can also visit Tambo Machay, a little palace with elegant fountains. Nearby, one can see the remains of a fortress that defended the road going down to Urubamba.

In the vicinity of Cuzco, the traveler must not fail to visit Chinchero, where a complex of palaces, buildings, and terraces, with monolithic walls fitted together, is seen half buried under a colonial town. The main attraction of this town is a very charming seventeenth-century chapel with a porch ornamented by a mural painting representing a battle between Spaniards and natives. Sunday mass at Chinchero, which attracts all the humble farmers in the vicinity, will leave the tourist an unforgettable memory, wondering whether he is awake and not dreaming of a trip to Tibet.

Past Chinchero, one approaches the Salkantay Glacier and reaches Moray, where the visitor finds himself in one of the most astonishing complexes of the Inca period. In Moray, three cone-shaped depressions dug in the soil to a depth of 33 feet are surrounded by circular terraces forming tiers. The diameter of each cone varies from 335 to 500 feet. At the very bottom, one sees snakelike pre-Columbian furrows, whereas Spanish furrows (traced with the plow) were recti-linear. The same snakelike furrows could still be seen around Chan Chan on the northern Peruvian coast near Trujillo a few years ago. There, while the slow airplanes of the period were landing, one could realize at a glance, in the oblique light of late afternoon, the immensity of the fields formerly cultivated by the Chimus.

It is unknown what purpose the cone-shaped terraces at Moray served. Like Saywite, they remain one of the mysteries of Inca agronomy. Of the hypotheses that have been formulated, I hold as plausible either that Moray was intended for the cultivation of precious plants from temperate lands, plants sheltered from the icy winds of the puna by sinking them into the ground, or the hypothesis of a testing center, a school of agronomy. Of course, those who find a religious significance in everything say that the complex had a sacred character.

From Moray one can walk down to the middle Urubamba Valley, where one must visit Pisac and Ollantaytambo. Pisac is a big cluster of buildings overlooking the valley. It is strategically well placed in the piedmonts of the upper cordillera near the glaciers that supplied the city with water. This cluster resembles Machu Picchu but is interesting from other points of view, perhaps for having been more mixed with the everyday life of the Incas than was Machu Picchu, as a result of Pisac's key position in the richest valley of the empire. One must visit old Pisac (the higher one), which is purely Inca, and be content to close one's eyes while passing through lower Pisac at the Urumbamba bridge, which is modern and dismally touristy.

The city is surrounded by the tiered farming terraces called *andenes* by Peruvians. These were irrigated not by the torrential waters of the Urubamba, but by the waters of the Lares glaciers, which overlook the region.

Going down the Urubamba, one sees on both sides of the river farming terraces bordered by walls of big stone blocks. These complexes should be studied to find out how the terraces were irrigated. They were certainly not irrigated by the powerful Urubamba's flow well below them, for I have not seen a single lateral canal, dam, or water catchment. The Incas' farming techniques demand more detailed study.

In Yucay one may visit the touching ruins of the palace or, better, villa of the Inca Sayri Tupac. The poor man was crowned in 1557, but died of illness or poisoning three years later. His villa, built in the beginning of the Hispanic period, still follows the Inca plan in part, with its sloping walls and trapezoidal gateways. However, the workmanship necessary to cut granite blocks had been lost. The building was made of unfired bricks and several years ago was still surmounted by a coat of arms in the European style. The failure to preserve this precious evidence of the transitional period is one more crime to impute to our society.

A late pre-Columbian stone mace. From the central Andes and coastal areas of Peru.

A late pre-Columbian silver object.

Still lower in the valley, one finally reaches Ollantaytambo. Although the fortress of Sacsahuaman is imposing, it cannot compare to this Urubamba stronghold, which is a strange monument, of a grandeur to leave one speechless. It is a blend of religious and military architecture and is typical of a world so different from ours, where war was still a ritual act performed according to rules prescribed by an ancestral tradition that was obeyed out of fear of the gods and spirits.

Ollantaytambo was built in a steep gorge perpendicular to the river valley. At the very top, joined to the rocks, are barracks or storehouses—high buildings with two-sided roofs. Below, the Inca village, with rectangular houses surrounding a big square, still survived until a few years ago. A little palace had survived close by. Its ruins are called "the Inca's bath."

Between these two extremes, immense and majestic terraces rise above one another to a height of three hundred feet. One can imagine how terrified the Spaniards must have been to see thousands of warriors gathered on these tiers waiting for the enemy. Legend has it that they were unable to capture Ollantaytambo because the stairways were too steep for their horses to climb.

On a crest overlooking the terraces, below the granaries, the ruins of a seemingly unfinished building may be seen. Enormous carved monolithic slabs stood there as if to form the gates of a temple. Were the artisans who made these slabs working for the Incas, or for the Tiahuanacos?

Where did these slabs come from, and how were they brought here? They weigh over a hundred tons each. When asked, tour guides say they came from a

The monolithic wall at Ollantaytambo, in the Urubamba Valley of the central Andes.

quarry at the bottom of the valley. It is hard to imagine the upward transport of such heavy monolithic pieces. Other people think these carved slabs were stolen from Tiahuanaco and transported to Ollantaytambo by water. But pre-Columbians had not invented a hoisting mechanism, and apparently they did not even know the principle of leverage. Regarding the transport of heavy blocks, therefore, I imagine that the Incas, like the builders of Stonehenge, used the technique the Egyptians employed to build their big temples: earth embankments covered the walls as high as the top, and the slabs and lintels of the doorways were slid up the embankments. When the last heavy piece was in place, the earth was removed.

The incomplete state of this templelike building dates it. It seems that the princes of Cuzco were unable to have it finished, perhaps because of the civil war.

From Ollantaytambo one travels to Machu Picchu by train, for the road does not go much farther northward. It turns eastward here and, rounding the Veronica glaciers, heads toward the hot lands of the Amazonas.

I have described only one itinerary that tourists interested in culture and monuments may take in the Andes. The Cuzco itinerary is the best one for travelers without much time. The tourist who can afford to spend more time may extend his investigations to Lake Titicaca, bordered by so many beautiful baroque churches, and to the Inca temple of Copacabana on the Island of the Sun. From there it is one jump to the ruins of Tiahuanaco, located eleven miles from the lake.

In the north-central Andes, the Incas did not have time to build much. However, they left us Huanuco, an irreplaceable example of Cuzco's organization, where one may still see what could have been either the temple itself or its *cella* (inner sanctum), the administrative buildings encompassed by a wall, and all around, the city itself with irrigated fields beyond.

Still farther north, near Cuenca, Ecuador, is the fortress of Ingapirca, which is presently in the process of being restored. This stronghold constitutes the last visible bastion of imperial power, for even in Quito, nothing Inca seems to have survived.

Great builders, the Incas did not have the time or the desire to develop the arts of statuary and mural painting. Their artisans barely carved a few serpents and pumas in low relief on funerary monuments, palaces, and houses. They also sculpted some stone vessels and dishes.

In Machu Picchu one does not see a single sculpture in the round. Two felines adorn the lintel of a doorway at Huanuco, but they remind one of Marca Huamachuco, a neighboring settlement that was active at the time of the Tiahuanacos.

The fabrics of the period were very well made, but they lacked originality of decoration. The Incas were content with geometric themes and contrasting colors.

Most of the gold objects disappeared in the melting down of some five hundred tons of precious metals that the Spaniards sent to Madrid. The remaining statues are some anthropomorphic and zoomorphic ones, generally representing llamas.

The chroniclers tell us that the interior of the Coricancha, the Temple of the Sun in Cuzco, was covered with gold sheets nailed to the stone walls, and that the Incas were carried in litters decorated with gold. The ransom of Atahualpa, who thought he could save himself by giving Pizarro enough gold to fill one room of the palace, was comprised of gold vases, dishes, plates, jewels, pendants, and statues of gods.

One finds in the Andes, as in Egypt at the end of the Neolithic period, stone objects copied from metal models. The copper objects, maces, pins, and tools such as knives and chisels to be found in the Andes are thought to be of Inca origin. When they are found on the coast, their presence is explained as being the result of barter or the passing through of troops from Cuzco. Let us recall, however, the villages of Ayabaca and Vicus, near Piura, where metallurgy dates back at least two thousand years. I myself found a spear thrower with a copper hook in a twenty-two-hundred-year-old tomb in Paracas. As early as the fourteenth century, copper objects were buried with the potters of Chichacara in the Chilca Valley. In Rupac, in the upper Chancay Valley behind Lima, one can still visit a site with enormous, magnificent houses three stories high and covered with overhanging tiled roofs. These houses surround a square that is decorated all along one side by a building with thirteen trapezoidal gateways. I have not, however, been able to find a single shard with Cuzco-style decorations in the area.

The princes of Cuzco probably put to work artisans from all the Andean provinces. They mastered extremely diversified techniques that were already established to varying degrees in everyday life. In many instances, these techniques had been in use for a long time. Metallurgy, for example, was practiced at the village level from the extreme north of the continent to the Argentine cordillera.

Furthermore, we must not underestimate the influence of the forced population movements that the Incas imposed—the creation of settlements or *mitimae* —which were partially made up of recalcitrant or unruly groups that the Incas wanted to get rid of. In this way philologists explain the pockets of Aymara speech that they find outside the territory formerly inhabited by the speakers of this language.

Sometimes the settlers of the mitimae established certain Inca traits in the territory assigned to them, but without adopting the decorative themes typical of their masters. For instance, the settlers could obtain their pottery from artisans who were already established there rather than using pottery with Cuzco-style decorations.

When we cast an overall glance at the Incas' achievements, we may be struck by their success in the realm of material creations. It is a fact that the Cuzco princes imposed modern norms of settlement and built many well-planned architectural complexes that were not just princely villas. On the other hand, they apparently did not have the time, or perhaps did not want, to impose their architecture on the conquered populations. In this regard they remind me as well of the feudal barons in the high Middle Ages who had chateaus built for themselves, and of the Germanic invaders in the centuries following the fall of the Roman

Empire, for whom country villas and garrisons were built outside the Gallic Roman cities.

One can also compare the Incas' achievements with those of the Roman troops after the short-lived conquest of Great Britain. The Incas did not build Hadrian's Wall, but their settlements recall those of the Roman legions on the Scottish borders and the Thames, their complexes of granaries, palace strongholds, and garrisons whose soldiers were supposed to work the land between skirmishes.

The Incas certainly contributed to reorganizing provinces torn by internal struggles and by the establishment of local feudalities that followed the weakening of the royal power of such rulers as those of Chan Chan. Certainly the Incas also must have tried to feed starving populations. And since the empire and its armies could survive only if the provinces were prosperous and productive, these armies acted as peacemakers as well as conquerors.

In this sense, the Incas undoubtedly proved themselves to be statesmen. However, as I have said, it would be going too far to suggest that they had deliberate policies toward creating an Andean nation, a state dedicated to the well-being of the people under its administration.

The Incas remind me of the Capetians, who started building the royal house of France while establishing the power of their own family. Let us not forget that the concept of the state serving the people developed only much later. At first, the state was the prince and his barons, to whom the commonwealth belonged. The masses had to grow to adulthood before they dared cut off the head of the patriarchal king and govern as they pleased. Apparently, the fifteenth-century Andeans were still overage adolescents. With the father Inca gone, killed by invaders, they were left gasping and incapable of taking the actions that would have saved them. They still needed masters, and by the time they realized that the new masters were worse than the old ones, it was too late—the Inca society had been destroyed forever.

Bearing in mind that the Incas were preliterate princes hardly out of the Stone Age, I conclude that they made a great contribution to the history of mankind. They organized the exploitation of Andean natural resources, appointed administrative officers, improved farming techniques, and tried to keep peace with the help of professional armies. They showed a will not only to conquer but also to organize, to make the best use of annexed territories. And above all, they ruled and administered, and did not exterminate other societies. The Incas appear to me to have been model princes in terms of benevolence if we compare their campaigns to those of Assyrian princes. The Inca system also calls to mind the policies of Rome and its harsh but organizing law.

The degree of spiritual development of the last Incas is not very well known. I suspect that their religious progress may have corresponded to a sudden awareness both of the inadequacy of having their people practice an exclusively animistic religion and of the beneficial effect of establishing a pantheism in which (to our minds) the sun god would play the role of Zeus, the king of the gods.

A typical Inca stonework fountain. From the Cuzco area.

Perhaps the Chimu princes were also just about to create a nation, or even a new religion, around Chan Chan. These princes dominated only a few valleys, however, and they must already have suffered severe reverses when the European invaders came, for Pizarro does not even mention their capital, whose ruins prove that a big city existed there. Who knows; perhaps Chan Chan had already been raided by bands from the upper Andes even before being occupied by the Incas.

The Chimus left many cultural developments in the central Andes: administrative organization, communications by road, agriculture, long canals that made possible intensive and extensive farming, domestic well-being, and maybe also trade and navigation. It is possible that people in the fifteenth century led a much more civilized life in Chan Chan than in Cuzco.

It cannot be denied, however, that the Incas exerted an influence on much of the Andes and that they far surpassed the other South American caciques and petty kings in their abilities as builders and organizers. It was not without reason that the Incas felt superior, not so much to the highly developed peoples of the lower central Andes (like the Chinchas, with whom they joined forces) but to the tribes they subjugated: the Cañaris, Mantas, and Huancavelicas of Colombia and Ecuador, the Chachapoyas, Mojos, and Lucanas of the southern Andes, and the Diaguites, Atacamanians, and inhabitants of the Argentine sierras.

To conclude this section let me relate one reaction of my Peruvian assistant, a first-rate archaeologist. A native of Cuzco, this young man is very proud of the Incas, to whom he attributes a civilizing effect throughout the Andes. During an exploration of Ecuador and Colombia, this young man encountered some natives who had remained untouched by modern life. He was unable to hide his disdain. "They're barbarians," he said. "They don't even know Quechua."

THE OTHER ANDEAN SOCIETIES

THE ATLANTIC ANDES AND
NORTHERN HOT LANDS

We know practically nothing about what happened during the first millennia of the Holocene epoch in the northern cordillera, which runs along the Atlantic. The scholars Irving Rouse and José M. Cruxent have simply shown that the natives of the northernmost Andes, the wooded plateaus that extend from the highlands down toward the Caribbean Sea, had lived in a preagricultural stage since at least thirteen or fourteen thousand years ago. That was before the end of the last North American ice age, called the Valders glaciation period in the United States. Therefore, in the sites of Muaco, El Jobo, Manzanillo, and Rancho Peludo we are confronted with vestiges of tribes that lived at the end of the Pleistocene epoch. The objects in these sites are found along with debris from such Pleistocene animals as sloths, horses, camels, mastodons, and so forth.

Debris from these late Pleistocene groups has also been found at the edges of lakes and swamps, in the coastal plain and piedmonts of mountain ranges, and in the *llanos* (grassy plains) around Lake Valencia and in the Orinoco Basin. The Atlantic Andes—the sierra region of Colombia and Venezuela—must therefore have been especially favorable to man. Rich in game and water resources, close to the sea and big rivers, they seem to have been less arid then than they are today, probably because they had not been deforested as they are today.

Later, between nine thousand and five thousand years ago, this area was inhabited by "meso-Indians," as they are called by classical authors, or "Mesolithic" peoples, as they are called in Europe. The ecology of these populations was based essentially on exploiting seafood and especially on gathering shellfish. The large animals of the Pleistocene epoch had disappeared by then. Berries, seeds, roots, and tubers played an increasingly important dietary role, as indicated by the presence of mortars and pestles in the villages.

This period is typified throughout the world by the formation of big shell mounds, piles of ashes, and the debris of dwellings and food. These mounds are characteristic of populations living essentially on aquatic animals they gathered from the seas, rivers, and lakes.

In the Americas, mounds of this kind may be traced in a chain stretching from Alaska to Cape Horn. Off the Isthmus of Darien, this chain divides into two branches. The eastern one continues first to the Guianas, then to Brazil, where the shell mounds are called *sambaquis*. The western chain goes down the whole length of the Pacific as far as the tip of Patagonia.

Furthermore, the meso-Indians were navigators, for traces of them have been found in Guiana, on Cubagua Island, in Manicuare, in El Heneal on the central coast of Venezuela, and in Ortoire on the island of Trinidad.

Pottery apparently appeared around forty-seven hundred years ago around the Caribbean Sea in places like Rancho Peludo, Barlovento, Puerto Hormiga, and farther south, in Valdivia on the coast of Ecuador. These places, then, are the earliest Neolithic sites presently known on the South American continent, if we accept that pottery means agriculture; that is, a productive Neolithic life as opposed to parasitic Mesolithic ecologies.

The period called neo-Indian began about three thousand years ago and lasted until about A.D. 500. In the north and northeast of the continent, the cultivation of manioc and other rhizomic plants then took the lead. Manioc consumption is attested to by the presence of the rough files needed to make them edible by peeling off their bitter and poisonous skins. On the other hand, corn (which was apparently brought from Central America) was slowly to become the major food on the Pacific Coast.

The inhabitants of these regions in this epoch apparently already had a complex form of social organization. They seem to have lived in bands, possibly in tribes grouped according to certain common traits and consanguinity, a concept based on theoretical as well as physical sharing of common ancestors.

However, an uncomplicated social life does not signify poverty. Many neo-Indian sites indicating some wealth have been found, from the banks of the Orinoco to as far as central Venezuela. The Caribbean islands were apparently settled during this period, as were the lower Amazonas and Guianas. These low tropical lands do not enter into the framework of this study, but I must cite them as being places where a very early Neolithic way of life seems to have occurred, with apparently favorable results.

In order to understand better how the neo-Indians lived, one need only come into contact with the noncrossbred groups now living as seminomadic shepherds in La Guajira. This peninsula juts out into the Caribbean Sea north of the Sierra Nevada de Santa Marta cordillera. Twenty-five thousand people, practically all immigrants who have abandoned the Orinoco Basin, still populate La Guajira. Their ancestors arrived in one of the many migrations of peoples from unfavorable environments who left their territories in search of better lands.

La Guajira is a territory of plains and hills covering some fifty-two hundred square miles. The region is dry and sterile, with a few prairies in the southwestern part, which are crossed by only a few wadis. The migration out of these wadis that originated the present settlement took place apparently some six or seven hundred years ago.

The Guajiros are brachycephals of medium height. Anthropologists think they are Caribs who came to the mainland in boats, driving out the Arawak population settled in what is now Venezuela. Other authors classify them as Arawaks.

The expelled Arawaks migrated eastward and westward, toward the Antilles and toward the Sierra de Perijá and Colombia, respectively. From the Arawaks the invaders adopted a few circum-Caribbean and Andean traits while communicating Caribbean cultural habits to them. Later, some of these Caribs moved westward toward La Guajira.

Formerly fishermen, the Guajiros are now nomadic hunters and shepherds. They are quite warlike and use poisoned arrows equipped with the stinger from a ray or a substance made from putrid toad glands, such products making the wounded person die within ten days from tetanus. Therefore, it differed from curare, a strychnine-based poison used by the natives of the Amazonas. It is said that the Guajiros are still cannibals.

The polygamous Guajiros treat their wives well; their family system is matriarchal. They like to drink, they go about in loincloths with their faces painted, and they sleep in hammocks in big huts that are often as large as 120 square yards. The huts have no walls, just some posts supporting a straw roof, and are scattered so as to be beyond the range of an arrow, as well as being well protected by cactus-thorn fences.

Among the cultural traits acquired by the Guajiros from Andean societies, one may note the customs of chewing coca mixed with lime, of spinning wild cotton, and of weaving very beautiful fabrics with multicolored decorations.

The arrow equipped with a whistle, which until now ethnologists have observed only in Japan, is also found among the Guajiros, who have another peculiar trait. The men use a flute making only one sound, leaving to the women the flutes with several holes to produce several sounds.

Let me add that these people practice secondary burial, putting the bones into funerary jars once they are stripped of flesh.

In the beginning of the twentieth century, the Guajiro tribe was still subdivided into thirty consanguineous groups, each having its own hunting territory.

Natives living as they did in pre-Columbian times have also survived on the slopes of the Sierra Nevada de Santa Marta, between the altitudes of thirty-three hundred and sixty-six hundred feet, elevations in which fog and cold begin to create an unpleasant climate. The summit is almost nineteen thousand feet high, but the inhabitable zone covers some fifty-two hundred square miles within a radius of ninety miles. Cliffs overlook the Atlantic from a height of about sixty-six hundred feet. In the south, the massif ends in the César Valley, which has a distorted indigenous name. This valley is still inhabited by Chibcha-speaking Chimilas, a forest tribe that has also acquired Andean traits.

About twenty thousand Ikas or Ijkas, two thousand Kogis, and five hundred Sankas still live on the slopes of the Sierra Nevada de Santa Marta. The best known are the Ikas, formerly called the Kabagas. They speak a Chibcha dialect that they learned through contact with Andeans. They are small, thin people with long hair, and they wear long cotton gowns. Sedentary, they now farm only on a limited scale, cultivating potatoes, tomatoes, manioc, sweet potatoes, sugar cane, tobacco, and coca. The rich earth of the César Valley was taken away from them by Colombian stockbreeders grouped around the diocese of Valledupar, so the Ikas' diet is rounded out by the meat of several animals they hunt with bows and arrows and traps: rodents, tapirs, and peccaries, but especially iguanas, which are their favorite food and chief source of meat.

Walking around in this region, one meets Ikas on the trails, pulling a cow

An Ika inhabitant of the Tairona area, Santa Marta, Colombia. His quarry of iguanas is strapped in bundles on his cow's back.

or donkey loaded with iguanas. One of my friends asked an Ika what he would buy if he had a lot of money. The man replied, "I would fill my house up to the ceiling with iguanas."

The Ikas are very timid. Until a few years ago, they used to leave their villages whenever a stranger approached. Against physically stronger beings, they protect themselves by sorcery, as do certain tribes in New Guinea. They are feared by their neighbors because they cast spells.

Today the remaining Ikas are grouped in three villages—Palomino, San Miguel, and Santa Rosa—which are composed of circular huts with vertical walls covered with cone-shaped roofs. These villages also include a rectangular house intended for visitors passing through and a church built by missionaries.

Some ethnologists think they see Mayan and Honduran elements among the Ikas. Actually, a tribe called the Palenques, a Hispanic name given to a group from Yucatán, existed south of the Venezuelan cordillera. However, modern authors reject any link of this kind.

The Ikas are probably Caribs who came to the region fairly late in pre-Columbian times and were driven toward the cordillera when Europeans took over the good lands along the César River. They speak of the other pre-Columbian societies of the Sierra Nevada as their ancestors, but this is probably because they, like the Guajiros, used to loot gold from the tombs of the Tairona populations who practiced metallurgy and created a highly developed material culture in the region many centuries before the Ikas entered the area.

The almost miraculous survival of these Ikas teaches us little about the ancient history of the region, for they were latecomers. To find out more about that history, we must return to the sources: the chronicles and archaeology.

The first contact between natives and Spaniards took place in 1501, when the Bay of Santa Marta and the Gulf of Cartagena were explored. The port of Santa Marta was not built until 1525, when the Spaniards had succeeded in establishing themselves on the continent after long struggles. Santa Marta, like Cartagena, had a tormented history, being the first to be destroyed.

According to the chroniclers, at the time of the Conquest the natives were living on the seacoast on a strip ninety miles long and below an altitude of thirty-three hundred feet. The invaders who came across them there found them engaged in gold metallurgy and barter. They called them the Chairamas, whence comes the name of the Tairona society, which, according to some ethnologists, means a place where metal is melted.

The mines and rivers that yielded gold washings seem to have been located farther west, in the Chocó and along the lower Cauca. According to legend, the Taironas controlled some production centers. I think, on the contrary, that they acquired the ore by barter and that it was the caciques of the Cauca and the Tumacos who dominated the gold-bearing regions.

The struggle between the Chairamas and the Spaniards must have been terrible. Spanish conquest of the area was never fully achieved. The Taironas withdrew to the mountains, where they finally disappeared, probably decimated by diseases and hunger.

The connection that some have sought to establish between these sixteenth-century Taironas and the archaeological remains to be seen around the Santa Marta massif is ill founded. I believe that the natives the Europeans met were in no way descended from the inhabitants of the pre-Columbian villages found by treasure looters. According to archaeologists, these communities were active some two thousand years ago. It is true that the chronicler Oviedo cites the expert skill the Taironas had in metallurgy, but we do not know what territory this writer was referring to when he mentioned the Chairamas. In the tombs of Coclé, a site near Panama, very beautiful gold jewelry has been found, comparable to the ones made by the Quimbayas in the Cauca Valley. It seems more logical to attribute these achievements to ancient inhabitants of northern South America rather than to later invaders, whether Arawak or Carib, who ravaged the earlier chiefdoms.

Ruins have survived of settlements the Taironas built of stone. These show that the material culture of the people must have been very different from that of the invaders coming from the eastern part of the continent. Archaeologists have found several Tairona villages: Tairo, Pueblo, Pueblito, which are all situated on crests overlooking the sea, as well as Posigueyca, their so-called capital, and Calabazos. The chroniclers knew of six such clusters and described them as located on high places that were hard to reach. All these villages have not been found, but the ones that are known have several common characteristics. One reached them by way of roads and paved stairways, some of which were sixty-six feet wide, and by bridges made of stone blocks. The villages were decorated with rock

The ruins of a Tairona house in Santa Marta, Colombia. Approximately one thousand years old.

carvings. Farming terraces rose in tiers all around, down toward the cliff that overhangs the sea. Today these villages' huts or houses, built of perishable materials, have disappeared, but their shapes and the places where they had been are still visible, outlined by circles of stones. The settlements also included artificial mounds, possibly for ceremonial use, and graves.

I have visited one of the Tairona complexes, known as Pueblito. It extends over about two and a half miles in length at an altitude of a thousand feet above sea level in a narrow valley and has revealed some two hundred houses that would suggest a population of at least one thousand people, and probably more.

This kind of excursion is disagreeable because of the insects that infest the jungle—mosquitoes, flies, and *garrapatas*, or ticks that implant themselves by the dozens in the tourist's skin as he travels on muleback along "roads" that sometimes have a sixty-degree slope. Fortunately, the mules know how to go down paved staircases with steps that are sometimes sixteen inches high.

Archaeologists and treasure looters have extracted from Pueblito some very beautiful decorative gold objects such as nose- and breastplates and jewels, as well as musical instruments, polished stone axes, and small, carved stone chairs like the ones found in Costa Rica and other places in Central America.

According to an Ika tradition, their ancestors were allies of the Taironas, "for whom our people built the villages." But one should still put all these events in their chronological place. Oral traditions often reduce the length of time between different cultural periods.

The Caribbean islands and the easternmost Andes, which stretch out east of Lake Maracaibo as far as the island of Trinidad, have been among the most decimated and persecuted South American territories. Here only a few groups who took refuge in the llanos or the upper Orinoco Basin have escaped destruction. This region seems to have been very prosperous and well cultivated before the arrival of Europeans. This area, populated by people who were strongly influenced by Andean traditions, managed to produce a typical hybridized culture that was a mixture of highland and forest ways of life.

The Andean influence is shown by the fact that their villages had been built either on mounds or on terraces protected from floods. Their villages contained up to eight hundred houses, made of stone, a number that suggests a population of at least four thousand people. Rituals were observed in a temple or in caves, their dead were buried in cemeteries, and their chiefs were carried in litters decorated with gold plaques. The chiefs sometimes had harems comprised (if we believe the chronicles) of up to two hundred women. The society was marked by social stratification. The peasants practiced intensive irrigated farming, since the rains were either insufficient or too irregular for dry farming. The cacique was often the shaman too. These shamans had rather highly developed religious concepts in that they sometimes considered the sun and moon to be supreme divinities.

At the time when Europeans attacked them, all these northeastern tribes had undergone strong cultural hybridization, which is evident when one studies their material cultures. The nose plate was already worn in Venezuela as in Ecuador, and clay statuettes were modeled as they were in Peru. Strong circum-Caribbean influences are also notable among the Caquetios and Jirajaras who, on the other hand, used the Andean vertical loom. Even the forest tribes were bartering with Andean societies. They even knew of the llama, and were obtaining gold in exchange for cotton.

All these people were exterminated by smallpox, hunger, and demoralization. As early as 1568, when the capital of Venezuela was founded, the aborigines known as the Caracas had all disappeared.

Before going farther west, let me note the forest groups that have survived down to our time in the Sierra de Perijá, a mountain range separating Colombia from Venezuela. These natives live isolated from the modern world and are still feared and respected as far as Valledupar, in the César River valley. About five hundred of them have survived, subdivided into Yokas, Dobokubis, and

Chakchés. Formerly, 185 consanguineous groups of them were counted. (The Spaniards gave the name *motilones* to several very distinct groups spread out between the Orinoco and the Chaco. This is not the name of a tribe, but a term meaning "primitive.")

The various consanguineous groups were Caribs who had come from the east, who lived in communal houses grouped into small villages, and had no contact with the outside world. Despite their wild character they were farmers. Their appearance is pygmoid, with an average height of fifty-nine inches for women and sixty-two inches for men. One may compare them to the Caribs who invaded the West Indies and drove out the Arawakans, who had themselves destroyed the preagricultural Ciboneys and are thought to have migrated south from Florida.

Just as obscure, poorly understood, and distorted is the history of the territories farther west, in an area extending from the mouths of the Magdalena and Sinu rivers to the Gulf of Darien on the Atlantic, and along the Chocó and the banks of the Atrato River on the Pacific Coast.

These lands were still prosperous and heavily populated at the time of the Spanish invasion. Practically everywhere in these territories, archaeologists have uncovered the ruins of villages built on mounds and of irrigated agricultural complexes established on terraced gardens. These ruins give us a glimpse of what must have been a normal existence in what is today an uninhabitable climate. The objects they used every day reveal a very acceptable standard of living, in complete contrast to the decline these regions experienced after contact with Europeans. Moreover, it is logical to consider that if the Caribs invaded these territories it was because they offered good farmland and all the amenities of a hospitable country.

Of all this, only ruins and desolation remained after about fifty years of colonization. As a result, tradition has transmitted to us an impression of an environment that was hostile to man—practically uninhabitable—where only some small poverty-stricken groups of natives had survived, persecuted by Africans who had escaped from slavery.

The chroniclers tell us of the hard struggle the European invaders had, settling in these lands, of the hardships and many reverses they suffered. It was only because of the natives' numbers and courage that they succeeded in surviving. In fact, they were never able to set up a coherent, organized defense. The struggle was carried on by tribes that operated continually but in an individual fashion. They were not yet psychologically prepared and able to form tribal confederations such as those formed for mutual aid in cases of grave danger by the natives of the northeastern United States.

In 1510, Alonso de Ojeda founded San Sebastian de Urubia, but this embryonic town was soon destroyed, as was Santa Maria la Antigua de Darien, on the Atrato River. It took Cartagena twenty-three years to become a permanent settlement. Similar difficulties faced colonial Mompox, which replaced the indigenous Mompox.

Thus, it was a life-and-death struggle, and once the Spaniards finally won, the native population was decimated. Within fifty years it had disappeared. Today the region is being cleaned up and settled. The Sinú and the lower Magdalena are bare of trees, and stockbreeders have settled there with their cattle. Cartagena now has 350,000 inhabitants, almost all Africans, living in dilapidated colonial houses amid baroque palaces and churches dating from the time of Hispanic splendors. Reichel Dolmatoff maintains that some natives have also survived in the countryside, as mestizos.

The Spaniards transmitted to us the names of the principal groups: Cénu, Calamari, Tolu, Turbaco, Buritaca, Mompox, and so on. These names have since been given to towns and villages that have grown up near the pre-Columbian sites.

Leaving the ocean and going southward, we enter the valleys of the Magdalena and a tributary, the Cauca. The Quimbayas' chiefdoms were established there at the time of the Conquest. The Quimbayas were industrious farmers, builders of roads and bridges, and clever metallurgists. They were used to the tropical, quite forested environment of the time, which today is terribly arid as a result of deforestation.

In what is now the province of Antioquia, Colombia, which was colonized by the hardiest Spanish peasants, when some landowners want to relax, they still go off with an axe on their shoulder to cut away the *monte*, to destroy the last few surviving trees. The monte was the settler's enemy, since it brought insects, took up good land, and so forth. A kind of rage against all savannah vegetation can still be noticed all over South America. One may question the wisdom of these practices in territories where the daytime temperature is sometimes over ninety-five degrees in the shade.

During late pre-Hispanic times, the Quimbayas came under pressure from the Paezes, who came from the east and crossed the cordillera in an attempt to settle in the Cauca Valley.

Neither big complexes, nor buildings of stone or fired brick have been found in the region. The country is fully tropical. People lived in villages of huts surrounded by palisades. The Cauca Valley's pre-Columbian peoples practiced a kind of agriculture that involved a high level of technology. Aerial photographs of the Cauca's banks reveal the existence of pre-Hispanic mounds built to subdivide gardens in areas that were watered and thus fertilized by mud when the river flooded.

According to Hernandez de Alba, the central complex of these Quimbayas was Buga. Other authors suggest it was Buritaca, near the present city of Cali in the province of Colima. Cali seems to be a distortion of the name of the Lili tribe, the remains of which have been found in the area.

Cieza de León describes the Quimbayas as being very well dressed and traveling on the Cauca River in boats. He adds that they did not build temples or worship idols. Another chronicler, Miguel de Estete, says that they used to make pilgrimages as far south as Pachacamac, near Lima.

The Quimbayas reportedly engaged in fights in order to obtain trophy heads and prisoners to sacrifice, and engaged in ritual cannibalism. They also played team games and some sports. Their culture thus appears to me to be a perfect mixture of well-marked Andean influences, forest traits, and typically Central American and Antillean elements. (A chronicler reports that they also wore tree bark, which was beaten and pulled off the trunks in sheets, but I have never noticed such a use of bark in Peru.) The Isthmus of Darien nearby must have constituted a very important gateway and trading area. Moreover, it was through Darien that the big animals of the Pleistocene epoch entered the southern continent. Later, products of the Quimbayas' gold metallurgy were exported over Panama as far as Honduras, where menhirs (upright monument stones) and monolithic statues have also been found.

Tradition has it that the cacique of Buritaca controlled all gold bartering in the region—jewels that went to Coclé and into Central America, goods delivered by the Pastos to the south, and the trading practiced with the Taironas of the Sierra Nevada.

These Quimbaya lands have bequeathed to us the prettiest and most delicate pre-Columbian jewelry, which one may admire today in the museums of Bogotá and Guayaquil. The ignorant and coarse conquerors who were looking everywhere for El Dorado, the Land of Gold, and went into the heart of the Amazonas in their search for it, never realized that in fact only the Cauca Valley deserved the name Land of Gold. Dredging for gold is still practiced today in the rivers of the Chocó.

In the Bogotá museum one may see molds and objects by which we can guess how the pre-Columbians obtained small objects and very fine statuettes by the lost-wax process. However, this field requires much more investigation before we can comprehend their techniques adequately. Gold melts at 1947 degrees Fahrenheit, and we are told that the pre-Columbians did not use the smith's bellows. Tradition says that they obtained high enough temperatures by placing their furnaces on the summits of exposed hills, where winds stirred up the flame, and by using bamboo tubes to blow on the fire.

With the Spanish occupation, dredging for gold was resumed on a large scale after the veins disappeared. Cieza de León described Santa Fe de Antioquia as "the big gold capital." When he traveled through the region, black slaves had already replaced the natives, who had been decimated by diseases and forced labor.

Grave robbing is still widely engaged in as a sport in these lands. The most astonishing thing about it is that after four centuries of looting, virgin tombs containing treasures are still being found.

East of Cali and the first ridge of the high cordillera lies the city of Popayán. In the eighteenth century, this town, named after the tribe whose last cacique was killed by Benalcázar, became more important than Santa Fe de Antioquia, which was too threatened by pirates and rebellious African slaves. Popayán also became a very beautiful colonial city, with numerous baroque churches. Today it is well preserved, all-white, and still with much of its charm and many of its beautiful eighteenth-century houses. The region's archives have been assembled there; in them one can consult primary sources of great interest.

It was the gold trade that made Popayán wealthy. At first the metal was shipped to Cartagena on the Atlantic coast. However, because this port was constantly attacked by pirates and was raided several times, it became too exposed. Mule convoys loaded with gold and also silver from the La Plata mines therefore set out from Popayán to go to the port of Callao in Lima, via Pasto and Quito. From there the vessels then left for Europe in convoys with heavy protection. This trade was officially reserved for the state, but merchants were not wasting their time—in the meantime they were smuggling spices, an activity which the Madrid administration seems to have winked at.

Before leaving the far north of the continent, let me say a little about the coast known as Chocó, the *Biru* of the sixteenth-century conquerors.

Among modern geographers and travelers, the hot and very rainy lands of Chocó no longer have a good reputation. Today the Chocó area, with its annual twenty-six feet of rain, its pumas and insects, is not liked by prospectors. I know one survivor of a low-powered airplane that crashed in the Chocó. Of the five passengers, three died insane and two kept alive by staying in the trees all night to escape the ants and wild animals until found by the search party.

The chroniclers called the inhabitants of the Chocó the Barbacoas, after the name of the huts they built, which resembled the ones still to be seen all along the Ecuadorian coast. These huts were very high, built on posts several yards above the ground, and were entered by means of movable ladders.

The Barbacoas had an abundance of gold, which they extracted from the rivers' sands. They went about naked with their bodies painted. They exchanged their gold, fish, and salt for other products, trading with the people of the Cauca Valley as did their neighbors of the Tumaco region farther south.

Today all the Colombian lowlands are inhabited by people of African origin, such as the three hundred fifty thousand blacks in Cartagena alone. In the region of Buenaventura, one of the modern Pacific ports, and in the Colombian province of Tumaco, natives have survived only as exceptions. Nearly everywhere else the Africans predominate, and after having invaded the hot lands they are approaching the heart of the Andes. Going by land from Quito to Bogotá one passes through villages where one could think he was in Africa.

The Chocó populations practiced milpa farming, in which they cleared jungle lands by burning, farmed them for a few seasons, then abandoned them. It would be astonishing if their hot and rainy country had not produced edible plants. The villages were located along the Patia and Mira rivers.

Their languages were either Chocó or Chibcha, according to their ethnic origins and the cultural traits they displayed, such as clothes made of beaten bark, stone chairs and headrests, the absence of weaving, the use of looped and twined fabrics, and rough pottery. The Chocó's inhabitants remind one of circum-Caribbeans whose social organization had remained at the stage of very small chiefdoms without any marked social stratification.

In order to reconstruct their social system, one can refer to the life-style of their neighbors the Cunas, who lived in the Isthmus of Darien and have survived on the San Blas Islands in the Pacific west of Panama. Regarding these groups, we know that in 1527, Nata, one of their chieftains, still commanded a village of forty-five to fifty huts, inhabited by 250 people. Furthermore, this chieftain controlled ten subchiefs. The whole complex, then, represented a little society of about twenty-five hundred people, living a more or less luxurious life, depending on their social status. The chieftains, who were polygamous, were carried in hammocks and had slaves as well as warriors in their service.

Going down along the coast toward the third parallel, below Tumaco, we enter a beautiful tropical forest in a region less rainy than Chocó and hot (but not too hot), with sea breezes and a large river. This region is known as Esmeraldas, the conquerors' Land of Emeralds.

A Colombian atlas classifies this region as subarid. Today the deforestation practiced by settlers bringing in cattle is causing serious damage. These cattlemen are replacing forests with pastures, and sand blowing unimpeded from the beaches is already invading the interior of the country.

The natives of Esmeraldas disappeared a long time ago. The only traces remaining of them are their kitchen middens, mainly consisting of shell heaps stretching all along the beaches. These natives were Andeans who had come down from the mountains and formed a lively circum-Andean society near the ocean. Coaque, Atacama, and Mateo, looted by Pizarro during one of his first trips, were described as prosperous communities of up to three thousand persons, with well-marked streets. Cieza de León noted that the province had a great abundance of gold and precious stones, especially in the Atacama area.

Cieza made this voyage around 1540. There could not have remained much gold or many emeralds in the region except in graves, which were very soon plundered with the help of African labor. It was only much later, it seems, that the Andeans participated (under European guidance) in looting the tombs of their ancestors, whom they now call *gentiles,* meaning pagans.

Near the important village of Cojimies, archaeologists have brought to light the ruins of what they call the Tolita complex. *Tola* means mound; *tolita,* little mound. These terms are used in Ecuador to designate artificial hills that supported a ceremonial center or a pre-Columbian building reserved for communal use. The most famous mounds are those found north of Quito at Otavalo.

At Cojimies one may see platform mounds, artificial hills that may have had a ceremonial purpose but in my opinion had simply been built for people to live on above the swamps and insects. Around them one could see enclosures marked with planted stone slabs, bottle-shaped graves, and storage bins dug into the soil. Countless mundane objects were found in these villages: metal plaques and masks with mythological motifs in low relief, jewels, millstones shaped like the Central American ones and called *metates,* stone chairs, engraved stone columns serving as bases for the posts supporting house roofs, anthropomorphic stone statuettes, female figurines sculptured in low relief or in the round, flat bars for filing off the skins of manioc, disk-shaped obsidian mirrors, and many more.

All these elements are characteristic of circum-Caribbean and southern Central American societies. It seems, therefore, that Esmeraldas, where one also finds Andean cultural traits, was invaded only by Chibcha-speaking groups that came down from the cordillera during late pre-Hispanic days.

Unfortunately, archaeologists have brought us only objects from Esmeraldas, whereas what we would like to know is the ground plans and sizes of the villages. We need more elements from which to reconstruct the inhabitants' lives, to estimate their numbers, and to study their agricultural techniques. Esmeraldas was a farming region whose basic food was manioc, complemented by seafood. Its so-called Tolita society has bequeathed to us about forty mounds; it would be quite useful to study them scientifically.

Today the natives of Esmeraldas are replaced by Africans who lead a meager existence. The arts and all the pleasures of life have disappeared in the area, and the new settlers live in poverty in villages that have remained distinct from the industrialized Colombian society. Today, with the pipeline bringing oil from the Amazonas, a little prosperity is fortunately going to revive the region.

A bit farther south, deep in the forests that grow along both banks of the Daule River, there still live several groups of Colorados and Cayapas, but there are hardly more than thirty-three hundred of them left. These people go about nude, or nearly so, their bodies painted with achiote, and live in isolated huts in the forest. Because some of their cultural traits are clearly Andean, some ethnologists see the Colorados as Chibchas who came down from the Andes. Another school sees them as early nomads who were forced by circumstances to become farmers and fishermen.

Finally, some anthropologists think that the Colorados are descendants of the Barbacoas of Chocó, whose territory is thought to have formerly been much more extensive, reaching down the coast to the vicinity of Guayaquil. However, the Barbacoas have linguistic affinities with the Chibchas, Paezes, and Pijaos who occupy north-central Colombia, which is to say once again, with groups that speak Andean languages. This would mean that the Colorados would be the survivors of a great Chibcha invasion that occupied the whole Pacific Coast.

Today, the last Colorados, whom I have visited, or the Tatchilas, who are not known to have clans, still live in the nude, in extended families of ten to twelve people. They refuse to live in villages, and go to the town of Santo Domingo, on the Daule, only to barter. The three hundred or so who are left practice milpa farming and have adopted the use of houses built on posts.

I visited the Colorados and was very much upset to see their nude women being photographed by tourists who hire taxis in Guayaquil especially for this sort of experience. Photographing a young woman nude in the rain, with her feet in the mud, is probably an unforgettable adventure for some people, since they pay a small fortune to experience it.

The Cayapas have been pushed farther and farther back toward the interior, to the foot of the Andes. There are three tribes of them left, totaling about two thousand people, who live around San Miguel de Esmeraldas. Rivet thought they were a remnant of Caras who had come down from the high plateaus of Otavalo and had abandoned the blankets and shirts worn when they lived in the cold lands. They are fishermen as well as farmers, and use canoes. They also go around nude, with their bodies painted red, black, or yellow, because of their belief that the color they smear themselves with is essential to maintain contact with the spirits of the waters and forests. They deform the skulls of their babies, blacken their teeth, and wear a silver-colored net on their heads.

Before leaving the hot lands of the northern part of the continent, let me say a little about the eastern piedmonts of the cordillera. There, in the forests, savannahs, and grassy plains of eastern Colombia one may still observe a mixture of marginal groups who have changed very little since the arrival of Europeans and who have remained very unresponsive to all foreign penetration. Some of these groups are thus still very primitive and dangerous. Others are more developed and have, for example, learned to travel in boats, but sometimes they still wear clothes made of bark. These marginal groups have adopted certain customs of the forest societies. The Betois, for instance, do a little farming, apart from devoting themselves to fishing, hunting, and food gathering. Moreover, they live in communities and build villages protected by fences. Other groups are much more timid and live a hidden life, guided by one of their elders. Of these groups, the best known are the Achaquas and Guaiqueris, who come to trade with the mestizos in the modern Colombian settlement of San Juan de los Llanos.

THE UPPER MAGDALENA: SAN AGUSTIN AND TIERRADENTRO

The Magdalena River, a thousand miles long, begins at an altitude of some sixty-five hundred feet in the heart of the northern Andes. In the immediate vicinity of its sources, one enters the San Agustín Archaeological Park. In San Agustín the Colombian government has built a hotel for tourists, where one can hire a mule and reach the source of the river in a few hours.

San Agustín is still in the hot lands. The nights are cool there, but the days are stifling. The vegetation is luxuriant, a mixture of savannah and tropical forest.

Upon entering the park, one immediately receives the impression of coming into one of the shrines not only of American archaeology but of human history. The terrain is undulating and covered with artificial mounds.

In the beginning of this century, San Agustín was considered an enormous cemetery. What had happened was that grave looters had opened the mounds, found the graves hidden therein, and brought to light the anthropomorphic statues that had been hidden in graves in passages roofed with stone slabs. As a result of this plundering, the statues appeared, and they are now visible on top of the mounds for visitors to enjoy.

Megalithic statues do not exist everywhere. The well-known ones are concentrated in the area of San Agustín and Tierradentro, which I shall describe shortly. There are a few of them in the Cauca Valley, among the Quimbayas. The gold jewels of the Tolimas in the Cali region reproduced themes comparable to those of the San Agustín statues.

A cemetery necessarily implies a nearby community. The formerly popular notion of there being sacred places to which the pre-Columbians brought their dead from great distances to bury them has been totally contradicted by the facts revealed by modern archaeology. Research in San Agustín during past years was found to reveal the existence of a large settlement. Now, investigators have recognized the presence of piles of debris and farming terraces indicating the existence of a rural community extending over an area some 165 miles long from Pasto to Tierradentro. Little by little, San Agustín is recovering its true face: a great ceremonial center surrounded and sustained like the Maya complexes by a population that lived scattered all over the vicinity.

According to radiocarbon datings, the San Agustín complex was active as early as some twenty-five hundred years ago, and was inhabited until about A.D. 600. Where had its inhabitants come from? Was the astonishing statuary art that they had mastered of local origin? As always in cases of this kind, one thinks of a migration. But from where—Central America? Polynesia? The Magdalena

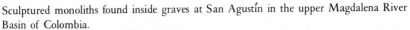

Sculptured monoliths found inside graves at San Agustín in the upper Magdalena River Basin of Colombia.

River obviously constituted a prime north-south entryway from the Caribbean islands and the Antilles, but one cannot fail to observe similarities in the statuary of San Agustín, of Easter Island, and of the Olmecs from the Vera Cruz area in Mexico.

As the excavations progress, new statues are found and the boundaries of the San Agustín park must be enlarged. It is now clear that the region must have supported a large population, an agricultural society that lasted for several centuries. The modern prehistorical school now tends toward the idea that two thousand years ago the San Agustín society was typical of the whole Magdalena River basin, being a megalithic and Neolithic society that, like the Mayas', did not use metal.

The statuary art of San Agustín must have had a long past, for by this time, statues had already been carved, in the round, the most common prototypes being representations of gods carrying on their backs a second small figure of mythological animals. Mexico aside, works of this quality are rare in the Americas, where only a few heads and monolithic statues are known: those of Chavín de Huantar in the central Andes, of the Callejon de Huaylas in the upper Santa Valley in Peru, of Collao around Lake Titicaca, of Tiahuanaco in Bolivia, those found in the puna near Lake Poopó in Bolivia, and the great figures of Easter Island, insofar as Easter Island can be culturally associated with the South American continent as well as with Polynesia.

According to Horst Nachtigall, the author who has studied the megalithic Andean cultures most thoroughly, one can observe an evolution there from simple, block-shaped menhirs to statues in the round, with all the intermediate stages. I wonder if this first-rate author has considered the problem carefully from the point of view of the evolution of styles and dissimilarities, and not only from the point of view of technical progress.

In crossing the cordillera that separates the Cauca and Magdalena valleys, and then in continuing eastward beyond Popayán, one enters a new hot-land region, an area of valleys watered by streams that originate around the summits of the Huila peaks. A string of villages of pure-blooded natives who do not yet speak Spanish can still be visited there over a sixty-mile stretch. This region is called Tierradentro, or "interior land."

To the east, around Garzón and Neiva, was the land of the Piajos, who are now extinct. The Pastos, who lived in the south near the equator, have been exterminated. Only the Paezes, who lived in the interior valleys of Tierradentro, have survived in their pure state.

Here again, the present natives do not seem to be the descendants of the people who occupied the lands when the San Agustín society was flourishing, but instead seem to be the successors of invaders from lower lands. Ethnologists think they are the remains of tribes that came from the east, the ones Benalcázar fought.

At the time of the conquest of what is now Colombia, these tribes were not organized into nations. We know they resisted the invader fiercely, not as a confederation but as courageous, isolated bands that carried on the struggle to the end. In 1577 these natives still managed to destroy the Spanish colony that had been created to exploit the silver mines of La Plata. The last convulsions of their revolt lasted until the beginning of the seventeenth century. Today there is hardly any evidence remaining of their existence.

Some interesting monuments have survived in Tierradentro. The largest ones are found in Iza and in the park of San Andrés, between the altitudes of four thousand and thirty-three hundred feet, in the Paez River Valley. These monuments bear witness to a social organization that was more complex than that of the present inhabitants of this territory.

In the San Andrés park one can visit underground rooms of some size, the only ones known in South America. Subterranean buildings in the Andes usually are very small houses or storage bins that were used as burial places.

When they were discovered by treasure looters, the underground rooms of San Andrés were being used as graves, but it is quite possible that they had been dug with another function in mind—as cult places, for example. Graves are found all over the area. They are quite different from the hypogeal underground living sites, and contained complete skeletons given primary burials. But only the remains of secondary burials, with burned bones and no skulls, were found in the underground rooms. Archaeologists thus consider that the hypogeal rooms had been reused, probably to hide the remains of high-ranking people. But as far as I am concerned, I am far from convinced that these remains were those of the people who had ordered the digging of the underground rooms. These rooms may have been broken into by pre-Columbian invaders. (We have found practically no intact pharaonic graves in Egypt—looting is an everlasting practice.) The funerary accoutrements with the skeletons that were buried in individual graves were richer and more complete than the furnishings found in the subterranean rooms: gold ornaments placed through the septum or on the arms, Quimbaya-style ceramic figurines, gold plaques, and necklaces of stone beads, shells, and animal teeth.

The hypogeae consist of one or two rooms of up to forty-three square yards in area, with a volume of up to ninety-one cubic yards. They were dug into white, chalky soil into which one descended by very steep, winding staircases whose entrances were blocked by stone slabs. The rooms had been carved in such a way as to leave intact some benches, niches, and half columns. The walls and ceilings were painted one, two, or three colors in red, black, and white. The decoration was essentially geometric: simple parallel lines, lozenge shapes, and rectangles. A restoration of one of the painted ceilings has, however, also revealed two faces of men.

Tierradentro also exhibited three-dimensional statues that call to mind those of Easter Island and represent anthropomorphic gods that are comparable to those of San Agustín, but less stylized. But the Tierradentro statues show a more realistic and individual treatment of the bodies and faces they represent.

The pottery that has been found in the villages of Tierradentro clearly differs from the ware generally found in Colombia. Here the decoration was made by applying modeled pieces or by the process of negative painting. In the Colombian process, the potter made the motif appear in areas that remained pottery pink, whereas the rest of the vessel took on a blackish color when the vegetable pigment in which it had been dipped became charred in the course of a second firing.

The sizes of the villages from this period and the areas of the farming terraces surrounding them indicate that a large and well-organized society had developed there. This society has not yet been correctly located in time and place. Archaeologists who have studied the problem see Tierradentro as a remnant of the San Agustín civilization in its highly developed and declining stage, very much marked by Andean and Cauca Valley societies. According to this view, Tierradentro would have flourished between A.D. 800 and 1400, the present Paez tribe having invaded the region and replaced the earlier inhabitants around A.D. 1400.

The Tierradentro society was poorer than the San Agustín. Here the funerary urns were made of earth, though gold ones are said to have been found in San Agustín. This mythology of gold is always cropping up to falsify the data. Deifying gold, thinking all buildings are temples, and calling all villages cemeteries are the three most baneful and most deep-rooted mental habits of specialists in American studies; and they accuse me of "desacralizing" archaeology.

We can learn something of the past by observing the present inhabitants of Tierradentro. Although they cannot tell us anything about the chiefs who had ordered the digging and sculpturing of the underground rooms, they do exemplify the kind of life that could have been led by the sixteenth-century populations practicing tropical agriculture between forty-six hundred and fifty-six hundred feet above sea level.

The present Tierradentro peasants still inhabit a territory that is about two thousand square miles. They farm according to the milpa (slash-and-burn) system and sow corn. Today, probably as in former times, each family lives in a separate hut with vertical cane walls and a four-sided straw roof. Each family tends about half an acre of corn complemented by a small garden, which is rotated every five to seven years. They also raise some livestock, and sometimes hunt and fish. They drink *chicha*, made from fermented corn, and chew coca. Formerly, the weapons used were big spears made of *chonta* (the wood of tropical-forest palm trees), blowguns six to nine feet long, and slings. Warriors took shelter behind shields made of tapir skins.

All this indicates a mixture of forest traits and typical Andean ones. Such a blend is probably a consequence of invaders who had come from elsewhere adopting certain customs from the early societies of Tierradentro.

The contemporary natives still are animists and listen to their shamans. They do not speak Spanish, but the Colombian government is trying to bring their children into schools and Christian churches. Charming chapels with straw roofs, built by Spanish missions as early as the sixteenth century, are still to be found in their villages next to the kindergartens and primary schools created by the Bogotá administration.

THE COLD HIGHLANDS OF THE NORTHERN ANDES

The tortuous northern upper Andes, intersected with deep canyons through which big rivers flow, do not lend themselves easily to a comprehensive description. Therefore, I must simplify and regroup to create entities that are somewhat artificial, to make this account intelligible and not too detailed.

Westward, toward the ocean, the descent from the high plateaus is very abrupt. In the east, or Oriente, the grassy plains extend as far as the high plateaus of Brazil and the Atlantic.

Westward, the Magdalena is very close by. In Girardot, at the foot of Bogotá, one is already at an altitude of thirty-three hundred feet, in a deeply tropical zone.

According to the chroniclers, this region experienced incessant movements of populations during the last pre-Hispanic century. Despite his lack of anthropological experience, Cieza de León suspected that the Muiscas, Chibchas, and other warrior-farmers (who were cannibals at times) were not the first inhabitants of the lands he traveled through. Ethnology and linguistics have now confirmed these intuitions. Here again, circum-Andean and circum-Caribbean traits are present. Arawaks and even Caribs from the forest must have come in successive waves and dislodged the indigenous populations of the valleys of Tierradentro, the high plateaus, and the *meseta* of Bogotá. (Colombians say *sabana,* which means plain. The meseta must have still been wooded when the conquerors arrived.)

THE PLAIN OF BOGOTÁ AND THE TUNJA REGION

According to the classical archaeological school, these high plains belonged to the Muiscas, a Chibcha-speaking people, at the time the Spaniards arrived.

The Muiscas or Chibchas supposedly formed a nation of about three hundred thousand people, a confederation of forty or fifty groups joined into five chiefdoms or kingdoms. According to Alfred L. Kroeber, there were a million of them. Tradition has it that in the sixteenth century the two largest chiefdoms were those of a *zipa* or king (centered to the south of Bacata, the future Hispanic Bogotá) and by a *zaque,* centered farther north where the modern city of Tunja has been built over the pre-Columbian settlement. The actual situation, however, must have been more complicated.

The Muiscas had progressed in social organization and constituted an embryonic nation. Perhaps population density had forced them to adopt a more structured way of life. Left to themselves, they might have been able to play a civilizing role in the northern Andes comparable to the one exercised farther south by the princes of Cuzco. In the time of Benalcázar, however, they were unable to resist the guns, horses, steel swords, and cannons of the Spaniards, and were cut to pieces after a very brief resistance. They did not use the bow (a forest weapon), but rather the spear thrower.

Beyond what the chroniclers' legends report, we know very little about the Muiscas. For instance, they have left us practically no architecture. It is only by hearsay that we know they lived in villages of circular huts with cone-shaped roofs.

As for artistic achievements, it is not certain whether they were the authors of the few rock engravings and carved monoliths found in their territory. These objects may date back to the earlier San Agustín period. Their pottery was mediocre. On the other hand, they wore beautiful fabrics and adorned themselves with very beautiful gold jewels. In the gold museum of Bogotá one can see the most beautiful specimens of this jewelry, one of which is a representation of the Dorado rite. During the course of this ceremony the *zipa*, covered with powder of the precious metal, set out on a raft and dived into the lake at an annual religious ceremony.

The gold museum at Bogotá was established by the Central Reserve Bank of Colombia in order to prevent the disappearance of pre-Columbian jewels by their being melted down and sold for the weight of the metal. The bank has been buying prehistoric gold at a premium since 1913. As a result, it now owns a first-rate museum housed in a beautiful building constructed especially for the purpose. It is worthwhile going to Bogotá just to visit this museum, and a visit to the archaeological museum in Guayaquil is also recommended, as the collection of jewels there is very beautiful.

Today the Colombian cold lands are inhabited by a much more mixed-blood population than comparable Peruvian and Bolivian areas. Apparently, many more Spanish small farmers immigrated to the northwestern than to the central Andes. In this respect Colombia has a few points in common with Chile. In Colombia, however, the Muisca element has remained dominant, whereas in Chile the indigenous element appears to be more regressive.

The pre-Columbian vestiges that have survived in the Tunja region, a fertile and densely populated province, are extremely rare. This region was the center of intense missionary activity, and very beautiful and interesting works have survived. There is mainly a heavy concentration of churches and monasteries, such as the ruins of the first chapel built by the conquistador Ojeda, the Ecce Homo cloister, and the little sixteenth-century practically intact town of Villa de Leyva. But the effort made by the Church to eradicate heresies during the seventeenth century not only completed the destruction of the Muisca society but also helped to eliminate the vestiges of the pre-Columbian past.

The northern Andes from Venezuela to Ecuador abound in Renaissance and baroque art treasures. Wherever one wanders there, one finds isolated churches almost lost in the countryside in what is now in the hot lowlands a totally Africanized country. These works of art, hard to get to, are generally forgotten and abandoned to the vandalism of merchants. The ignorant people in charge of them have been giving away paintings by Italian Renaissance masters to passing foreigners in order to install an electric organ and neon lights in the choir of the local church. Corrugated iron is everywhere replacing the lovely thatched roofs, and the floors have been covered with cement. Near Valledupar in the César Valley there is a little forest village populated entirely by Africans. The head of the community told me that the inhabitants had risen en masse, machetes in hand, to defend the altar paintings of their church when the priest agreed to sell these Renaissance works of art to a passing merchant. This community leader lived quite well; his register of visitors indicated the large fees he had charged for granting religious intervention toward obtaining recoveries and even miracles. Furthermore, visiting this personage was obligatory, and entering his house meant one had to pay his fees, since the machetes were not far away.

OTAVALO, QUITO, AND THE HIGH PLATEAUS OF ECUADOR

Going southward past Pasto, one enters what is now Ecuador, inhabited by several million natives who form pure or scarcely mixed ethnic groups. Meeting them and observing their customs is no problem. One comes across them on market days, holidays, and during processions in the communities outside of which they live, working in the fields or in the city for the benefit of economically more highly developed individuals.

Practically nothing is known about the early history of Ecuador, where only two preagricultural sites have been studied, El Abra and El Inga. Clearly, archaeologists have not done much investigation here. Fieldwork is indeed difficult in a region that suffers from torrential rains and continual earthquakes. However, many stone artifacts, the work of a single society, have appeared on the surface of a hill at El Inga. Other comparable sites must have survived, and this should encourage research.

Archaeologists do not go on long walks often enough. One must be able to forget the scenery and look at the ground as though looking for four-leafed clovers. Thus, after a ten-hour walk, I found some obsidian arrowheads on the banks of Lake Parinacocha in the upper Andes of central Peru. These arrowheads were interchangeable with some I had picked up in Pampa Colorado, which is 120 miles farther west, on the seacoast.

The information becomes a little less scanty with the appearance of the society of the Valdivias, which I shall discuss later. This coastal society seems to have been active from 2500 to 1500 B.C., after which it seems to have been succeeded by the Machalilla society, between 2000 and 1500 B.C. Then, starting in 1500 B.C., the tribes that left us traces of the Chorrera society seem to have little by little come to dominate the coast and to colonize the regions of Guayas, Manabí, and, finally, Manta Bay and Caráquez Bay, creating what archaeologists call the Bahia or Bay Culture.

According to some researchers, Asiatic influences continuously made themselves felt on the Ecuadorian coast, and probably also in Central America, until about 200 B.C. These researchers say the arrival of Asiatic elements is proved by the presence of objects of Indonesian or Malaysian origin. But the impact of such migrations is a very controversial subject.

In the course of the following centuries, the coastal Ecuadorian societies seem to have declined, perhaps as a result of a climatic cycle that created unfavorable conditions for agriculture. Here again, the last pre-Hispanic centuries show the effects of migrations from the upper Andes and a phenomenon of concentration in fewer, larger settlements. Finally, the Incas entered Manabí, but only for a brief period, perhaps twenty-five years at most.

The history of both the ancient and middle periods of the Ecuadorian upper Andes has remained almost totally obscure. The only thing we know is that the high plateaus were inhabited by tribes who practiced a technologically advanced agriculture and built planting terraces and irrigation systems. Apparently, these populations were constantly harassed by warlike groups who came up from the hot regions to invade their lands. To these people the Spanish invasion may have appeared to be just one more raid, and the pacification that immediately followed the Conquest may have seemed a blessing. All resistance quickly stopped, therefore, with the poor Caras and Cañaris of the high plateaus believing they at last had peace. Thus, in 1547 the Italian traveler Benzoni could comfortably visit the country and meet the cacique of Colonche, on the Pacific Coast.

To sum up, the population pattern when the Incas occupied Ecuador may be seen as follows.   Bear in mind that the migrations that occurred, during the last pre-Columbian centuries as well as during the first centuries of Hispanicization, are illustrated by the complete name changes we may observe. The modern provinces bear pre-Columbian names that no longer correspond to the names the chroniclers reported. Thus, as discussed later, Pichinchas are living on the territory of the Panzaleos, Pastos in the province of the Carchis, Tungurahuas on the lands of the Purujas, and so on.

The Amazonian lowland territories (the Oriente) were inhabited by very primitive tribes, of whom the best known—those living in the south—have entered history as the Jivaros, discussed later. As late as 1540, Cieza de León noted that the Jivaros were still trying to invade the high plateaus, mostly to loot.

The Pacific Coast was densely populated by the Caráquezes, Mantas, Huancavelicas, and Punas, to whom I shall also return.

In the northern Andes one would have met the Pastos, an unpleasant group restricted to what is now the province of Carchi, with the cities of Pasto in Colombia and Tulcán in Ecuador. And around the towns of Ibarra and Otavalo, in the province of Imbabura, one still finds descendants of the Caras.

The central Andes, the region of the active volcanoes around what is now Quito, as well as Cotopaxi in the provinces of Tungurahua and Pichincha, were divided between the Panzaleos and Purus.

Farther south, the Cañaris lived in the Azuay area, and the Paltas were where the colonial town of Cuenca was later built.

Some evidence of the Cuzco princes' presence is found in the high plateaus, where active volcanoes still rumble. The best examples are the fortress of Ingapirca and a number of *tambos* (garrisons equipped with silos and storehouses), as well as the Tomebamba complex, all near Cuenca. The Incas' palace in Quito has not survived; even its ruins have been destroyed. The hewn stones used to build its walls must have been reused to build the Hispanic churches in what later became the Ecuadorian capital.

In the sixteenth century, Ecuador had not yet progressed. Cieza de León, who visited the plateaus ten years after the conquest and the official founding of the Hispanic town of Quito, describes this city as a big, poverty-stricken village where a few Spaniards lived with their livestock.

I have found only two references to a tribe bearing a name that sounds like Quito: the Quijos, who lived to the east in the hot lands; and the name *Iquitos*, a town located on the bank of the Amazon in what is now Peru.

The most important pre-Columbian monuments have survived farther north, in the region of Otavalo. Here one may visit the *tolas*, big mounds topped with platforms reached by way of stone staircases. Today these tolas are covered with grass, but the excavations carried out several years ago by a German archaeologist allowed me to verify that the platforms must have served as bases for buildings, probably temples surrounded by storehouses, whereas the encompassing tiers could have either held buildings intended as dwellings places or served as farming terraces. The tolas are attributed to a Caras group that seems to have subsequently gone down to the Pacific Coast and occupied Esmeraldas.

THE COOL ECUADORIAN COAST

The general atmospheric circulation and the rising cold waters whose effects are felt along the coasts of Chile and Peru also make the coast of Ecuador arid as far as the zone where the equatorial countercurrent brings warm waters close to the continental shores.

The two systems meet a little below Esmeraldas, around Coaque. Cojimies is still hidden in a deep forest, though just a little lower down, where the province that the natives called Manabí begins, Caráquez Bay is already cold in winter. The Spaniards called the inhabitants of the Indies the *canaques* or *caraques*. This is an Arawakan name that reappears all along the Pacific. Similarly, one finds an An-con in Peru and another in Panama. These names remind me of An-Kor in southern Asia. There is also a Pisco in Peru corresponding to Piscop in Haiti.

If we draw a line along the second parallel south from the ocean to the upper cordillera, we would come across four climatic zones:

• An arid floor, dried out by meterological conditions that prevent any precipitation. This zone is now untimbered, and the soil there is becoming unfit for agriculture. Without the protection of a savannah, it is being washed away and ravaged by wadis whenever heavy rains occur in the cordillera.

• A hot, tropical floor.

• A cool floor that is, botanically speaking, still tropical.

• Finally, the puna, the grassy, alpine upper Andes, locally called the *paramos;* an area where volcanoes emerge.

The pre-Columbian sites of Manabí were all located in the arid floor on the terraces found along the seacoast. But the villages were actually located along interior sections of the coastal strip, on the green, wooded hillocks that survive on some rain brought by easterly winds from the Atlantic. In pre-Columbian times, Manabí was a country of savannahs and forests, intersected by rifts where watercourses coming down from the high Andes flowed during the rainy season. It was an economically prosperous region, a fact attested to by the density and richness of the archaeological remains that have survived there. As a result, it interested the Incas, who annexed and dominated it during a short period, ruling the country from the high Andes, where they relied on their Huachalla fortress. The chroniclers thought that the princes of Cuzco were attracted by the abundant fish found in the cold waters along the Manabí coast and also by La Plata Island, located a good distance out to sea from Machalilla and thus important from the point of view of navigation.

A report dated 1526 still described Manabí as a very prosperous zone, with many large, fortified settlements. This whole section of the Ecuadorian coast was an active navigation and trade center. The lands must have been poor, but the sea offered many resources. Erect stones, menhirs, lizards carved in stone, U-shaped stone headrests typical of Central America, and a great many jewels have been found there, indicating continuous trade.

The heart of Manabí may have been the natural port of Manta. Rivet called the natives he observed in this area the Mantas. Between the Mantas and the Esmeraldas, however, the Spaniards found the Caraquezes, who dominated the lovely bay of the same name where the Chone River meets the sea.

The farther south one goes, the more accentuated the aridity becomes. Because of temperature inversions, it can no longer rain, and the winter becomes a season dominated by fogs and cool winds.

On the mainland, opposite La Plata Island, archaeologists have excavated the pre-Columbian villages of the so-called Machalilla society. They succeeded the Valdivia society, discussed below.

After crossing the Colonche River, one reaches the Santa Elena Peninsula, the waters of which abound with fish where maritime activity was the most pronounced. (The Galapagos archipelago, located nine hundred miles out to sea, was likewise known to the pre-Columbians, who left fragments of their pottery there.) This is the country where the Spaniards met the Huancavelicas, a tribe bearing a name that appears in several places in the upper Peruvian Andes.

The Santa Elena Peninsula was once fertile and prosperous. Now it is in the last stage of deforestation, and the aridity of the region is becoming more and more accentuated. The livestock breeders who settled here have destroyed the savannahs that protected the soil from evaporation, and in destroying the rich plant life they also changed the climate.

Photographs taken by archaeologists fifty years ago show the pre-Columbian sites of the region to be still covered by trees. To revitalize the region, it would be necessary to construct a canal bringing the warm waters of the Guayas River to the peninsula. These waters are wasted anyway, since they flow into the Gulf of

Guayaquil. The construction of such a canal would present no difficulties, since the land is flat, and it would make this coast very rich.

The effects of the cold waters are increasingly felt as one nears the tip of the peninsula. Their influence is observable as far as Guayaquil, where, despite the proximity of dense tropical forest and the existence of an enormous mass of warm river waters forming Guayas Bay, the winter is cool from May to November.

Here the vegetation gradually changes from savannah to tropical forest. The region was heavily populated before Hispanicization. Remains of the pre-Columbian agricultural systems can be found practically everywhere, either on the slopes of the lower Andes, where farming terraces still protrude through the vegetation, or on the terraces overhanging the ocean, which were Ecuador's principal centers of oil exploitation until just a few years ago.

From what we know of Ecuadorian archaeology, I would guess that the pre-Hispanic settlements were of two complementary types: farming villages and fishing camps or villages. I have eaten delicious spiny lobsters and enormous oysters on the peninsula. Seafood is still abundant there.

In Valdivia, also on the Santa Elena Peninsula, Emilio Estrada discovered one of the earliest South American archaeological sites containing pottery. Valdivia and the surrounding sites, where ashes and debris stretch over numerous acres, must have been a major population center. The Smithsonian archaeologists who worked very hard in Valdivia, Evans and Meggers, think the settlers in this site were living in a terminal Mesolithic age that was still preagricultural but was already using pottery. In my opinion (and in this I agree with Bosch Gimpera), the Valdivians must have been a Neolithic society of people who cultivated plants for food. The plant debris must have disappeared because of the humidity, and it will be necessary to study the pollen to be sure. Moreover, the site contains many delightful little female statuettes more typical of a farmers' village than of a Mesolithic settlement.

Evans and Meggers were also impressed by the similarities they saw between Valdivian pottery decoration and the contemporaneous Jomon pottery of Japan. They think Valdivia may have been the landing point of a Japanese immigration, which would explain the sudden appearance of a population for which no antecedents have yet been found and of which not even Valdivia seems to have been the point of origin. Evans and Meggers seem to suggest that the shapes and decorations typical of Valdivian pottery appear and disappear abruptly without undergoing perceptible development.

Observations of this kind reinforce the theories of authors who consider that the cultural changes we observe in South America were the result of transpacific migrations. Authors like Heine Geldern and Covarrubias have shown us examples of Indonesian decorative motifs that are found among the Mayas, Japanese motifs in Valdivia, and Chinese motifs in the Chavín art of Peru. (Let us recall that Jomon-type vessels with a round base and a square neck are found even in the Neolithic sites of central Europe.) I would personally add perhaps even African themes that are noticeable in the basin of the Amazon.

Other authors, however, treat the appearance of comparable traits as the consequence of a multilineal cultural evolution, the origins of which should be found within a common but very early Asiatic tradition. The matter is still being debated.

THE GUAYAS: A GEOGRAPHICAL BOUNDARY

Past the Santa Elena Peninsula, one gradually reaches a temperate zone which rapidly mingles with a very warm tropical forest. Here the waters of the big rivers that run into the Bay of Guayas counterbalance the effects of the cold waters of the Peruvian current. The Guayas thus forms a barrier of jungle and swamps that separates Ecuador from the arid central Andes.

Until recently it was supposed that this region had formerly been unpopulated and unattractive to the pre-Columbians. New studies, however, have indicated that the vicinity of Guayaquil was settled, at least during the last pre-Columbian centuries, by farmers who left traces of their activities in the form of farming terraces rising one above another on the hillsides. In 1573, Guayaquil still had only 152 inhabitants. They were Creoles, or people of Spanish origin, in contrast to the natives of the country.

Opposite Guayaquil, on Puná Island, there existed a very heavily defended place that the Spaniards had a hard time destroying. According to Agustín de Zarate, "The Puná were rich, warlike, and socially well-organized; they used 'balsas,' rafts made of straw and the trunks of very light tropical trees, which could transport fifty men and three horses; on their island was a temple with a formidable idol. . . ."

This coastal strip, favorable to maritime barter, was not propitious for communication by land, because of the several hundred miles of swampy forests that stretch between what is now Guayaquil and the outskirts of Tumbes in Peru. As soon as one nears Tumbes, however, the scenery becomes Andean again, and the cordillera once more comes down to the seashore. In pre-Columbian as well as colonial times, people going from Peru to the northern countries thus had to go either by sea or through the high Andes, over the Inca road connecting Tumbes to Cuenca and Ingapirca. Some sections of this road have survived, parts that must have passed through what are now the towns of Zarumilla and Loja.

The history of the central Andes begins with Tumbes. It was a fortress defending the north coast of Peru in pre-Columbian times. It was conquered by the Incas a few years prior to Pizarro's arrival in the area.

THE FAR SOUTH: THE ARCHIPELAGOS, PATAGONIA, AND TIERRA DEL FUEGO

The highest summits of the cordillera, over twenty-three thousand feet high, are found in the southern Andes. The highest mines in the world are operated here. Ten-thousand-foot-high peaks are still to be found as far south as the fiftieth parallel, and a mountain eight thousand feet high rises in the island of Tierra del Fuego, at the very tip of the continent, where glaciers enter the ocean.

From the forty-fourth parallel south, the area off the coast is broken up into a multitude of islands, the Chilean archipelago. The largest island in the complex is Chiloé.

The Far South is of great interest from the point of view of prehistoric human geography. Patagonian caves were inhabited during the high Holocene epoch, and immigrants from Australia by way of Antarctica may have entered the continent through the island of Tierra del Fuego. Subsequently, these regions were settled by other groups who seem to have come from the eastern slopes of the Andes, maybe from quite far away. Later still, the moist, wooded lands of what is now southern Chile were invaded by more highly developed people, the proud and courageous Araucanians, to whose history I shall return. They established themselves from the Maule River to the forty-third parallel.

At the southern tip of the continent, just a few decades ago, some researchers were able to share the life of the last Patagonians, the last descendants of groups that have since disappeared. Observing them has taught us a great deal about the ecology of bands that live by collecting, hunting, or fishing, to the exclusion of any agricultural activity.

Finally, let us not forget that the Andes are flanked far out in the Pacific by Easter Island. It was already populated when it was invaded by immigrants from Polynesia. It must have formed an early bridge between Asia and South America.

Archaeology reveals an invasion of Polynesian origin, from already inhabited islands, but does not tell us who the previous inhabitants were, where they had come from or when. The original settlement of the island remains a complete mystery, and here we are confronted with another exciting problem of American prehistory, for this first migration occurred quite long ago. Easter Island being miles from any coast, one can no longer maintain that groups living in a very simple style could not have been excellent navigators on the high seas. The great figures carved out of volcanic tuff, or tufa, must be the work of later Polynesian conquerors.

In August 1520, in the middle of a harsh winter and amid storms, Magellan's ships entered the strait that bears his name. This strait, bordered by rocks and covered with ice and snow, separates the continent from a large island, the coast of which was illuminated at night by hearths in the natives' camps. (On glacier-covered Santa Inès Island, one would think he was in Greenland, whereas the corresponding latitude in the northern hemisphere is actually that of Scotland.) So the island was named Tierra del Fuego, Land of Fire. After weeks of extreme hardship, on the memorable day of November 28, the fleet finally entered the Pacific, rounding the continent for the first time.

The Patagonian territories did not suit the sixteenth-century Europeans, who were not prepared to survive in such an environment. Attacked by natives defending their hunting and fishing grounds, many of Magellan's sailors were killed or died of hunger. The boats were badly damaged by storms, and only a remnant of the fleet made its way home via the Philippines. But Magellan never reached home to enjoy the triumph, for he was killed in the Philippines by natives. With the only remaining vessel, the thirty surviving men tightened their belts and managed to return to Lisbon.

The route opened by Magellan through the strait is so difficult for sailboats that it was finally abandoned. As early as the eighteenth century, ships were passing around Tierra del Fuego south of Cape Horn and as far as the fifty-sixth parallel.

It was around 1579 that Europeans came into contact with the natives of Patagonia. At first this contact was friendly, but soon it became disastrous following attempts at colonization and the introduction of European sheep, which the Patagonians started hunting, calling them white guanacos.

Today there are no true Patagonians left; only a few mixed-blood individuals have survived. All the purebloods have died—first hunted by colonists, then confined in restricted areas by missionaries, who tried to "civilize" them. The survivors, who were crowded together, living an existence different from their traditional way of life, soon disappeared, killed off by alcohol, mental disorder, and disease.

The Patagonians were very well adapted to a cold, rugged country of lakes, bushy savannahs, and forests. It is more or less rainy there according to the area, and it sometimes snows even in the summer. The few Europeans capable of recording scientific facts have described them as being light-skinned men who painted their bodies red and smeared them with grease in order to protect themselves from the cold—rough-haired men, with thick, bushy, black, wiry hair, and always with a hunting weapon (a bow or a sling) in hand.

In addition to the mainland, the Patagonian complex comprises four groups.

TIERRA DEL FUEGO, THE MAIN ISLAND

Triangular and about nineteen thousand square miles in area, Tierra del Fuego was inhabited by the Onas, a people made up of two tribes, the Selk'nams and Haushes. The Onas were big, handsome men who dressed in vicuña skins— land people who lived from gathering and hunting in the prairies and forests. Their game was mainly guanacos, foxes, and coypus, web-footed aquatic rodents.

The Onas did not use boats, so it is supposed that they came from the continent, thanks to the good-neighbor relations they had maintained with the Tehuelches of the mainland as well as the Yahgans and Alacalufs, their neighbors in the archipelago.

The Onas practiced neither agriculture nor stockbreeding, but they had domesticated the dog, did hunt mammals with bows shooting arrows with poisoned stone tips, and they trapped birds. They also fished from the shore and in rivers. They made *charqui*, meat dried by fire, typical of the Peruvian Andes, and preserved mushrooms.

In order to protect themselves against the cold, the Onas used to build shelters by stretching red-painted guanaco skins in the path of the wind. For longer sojourns they settled in tepees, conical huts covered with branches, and a much bigger tepee was built for ceremonial purposes. Certain North American natives such as the Sioux are also depicted as living in tepees that were dismantled and transported from one camp to another.

Men and women alike dressed in long skin cloaks that came down to the ankles. During extremely cold weather, they wore long strips of cloth wound spirally around their legs from the ankles to the knees. On their feet they wore moccasins, often equipped with branches in order to keep them from sinking into soft snow. The men wore a triangular cap on their heads and the women wore an undergarment and a loincloth, both made of leather.

The Onas removed their body hair with two shells forming a pair of pincers, but they wore the hair on their heads long and disheveled, though they possessed combs. They painted red, white, black, blue, green, yellow, or slate gray stripes on their bodies, and they wore necklaces, pendants, and bracelets as either ornaments or amulets.

They did not know how to weave or make pottery. Instead of ceramic containers, they used skins and baskets, leather buckets, and bladders.

The Onas' mythology provides an interesting indication about the history of the human settlement of Patagonia. According to tradition, an ancestral god, K'aux, gave each Ona family one of the thirty-nine hunting territories he had established in the area. According to the standards usually applied by prehistorians, this figure would represent about thirty-nine thousand people, or a density of .32 inhabitants per square mile.

How many Onas were there before contact with Europeans? Apparently two to four thousand were still alive at the end of the nineteenth century. In 1920 only one hundred remained, and since then they have died out completely.

THE CAPE HORN ARCHIPELAGO

This area was inhabited by the Yahgans, who lived in wooded islands bordered by cliffs and along the southern coast of Tierra del Fuego. These Yahgans, or Yamanas, as they called themselves, had been known since 1624. They spoke five dialects of a language once thought to be original, unrelated to other American languages, but which has by now been linked to the Andean group. Although the Onas had words for the numbers from 1 to 6 and for 10, the Yahgans used only the numbers, 1, 2, and 3.

Like the Onas, the Yahgans had domesticated the dog, but they were not really land people. Equipped with boats and using harpoons like the Eskimos, they lived off the ocean, on seafood, fish, sea mammals, and birds. For vegetables they ate herbs, celery, and mushrooms. Objects decorated with modest artistic themes, and made of multicolored dots and lines, were observed among the Yahgans. With regard to dress, see the description of the Onas. The differences were minimal.

There were no permanent villages. People led isolated lives in camps of two or three families, in cone-shaped tepees. Fire was obtained by a spark produced by striking two stones together. This technique distinguishes the Yahgans from the majority of South American groups and from Eskimos, who obtain fire by quickly rotating a small stick in a cup that contains highly flammable plant matter.

It is thought that there were still over twenty-five hundred Yahgans in the nineteenth century, but today they have died out completely.

THE WESTERN ARCHIPELAGO

The western islands were inhabited by the Alacalufs, who lived in a much harsher environment. According to José Emperaire, the west coast of the extreme south of the continent remained blocked by ice until about seven thousand years ago. Therefore, the Alacalufs must have arrived in the archipelago fairly recently, whereas the Onas could have entered the east coast of the southern tip much earlier, possibly before the last glacial period, the Valders.

The Alacalufs were little people. Their height ranged between 60.9 and 62.5 inches for men and 56.9 and 57.7 inches for women. Their appearance was truly Asiatic, with thick black hair, mongoloid spots, and very little body hair. They, too, painted their bodies, but only with black and white paint.

These people lived in hemispherical rather than cone-shaped huts, which were made of curved branches covered by straw. They lived totally dependent on the ocean for protein from fish, shellfish, and sea mammals. They, like the Eskimos and the Yahgans, used the harpoon. Their boats were made of boards sewn together. They traveled the year round on such boats, diving from them without discomfort even in winter into the icy water, to gather a meal of blue mussels.

For other details relating to their material life, see the description of the Onas and Yahgans. The equipment of the three groups was generally rudimentary, except for hunting and fishing gear. Even bone fishhooks were not used until late. In earlier times, fishhooks were made by filing down blue mussels or bending acacia thorns into a curve.

Contacts between the Alacalufs and Europeans were infrequent until the nineteenth century. Several thousand Alacalufs must have existed a hundred years ago, but today there are only two or three hundred left, and they are of mixed blood.

THE CHONOS

Known since 1553, the Chonos lived to the north of the Alacalufs, between the archipelago and Chiloé Island, which was settled by the Araucanians, discussed below. Here the environment was a little less harsh and the Spaniards attempted to colonize their territory, known as the Guaitecas Islands during the Hispanic period.

The Chonos were in continuous conflict with their Araucanian neighbors, to whom they sold slaves captured from the Alacalufs.

The language of the Chonos has been lost, but it is thought to have been related to the language of the Araucanians. According to documents left by the Jesuits, there were hardly any more than five hundred Chonos left in the eighteenth century. The last survivor was seen in 1875. The disappearance of this little people is particularly unfortunate since the Chonos are thought to have engaged in gathering, and maybe even cultivating, potatoes, the tuber that subsequently became so important in the pre-Columbian world of the central Andes.

THE PATAGONIANS OF THE MAINLAND

The territory extending at the bottom of the eastern slope of the Andes between the fortieth and fifty-second parallels and about a thousand miles long is only partially hilly—its easternmost part is covered by a moist prairie. As one walks down from north to south, the terrain changes. At first one goes through dry, brushy savannahs, but later, approaching the sea, the land is forested.

The earliest natives known to have lived in this territory were the Puelches and Tehuelches. Among the Tehuelches, a band included 150 to 300 individuals, or at most 60 families, but sometimes only 25. Five families would share one tent. Therefore, a camp contained no more than 12 tents, and bands of 500 people were rare.

Each band lived in one territory, but sometimes four bands (or 500 to 1,000 people) coexisted in the same territory. The territory was then subdivided so that each family could control its own area.

A few Araucanians were also in this area of the mainland, following a migration that originated west of the Andes. But this episode occurred late, in the eighteenth century. At that time there were ten to fifteen thousand Tehuelches and perhaps as many as ten thousand Puelches. Today they have all died out or been absorbed into the Argentine population through crossbreeding.

These natives were basically hunters, using bows and arrows and dogs to hunt guanacos, ostriches, deer, and rodents.

They also used the bola, the weapon of three stones attached to the end of a small cord. Bird noted the presence several millennia ago of such bolas in Patagonia, and we find them among the pre-Columbian objects typical of the Collao and Tiahuanaco areas. More recently, bolas have been found in the *sambaquis* or shell mounds of the Brazilian coast, together with cigar-shaped weights for fishing lines and small perforated maces like the ones I have found in villages of the upper-central Andes in strata nine thousand years old. Bolas, therefore, are a very early type of equipment.

Food gathering, however, played a much greater role among the Puelches than among their neighbors the Onas, and they also ate freshwater mollusks. They lived in camps each grouping a few families and did not practice agriculture. The piedmonts could provide sufficient resources only for small nomadic or semisedentary bands, like the Puelches and Tehuelches, in the anthropological classification of "marginal" tribes.

These bands had neither social stratification nor chiefs. In North America, ways of life comparable to those of the Tehuelches have been observed. The Shoshones of Nevada are an example. On the other hand, South America apparently did not have bands who lived like the Eskimos.

Going northward, and moving away from the cordillera, one enters dry, grassy pampas and the cool, moist grasslands that today make up the province of Buenos Aires. The inhabitants of these pampas were undoubtedly in contact with and influenced by various groups: inhabitants of the high inter-Andean valleys, the Araucanians, and Guaranis, who lived in the Chaco, the savannah along the Parana River. The Guaranis were active traders with distant territories. They probably taught the art of making pottery to the inhabitants of the pampas. The latter probably obtained their pre-European metal objects from barter with the metallurgists in the inter-Andean valleys, Mendoza Valley, or even from what is now Bolivia.

THE ARAUCANIANS

The Araucanians lived on the western slope of the cordillera as far south as the southern tip of Chilóe Island in central Chile, as it is called by geographers, between the thirty-seventh and forty-third parallels.

Coquimbo, on the thirtieth parallel, forms the southern boundary of the Chilean desert. After this boundary, the climate becomes progressively less dry. After crossing the Bío-Bío River and entering the city of Concepción, we enter humid Chile.

The hilly southern part of central Chile receives heavy rainfall all year round. The flora there consists mainly of birches and cypresses. I have always been struck by the fact that the Araucanians formed a vigorous society, whereas the inhabitants of northern California and western Canada, who lived in a comparable environment, never practiced agriculture.

Traveling upward from Araucanian lands by way of the valleys entering the cordillera, one used to come across the Pehuenches, marginal bands who lived mainly off the seeds of the araucaria, a pine tree that forms big forests. In the seventeenth century, these Pehuenches spoke Araucanian, but they must have originally belonged to a different group that was either Tehuelche or Ona.

The Araucanians were mentioned for the first time in Alonso de Ercilla's epic poem *La Araucana*, written between 1569 and 1589. The Incas had called them the Aucas, which is the Quechua word for *rebels*.

During their pre-Columbian history, the Araucanians infiltrated lands to the east of the Andes, south of the town of Mendoza, then proceeded from there into the Argentine pampa.

The western Araucanians, the ones who remained Andean, formed three groups: the Picunches, the Mapuches, and the Huiliches. Each group spoke a dialect related to the same linguistic family, an independent language that belonged to the south Andean group.

Estimations as to the number of Araucanians living at the time Europeans arrived vary from five hundred thousand to two million. Whatever the figure, it is clear that their country was densely settled until they made contact with the Spaniards. Today there are three hundred thousand Araucanians, and they are increasing in number.

The Spaniards apparently first obtained information regarding these populations by questioning the Incas. According to tradition, the Inca Tupac Yupanqui was the first to try to invade Araucania, around 1450 to 1480. This campaign, however, ended in the defeat of the Cuzco troops. The southern border of the empire was then fixed at the Maule River, around the thirty-second parallel, a little to the north of the present cities of Concepción and Talca.

Almagro was the first Spaniard to encounter the Araucanians. It was not until much later, however, in 1541, that Pedro de Valdivia invaded the northern part of the Mapuches' country and built the line of forts that bear his name, right in the middle of the enemy's territory. In 1558, Hurtado de Mendoza advanced as far as Chiloé, but the next forty years witnessed fierce struggles that ended in the death of the Spanish governor, Garcia de Loyola, and in the almost total destruction of the Hispanic colonies. Thanks to captured horses, numerous Araucanians were then able to take refuge in and settle on the eastern slope of the Andes, and subsequently to invade the pampas from which, in the eighteenth century, they were still threatening the city of Buenos Aires.

More peaceable relations between the Araucanians and European immigrants were not established until the end of the eighteenth century, and the total pacification of the region, still interrupted by revolts, dates back only to 1882.

Given the environment, it was normal for the Araucanians to engage in an economy centered essentially on the exploitation of plant resources. Hunting seems to have played a minor role. They ate little meat and led a sedentary life, having formed in very early times strong farming communities. Thus, it is unlikely that they learned to farm as a result of contacts with the Quechuas of the highlands or following Inca raids. It is possible that one day Araucania will be shown to be one of the first agricultural centers of the New World.

Their corn still ripens as far south as Chiloé, and potatoes, of which they were familiar with as many as ten varieties, beans, gourds, red peppers, quinoa, oca (a wood sorrel), peanuts, strawberries, and many other unidentified fruits and seeds were also grown in their gardens.

It does not seem that farming was done according to the slash-and-burn system. Of course, the land was cleared by burning, but according to one authority it was reused after having been allowed to lie fallow for at least three years following one year of production. But I think the slash-and-burn method requires much longer periods of rest for the earth.

Irrigation by canals was practiced in the northern part of the territory, which is already semiarid. The use of fertilizers, however, apparently remained unknown there.

Women did most of the field work, using wooden spades. Crops were supposed to have been harvested on a communal basis.

In addition to cultivated plants, the Mapuches ate a wide variety of wild green vegetables, berries, fruits, tubers, and seeds, mainly pine nuts, hazelnuts, and the like. Apparently, they did not lack food; until the arrival of Europeans, they seem to have escaped the famines that were so frequent in arid regions. Besides, let us not forget that they lived near the sea.

The Araucanians raised two kinds of domestic dogs, and the Spaniards found llamas in their villages. Camelids, however, may have been an Inca importation.

Although the Mapuches lived sedentary lives, they followed a settlement pattern different from that of the Quechuas and Aymaras, who were city builders. A few families joined together to form hamlets far from each other, for fear of evil spells. Each hamlet apparently consisted of people related to each other and led by one member of the community. As among the Carib tribes, some of their villages were protected by fences and may have served as places of refuge.

The houses were rectangular, oval, or polygonal. They were sometimes as large as 140 feet long by 30 feet wide and 15 feet high, with one to eight doors. Valdivia described these houses as being covered by a four-sided roof supported by a strong, lengthy central beam, the whole framework being covered with hay. The walls were made of bamboo slats and the interior was subdivided by partition walls. These houses were built for multifamilial occupation.

On the average, thirty to forty people lived in a single building, but the chroniclers tell us that in some cases as many as ninety lived in one house. Some sort of privacy was established inside by the partitions. Each family maintained its own hearth. Fires were started by using the rotating drill rather than by striking pieces of pyrite together, which was done by the Patagonians. As usual with most pre-Columbians, they probably did not use furniture.

Similarly, we know very little about the pre-Columbian dress of the Mapuches. Today their way of dressing is influenced by European styles. It is thought that in pre-Columbian times they could have worn the *unku* or Andean shirt, a loincloth, and a *chuyo*, a pointed wool cap covering the string that held their hair. They went barefoot, removed all their body hair, and neither painted nor tattooed their bodies. Their ears were pierced so that each could hold a ring, a practice that may have been introduced by Europeans. Contacts established later with the highland peoples introduced them to the use of *tupis* or pins and other metal ornaments.

Clothes were woven on small looms, or twined or looped. Weaving was probably introduced through contact with the upper Andes, as was the use of pottery and metal objects.

The elements necessary for a valid reconstruction of the social and political organization of the Araucanians are missing. It is thought that they were not ruled by some central authority and that they chose high chiefs only in exceptional circumstances, such as in wartime. Furthermore, we know that they were very belligerent and the different groups fought with each other frequently, not for the purpose of conquest, but rather for prestige and to obtain prisoners. The captives were then ritually tortured and sacrificed and their skulls were used as cups for libations. Cannibalism was probably practiced.

Battles were fought with bows or spear throwers and long reed arrows equipped with wooden or stone arrowheads, as well as with wooden maces, slings, and flint axes. The chronicles tell us that they used reed rafts called balsas and canoes made of three boards bound together, over which a sail was hoisted. The canoes could carry eight to ten oarsmen. It is also claimed that they had boats capable of transporting up to thirty people, but all this is rather difficult to believe, since it has not been proven that pre-Columbians from Chile were then trading by sea by using sailing vessels.

The Araucanians also differed from the natives of Patagonia in that they engaged in sports and were in the habit of organizing contests and music festivals. They played a kind of hockey or entertained themselves by moving about on stilts. Games of chance were very popular with them and they drank heavily. Apparently they had never heard of smoking or taking snuff, which is strange, because the Atacamanians farther north were using smoking tubes and tobacco tablets. On the other hand, they seem to have been interested in problems of cosmogony and astronomy. They observed eclipses, kept a calendar of twelve lunar months, and had divided the day into twenty-four hours. But again I have reservations as to the indigenous character of these cultural traits, which have been reported by modern Chilean authors. In surviving the invasion, the Araucanians became acculturated and adopted numerous European customs. On the whole, they clearly surpassed their southern neighbors in the intellectual sphere.

The Spanish invasion resulted in the decay of the Mapuche society. The Araucanians turned out to be the only South American society with the courage and power to resist the Europeans for three centuries, after which they survived by crossbreeding and adapting to present conditions of life in Chile. Thus, theirs is a rather exceptional case in Andean history. The Araucanians are to be considered in the same category as the inhabitants of the high plateaus in Bolivia, Peru, and Ecuador who have survived while retaining the character of the original tribe. Despite the efforts of missionaries, the Araucanian culture has remained very original, scarcely influenced by European ways of life.

Of course, their political power as a nation was destroyed. Uninterrupted wars caused depopulation, as the Mapuches, busy with fighting, did not produce enough food anymore. Disease and the permanent state of revolt lasting until at least the seventeenth century killed off the Mapuches. Where the chroniclers had spoken of troops of a thousand warriors, only bands of fifty armed men were mentioned by the end of the sixteenth century. Chiloé Island, which could have fed a population of perhaps fifty thousand people, was the first place to be depopulated, the Mapuche farmers being taken captive to be sold as slaves.

But physically and culturally the Mapuches are still present in Chile, where they now form a not-negligible portion of the population.

THE DIAGUITES AND THEIR NEIGHBORS

The Andes that extend from the Argentine province of Salta (around the twenty-fourth parallel) to the mountainous part of the province of San Juan (around the thirty-second parallel) were inhabited at the time the Spaniards arrived by people the conquerors called the Diaguites. There were perhaps some twenty thousand of them.

The Diaguites are known to us through Narvaez's *Relación,* his very detailed 1583 account, and then through descriptions by the mission fathers. In the sixteenth century the Diaguites occupied the whole Argentine cordillera except for the Córdoba region, where the Comechingons continued to live. Very warlike, the Diaguites resisted Jesuit infiltration for a hundred years and several times destroyed the outposts of the Spaniards who were trying to take possession of the country. The texts tell the history of the founding and prompt destruction of these missions: Ciudad del Barco in 1550; Córdoba de Calchaqui in 1559; Cañete in 1566; Salta, Talavera, and San Miguel de Tucumán in 1582; La Rioja in 1591; Londres in 1607; Santa Maria in 1617. San Miguel de Tucumán was again destroyed in 1685, and then transferred to Tucumán itself. Only the early towns of La Rioja, Pomán, Salta, and Catamarca have survived. The first seven European expeditions among the Diaguites failed, their leaders being killed by the natives or assassinating each other.

The Diaguites were already Quechuanized in the sixteenth century. The place names in their territory are all thoroughly central Andean. Finally, they worshipped the sun.

The Diaguites were encountered as far as the eastern piedmonts of the arid Andes, near what has since become Santiago del Estero, where about twenty inches of water fall annually. To the west, they had crossed the cordillera and reached the Pacific Coast.

All over the arid Argentine Andes, the Diaguites have left us the ruins of their small fortified settlements, located on easily defensible crests. Narrow paved roads led up to these sites, which are always found near a river or spring. The settlement pattern here was in strong contrast to those of the Patagonians and Araucanians: isolated houses typical of the semiarid Andes have survived. The Diaguites had built dense settlements typical of the highlands.

Archaeologists have observed four types of Diaguite settlements:

• *Pueblos viejos,* or villages, a general name given to pre-Columbian ruins. These villages were made of rectangular houses irregularly placed but forming small groups of buildings joined side by side. Dry stone masonry was used for the walls, which were as high as a man was tall and supported a roof of branches held up by posts.

• *Pucaras,* or strongholds. Located at strategic points, these light fortresses commanded access to the principal valleys or gorges and formed complex defensive systems sometimes surrounded by seven concentric circles of walls high enough to protect archers, with openings to allow attack or retreat. These walls were often complemented by cylindrical towers. In the pucaras, water was obtained from wells or, if there were none, from cisterns.

• Fortified complexes. These seem to have been large camps whose defensive walls surrounded a great number of houses and silos. People from various villages could retreat there.

• Farming terraces. Farmland had to be terraced to retain rainwater and keep the soil from being washed away. In contrast to other groups in the vicinity, the Diaguites practiced only "dry" farming, that is, without irrigation. They seem to have practiced what is called arroyo flood farming, a technique that consists of directing the water of occasional rains to the fields by means of short canals and light dams.

When the Spaniards arrived, the Diaguites were well dressed. Their clothes were made of llama or vicuña wool. They wore long shirts and sandals.

Their art has come down to us in the form of rock carvings, which are often painted with red ocher, and pottery. The best-known style is the "Santa Maria" urn, with a wide neck and side handles.

The Diaguites practiced a highly advanced Andean type of metallurgy. The missionaries described how they worked. Copper ore pulverized on stone mortars was mixed with zinc, gold, and silver. It was then melted in hearths, which were fed oxygen by the wind, and poured into molds. As in the Peruvian Andes, the most common objects made were the chisel, the *tumi* or knife, the *tupi* or pin, a little axe, and tweezers. Gold was beaten into very thin sheets used to decorate masks and jewelry by applying the repoussé or reverse-hammering technique.

Their stonework was also highly advanced. They have left us hafted hatchets, polished-stone chisels, star-shaped maces, all kinds of vessels, and mortars.

A comparative study of the objects the Diaguites used in everyday life shows that some shapes were typically Tiahuanacoid, whereas others, like the pottery aryballos, or large water jar, were typically Inca. The fact that such traits belong to societies very far apart chronologically indicates that the Diaguite society lasted at least five hundred years and possibly more.

It was the western group, which had migrated to the Pacific slope of the Andes, that was most marked by highland traits. At the beginning of the twentieth century, archaeologists thought that, upon its arrival on the Pacific shore, the Diaguite society was influenced by the society known in Peru as the Ika-Chincha chiefdom, which is thought to have succeeded the Nazca political system. Accepting this theory would mean that the Diaguite migration should be placed between the eleventh and fifteenth centuries A.D. But I would like to suggest that the coastal societies of southern Peru have been subject to the influence of groups who had come from the eastern slope of the Andes and in earlier days maybe even from the forest. Such groups could have gone north along the Pacific after they had crossed the Chilean cordillera.

The Diaguites must have formed a stratified society dominated by a warrior class. For example, the decorative motifs on their pottery represent men wearing feather headdresses and armed with spear throwers and long spears. Such traits reinforce the impression of their general insecurity we may feel when visiting their fortified villages and pucaras.

The Spaniards had constant skirmishes with the Diaguites before the latter were wiped out by disease. Each man was equipped with a bow, fifty arrows, and a mace. This information contradicts the scenes depicted on pottery, which show spear throwers rather than bows. It might reveal one more case of the constant migration of forest peoples crossing the Andes and exterminating already weak local societies. The fortified villages and pucaras may correspond to a defensive phase during which the Diaguites were fighting invaders from the hot lowlands, a phase that must have occurred well before the Spaniards' arrival. If this was the case, the Spaniards met not the true Diaguites but the immigrants.

According to Father Bruch, the Diaguites practiced circumcision. Let us recall that Mochica vessels from northern Peru depict circumcised prisoners.

From what the chronicles tell us we may suppose that the Diaguite society had no form of central government and was made up of numerous bands, each governed by a cacique. These bands were continually at war with one another. By the time the caciques realized the dangers of the European invasion and tried to unite their people and stir them up to fight against the Spaniards, it was too late.

South of the Diaguite territory, but still to the east of the cordillera, in the region of Córdoba, there seems to have lived another small group, the Huarpés, who may have been related to the Diaguites.

The Huarpés were described as tall, thin men with brown skin and a lot of hair. These details were given by Father de Lizarraga, who visited the region in 1589. Actually, our knowledge about these people is quite vague. For instance, some chronicles speak of the Huarpés as fishermen-farmers who practiced canal irrigation in the Mendoza region and lived in houses dug out of the ground at the edges of ponds. However, other authors describe them as hunters who might sometimes run as long as two days after a rhea, an American ostrich.

To the east, around Santiago del Estero, lived another society that archae-ologists call Chaco-Santiagueno. These Chacos were settled in savannahs by rivers with intermittent flooding and an aridity that meant the inhabitants could not live far from water sources. The Chacos were also farmers and lived in fenced villages composed of compactly grouped huts covered by thatched roofs.

In this region, explorers noticed continuous strips of elliptical mounds up to 165 feet long on stretches of land varying from half a mile to two miles in length. Unanimity as to the nature of these mounds is far from established. Some ar-chaeologists consider them to be the products of natural erosion, rather than man-made embankments.

The Chacos were importing a few metal objects from the highlands at the time of the Conquest, but on the other hand they were using the bow and wear-ing feather cloaks, traits characteristic of forest peoples. We know through the Jesuits that some Chacos had already learned Quechua. We may thus include the Chacos with the circum-Andean tribes.

In the province of Salta, archaeologists have observed remains of a society that they have described under the name of the Candelaria culture. Typical ruins of this society were found in the last spurs of the eastern Andes, from Jujuy to Tucumán between the twenty-fourth and twenty-eighth parallels, in such great numbers that I must suppose either that the region was very densely settled for a brief time or that a less numerous but static population lived there for several centuries.

Unfortunately, very little is known about the Candelaria society, which is mainly distinguished by the characteristic shapes and decoration of its funerary urns. Their objects in everyday use seem to have been borrowed from the Diaguites.

I am told that the Candelarias smoked bent pipes. If it is confirmed someday that these pipes had already existed in pre-Columbian times and do not represent an acculturization trait resulting from Hispanicization, this would reveal a cultural element that would be exceptional in the upper Andes, where use of the pipe is still considered to have been totally unknown.

The Comechingons lived much farther south, in the provinces of Córdoba and San Luis, from approximately the twenty-ninth to the thirty-fourth parallels in an area of about twelve thousand square miles. This is a wooded country traversed by numerous watercourses whose irregular flow made irrigation indispensable for farming.

The first Europeans described the Comechingons as having beards (a rather unusual attribute on this continent) and wearing long wool tunics.

A historic document, the *Probanza* or judicial inquiry of Pedro Gonzalez, presented to the Cuzco authorities in 1548, provides us with numerous interesting points about this people. Thus, we know that the Comechingons lived neither in stone houses nor big villages. Farmers, they established small, isolated half-underground huts wherever they found water to irrigate their cornfields. According to the account of the governor, Jeronimo de Cabrera, the Comechingons practiced both irrigation by canals and flood agriculture. This assertion is disputed by modern geographers, who find the region too arid to permit irrigation. However, these geographers are not taking sufficiently into account the subsequent deforestation that must have reduced the hydrological resources. The chroniclers add that in time of crisis the Comechingons were able to mobilize as many as forty thousand warriors, but this figure seems highly exaggerated, as it would compare with an Inca army.

Comechingon pottery was mediocre, and apparently metallurgy had not reached them. Their tools, made primarily of stone, consisted of mortars, millstones, projectile points, knives, and bolas.

In the realm of fighting methods, the Comechingons did something unique for pre-Columbians. No less than three chroniclers tell us how they fought at night, in well-formed groups, with bows, protecting the napes of their necks with leather, with their faces painted half black, half white. Night battles constitute an original trait in an animistic world in which people were terribly afraid of meeting spirits who, they believed, went about after nightfall.

North of the Candelaria group, above the twenty-fourth parallel, one enters the punas that extend between Jujuy and San Pedro de Atacama. These regions have a continental climate. A large population lived there in a poor environment, up to an altitude of thirteen thousand feet. On the other hand, the account of Matienzo's trip into the Argentine cordillera in 1566 describes the depopulating of the region after Hispanicization. The journey covered about 345 miles or 16 to 32 miles in a day, the average distance being 20 miles. These distances illustrate how far apart the main stopping places, tambos, or reasonably large villages were by this time.

This population consisted of groups with diverse names who were farmers and great builders of *andenes,* an Aymara name for farming terraces supported by heavy stone walls, which kept the soil damp by retaining water and preventing erosion caused by rainfall. According to other specialists in Peruvian studies, *anden* is not an Aymara or Quechua word but simply comes from the Spanish verb *andar,* meaning *to walk.* The *andenes* were also used as roads.

Contrary to what most uninformed people think, the creation of terraces reduces the area of cultivable surface instead of increasing it, since it limits it to the length of one of the short sides of the triangle instead of the hypotenuse. However, the advantages of terraces—especially the advantage of creating structures capable of retaining humidity—amply compensate for this small drawback. The bottom of each terrace was first covered with an impermeable layer of silt, over which the topsoil was spread.

These farmers may have been immigrants who had come down from the highlands of what is now Bolivia. They could have been a colony the Incas had established there, for many cultural traits typical of the Arequipa region in Peru and of the shores of Lake Titicaca have been observed among them. Thus, the stone blades of their spades (of the so-called Humahuaca type) are interchangeable with the ones I found in our excavations in the Peruvian highlands. The same remark applies to their wooden farming tools, their underground silos covered by corbeled roofs made of stone slabs, their bolas with three stones fastened to one small cord, their slings, their gourds decorated with fire-engraved motifs, and their musical instruments, one of which was the panpipe. Their pottery was also typically Andean, as was their custom of living in stone houses and building pucaras.

The chroniclers tell of the existence of other, nomadic, groups in the neighborhood. The Tonocotes, for example, numbered about thirty thousand and were divided into five subtribes. The Lules and Suris, who hunted ostriches, were also nomads.

THE ATACAMANIANS

It was through the Atacamanians that permanent contact was established, by way of the coast, between the populations of southern Peru and the tribes of central Chile, the Diaguites and Araucanians.

The Atacamanians spoke a language unrelated to that of their neighbors. They inhabited a territory that now constitutes the Peruvian and Chilean provinces of Tacna, Arica, Tarapaca, Antofagasta, and Atacama, an area extending east-west from the puna to the coastal desert.

The puna of Atacama is extremely arid, with only ten to twelve inches of annual rainfall. The pond water is salty. Violent winds blow there and the nights are frosty, even in summer. Thus, not much grows on this puna but small bushes.

Today these highlands are untimbered, but we are told that in the sixteenth century corn was still being grown on a large scale where today only camelids live. Acacias and other shrubs there formerly provided the seeds and nuts that formed a large part of the pre-Columbians' diet. Once more we realize how deforestation causes aridity and ruins all possibilities for farming.

Walking down toward the ocean means crossing the three-thousand-foot-high plateau that separates the upper Andes from the completely dry coastal range which extends over about 580 miles here, from the eighteenth to the twenty-seventh parallels. This coastal desert is one of the driest regions in the world. Therefore, life on the coast was concentrated in little oases, the largest of which did not exceed fourteen square miles. Thus, this territory could not have supported a dense population and the Atacamanians could never have been very numerous. An eighteenth-century census indicated 1,632 tributaries, or about ten thousand people in the oases and the Puna de Atacama. In the beginning of this century, Alcide d'Orbigny counted seventy-five hundred people there.

To the east, the Atacamanians probably infiltrated as far as the regions of Jujuy and Salta, where they practiced a dry agriculture. According to a document written in 1787, Atacamanian was still spoken as far as Tucumán at that time. Since then, the local dialect has disappeared. Now the people there speak either Aymara or Spanish.

To the west, past the coastal range, shell and refuse mounds covering the villages of little groups of fishermen have been found along the Pacific shore, and it is now known that some fishermen had lived there in very early times. Junius Bird has established that some of these villages date back to the high Holocene.

During subsequent periods, some of them much later, these villages were reoccupied by other fishermen, who rounded out their diet with corn and used a style of pottery decoration reminiscent of the so-called Churajon or Arequipa pottery of Peru.

In the nineteenth century, little groups of Chongo fishermen still lived on the coast in huts supported by whale ribs and covered with skins. These people used reed rafts for fishing and ate the roots of rushes, which is singularly reminiscent of the Peruvians who lived in Chilca six thousand years ago. The Chongos are thought to have been Urus who came down from the shores of Lake Titicaca, but this hypothesis is disputed.

Very long gaps still remain to be filled before we can suggest a valid history for this coastal strip. Has it been uninhabitable for several centuries, to be reoccupied only during more favorable periods? A great number of place names in northwest Argentina, Bolivia, and around Lake Titicaca sound like Atacamanian names. On the other hand, excavations carried out in the Argentine province of Salta have revealed successive occupations; the archaeological sequence indicates an evolution from a purely Atacamanian society to a Diaguite society influenced by the Incas, with an intermediate Atacamanian-Diaguite phase followed by a pure Diaguite phase preceding the final Incanized Diaguite stage.

With some experience of geography in arid lands, one can easily see that the Atacamanians' territory gradually became drier, then extremely dry. Savannahs of acacia and tamaruga trees lie buried beneath the sand all along the Pacific coast. Higher up in the arid cordillera, the ruins of numerous pre-Columbian villages are found near springs that are now dry. Furthermore, it is well established that alpacas and even vicuñas used to approach the coastal oases and live in nearby lomas, where vegetation lives upon condensed fog from the ocean. Moreover, some eighteenth-century maps indicate that streams that are dry today were still flowing into the ocean at that time.

Excavations carried out in the Taltal region revealed highland cultural traits as well as ones that indicate contact with forest peoples. Let me cite examples observed while excavating Paracas: combs, carved tablets for taking snuff, small wooden bells for games, shirts, *chuspas* (carrying bags made of fabric with multicolored stripes), the drinking of chicha, the wearing of breastplates as undergarments, panpipes, *quenas* (flutes with one tube), bull-roarers, headdresses of flamingo feathers, and the wearing of multiple braids decorated with cords of colored wool. But in spite of these upper-Andean characteristics, the use of bows and arrows and many other details link the Atacamanians to the forest, even though their pre-Columbian houses were also Andean in type. The houses had no doors and were small (about ten by thirteen feet), grouped in units encircled by a wall, with the total comprising a village that was seven to twenty acres in area.

The Incas exercised total control over the Atacamanians, whose territory had already been considerably reduced by the Diaguites. The chroniclers tell us that the coastal oases served as bases for Cuzco troops as early as the fourteenth century.

The Atacamanian language has not yet completely died out. Known as the Kunza dialect, it is still used by a few people who live in the Puna de Jujuy. A dictionary containing about eleven hundred of its words has been written. Thus, we know that Atacamanian was different from Aymara and Quechua.

Perhaps it was the poverty of their environment that led the Atacamanians to develop barter on a large scale. As a result, they served as liaisons as well as merchandise carriers and organizers of llama convoys in the southern Andes. These convoys traveled along trails that were ten feet wide and bordered by stones, of which several sections are still visible in southern Peru and northern Chile. Their convoys carried dried fish to the upper Andes and brought back edible mimosa seeds gathered on the eastern slopes of the cordillera. They bartered salt, red peppers, wool, imported metal tools, and tobacco. Actually, it would be better to say "a plant that was either snuffed or smoked." Bird found tablets and tubes for taking snuff in the region's graves. Since I have found the same objects on the Peruvian coast, in graves that are thirty-five hundred years old, it seems that there was a very ancient tradition that was common to several Andean peoples. But the existence of tobacco has not been proven.

THE HOT LOWLANDS OF THE SOUTHEASTERN ANDES

In order to complete this tour of the Andes, we must take a quick look at the peoples who lived along the hot piedmonts in the southern half of the cordillera.

A study of the lowlands in the eastern part of the continent has no place in this book, for they are not part of the Andes. Let me simply recall that according to Clifford Evans there were two areas that were settled in this part of the world, one being the Amazonas and Orinoco Basin, the other the southern plains. In the latter, the most heavily populated and most frequented center was the Paraná Basin. There archaeologists have found sites belonging to marginal prefarmers, ignoring the use of pottery that may date back to the high Holocene or earlier.

According to Evans, the Tupis and Guaranis came in great numbers from Brazil and settled in the region around A.D. 800. Europeans encountered their descendants there, living in small fortified villages and eating corn, squash, and fish. Without going into details, let me indicate a few characteristics of these peoples. For instance, on the island of Marajó, at the mouth of the Amazon, archaeologists have found the remains of the same type of house on piles as was built by the groups living on the Ecuadorian coast when Europeans came. Similar houses are still being built today. Corrugated roofs and cement are used now, but the basic principle remains the same.

Even in eastern Brazil, among the Gês, Tupis, and Guaranis, ethnologists have observed cultural traits that are typical of the Africanized Ecuadorian coast. Traits such as wearing a cover over the penis, engaging in collective games and sports, and so on are found practically everywhere in South and Central America, New Guinea, and Australia.

Such facts support the thesis of the diffusionist school and speak in favor of very large, distant migration, probably within continents and from one continent to another. The practice of circumcision should be studied in great detail, because it could indicate early contact with Africa and not just South Asia.

I have already spoken of the Puelches and Tehuelches who inhabited the far southern temperate lands. Along the western frontier of what is now Argentina, around the twenty-second parallel, lived the Chiriguanos. They were Guaranis, a tribe with Caribbean customs who had settled in the lower Andes in protohistoric times, around 1470 or 1475. Therefore, according to Garcilazo de la Vega, they had arrived during the reign of the Inca Tupac Yupanqui.

The Guarani invasion is thought to have taken place in four waves, along the thirteenth parallel. Starting out from the Chaco, their bands went up by way of the Pilcomayo River, reaching the outskirts of what has since become the region of Sucre, in hot Bolivia. There they encountered a people known as the Chichas, but the name of this group seems to be a deformation of *Charca*, the name of a tribe that inhabited the region of Oruro, Cochabamba, and Potosí in the cold Andes.

Apparently, these Guaranis finally conquered all the lower Andes, from the Bermejo River in the south to Santa Cruz in the north, and came into contact with the Mojos, who had settled farther north. Furthermore, it is historically known that several tens of thousands of these Guaranis made trips of over six hundred miles and were a permanent menace to the highland cities like Cuzco and Machu Picchu. They were attracted by the wealth of the inter-Andean valleys and in search of women, salt, wool, and metal objects. The Guaranis finally seem to have settled at the foot of the cordillera, in order to remain near Andean populations they could plunder during occasional raids.

Sarmiento de Gamboa tells that these raids were so harmful that Huayna Capac had to build three fortresses to guard the approaches to the highlands. This may be Incahuasi, whose ruins have survived. Erland Nordenskjöld, Stig Ryden, Hermann Trimborn, and other archaeologists have described the numerous Inca and Tiahuanacoid ruins that may still be seen in Bolivia at the edge of the forest. I have visited some of them myself. Some difficult but important archaeological work remains to be done there.

These Inca fortresses were unable to save the Chanés, who were peaceable Arawaks and excellent farmers. They lived at the foot of the cordillera, where they tried in vain to protect their fields of corn, manioc, peanuts, cotton, and all the products they ate and bartered with the people of the highlands. The Chanés were completely destroyed by the Guaranis, in spite of their defensive efforts and fenced villages.

When the first Spaniards tried to penetrate the lowlands, they encountered similar problems. At first Nuflo de Chavez founded Santa Cruz de la Sierra, not far from the present city of the same name. This outpost was, however, destroyed by the Chiquitos, a barbarous people who were not Guaranis but were warlike farmers who lived in huts grouped in villages heavily protected by fences.

A group that lived on the western shore of Lake Titicaca was also called the Chiquitos. The Mojos lived on the eastern shore. Both of these names are found farther east, in the forest.

The first-mentioned Chiquitos used curare-poisoned arrows that terrorized their enemies. The astonished Spanish chroniclers tell us that they engaged in sports and ritual games, played the flute at dawn, and drank chicha like true circum-Caribbeans, though they spoke a different language.

Next to them lived the Yuracarés, the Mosotenés, and the Chimanés, who also used to attack the people of the highlands but nevertheless were industrious people who built canals, dikes, platforms, and mounds on which they placed their villages in order to escape floods. Some of these groups paid tribute to the Incas, who had tried in vain to take possession of their territory. Thanks to Metraux, we know many details about them. For instance, we know that they cultivated several fields at a distance from their villages, that they lived in rectangular houses with two-sided roofs built aboveground on high posts, and that they decorated their faces and clothes with seals made of beaten bark. Thus, these people could have been moved over to the Ecuadorian coast, where they would have blended right in culturally with the inhabitants of the hot shores of the Pacific.

The most astounding thing for me was to find that their rectangular wicker baskets, decorated with elegant twill weave motifs, were interchangeable with those of the Tiahuanacoid period that I dug up in the Castillo fortress, in the Huarmey Valley on the Peruvian coast.

It may be that some Arawaks destroyed and plundered the Tiahuanaco society, after which they went down to loot the coastal cities, taking along the beautiful pottery they had found in the palaces and temples built around Lake Titicaca. We may speculate, as long as we don't state our speculations as facts.

To the east of La Paz, in the hot lands, were the Lekos, who (we are told) spoke Lapalapa. This name is also found in Chilca, on the central coast of Peru.

Farther north, in the seventeenth century the Mojos were grouped on the upper banks of the Rio Béni, directly at the foot of Lake Titicaca. When missionaries reached them, there were six thousand Mojos left, grouped in seventy villages and trading with the Aymaras of the highlands by using the Mosotenés as intermediaries.

These Mojos attracted the attention of various researchers and were the subject of somewhat more-thorough studies, so we know that they too built their villages on mounds in order to escape floods produced by the torrential rains. These mounds were linked by an interconnecting system of passages ten feet wide and two feet high. During the dry season, traveling was by canoes dug out of tree trunks, along man-made canals that were sometimes three miles long.

The villages were heavily defended by hidden traps, fences, and by an encircling ditch. The huts were round. Meals were prepared outdoors, under rectangular cane roofs covered with mud.

Like other forest peoples, the Mojos slept in hammocks. But they wore long cotton shirts decorated with bright colors, tufts of feathers, bracelets, necklaces, rings, metal plates, and labrets, small polished objects sticking out of the chin through a small hole. The women adorned their hair with ribbons, and both sexes painted complicated designs on their bodies.

According to the chroniclers, the Incas (in this case Topa Yupanqui) did not succeed in dislodging the Mascos, Araonas, and Tacanans who lived east of Cuzco and used to walk as far up as the upper Carabaya Valley to plunder. They were called barbarians, but were already speaking Quechua when the Spaniards first met and decided to exterminate them. But that took a long time—three attempts at colonization and the establishment of small towns or outposts failed, the last being burned down in 1542. Even after colonization succeeded, there were frequent revolts. These "barbarians" were surely different from the Mojos.

Scattered marginal groups had also survived in the neighborhood. One such group was the Sirionos, who went about nude, were seminomadic, and did almost no farming. The missionaries never succeeded in subduing them.

Allan Holmberg explains this stagnation as the result of cultural and psychological factors, one of which was constant hunger that created a state of anxiety. The response was aggressiveness that was worked off in sexual activity. Moreover, the search for food caused extreme exhaustion, for it meant forced marches and exposed people to serious dangers like being hit by falling trees, drowning in swamps, having wounds become infected by thorns, or being bitten by animals. So the Sirionos must have lived in a constant state of depression caused by the impression that they could never dominate an extremely adverse environment where the lack of resources would inevitably cause the tribe to fail.

Among cultural factors, Holmberg cites the technical inferiority of their weapons, which were unsuited to their environment, and their ignorance with respect to the accumulation and preservation of food reserves.

This incapacity to calculate, foresee, and build up reserves is typical of peoples whose social structures have been shattered, and I have often observed it among the Andeans. To be a good farmer, one must be a good boss; but during four hundred fifty years of colonial domination, the Andean has been reduced to a state of peonage, of unskilled labor. Other peoples also (especially Moslems, who believe that Allah will provide) consider that creating reserves is a sacrilege, or at least useless.

For years I tried to teach my Andean assistants, foremen, mechanics, and others that it is useful to foresee the eventual lack of essential products, and that maintaining a reserve of such items would eliminate dangers and loss of time. But each time, my insistence met with reticence, laughter, annoyance, or a negative response expressed more or less openly.

Holmberg has established the activities schedule of a group of Sirionos during a twelve-month period, which gives a picture of the everyday life of such people.

January: hunting, gathering; few agricultural activities; a sedentary life; the rainy season.

February: harvesting of corn, which was planted in November; a sedentary life; the rainy season.

March: gathering of wild fruits; a sedentary life; the rainy season.

April: nothing; the rainy season.

May: harvest of *chuchio* (scientific name unknown); preparations for hunting; sometimes a second corn harvest.

June: hunting; food gathering; nomadism; migrations.

July: nomadism.

August: nomadism or harvest. Sometimes there is a third corn harvest and a second harvest of *camotes* (sweet potatoes). Alcoholic beverages made from a honey base are prepared. Festivals.

September: festivals.

October: preparation of the soil for sowing; hunting; food gathering.

November: corn, sweet potatoes, and manioc are planted.

December: heavy rains. This month is devoted exclusively to hunting.

Going farther north and leaving behind the *yungas*, the Bolivian hot lands, we enter what Peruvians and Ecuadorians call the *montaña*, the hot country of wooded hills that makes the transition between the cordillera and the Amazonian lowlands. There, modern missionaries tried to reorganize the Chunchos, a group formed by remnants of migrating tribes that broke up and scattered along the piedmonts of the Andes. They spoke various languages: Arawak, Carib, Jivaro, Tupian, and so on. It was among the Chunchos that linguists have counted the largest number of different American languages.

These Chunchos formed a distinct contrast to the Quechuas of the uplands. They did not go up into the cold forest, but lived below thirty-three to thirty-nine hundred feet, where they formed a kind of buffer between the Quechuas and the Amazonians, for they did not fully belong to either world. Farmers, they grew manioc to obtain chicha from it (alcoholic beverages are ultimately the sole resource of groups living in hot-land regions where the water is not fit to drink in its natural state) but they also hunted and fished. They used blowguns, spear throwers, and bows, but not slings. They were to be found either isolated in the forest, in groups of fifteen to thirty people, or clustered in little villages.

The best-known of the Peruvian montaña groups were the Campas, who could have been proto-Arawaks like the Piros, Machiguengas, Amneshas, and others. These were very early tribes whose survivors can be found in the gorges of the Ucayali, Madeira, Apurímac, Urubamba, Pachitea, Perené, and Ene rivers.

Three years ago I visited the last Campas of the Urubamba, with Dominican missionaries from Rosalina acting as intermediaries. I saw only poor, discouraged people suffering from tuberculosis and alcoholism and living with very reduced means on staples of bananas, manioc, and some fish. These Campas also were dressed in long cotton robes. They still made a little pottery, but they were mainly noted for using a great variety of carrying bags. I found some lying on mats on the ground or in low rectangular huts with thatched roofs supported by short posts. These huts are sometimes grouped in little villages or isolated in the forest along rivers. In order to obtain a few metal objects, the Campas barter with people who come down from Cuzco or the town of Quillabamba.

East of Lima, along the Ucayali River, I came across Shipibo Arawaks and Panoans, the remnants of energetic groups who on various occasions managed to destroy the outposts of the missionaries who tried to "civilize" them.

Their neighbors, the Cashibos and Amahuacas, have also remained very primitive. They go about nude, deform their children's skulls, blacken their teeth, pierce their noses, lips, and ears, and tattoo themselves with long, cobweblike designs. The natives of the Tingo Maria region, on the Monzón River, still imitate these designs when they decorate the poor-quality pottery they sell to tourists.

The Huallaga Basin, whose temples and preceramic Chavín villages I have already discussed, was apparently also reinhabited during the last prehistoric centuries by immigrants from the east, who infiltrated as far as Huanuco, at an altitude of sixty-six hundred feet, on the one hand, and on the other hand, as far as Tarapoto, in the heart of the Amazonas. Sixteenth-century missionaries have left us records of a population of several tens of thousands of people who went about nude, with their bodies painted. They called them the Motilones, which means *primitive,* but in fact they were farmers.

This population was rapidly decimated by disease. Its survivors now make their living by bartering coca and salt, going from place to place in their struggle to live.

Other, more primitive, groups, the Chonzos and Cheberos, tried to survive by hiding in the mountains around Moyobamba and Concepción. Here we are not far from the equator, and several forest groups have survived in these territories by their knowledge of tropical farming. Such groups are now surrounded by Quechuas who have come down from the cold lands, but one can still encounter some Chonzos in Bagua on the Marañón River. Incidentally, while visiting a modern cattle farm in Bagua, I found a pre-Columbian irrigation canal whose banks were littered with fragments of Inca-decorated pottery. The Bagua region is a dry spot in the montaña. It provides a strong contrast to Pucalpa, very near it on the Ucayali, where six and a half feet of rain fall annually.

The Jivaros, a largely un-Quechuanized forest people, have survived from Chachapoya in the Marañón Valley to east of Guayaquil, between the fifth and second parallels. The Incas managed to defeat the Cañaris living in the Ecuadorian highlands, but failed in their enterprises against the Jivaros. The Incas tried to get rid of the Jivaros because they used to walk up and raid the highland villages. According to the chroniclers, the Jivaros even reached Loja and perhaps even what is now Cuenca, in the highest inter-Andean valley of Ecuador. From then on, contacts with the Jivaros were limited to bartering.

The Jivaros went about nude and slept on platform beds raised above the ground in big, elliptical, communal houses. They were farmers, of course. Their social life was complex, and they practiced numerous rites. They commonly elongated their earlobes, like the Malais of Borneo, and used a wooden drum based on an African model. This use may have been acquired since the arrival of blacks in the Guianas. Nevertheless, I have found big pottery drums among the Marangas in the Chillon Valley and also have a drum from Chilca, made of bark and skin.

The Jivaros have also entered history as specialists in the shrinking of human heads. They are still actively engaged in this specialty, now selling to tourists monkey heads instead of human skulls.

Let me also mention the Zaparoas, a very simple people who went about nude, and the Quijos, who spoke Chibcha and were farmers and metallurgists. Living on the Napo River, they had contact with other Chibchas, the Panzaleos of Latacunga in upper Ecuador. There were thirty thousand of them in the middle of the sixteenth century, but now they have almost all disappeared.

·4·
ARCHITECTURE
AND
ECOSYSTEMS

The Andean societies are remarkable for their creativity in the most varied fields. They adapted to a difficult environment by successively inventing diverse types of ecosystems.

Architecture developed parallel to these ecosystems, evolving from the little familial hut to the gigantic palace. And the populations' settlement patterns evolved in a parallel fashion, passing from hamlet to village to town and at last to being a city.

The evolution of architecture, ecosystems, and settlement patterns did not necessarily happen concurrently. Some societies built palaces while others continued to live in little huts. There was also a cyclical evolution, with phases of peaceful life alternating with periods in which villages were fortified. To help readers follow these developments, I shall describe them broadly and without going into technical details.

ARCHITECTURE

Pre-Columbian architecture has been the subject of extensive studies in Mexico and Central America. But in the Andes we suffer from a great backwardness in this field, which I think has two causes.

One cause, already mentioned throughout this work, is the lack of interest shown by modern South Americans in the remains of a past they still hesitate to accept as theirs. Up till now, only J. C. Tello, the father of Peruvian archaeology, and a few architects have been interested in the ancient buildings. Even important monuments have been totally neglected since Wendell C. Bennett wrote an essay on pre-Columbian structures in his *Handbook*.

The other cause is that it is deceptive to imagine that one can draw up the ground plan of a building without first clearing away the rubble, remains of fallen walls, and other matter like melted crude clay, mortar, and windblown dust or sand. Such materials usually hide entire buildings. How can one know their exact shapes when their walls are in ruins? One must find the bases, which luckily are almost always intact. The first line of blocks, stones, or unfired bricks is practically always set in a little trench, and as a result it is less exposed to destruction.

Now cleaning and preparing a building with an eye to drawing up its ground plan is a long, expensive, tricky operation, and whoever ventures into it takes on responsibilities. For instance, sections of a wall ready to collapse are often supported by the rubble around it. I have escaped from being hit by entire stone walls up to twenty feet high that fell when some of the fallen stones at their bases were removed. The risk of being the one responsible for the final destruction of a building is even greater when the archaeologist starts tampering with buildings made of unfired bricks. The pre-Columbians used to plaster their walls with clay, cactus sap, and mineral pigments, and to renew this protective covering quite frequently. Now that the walls are not maintained, the only bricks to have survived are the ones protected by the dust that has eroded and crumbled off the upper parts of the walls. On the coast, beach sand carried by the wind also helped protect buildings by burying them.

Even more serious is the situation with monuments decorated by high reliefs, as is the case with several buildings in Chan Chan, Peru. Here, the authorities decided to bring to light these sculptured façades, but did not provide for stabilizing the crude bricks. This is now causing irreparable damage. Moreover, most of these buildings were painted with pigments and ochers. I am familiar with painted walls at Tambo Colorado and Pachacamac, to cite only two monuments, which were completely covered with red and yellow pigment. Wind and dampness have now eroded the paint. At El Paraíso, I have discovered sections of walls painted white, black, red, and yellow. All such decoration disappears in a few years once it is exposed to the air.

Finally, in an even more serious crime, no one bothered to save the remarkable and imposing mural paintings covering the walls of several monuments. Nothing remains of Peñamarquilla, and only a small fragment, fortunately reproduced by Ducio Bonavia, reminds us of the splendors of a deployment of Mochica warriors.

At La Huaca Culebras, in the Chillon Valley, I copied the ninety-two feet that had survived of a frieze painted along the surrounding walls. However, the section I could reproduce represents only a fragment of what formerly existed, for the outer walls of Culebras were nearly two thousand feet long. Today their destruction is accelerated by tourists and other ravagers of archaeological sites.

As a result, very few ground plans of the large buildings that can be seen virtually everywhere in the central Andes have been drawn up, to say nothing of profiles and drawings of architectural features such as corbeled roofs, passages, and stairways. It seems astounding that not a single mission or institution worthy of the name has ever cataloged such a valuable heritage. This neglect reflects all the more credit on the accomplishments of individuals like Captain Guillen of the Peruvian army, who sketched a rough map showing several hundred buildings. This document gives one an idea of what may have been the density of stone structures in the territory comprising the two slopes of the Andes and now constituting Peru and Bolivia.

The building of large monuments stopped south of the central Peruvian coast, with Cahuachi in the Rio Grande de Nazca. Some Bolivian monuments are found farther south, but in the cold highlands there are no large monuments. Arid Chile and the Argentine Andes have revealed only medium-sized structures, generally villages or small clusters of buildings that are sometimes fortified, sometimes not.

To the north, Ecuador also has revealed few imposing structures, usually high platforms that were probably ceremonial in character. Subsequently, the Incas built a few tambos and palaces, of which only Ingapirca, near Cuenca, has survived. In Colombia, we know only the underground rooms of Tierradentro and the archaeological park with its monumental statues in San Agustín.

The tropical lands have not left us monuments, which is quite natural, since buildings were made of wood there. The only architectural examples we have from the Caribbean Islands, the Guianas, and Brazil are the natives' houses that have survived there. Nothing, however, indicates how many centuries or millennia their architectural tradition goes back. And these present-day natives may not be descendants of the people who first wandered through these lands.

In Peru and Bolivia, thanks to the courageous European travelers of the nineteenth century, we can consult some rough sketches of monuments, most of which have since disappeared. The Inca buildings in the region extending from Machu Picchu to Cuzco are fortunately now in the process of being saved, thanks to the efforts of the authors of the Copesco plan, a plan elaborated by His Excellency the Peruvian ambassador Alberto Wagner de Reyna, M. Ali Vrioni of UNESCO, and myself. This plan has led to obtaining very considerable funds lent by the International Bank for Development, which will enable the implementation of a monumental tourism program and repairing of the principal pre-Columbian and Hispanic monuments of the territory in question. Unfortunately, similar reports cannot be made for buildings in other areas: Chavín de Huantar, the most prestigious monument in the central Andes, is far from being completely explored. And El Paraíso, one unit of which I have restored, was seriously affected by the earthquakes of 1970 and 1974.

After realizing that the study of Andean civil architecture was only in its infancy, I decided to undertake a systematic analysis of prototypical dwellings characteristic of each ecological sociocultural period. This program is developing satisfactorily, but the theme is so vast that it will take the work of several teams to bring it to a satisfactory conclusion. Furthermore, I preferred first to devote my energies to the arid lowlands. The rainy cordillera and the western slopes have not yet been the subject of the explorations and studies that are prerequisites for any classification. However, I have helped set a fashion, and texts are appearing to indicate that several other researchers are moving in the right direction at last.

I have learned from experience, moreover, that even the simplest architectonic details constitute fundamentally diagnostic elements in the fields of chronology and the diffusion of cultures. Construction techniques circumscribe the influence of a society in time and space, as well as the diffusion of artistic styles. No two societies in the central Andes built in the same way. Modifications of forms and techniques, accompanied by variations in settlement patterns, occur every time we see traits indicating changes in the sociocultural pattern. The strange thing is that in this sphere, as in others like agriculture, techniques do not evolve. Each society remains traditionally attached to its own methods. In studying architecture and the appearance, then abrupt disappearance, of styles and building techniques, one realizes again that the Andes experienced continual migrations and upheavals that resulted in fundamental changes, as in Mexico.

Such a vast theme cannot be developed in this work. However, I thought it useful to report the essential results of my investigations in a field that is still largely unpublished. One conclusion that can be drawn is that the evolution of architecture seems to confirm what the economic history of pre-Columbian Peru apparently teaches us, namely (and this will come as a surprise to no one) that developments in the construction and grouping of dwellings and monuments are connected with the improvement of ecosystems. Thus, architecture using stone appears only in the final or classical phase of agriculture without corn. The earlier farmers still lived in little huts made of plant materials, as did the prefarming communities of food gatherers.

An important social phenomenon occurred in the arid Andes about four thousand years ago. About 2000 B.C., the Andeans began constructing buildings with a communal or ceremonial function. But they were still not building comfortable familial houses. Private lodgings were poor for many centuries and, with some tribes, until Hispanicization. The small forest tribes often lived in big houses that sheltered several families. As I have just said, however, we do not know how far back this tradition goes.

A village in the high Andes of Colombia. Compare these dwellings with the reed huts used during pre-Columbian days.

A contemporary house in the lower Andes of Colombia.

The transition to urban life, to the phase when big princely buildings and large familial houses were built, was apparently connected with what I call the second Neolithic revolution, which led the societies of the arid Andean coast of Peru to an intensive and extensive agricultural exploitation of large territories that had been deserts until then. (For more information on this subject, see the section below entitled "Ecosystems.")

It is true that large monuments such as the big ziggurats of Moché and of the Akapanas of Tiahuanaco were built earlier. These buildings, however, have a religious character. It is also true that the palace complex, paired with a ceremonial center, storehouses, and possibly artisans' workshops, seems to have existed very early. Certain complexes like El Paraíso or Huancaca of the Gallinazos in the Viru Valley call to mind predynastic Egypt. However, they are far from being the urban concentrations that were discovered in the immediate vicinity of the big palaces of Chan Chan, Cuzco, Cajamarquilla, Pacatnamu, and Pachacamac, to cite only the best known. Only after the twelfth to fourteenth centuries A.D. do the coastal valleys and upper-Andean piedmonts become peopled with towns and villages containing beautiful high familial houses equipped with patio, cellar, and storehouse.

One is therefore tempted to draw a parallel between the progression of comfort (seen in terms of an increase in the habitable floor space available to a single family) and a better and more complex social life. However, hasty generalizations are dangerous. Tradition seems to have been just as important. For example, the habitable space in the huts we find in the preagricultural villages of the Andean high Holocene is twelve square yards on the average. This is reminiscent of the pit dwellers of the southwestern United States, who grew corn and lived in the same way during some periods—with only two and a half square yards per person.

When Nazca fishermen arrived in Paracas, they built spacious collective houses with several rooms grouped around a patio. It is not clear if these Nazcas replaced the fishermen who had lived there in square individual huts made of mats, with flat roofs and a surface not exceeding twenty-six square feet. Or had these fishermen changed their life-styles?

The *choza*, or square hut, has survived down to the present. It is the dwelling of Andeans who come down to the coast and settle in the outskirts of a city until their salary permits them to build a brick house, and then finally one of concrete. Some Lima suburbs exhibit the immigrant's progression in social success in the following architectural stages:

Stage One: The foundations are missing. Rags, cardboard boxes, sheet metal debris, and the like are resorted to.

Stage Two: Resources are still minimal. If they can, people build themselves a cabin with a roof and walls made of mats.

Stage Three: The house is made of bricks.

Stage Four: The concrete house clearly indicates success.

The appearance with the Nazcas of new mythological themes (as well as other evidence, such as the disappearance of individual weaponry and beautiful clothes) leads me to believe that these people had exterminated or replaced the earlier inhabitants of the Paracas Bay area and built new dwellings corresponding to their own traditions.

Still later, we find the settlers in the lomas living comfortably in good stone houses, until suddenly an invasion by people called the Puerto Viejos destroyed the previous life-style. The Puerto Viejos are responsible for constructing quite large clay-brick buildings, perhaps under order of the princes in nearby Cañete. But, expressing no sense of comfort, they lived in little underground rooms of about ten square feet. At the same time, their contemporaries and neighbors in the Lurín Valley were living in beautiful high houses that were thirteen hundred square feet.

One must be just as careful when trying to interpret the pre-Columbians' motives for choosing such and such a building material. Here again, tradition as well as the absence of certain raw materials in the vicinity may have played a role. Why did the Nazcas, an eminently coastal society concentrated exclusively in the lower valleys of south-central Peru, build with stone when they had an abundance of clay near at hand? But on the other hand, other groups continued to build with unfired brick even when they had no lack of stone.

In some valleys, changes from one tradition to another, linked to environmental changes, can be noted. We know that the environment here is governed by altitude, which limits to only one type the farming that can be practiced at any chosen climatic floor. At a high altitude the round house predominates. This type of dwelling is totally enclosed and consists of a cone-shaped roof made of branches and straw resting on a stone half wall. Rectangular houses appear at a lower altitude. This kind still has stone walls, but they are not as high as a man is tall. Their roofs are supported by wooden beams and posts that provide much better ventilation than the round type of house. This change does not seem to correspond to a boundary between two climatic levels; instead, an overlapping tradition exceeds the physical boundaries. On the other hand, who would have been the ones to introduce the big oval or circular buildings one sees in the Andes? Such buildings remain a rarity in a land where stone buildings were either rectangular or square. As prototypes of big oval buildings, let me note the building of Chanquillo, in the Nepeña Valley, and of Sondor, which was cited by Charles Wiener.

Finally, the observant traveler will not fail to notice that some traits typical of the hot lands and the eastern part of the continent also appear on the west coast, in tropical climates as well as in arid and cool zones. The most obvious example is the flat-roofed houses built on piles that can be seen in the Guianas and around the Caribbean Sea. Similar houses are also set up in the desert sands of arid Ecuador, where the dry climate, unlike the tropical one along the Pacific coast of Colombia, does not seem to justify their existence. Let us not forget, however, that similar houses may be seen in Polynesia. Where was the tradition born —in the east, or the west?

The round house with a cone-shaped or dome-shaped roof is generally associated with cold lands. It is typical of the rainy upper Andes, where it can be seen from Colombia to Chile. But let us remember that we see the same house, but built out of plant materials, in the hot Amazonas. And the long, oval house, with a two-sided or dome-shaped thatched roof, which is typical of the Chaco or the Guianas, passed through the Andes. It is found again, made of bamboo slats, among the Araucanians.

Let us now consider the house with a two-sided roof. Its appearance in the western Andes seems to have followed the Inca invasion. Wherever one sees a gabled roof, one knows one is dealing with people using pottery in the Cuzco style. Where did the Incas come from, and where must one look for the origin of the tradition of the gabled roof? Examples of such buildings may be seen in Polynesia and the Amazonas. Was this a result of multilineal evolution, or of diffusion? The debate will never end. One can of course imagine the landing of Polynesians who climbed the cordillera and conquered the Cuzco Valley before conquering the entire Andes, but this seems rather farfetched. However, the Cuzco house with a gabled roof looks like the stone counterpart of the same tropical house made of wood. It is thus a simpler hypothesis to consider the Incas to be a group that came up from the hot lands in search of women, metal, and other attractions and entrenched itself around Cuzco.

One could also refer to the Polynesian migrations to explain the architecture of the Tiahuanaco society, an architecture so foreign to the Andes. But would the Polynesians have been able to forge copper and make the monumental hinged doors of the Akapanas? Would they have been able to cut monoliths and carve them with the precision, rigor, and purity of line that make the temples of Tiahuanaco unique in the history of the Americas?

Whatever the answers to these important questions, it is undeniable that the architecture of the western Andes came under foreign influences. It is thus wise to consider all the possibilities, but especially the influence of the east. Unfortunately, we still know almost nothing about the history of Amazonian architecture in early times. Our knowledge in this field does not go back much farther than the sixteenth century, the period of contacts. Are the Amazonian traditions ancient? How did the inhabitants of the Guianas live two thousand years ago? We do not know. And since plant materials do not survive in these regions' climates, we may never know any more about them than we do now.

ECOSYSTEMS

"Ecology" was proposed as early as 1886 to define the science dealing with relations between organisms or between communities and their environment. "Ecosystems" designates the whole that is constituted by a biological or "biocenose" community and the physical or "biotopic" milieu in which it lives.

Walking along the valleys and gorges that lead us between two Andean ridges from the ocean to the upper cordillera is one of the most gratifying experiences to be had. This is so not only for the archaeologist in the classical sense of the word (the seeker of monuments or objects) but also for the ecologist, the geographer preoccupied with the problems of prehistoric human geography and the problems that confronted the Andeans when they were adapting to life first as gatherers, then later as farmers in arid lands.

There are countless archaeological sites in the Andes. I have suggested a figure of one million for them, and so far no one has contradicted me. Thus, the Andes must have been densely populated, at least during certain periods. However, the peoples in question were preliterate and lived in a Neolithic age, with primitive, almost nonexistent technological means at their disposal. Today, Peruvians survive only with the help of big dams, hydro tunnels, and pumping stations. How did the principalities and rural communities of pre-Hispanic days feed so many inhabitants?

Various suggestions may be formulated. Larger land surfaces were used to produce food. Cotton not being an exportable material, only enough was grown to clothe the inhabitants. (Furthermore, a great deal of wool was used.) Products for family consumption—corn, beans, peanuts, and so on—were raised in the absence of sugarcane plantations.

However, let us not forget another factor that has been revealed by a number of experts, first by ecologists (mainly Joseph A. Tosi), then by the Peruvian governmental office in Lima in charge of evaluating natural resources (the National Office of Appraisal of Natural Resources of Peru), and finally by Carlos Peñaherrera in his *Atlas of Peru*. These experts show that only a small proportion of usable land is developed today in the territories that concern us. This point having attracted my attention, I undertook a methodical exploration of the remaining uncultivated lands along the arid coast between the seventh parallel and the Chilean border. I then discovered that quite a large part of these lands was formerly developed. (In this regard, see Chapter Three, which gives examples of vast farming systems on terraces complemented by wells and thousands of silos.)

The contrast between the pre-Columbian past and the present, from about 1530 to now, is striking. Formerly, not a patch of usable ground lay fallow. In the Chilca Basin, which is extremely poor and some 480 square miles in area, I have noted 1,250 places that were inhabited or reinhabited by people who built hamlets, villages, or clusters of buildings there. But today, only some 1.5 million acres out of 50 million on the coastal strip are used, and the rest is desert.

In the first half of the twentieth century, the only places that were still settled were the high inter-Andean valleys like Collao, the puna in the neighborhood of Lake Titicaca, the big industrialized farms along the coast, and several unimportant towns and straggling villages. Except for a few haciendas or estates whose owners had practically appropriated all the usable lands, the coastal valleys were empty.

Today, because of the agrarian reforms instituted by the revolutionary government of Peru, the situation is somewhat different. Several million Andeans have left the highlands and occupied the lower valleys, from which the previous landowners have been expelled. However, these invasions had bearing only on land already under cultivation. The highland immigrants resettled the green areas of valleys, in which only a few hundred people had lived for four centuries, reduced to being unskilled laborers on farms that sometimes extended over thousands of acres. To the present the reform has not yet changed the desert condition of the immense surfaces that had formerly been cultivated and that today are still completely neglected. Food shortages are now deeply felt in Peru, and people are asking what happened. Today in Lima, people eat potatoes from Holland, zebus (crossbred Asiatic oxen) from Colombia, dairy products from Denmark and New Zealand, fruits from Chile, and so forth. I think the authorities underestimated the dangers that would result from an action that was obviously necessary but was, for psychopolitical reasons, carried out in a very abrupt manner. The official reasoning followed these lines:

First, an extremely small leading group held all the economic power and did not accept any reform.

Second, it was abnormal for 95 percent of the cultivated lands to be owned by 2 percent of the population.

Third, a thorough reform thus was necessary. The Andean, a peasant by nature, had to be resettled on good lands, since those of the high plateaus were now exhausted and were no longer productive in any way.

Finally, in order to carry out this reform, it was necessary to neutralize the ruling class, and in order to do this it was not enough to strip them of their lands. The landed proprietors had taken precautions—they controlled industry, domestic and international big business, and the media. Thus, it was necessary to expropriate almost all the means of production, exchange, and communication. This change was made peacefully, but because of a lack of thoroughly prepared new leaders, this policy resulted in serious economic disturbances.

To begin with, stripping the ruling class, without compensating it in an acceptable way, created a climate of revolt that, though perhaps unimportant in respect to internal policy, nonetheless provoked the departure of a good part of the intelligentsia. Thus, it led to an absence of capable, salaried staff—people greatly needed in countries in which a middle class has barely begun to emerge.

Furthermore, the Andean states are now faced with ever-increasing housing and food needs for a population that suffers from a galloping birthrate and that, after emerging as it were from the Stone Age, insists on being incorporated immediately into a highly mechanized consumer society. How much will the dwellings cost that will have to be built for millions of Andeans by the year 2000, and even well before then? It would be unwise for the Andean states to cut themselves off from foreign sources of aid that would be helpful in this regard.

With respect to food, the agrarian reform inevitably led to a serious situation. Four hundred years of domination—first imperialistic, then personal and commercial—transformed the great majority of the Andes inhabitants into day laborers, unskilled workers who are unable to do more than turn the earth with a shovel. Very few people in Peru know how to sow, reap, irrigate, and use fertilizers and pesticides judiciously. In effect, the land—which used to produce exportable commodities such as sugar and cotton—was given to cooperative groups of Andeans who had forgotten the arts of being peasants and stockbreeders. Being a peasant in an arid land is an extremely difficult art; it is hard to resist the temptation of transforming ones pedigreed bull into Sunday steaks.

Finally, it is remarkable that up until now no new land has been developed. Big irrigation programs are being studied, but those being considered have been talked about for twenty years. Immense virgin territories such as the Chao and Viru are still deserts. No effort has yet been made to rehabilitate lands that were formerly cultivated or used for pasture. If the experts' calculations are correct, these lands represent a surface at least half as large as the area now under cultivation. In other words, developing them would make it possible to add 25 percent to the present food production, the other half being that which is brought down from the highlands.

Once again, we may observe that economics and politics are two distinct sciences. The concept of dealing with the problems of government according to purely economic criteria is abstract and impractical. The human factor and emotional elements must be taken into consideration, just as getting too far away from certain fundamental principles regarding the economy creates perilous situations.

It seems, then, that it would be in the interest of government leaders in Andean countries to turn more toward the past and draw their inspiration from it, but not copy it. The point is not to redo history and return to the Neolithic age. Ecologists know from experience, however, that thorough study of the past permits formulating norms that can help govern the rational exploitation of natural resources. This is typically the case in Peru, where we know that the pre-Columbians were able to nourish themselves without spending half a billion dollars to import food every year.

THE PREHISTORIC ANDEAN ECOSYSTEMS

In the introduction, I indicated the geographical diversity that characterizes the Andes. This diversity is naturally reflected in respect to ecosystems. A farmer in the coastal Viru Valley would obviously have to solve problems different from those of a farmer settled in the Cuzco Valley, or one who was practicing *milpa* agriculture on the eastern slopes of the cordillera.

Because of these convictions, the existence of big macroclimatic areas must be taken into account when considering well-conceived programs dedicated to ecosystems, prehistoric or otherwise. Establishing such programs will lead to the undertaking of regional studies along the arid coastal strip, in the semiarid western slopes of the Andes, in the cold and rainy highlands, and in the hot and rainy lands of the Amazonian slope.

Food production and herding are governed not only by macroclimatic or general conditions; we must also consider the effects of latitude and altitude. Glaciers are to be found melting in the ocean in Patagonia, but east of Lima one must climb to sixteen thousand feet to touch snow. Thus, ecologists are observing the effects of local climatic changes and even microclimatic conditions, which makes their task difficult. For example, nothing bears as much resemblance to a coastal Peruvian valley as any one of its neighboring valleys, of which there are some fifty. But on the other hand, nothing differs as much from the lower, coastal, and totally arid phytoclimatological floor than the lomas or the next (completely arid) floors of the middle valleys.

The best answer in such situations (in my opinion, and my suggestions have been accepted by the Peruvian authorities) is to consider ecological studies to be regional in character, but to have them cover territories extending from the glaciers down to the Pacific. Only studies of this nature will provide us with information about transhumance, trading activities, migrations, and the occupation of various floors by peoples who were related, a phenomenon brought to light by John Murra. It is not necessary, at least at first, to study the macroclimatic territories as a whole. One can extrapolate from results acquired while studying phytoclimatic floors characteristic of one valley, and establish norms valid for a group of valleys. Of course, one must take into account the corrective factors constituted by the latitude and by altitudinal levels. These two factors clearly modify the mesoclimatic conditions of valleys that at first glance seem to provide comparable environments.

So far, I have only been able to carry out a few studies of this type, but other teams are now proceeding in the same way, and all serious researchers have now accepted the notion of looking at a territory rather than a place. In this respect we are following the lessons of my pioneering teacher Gordon Willey, who, as early as 1945, wrote a model monograph about settlement patterns in the lower Viru Valley. Should they follow this principle, prehistorians will have at their disposal after perhaps ten years a body of valid data that will enable them to begin to grasp what life in the Andes may have been like between ten thousand and five hundred years ago.

I first concentrated my own efforts on a totally desert zone having no surface water resources. This region extends from the southern bank of the Pisco River, across the Paracas, Ica, Nazca, and Marcona deserts, and down to the Acari River. The Acari forms the northern border of the Peruvian Far South, a very different territory, where life is conditioned by imperatives that are distinct from the ones that condition existence in the Middle South, which extends from the

Chincha Valley to the Acari Valley. Subsequently, in a second stage I undertook a study of the dry gorge of the Chilca Basin from the glaciers to the ocean on the central coast of Peru. This study complemented the one done by Willey of the coastal half of the Viru Valley in that it included the highland ruins and caves.

Simultaneously, I undertook the study of various high Andean territories, beginning with the cradle of the Inca empire, the Cuzco Valley, then Collao and the upper Urubamba Valley.

Detailing the results obtained in the course of these studies would naturally require several volumes, so I shall recall here only the essence of what I learned from this research.

PREAGRICULTURAL TIMES

My research enabled me to demonstrate that Paleolithic people or, to use more-modern terminology, people who practiced neither agriculture nor stock-breeding, did not necessarily live in wandering bands that spent their time hunting. This fact was already suspected by a few researchers and was mentioned by François Bordes as well as others. Now I have proof of the existence of a sedentary life independent of any neolithization and independent of the transition from a life of parasites to a life as producers. I know that groups not practicing agriculture already lived in large communities for long months each year, and maybe all year round. Since at least ten thousand years ago, nomadism in the Andes has no longer been the issue; transhumance, possibly. The controlling of various floors at various altitudes—of lands providing diverse products—is also a possibility. However, the notion of wandering bands of hunters will now have to be considered obsolete.

What we see, on the contrary, are traces of large groups—communities of one thousand, two thousand, or more people—devoted to the systematic exploitation of resources in certain territories that were perfectly defined by the possibilities they provided. Such territories can be quickly summarized as the puna, the grassy plateaus surrounding the high summits of the cordillera; the lomas, or coastal oases in which vegetation is sustained by fog, and the seashore.

As I explained when I first published an analysis of the phytoclimatological levels one finds when climbing the cordillera, the preagriculturalists, for hydrological reasons, could live only at certain levels. The lower coastal plains were useless to them, though drinking water is often accessible there as a result of the resurgence of the water sheets right next to the ocean. The lower and middle valleys were also uninhabitable, as the rivers and streams remained dry several months a year there.

We can thus discern the outlines of a first ecosystem that seems to have been centered on three points.

First there is hunting, probably seasonal, which provided bones used to make tools, skins and sinews in which to dress, and, secondarily, meat. Even on the seacoast, the skeletons I found in the Paracas ossuary, for example, were dressed in vicuña skins. Hunting must have been practiced in the grassy puna. Also, wild animals occasionally go down to the coastal lomas, where I have seen deer and bears. The wooded lower valleys were probably also inhabited by game before they were exploited by farmers. However, archaeologists have not yet found preagricultural camps in such areas. The reason may be the profound changes these valleys underwent in the course of the following millennia as a result of intensive farming.

The second element is the gathering of plants that supplied edible rhizomes, tubers, and possibly bulbs and leaves. Lupine, quinoa, various cactus fruits, the seeds of an unidentified graminaceous plant, wild tomato seeds, alder seeds, rhizomes and tubers of jiquimas, sweet potatoes, manioc, and a plant of the genus *Solanaceae* resembling the potato constitute the essential plant foods seen in the excrement of the preagriculturalists. According to botanists all these plants grew without human intervention.

Third is seafood. Fishing was practiced in very early times. I have in my possession fishhooks and nets that are ten thousand years old. Someday we may be able to establish that fishing was already engaged in before the last glaciation.

Fishing, as important as it was, contributed only part of the food of marine origin. There is hardly a village on the coast in which the debris of fish, mixed with the debris of other marine animals of all kinds like sea lions and dolphins, is not topped by enormous quantities of shells. The preagricultural site of Paloma, for instance, contains thirty thousand tons of shells.

The large number of shellfish that lived along the coasts in conditions such that gathering them was easy may very well have been one of the factors that played an important role in the evolution of preagricultural Andean societies. Indeed, as time passed, shellfish apparently supplied an ever-increasing proportion of the proteins consumed daily. This growing consumption of seafood seems to correspond to an increasingly pronounced decadence in the art of making stone tools and projectile points, which might indicate less interest in hunting.

The sea provided the settlers with such abundant food that they gave up moving from one territory to another and just went on living a sedentary life by the sea. Now did this result in degeneration or simply weaken the societies, or did some environmental change destroy their shellfish beds or sources of drinking water?

We shall never know, and can only speculate, about whatever happened. We note the disappearance of the inhabitants of the big preagricultural villages, and of all the Peruvian settlers living in a prefarming horizon, fifty-five hundred years ago. They were replaced by groups with ecosystems that were already centered, at least in part, on growing edible plants.

Authors like the archaeologist R. S. MacNeish suggest that on the Andes' eastern slopes, where the resources provided by the ocean were not available and the fauna were scarce, such a situation may have obliged the populations to turn much earlier toward gathering plants, and toward agriculture and the domestication of camelids. In the meantime, the meager agricultural resources offered by such territories would have favored the establishment not of big villages but of small, mobile groups obliged to travel from camp to camp, according to the season.

Theories of this kind are quite entertaining, but the moment they remain, if not pleasant fantasies, just working hypotheses. I shall thus stick to the facts, which seem to indicate that the end of preagricultural horizons was announced on the western slope of the Andes by such signs as the decadence of the stone industry, the absence of meat obtained from land mammals, and the disappearance of big villages. The latter were replaced, beginning six thousand years ago, by modest communities that lived on cultivated plants and whose inhabitants wore cotton clothing.

Documentation regarding humid Chile, Argentina, and Colombia is lacking. So far, only Pleistocene prefarming sites are known in Venezuela. The high Holocene there is very poorly known, as it is in all the Caribbean Islands.

Groups of preagriculturalists were certainly numerous on the western slopes of the Chilean and central Andes. In saying this, I do not mean to insinuate that all the Andean valleys going down to the Pacific were continuously inhabited between ten thousand and six thousand years ago. Our chronological table is still very incomplete and contains considerable gaps. Sometimes we find villages dated as being ten thousand years old, then nine thousand years old, seven thousand, and finally sixty-five hundred years old. Furthermore, the imprecision of carbon 14 dating does not yet permit us to establish an exact chronology. However, I have already observed a substantial enough number of facts to suppose that about fifty valleys in central Peru and arid Chile were inhabited by groups that were formed by as many as two thousand people, and this already before the appearance of agriculture on the coast.

When reduced to the square mile, such figures are quite reasonable, since the territory in question represented a surface of about four hundred thousand square miles. These figures thus would indicate a density of about .15 inhabitants per square mile, as compared with the density that has been observed for the Amazonas. Here, however, its aridity notwithstanding, the environment may have been more favorable for intelligent people skillful in using the resources of a dry territory.

When studying the Andean territory with a critical eye, one soon finds that only about one-tenth of any land surface at most is fit for human use; normally, 90 percent is totally sterile sand and rocks. Such a pattern has unexpected consequences. During certain periods (whose duration we do not know), some areas show a density of twelve inhabitants per usable square mile. At first glance such figures seem excessive, but they do in fact agree with the ones I obtained in a thorough study of the Chilca Basin where, around the fifteenth century A.D., about three thousand people seem to have lived by agriculture and herding, on about four hundred square miles. Moreover, these figures correspond to an agricultural horizon. It is normal that they should be ten to twenty times higher than those observed for previous horizons, during which the inhabitants ate only by gathering tubers, seeds, and seafood.

ARCHAIC AGRICULTURE

This name applies to the horizon during which the pre-Columbians limited their techniques to exploiting the natural resources of a valley or several valleys without going so far as to try to modify the environment and colonize new lands by building large hydraulic works.

Archaic agriculture, which was apparently practiced on the eastern slopes of the cordillera as early as some eight thousand years ago, appears on the Pacific Coast about six thousand years ago, according to my own data. But archaic agriculture does not seem to have met with much success in the western lowlands. I have found very few villages belonging to this period, and my detailed study of them yields no data that would allow me to assume that an apparent attempt to colonize these completely arid lands (a most difficult task) was successful. Rather, the facts indicate that these early farmers, who seem to have created only very fragile ecosystems, must have failed. In the absence both of rain and water reserves, these farmers' harvests were subject to the vagaries of flooding by the little rivers and watercourses that had a single yearly flow, because these were the only ones that could be exploited at that time. We can guess at the distress of these pre-Columbians when drought or too heavy a flood destroyed their crops. This hardship would have affected the peasants themselves and their village chiefs, who were responsible for storing food and seeds and distributing them in the course of the year. Although we know too little about how these first farmers were organized socially, the substantial information we have about the environment in which they were struggling does not let us feel optimistic about their future, and archaeology seems to confirm this pessimism.

We should not let our vision be falsified by accepting what we read by the chroniclers. Practically all they have reported was facts observed during the feudal and totalitarian regime of the Incas, when millions of farmers and herders were living in the central Andes.

In order to try to understand what may have happened in the Andes before the imperial venture of the princes of Cuzco, we generally proceed by way of comparisons with what we know of Mesopotamia, Iran, and predynastic Egypt. Such comparisons obviously give only theoretical results, but they do facilitate an understanding of certain situations, since in both cases we are faced with problems regarding agriculture in arid lands.

One thing, however, is certain, since it left visible traces. The Andeans constructed the largest buildings that preliterate Neolithic peoples have ever created. Whereas the surface area of Athens in Pericles' century did not exceed 375 acres, Pachacamac, a Peruvian city that should be compared with a Mesopotamian city before Sumer, covered an area of 563 acres.

Now let us look at complexes such as that of Viracocha at Rach-tché, the palace of the Huancacas in the Viru Valley, and the seven complexes of El Paraíso, which contain several hundred rooms (though they date back to the period before corn farming). What do they remind us of? Looking at them, I cannot help thinking of the storehouse-temple-palaces of the predynastic Near East.

Nothing, therefore, prevents me from supposing that in the chiefdoms of the arid Andes the princes also had a good part of the harvest—perhaps the whole harvest—delivered to them, and then redistributed it. The positions of these chiefs thus could have been very much threatened in case of famine.

On several recent occasions I have myself witnessed catastrophes that did not have such tragic consequences, as a result of different distribution systems used now. But let us imagine what we experienced in the Viru Valley in 1973 would have meant to a peasant living there two thousand years ago. In 1973 the river flooded so late that the crops were about to die from lack of water. Then, at the end of December, the gorge suddenly released its waters so violently and in such quantity that all the cultivable lands of the lower valley were washed away. I suppose that the arid Andean lowlands periodically went through similar serious crises, even catastrophes, that destroyed entire populations for lack of means to transport food, a means that might have been available in other areas. This supposition is confirmed, moreover, by the fact that vast territories reveal alternating cycles of dense habitation and complete abandonment that sometimes lasted several centuries.

Today, motor-driven pumps are coming to the aid of farmers. They permit sowing of fields in the spring and waiting for the summer flood with less anxiety. In the time of the Gallinazos, however, one could sow only in earth that had been moistened by floodwaters. Thus, a flood that came late or insufficiently or too heavily upset not only the lives of people in the valley in question, but also lives in neighboring valleys, since the mechanism of floods is controlled by weather factors that affect an entire region rather than just a small area. As a result, people could not even expect help from valleys adjacent to the north or south. Once the flood was over, one had to wait twelve months before being able to sow again, and sixteen months before one could reap a harvest.

Obviously, not all crises must be attributed to natural events; people must have also played their roles. However, strong and well-fed populations are better fit and more eager to defend themselves than are starving groups. Let us recall the fall of the Mayas' sociopolitical system, attributed to invaders who came down from the high plateaus. Perhaps these invaders would have met strong resistance if the society attacked had not been in a state of crisis.

In my opinion, the first farmers of the arid slopes of the Andes, like their preagricultural predecessors, were able to survive only because they knew how to elaborate bi- or tripolar ecosystems centered not only on farming and herding but also on the sea. This importance of the sea's role is revealed over and over again. All along the coast, on terraces and cliffs overlooking the ocean, the archaeologist finds an almost uninterrupted series of fishing villages. Wherever fishing villages are not found, it is because there was no drinkable water. Thus, some very beautiful fishing territories remained practically virgin until recently. Lone fishermen could go fish in remote places after a long walk carrying a jar of water. (The *cantiflora* appeared around A.D. 450, with the Maranga society. Comparable to the *boille* used by dairy people in the Alps to transport liquids, it had a flat side that was rested across the shoulder blades.)

Villages could not be built away from some well. On the other hand, pre-

Columbians would build villages in practically every place that drinking water became accessible. Today the presence of fresh water is revealed by the existence of either a carpet of salt-meadow grasses or by bunches of purslane. The underground water is generally found six feet below the surface of the beach. And today these territories, so interesting to the researcher because they have remained intact, are traveled through in every direction by trucks carrying fishermen or fish merchants. This means that the coastal deserts have taken on a very different appearance and easier access has, moreover, tragically fostered the systematic looting of pre-Columbian sites that were still intact twenty years ago.

Some of these villages could have sheltered up to two thousand people. Because these are found up to thirty miles away from running surface water, they would have been located away from any cultivable land. Watercourses would hardly have been useful to these villagers, for streams with an intermittent summer flow would not have provided the necessary drinking water during the dry winters. A pond or marsh was valued much more, for it provided water all year round, without wells having to be dug and maintained. Immense complexes like Las Haldas (described on page 112) are located many miles away from rivers or ponds. These people could live only by tapping the subterranean water sources. We are entitled to wonder why the pre-Columbians clung to such a hostile territory—a barren plain where only Tillandsias grow—for five thousand years.

Again, the answer may lie in what was obtainable from the ocean. Las Haldas offers incomparable fishing resources. According to a document from the ministry of agriculture, the sea is more full of fish out from Las Haldas than anywhere else along the Peruvian coast. Furthermore, patches of vegetation existed that were capable of living on brackish water, which shows that subterranean freshwater sheets existed along the beaches in the area. It is probably to this combination of favorable circumstances that the occupation of Las Haldas by early Holocene settlers and the building of an early Neolithic ceremonial center there must be attributed. Under the big temple built by the Chavíns around 500 B.C. I found, buried under several yards of preceramic detritus of a much earlier date, a large structure that must have been built by settlers who lived there thirty-eight hundred years ago. This structure, which is much too large to have served as a dwelling, is surrounded by a multitude of small houses bordered by low stone walls. It obviously must have been built for communal or, according to the people who assign a religious significance to every building of the past that is of any importance, for ceremonial purposes. Such people, whom I call sacralists, will also label as ceremonial the big complex built 1,330 years later by people bearing the stamp of the Chavín society. Indeed, there is no doubt about the ceremonial character of some aspects of the Las Haldas Chavinoid complex, especially the succession of artificial terraces that form a system 1,250 feet long and rising 130 feet above the rocky cliff to overhang the ocean, facing the setting sun. However, I think Las Haldas may also have played a very important economic role, perhaps as a fish market.

Las Haldas should be studied in connection with the ruins left by the Chavín society in the northern Peruvian valleys east of the ocean. These valleys are the ones that contain the greatest concentration of monuments from the period, including the most important in terms of size and sociocultural or political importance. These monuments had been built in a territory made up actually of just a few very poor valleys. The princes or high priests of the Chavín cult had in this region at most some eighty thousand cultivable acres. These were made up of lands where agriculture was subject to the irregularities of flood farming dependent on secondary rivers.

How many people could this territory have sustained? On the basis of only one corn harvest a year, complemented by beans and peanuts, one can hardly imagine a figure higher than 21,000 families of five people, or some 100,000 inhabitants. Such a figure seems quite low when compared to the massive Chavín complexes. To repeat, I do not know if it was in this case a question of political domination or simply of religious influence. In the central Andean areas where the impact of Chavín was felt, all the sites inhabited between 800 and 500 B.C. bear the stamp of the movement in one way or another. Our ignorance on this point does not, however, prevent me from observing how weak the resources of this territory appear today, compared to the massive achievements of its inhabitants.

Obviously, one can bring in various factors, such as barter, the levying of taxes, or simple looting, in order to explain the power of Chavín. In my opinion, this power can also be explained by taking into account two more elements.

The first is the contributions of the sea. Las Haldas, located between fifteen and thirty miles west of the big command centers in the Casma, Sechin, Nepeña, and Huarmey valleys, may have functioned as the supplier of what could not be provided by farming in valleys where production was limited by irregular annual flooding.

The second element is the fact that the Chavíns had been practicing an archaic but diversified agriculture that had already reached a certain level of technology. Fifteen years ago, before modernization of the coastal farms began, one needed only to visit the Sechin or Huarmey valleys to realize that, independently of flood agriculture, the Chavíns must have practiced on a large scale an agriculture comparable to that of the Pacific's Melanesians. They took advantage of all areas with black earth where subterranean water accumulated close to the surface. Let us imagine these lower northern valleys as they used to be: wooded, covered with savannahs, with a resurgent water sheet appearing practically everywhere in the vicinity of the ocean. Clearly, an industrious people would have been able to draw maximum benefit from such natural resources.

An analogous situation may be observed during the succeeding politico-cultural period. The Viru Valley, poor in river water, then became covered with enormous architectural complexes built by the Gallinazo society. Now if one studies the environment in which these complexes were located, one discovers that the Gallinazos not only exploited the yearly flood but also the underground water, lagoons, and marshes.

The Mochicas' history is too poorly known to enable me to formulate theories regarding the centuries that followed. I shall simply recall that Moché, the pre-Columbian "capital" with its immense ziggurats, was surrounded by ponds and marshes and located where the middle valley opens onto the plain, instead of being found in the lower plain where Chan Chan, the Chimus' capital, was built nearly two thousand years later.

It would be advisable to look for Mochica pottery along the old canal systems that have survived. This would give us an idea of the size of the territory that this society was able to irrigate. But it would first have to be verified that these canals really are the work of Mochicas from the classical period, and not of a Mochica society that already bore the stamp of Tiahuanaco.

INTENSIVE AND EXTENSIVE ADVANCED AGRICULTURE

In Chapter Three I explained what I meant by these terms. Apparently, what I call a second Neolithic revolution occurred on the dry coast of the central Andes (and there only) perhaps a few centuries later than the phenomenon occurred in the southwestern United States.

This revolution, technological and probably also social in character, made possible the colonization of vast territories that had formerly been unused. For example, let us recall that after the rulers of Cañete built lateral canals twenty-four miles inland to collect water, the acreage under production in the valley increased tenfold, from about 3,750 to 37,500 acres.

Instead of dwelling on all the sociocultural implications of such an important phenomenon, let me simply recall that the arid lower Andes took on a very different face during the last pre-Columbian centuries, after the construction of such big hydraulic works. Big valleys that were formerly sparsely inhabited then became very densely populated, and large cities appeared at several points in the desert.

However, as important as these achievements were, they do not seem to have favored the birth of a solid new sociopolitical order. Their result was apparently fragile and lasted too short a time to produce profound modifications in societies as traditional and set in their ways as those of the Andes. Perhaps the southwestern United States underwent a comparable cycle.

Curiously enough, the majority of American studies specialists have not emphasized the development of this second Neolithic revolution and have not mentioned that entire basins, such as the Pisco, Chicha, and Cañete, which had been practically uninhabited during preceding centuries, suddenly assumed an unquestionable importance around the thirteenth or fourteenth century A.D., after the long canals were built.

But on the other hand, we must not forget that basins like the Chillon, which are fertilized only by a single annual flood but have also benefitted from an important flow of resurgent underground water, also experienced material prosperity and a dense population, shortly before the arrival of the Incas. To become aware of this, one need only take inventory of the villages with large, comfortable houses that have survived in the lower Chillon Valley. These houses have not been precisely dated, but I believe they must have been built around the four-teenth or fifteenth century A.D. Have we once more exaggerated the importance of technology at the expense of favorable sociopolitical conditions like good gov-ernment and peaceful existences?

Furthermore, it seems to me that we are once more confronted with facts that tend to prove the existence of very diversified ecosystems. It is clear that the inhabitants of the Chillon and Rimac basins harvested fields irrigated by the an-nual flood. However, we should not forget the existence of the big villages, whether open or fortified, to be found at the entrance to the puna, in the upper part of all the hydrological basins on the central coast. A careful examination of the ruins and environs of these quite numerous villages belonging to the last pre-Hispanic centuries indicates intense herding activity. This is proved also by a much wider use of wool as either a complement or a substitute for cotton, even on the coast. Stockbreeding must have played a very important role in the fourteenth and fifteenth centuries A.D. On the other hand, the lomas were once again densely reinhabited, certainly by farmers (otherwise, what purpose could have been served by the thousands of linear feet of terraces bordered by stone blocks weigh-ing thousands of tons that were built then?), but also by herders.

The only present nomads in Peru are the *chivateros* or goatherds, who migrate seasonally in the central Andes, going from the puna to the grassy pied-monts, then down to the lomas during the southern winter. They may well be the survivors of a very old line of herders.

The dry Huarangal gorge flowing into the Pacific forty-two miles south of Lima still has a surface of about thirty-seven hundred acres that is covered with vegetation between June and November, a period in which three families of a few people each sojourn there. They graze cows, goats, and sheep there and water their animals with the help of two pre-Columbian wells that still provide a little water. Now let us imagine the Huarangal gorge covered with trees, as it used to be. It would then have been able to provide forage for one hundred to one hundred fifty camelids. This figure, based on four acres of grass per animal, is conservative when compared with the needs of one llama, about one acre per head (source: Peruvian minister of agriculture, Lima). At any rate, only herding activities can explain why villages with adjoining corrals existed at the eastern, upper end of the gorge, in a defensive position around the twenty-six-hundred-foot perimeter where the loma vegetation dies out.

The existence of these villages would be poorly explained if we took into consideration only the lands suitable for farming, which represented at most only five hundred acres. This alone could have fed not more than some 130 families. Such figures probably explain why the inhabitants of Huarangal ate marine shellfish, of which their kitchen middens remained full until the arrival of the Spaniards, when the Chilca and the coastal canyons were deserted.

Establishing a map showing the migrations of these pre-Columbian herders would be a nice task for archaeologists. Where did the llamas that fed in the Omas Valley in the winter spend the dry summer months? After December, the gorge must have been uninhabitable for camelids, for the vegetation is burned by the sun and disappears. Maybe someday the pottery so typical of the Cuculi and Puerto Viejo populations who inhabited Huarangal and its surroundings in the fifteenth century will be found in the upper Andes. This would indicate transhumance between puna and loma. Up till now, no researcher has taken the trouble to walk over the Huarochiri area, the puna east of the Chilca canyon, in search of traces of transhumant peoples comparable to today's chivateros.

Specialists in American studies do not all agree that these populations migrated seasonally with their herds. There is obviously the problem of the physical transfer of llamas to cooler lands during the summer months. Perhaps a few families of herders were enough to take livestock up to the puna the way Alpine shepherds do who lead cows to European mountain pastures. These few people would have left rare traces, which would explain why their changes of location have not been reconstructed by archaeologists.

The camps of modern farmers, however, are easy to find. Littered with plastic, sheet metal, scrap iron, rubber, they are recognizable at a distance. Modern materials are unfortunately more indestructible than those the pre-Columbians used.

Other authors such as John Murra propose a different theory, suggesting that Andean groups could have controlled several territories located in varying climatic levels. In this way the group would have been assured of the complementary resources offered by each level and could have obtained such products of cold, temperate, and hot lands as salt, coca, hay, leather, lupine, and so forth, as much for their own consumption as to barter.

Finally, other researchers think, more simply, that bartering was much more frequent and developed at that time than is generally supposed.

Walking over the arid and semiarid Andes in Peru, Bolivia, Argentina, and central Chile presents one with hundreds of subjects that bear reflection. The Huarangal canyon seems typical of an already very specialized system adapted to the environment and entirely centered on the exploitation of lomas. Other villages, such as Rupac and Chiprac in the upper Chancay Valley about sixty miles northeast of Lima, clearly typify the tripolar Andean ecosystems, remarkable creations of groups that may have lived for thousands of years in hostile territory by making the most of unstable resources.

A study of the settlement pattern of villages and clusters of buildings informs us as to the sociopolitical state of the region during specific periods. Inca places are unfortified and are often located at the bottoms of valleys. They seem to have controlled traffic along the main roads. Apparently, the Incas relied on their armies rather than on fortifications. But in troubled times the villages were perched on hilltops and were surrounded by high defensive walls.

In Chiprac, the puna and its pastures for llamas extends as far as the horizon above the fortified village, which is placed in a strategic position on a rocky mountain peak and is encircled by thick, high, defensive walls. Below, starting about ninety-two hundred feet, lie the terraced planting plots that fill the valley, which is sheltered, temperate, and watered by springs and a tributary of the Chancay River. The water supply here is sufficient, though the ocean is visible from the puna. Although the ocean is somewhat distant, contact is maintained with it and it helps feed the inhabitants, whose houses all contain shells from the Pacific.

THE INCA ECOSYSTEMS

Much research is still needed before an economic evaluation can be made regarding the results of the second Neolithic revolution, in which the big hydraulic works were achieved that made possible the domination of vast new planting territories.

This revolution must have had positive results, even if only in permitting the existence of big cities, which had formerly been unknown on the arid coast. Was the development of extensive and intensive agriculture the cause—or the consequence—of the evolution toward urban life? This is like the problem of the chicken or the egg. Did population pressure oblige the princes to build canals, or did the valleys become overpopulated when new lands made possible the feeding of more people, or at least attracted too many immigrants?

The Incas seem to have been able to take possession of, then control immense coastal territories without meeting tough opposition. This leads one to think that the coastal chiefdoms probably had not escaped one of the cyclical crises that plague the Andes and all other arid lands. Maybe the lower valleys were experiencing the phenomenon that affects them again today. When poorly drained lands are heavily irrigated, salts in the subsoil rise to the surface and destroy plant life. We have historical and contemporary examples of this phenomenon: that of Roman Egypt, whose lands, overirrigated on account of an enormous demand for wheat, were ruined by salt; and that of contemporary Peru, where government agencies acknowledge their anxiety over the gradual salinization of the coast. According to the latest figures, salt there is ruining up to 40 percent of the 1.5 million cultivated acres.

Historical precedents such as these teach us that the pre-Columbians, by diverting streams into insufficiently drained areas, may have reduced to famine the settlers who had been attracted by new cultivable land that was extremely attractive at first sight.

Finally, let us not forget that the coastal chiefdoms may have suffered from a destructive process typical of so-called hydraulic societies. One will recall that the political system of such societies is fundamentally centered on the control and distribution of water resources, a predominant factor in the production of crops and thus in feeding the masses. Let us imagine, for instance, the Cañete Valley, whose 37,500 cultivated acres were able to survive only because of two irrigating canals, whose uptakes were located twenty-four miles to the interior, at an altitude of twenty-six hundred feet in the middle valley. It would have required only a small band of guerrillas coming down from the neighboring highlands to seize control of the uptakes and dictate their terms. The survival of the entire irrigation system, the survival of all the cultivable lowlands, and the lives of a population of about fifty thousand people would have been entirely in their hands.

This example is perhaps not well chosen, however, for the prince of Huarcu (now Cañete) was apparently one of the only ones to resist effectively the armies and diplomacy of Cuzco. Thus, he seems to have remained powerful. But where did he himself come from, and when did he begin to dominate his territory? Very likely he had come down from the highlands to destroy an established society. The well-known example of the Aztecs shows how such operations were carried out.

Archaeology reveals that during late pre-Hispanic times the lower coastal valleys had apparently been dominated by chiefs that did not belong to the coastal societies. The so-called Chancays in the Chancay and Chillon basins, the Huanchos in the Rímac Basin, and so on, seem to have been strangers in the region. Pachacamac had already been looted when Pizarro entered it, and the Inca site of Tumbes had been destroyed by the natives of Puná Island.

I am inclined to consider that coastal Peru fell into the hands of warrior bands and also suffered a serious cultural setback when Inca generals and administrators came down from Cuzco. With the arrival of the Incas' civil servants and armies, different concepts and mechanisms seem to have been introduced. It seems (and this is one of the most astonishing aspects of the actions by the rulers of Cuzco) that the Incas were able to conceive and implement a plan to systematically exploit an immense territory on an imperial scale. In that sense, only the Incas introduced notions that appear to have been new in the Andes. They developed barter as much inside the empire with allies as with outside territories: Ecuador, maybe Colombia, Chile, and the eastern hot lands. Such barter involved building outposts at the edges of the forest, in Bolivia to the south, and among the Jivaros to the north. And from their enemies the Incas exacted permanent levies of tribute in workdays, crops, raw materials, and maybe even manufactured goods.

Unfortunately, the Inca experience was too short for its results to be fully determined. In the course of the fifty years or so that their maximum power lasted, the Incas were able to attend only to the most urgent tasks: to eliminate unruly tribes, to supply strong points, perhaps to help populations who were victims of the elements and whose production was useful to the empire, and, finally, broadly speaking, to levy by will or force what the Inca required to supply the needs of his close relatives, domain, and armies.

When studying the centuries of the Incas' rule, the point is not to appraise an ecosystem but rather to look into what they did with it, which was to seize the existing resources and to develop as fast as possible all land that could provide raw materials or food. In this field, one might go on to useful comparisons with what one may observe about post-Roman Europe.

In my opinion, therefore, the Inca phenomenon constitutes a new achievement in the history of the Andes. Garnering food in northern Peru in order to carry on war against insurgent populations in the south constitutes an act of highly advanced policy. Such events deserve a separate book. Who will write a treatise on the diplomacy and war policies of the princes of Cuzco?

·5·

CONCLUSIONS

By now it should be clear that the pre-Columbian Andeans created highly original societies characterized by numerous particularly outstanding traits. It is thus not necessary to review these features here, but merely to formulate some final remarks.

The South American pre-Columbian societies appear to me to be fundamentally traditionalist, complex, ultraconservative, and hermetic. Being Asians, Andeans are reticent. If we coldly analyze our sources, we must admit that we really know very little about these people. What the chroniclers tell us and what the mixed-blood people of the two worlds (such as Garcilazo) wrote are unreliable. Moreover, these authors were referring only to Inca times, and I have emphasized what in the policies of the princes of Cuzco was original and not in conformity with the ancient traditions of the preceding Andean societies.

As we can hardly count on the chroniclers' texts, it seems that researchers from all countries should apply themselves without delay to collecting all the lessons we can draw from pre-Hispanic ruins, monuments, clusters of buildings, villages, and hamlets. Once these have disappeared, we will no longer have any sources of information.

Luckily, these ruins have survived by the hundreds of thousands in the Andes. Furthermore, Peru constitutes a unique territory for the study of prehistory for, contrary to what the Near East experienced, the Inca empire was destroyed when it was still composed of Neolithic tribes hardly touched by the use of metal. This means that visible upper strata of prehistoric remains in the Andes correspond to what we find in Egypt or Palestine under the debris of five thousand years of later reoccupation.

Traditionalism appears in several ways, first in the way Andeans think. A fundamentally animistic conception of the events of life continually reappears and cracks the varnish imposed by a very superficial Hispanicization and Christianization. At first I had judged them to be stubborn. Now I see them as prudent and reluctant to adopt new outlooks that might be dangerous.

Then let us recall the ultraconservatism that exists with regard to concepts relating to social life. Even when they are uprooted, after coming down to the coastal cities Andeans try to reestablish old bonds created by the concept of the extended family. All pretexts are good, such as the practice among peasants and workers of constantly regrouping people in a framework of consanguinity that is not physical but abstract, psychological. The bonds go as far as *consuegro* and *consuegra*—people become related to the parents of their child's spouse—or through christening a child become related as *compadre* or *comadre*.

I shall never forget a scene that occurred in my garden. A fisherman came to offer me some fish. My foreman, who was passing by, recognized him. "Compadre!" he said, stopping and tipping his hat. After a small bow, the two men advanced three steps. They bowed again, took three more steps, and embraced each other. "This is my 'compadre,'" said Don Alejardro, my foreman, showing pleasure and respect at the same time.

Family life, or rather its hierarchy, also expresses all the contradictions resulting from a blend of ancient traditions marked by a profound and total disdain for women and by the Mediterranean type of mother cult.

In the high Andes, modern life is now dismantling the old *ayllus,* or family units. The earth is too poor; it is no longer exploited communally, though the ancient communal sentiment tries to survive. Thus, though the fields are now privately owned, cattle sometimes remain the property of the *ayllu,* the community, and pasture rights still belong to the group.

Traditionalism also appears in the realm of art and folklore. Let me not speak of modern folklore, for it is dead. Its products—comtemptible copies of prehistoric objects—have nothing in common with the fabrics or ceramics of highly talented pre-Columbian craftspeople.

I wonder if we should not link the disappearance of artistic talent and the death of folklore with the destruction of traditional moral and religious values. In the societies of the central Andes there apparently existed certain archetypes, mythological themes that tended to reappear on various occasions after disappearances that seem attributable to the influence of foreign, or at least new, religious factors. Among these archetypes, the most obvious one is that of the fish (or serpent?) with two interlocking or inverted heads, "the interlocking fish heads," a theme that appeared as early as the period of preceramic agriculture without corn.

This motif disappeared with the Chavín society, which apparently imposed other gods or demons. As soon as Chavín came to an end, however, the interlocking fish heads reappeared, to vanish again under the impact of the Tiahuanacos, who seem also to have taught a new cult. Once the Tiahuanacos were absorbed, coastal societies returned once more to their traditional motifs. The fish reappeared, but it was now placed side by side with the pelican or other sea birds. These birds are symbols of fertility, since their excrement (guano) was used as fertilizer. And even when the Inca influence made itself felt in the lowlands, the inhabitants of the coast still sewed little rectangles with fish decorations onto cloaks decorated in the Cuzco style. In doing their best to destroy what they called pagan beliefs, the Spaniards managed to eradicate the archetypes and thus killed the art.

A somewhat comparable situation can be observed when studying the evolution of themes belonging to invading groups, whether these had a pan-Peruvian influence like the Chavíns or whether they dominated a few valleys like the Chancays. The mythical archetypes of such groups disappeared as soon as the societies that introduced them were destroyed. If, however, the society in question lasted a long time, one may observe not the stylistic evolution one might expect but a very peculiar process of degeneration. The themes and motifs gradually fragmented, before being totally forgotten. In such cases, the first stage is characterized by folkloric or religious themes developed in the form of perfectly drawn, painted, or sculpted motifs that are usually stylized. This in itself is strange, because stylization is normally a late stage and not a point of departure. Some realistic forms show up during a second stage.

A decadence in execution can be noted in the third stage. Potters copied without knowing what they were supposed to be representing. Perhaps they no longer knew how to copy the models because the models no longer existed.

The fourth stage is distinguished by artisans using scarcely recognizable elements that survived from the motifs of earlier compositions. Such elements were used simply to fill empty spaces. No longer able to create, the potter or weaver covered surfaces with randomly placed motifs. The original themes became barely recognizable.

In the fifth stage, everything became confused. Decoration now consisted of a series of lines and spots that no longer pretended to represent anything and did

A large ceramic drum. Note the leather thongs used for stretching the drumheads. From the Early Lima period, A.D. 450.

not even create a simple geometric pattern. This process is particularly easy to observe in Nazca pottery.

To summarize quickly, pre-Columbian patterns seem to appear in a fully realized state, then soon afterward they become stereotyped expressions. We fail to discern any creative evolution, and changes lead only toward a decadence of the original themes. The only new contributions occur during the realistic stage, from which the flower, plant, and animal representations might be interpreted as an escape from strictly mythological patterns. And when we compare the pre-Columbian societies with civilizations of the Near East and Far East, we cannot escape the fact that the pre-Columbians developed five thousand years late.

However, let no one be mistaken about my views. I do not mean to deny in any way that the Andean societies (or Mexican societies to a still higher degree) attained a certain finished form of original civilization. As Jacques Soustelle has said, Mexico was a highly civilized country, with its own embryonic writing, and was highly advanced, thanks to the work of the Mayas, in the fields of mathematics and astronomy. The Peruvians had invented mnemotechnic systems for recording figures and were about to create their own system of writing.

Peoples invent writing when states are organized and their leaders need to know at all times the resources of the country, the state of food stocks, and the distribution that must be made—in short, when leaders for administrative purposes need secretaries who know how to read, write, and count.

Compared with China and the Near East, however, the Americas were unquestionably late to develop intellectually and technologically. During my years of teaching, I have repeatedly heard the same questions in this regard: What are the causes of this lateness? Why did this enormous, rich continent remain at a Neolithic stage? One can approach the problem from various angles, if it is well understood that I refuse to bring in the notion of degrees in the intrinsic worth of the human material, because I see no valid criteria for appraising worth. People remain people, no matter who or what has conditioned them; conditioning can make cowards or heroes of men. In this regard, the best example that comes to mind is the attitude of French soldiers during the First and Second world wars.

Once the notion of "superior" and "inferior" groups has been eliminated, one cannot help thinking that the failure of certain societies, as against the material progress of others (ultimately a temporary progress, since they too eventually were engulfed in crises and disappeared), could be attributed to an intrinsic process of self-destruction. Steward explains the ultimate decadence of the South American chiefdoms by considering that they had been exhausted by incessant fighting, with the elites losing control of the sociopolitical life. This resulted in a breakdown of traditional frameworks, in a lack of manpower for agricultural tasks, and in the invasion of food-producing territories by less-advanced bands. What Steward has not developed is the idea that the internal structures and dynamics of human groups may unconsciously lead them toward self-destruction in much the same way as whales and dolphins may suddenly seem to go berserk and swim toward a beach, where they become stranded. They will die even if helped and brought back to deep water.

The Andean societies remind one of ants, rebuilding with perseverance and tenacity what the elements were constantly destroying—let us remember that South Americans live in a hostile and dangerous world. But ants are not clever, and the Andean people are very intelligent. They have demonstrated a deep capacity for adaptation to essentially fragile mesoclimatic situations in an environment that, generally speaking, should have permitted only a marginal existence.

This tenacity is an innate trait among the contemporary population of Peru. In Lima I have experienced three earthquakes. After each quake, when the panic is over and the tears have dried, the entire population begins to rebuild what has been destroyed so many times and will be destroyed again, maybe a few days later. "C'est la vie," people imply, and gaiety returns.

That being said, the Americas' geographical isolation probably also constituted one of the fundamental causes for their slow development. With the putting into practice of stockbreeding and agriculture, American groups created conditions for civilized life as early as their brothers of the Near East, India, China, and Mexico. However, a lack of continuous physical contacts with different peoples may have deprived them of the element of competition that comes with exchanging thoughts and methods. Such exchanges are made in the great travel corridors such as formed notably by the Near East, an obligatory gateway with respect to connections between Europe, Africa, and Asia. The South American societies, on the contrary, lived in isolation. With two exceptions, the Chimu kingdom and the Inca empire, they experienced only the first stages of their Neolithic development, not evolving further than military or religious chiefdoms that were constantly destroying themselves in the course of domestic fighting. We know through the chroniclers that the forest villagers were slaughtering each other in the same way, thus preventing any progress.

I nevertheless think it likely that despite their traditionalism when Europeans invaded, the two Americas were on the eve of a philosophical and religious revolution, a conversion to new modes of thought, at least among the elite. The princes of Cuzco seem to have already tried by then to impose a theocracy in the form of a monotheistic sun cult in which the Inca personified the sun, the supreme god. This solar monotheism would have little by little replaced animism and a pantheon of naturalistic deities. Perhaps the division, the lack of cohesion in the face of European adversaries, could have come in part from a kind of disjunction, a loss of faith, a disaffection from or fear of the new practices introduced by the Inca to replace antiquated ceremonies. Didn't a comparable phenomenon occur in Egypt with the attempt at monotheistic reform by the pharaoh Akhnaton?

Akhnaton or Ikhnaton is the surname taken by the pharaoh Amenhotep IV in order to eliminate from his given name the name of the god Amon. Amenhotep, who reigned from 1379 to 1362 B.C., was the earliest idealist to transmit his views to us. He attempted a religious revolution that if it had succeeded could have modified the course of Egyptian history by reviving thought and liberating it from the yoke of a religion in the process of ossification. Who knows; perhaps art itself could have been revived. As early as 1400 B.C., intellectuals showed a disaffection for the naturalistic pantheon and an inclination toward a conception of a sun god reigning over the other divinities. From there it was natural to pass to the notion of the pharaoh as a personification of the sun god, to a universalism expressed in terms of imperial power. As soon as he was on the throne, Amenhotep lost no time in setting up the cult of Aton, the sun god, and combatting the polytheism represented by the rich and powerful clan of the priests of Amon.

Despite all his efforts, Amenhotep failed before the hostility of the priestly clan and the attachment of the people to the traditional cult of Osiris. Then again, the army severely judged the disasters that occurred in Egypt's foreign policy. Busy revolutionizing thought and the arts, Amenhotep neglected the borders. Worn out, perhaps, by an intense personal life, he died at the age of thirty, the first prophet of monotheism and an internationalist conception of the world.

This question reminds me of the problem that has always preoccupied my readers and students; namely, how were Pizarro and a few companions able, all by themselves, to conquer a territory that extended over four hundred thousand square miles, populated by people so gifted in producing, building, working, and surviving?

First let us recall that none of the various Andean societies seem to have lasted long. (The Near East also experienced the sudden and total disappearance of powerful societies. Let us recall, for example, the fate of the Hittite empire.) Chavín provides an excellent example, since we know fairly precisely the dates of its appearance and disappearance. Chavín lasted only about three hundred years —how short, compared to the immutability of the Egyptian systems! In Peru, the Chimu kingdom seems to have been in ruins already when the Incas incorporated it into their empire. And the empire lasted only a few decades before being engulfed in civil war and falling at last into such a tragic sociopsychological condition that it was unable to resist one hundred fifty foreigners.

The atmosphere of civil war that prevailed around A.D. 1530 clearly did not favor the development of civic spirit. However, I do not think that is the real point. I imagine, rather, that people did not realize the terrible danger threatening the Andes, the danger of a complete destruction of the social structures and the disappearance of more than 90 percent of the population. During the first months, the war against the Spaniards must have been regarded as one of the usual conflicts that occurred regularly in every peasant and warrior society in a preliterate world. Let us recall, moreover, the psychological difference that must have existed between men belonging to a preliterate Neolithic cultural system and their conquerors—ruffianly soldiers, certainly, but heirs to a Mediterranean civilization and emissaries of a monarch whose vocation was to govern in the name of an unrivaled religion. This distinction would in itself have resulted in a shock powerful enough to shatter all the social structures of the New World, which, incidentally, was very poorly named, since it was living for the most part in the Stone Age.

Furthermore, the assailants and defenders did not fight the same way. The former were carrying on a war of conquest whose object was to enslave the vanquished peoples; the latter were carrying on the type of war that Andeans were in the habit of conducting. Their wars had varied purposes, certainly, but they were as much ritual as economic or political in character. They ended not in exterminating the enemy but merely in the fall of one society, the entering of the defeated into a new alliance, payment of a moderate tribute, and capture of a number of prisoners.

Mexico and the Andes differ in this respect. In the sixteenth century, South America still contained groups who practiced cannibalism, probably as a ritual with a view to absorbing the virtues of the people whose flesh one was eating. However, human sacrifice was apparently practiced only rarely and called for only a moderate number of victims, whereas it played a fundamental role in Mexico.

John Hemming's work on the end of the Inca empire gives moving details of the battles conducted by these Andeans. His descriptions remind me of the Gauls struggling against Caesar's legions—courageously, but in a disorganized way, displaying a strategy that could hardly succeed against a determined assailant. Thus, for example, the Andean peoples were afraid of the night and did not continue their attacks after nightfall, for fear of the spirits they thought they risked meeting in the dark. (Benalcázar was attacked at night while he was trying to reach Quito. However, active volcanoes light up the darkness in these regions.) With their overwhelming majority of men and arms, if they had continued fighting after sunset, they would have easily disposed of the small band of Spaniards. Let us remember the defeat of General Custer.

Opposed to the defensive side's animistic psychology, whose rules of the game corresponded to a very different conception of war conducted almost as a sport, was a small group of adventurers of undeniable courage and strength of character. They terrorized their adversaries, at least during the first encounters, by mounting horses and cutting off heads and body parts by great thrusts with steel swords. These men were determined to make a fortune, to secure total control of a country they believed to be enormously rich.

The code name of this enterprise could have been Operation Grand Illusion. The gold quickly disappeared from Peru, and there was very little of it in Mexico. Silver was not exploited until later, and even the mountain of silver in Potosí was soon exhausted. The Spaniards were unable to develop the mining resources that today constitute the wealth of the South American countries.

In addition, the Andeans apparently suffered from the contradiction that resulted on the one hand from their fundamental traditionalism—a conservatism that was probably rigidifying in the socioeconomic sphere—and on the other hand from the living conditions imposed on them by an environment that offered only marginal possibilities, at the mercy of the slightest mesoclimatic alterations. As an example of the influence of such conditions, let me recall that field archaeology has taught me that when a group was no longer able to apply its traditional techniques in a given territory, it abandoned the area. What became of such groups? We do not know, and what's more, have never found traces of them in other areas. In all cases I have studied, when the territory in question was reinhabited, it was by other groups applying different techniques and thus choosing another climatic level or another hydrological system—a rainy upper valley, the coastal lomas, the lower valley—where farming could be practiced with the help of a stream that flooded annually, or the lower plains, when the water sheet was accessible there. Perhaps more flexible and adaptable groups would have tried to use the resources of another level and would not have disappeared.

Nothing in the history of the Andes favors the concept of societies shaped by the environment. On the contrary, Andean societies of arid lands appear to me to have been groups struggling to assert themselves with courage and perseverance in hostile surroundings. As Gordon Willey remarked, it was not the environment that created the Maya monuments; if these monuments exist, it is because Mayas built them. And as Franz Boas said, "The milieu does not have creative power." The creative capacities of the Andeans were amply revealed, moreover, in the cold upper Andes as well as in the sands of coastal deserts. In other words, the Andean societies erected comparable monuments in totally different environments. If it was the milieu that had favored the erection of the palaces of Cuzco, why did the hot desert sands give rise to the palaces of Chan Chan?

And during all these millennia, the tribes living in the tropical lands and grassy pampas created nothing, while certain hot lands, like the banks of the Orinoco or the Atrato Valley in Colombia, saw the flowering of a prosperous agriculture in complexes that were producing up to three harvests a year. I am thus inclined to think that it was those who wanted to build who did.

Arnold Toynbee explained that the societies who went through difficult periods struggled to improve their condition, but if the living conditions became too harsh, these societies sank into neglect and gave up struggling. I wonder about, and am more and more attracted toward, a structuralist concept of evolution regarding the dynamics of societies. I have a feeling we still do not understand what pushes societies along or leads them toward stagnation and destruction.

When it comes to comparing stagnant and lively societies, a writer named Edwin N. Ferdon, Jr., has confined himself to a much more positive approach, and I admire his work. This author reminds us that all over the world the richest lands are not those that gave birth to the most highly developed societies, but that the early, original centers of agricultural civilizations were in territories hard to exploit: arid Egypt and Mesopotamia; the Chinese lowlands of the Yangtze; the high Mexican plateau, cold and arid; and finally, the coastal desert of Peru. On the other hand, the big, rich plains such as the pampas of Argentina and of the United States produced nothing.

I tried to test Ferdon's theory as follows. First, I divided up the South American continent into geographical regions corresponding to territories occupied either by one society or by little groups living in the same way during the last pre-Columbian century. Then I gave each region a number of points, taking into account its economic potential considered from these points of view: usable lands; climate; water resources; resources from the ocean, lakes, or rivers; game; the possibilities of stockbreeding; other resources, particularly mines, and finally its topographical position in respect to approaches and intercommunications.

Furthermore, I subdivided into cold, temperate, or hot regions the societies that inhabited areas with very different climates. Each heading was then assigned a coefficient of 3, 2, or 1, according to the quality of the resources in question: excellent, mediocre, or nonexistent. For example, in orographic matters (the study of mountains), the regions endowed with large flat surfaces were assigned a coefficient of 3; the steeply sloping and difficult lands, a coefficient of 2; and the very wild and uneven lands, or lands with very little usable surface, a coefficient of 1.

In climatic matters, I applied the coefficient 2 to lands that were too hot or watered by rains that were poorly distributed during the year, and a coefficient of 1 to hot territories in which agriculture was practiced according to the slash-and-burn system, in view of the drawbacks of this technique.

As a result of this work, one can see that there are thirty-six geopolitical regions in South America, listed in decreasing order in terms of their economic potential.

1. Cold Colombia. 22
2. Cold northern Ecuador 18
3. Cold southern Ecuador 18
4. Araucania 18
5. Atrato, Chocó, Tumaco, Darien . . . 17
6. Tierradentro 16
7. Esmeraldas 16
8. The Chaco 16
9. Patagonia 16
10. The Chilean archipelagos,
    Tierra del Fuego 16
11. Tumbes 16
12. The Antilles, Trinidad 16
13. The Guianas 15
14. The Sinú, lower Magdalena,
    and César valleys 15
15. Hot, coastal Brazil 15
16. The Brazilian plateaus 15
17. Coastal Peru 15
18. Cool, coastal Ecuador 15
19. The Guajira Peninsula 15

20. The Manabí 14
21. The llanos 14
22. The Guayas 14
23. The San Agustín savannah 14
24. The central Orinoco Basin 14
25. Atacama (puna, plateaus,
    and coast) 14
26. The central Amazonas 13
27. Sierra Nevada de Santa Marta 13
28. The Venezuelan cordillera 13
29. The cold eastern slopes
    of the Andes 13
30. The cordillera of the Diaguites 13
31. The mouth of the Amazon 12
32. The mouth of the Orinoco 12
33. Sierra Perija 12
34. Arid central Peru 12
35. The hot eastern slopes
    of the Andes 11
36. Cold Bolivia and Peru 11

This table invites several observations. For one, it confirms Ferdon's theory that the richest lands do not necessarily favor the development of complex societies.

For another, it shows that well-endowed territories, such as cold Colombia, Ecuador, Araucania, the Isthmus of Darien, Tierradentro, Esmeraldas, San Agustín, and the lower Magdalena Valley actually did become rich agricultural lands, whether in a hot or a cold milieu. Furthermore, these territories experienced very different forms of social organization: a regime of fortified villages in Araucania, chiefdoms in hot lands, big chiefdoms that were perhaps on the way to creating a kingdom in upper Colombia. Despite these facts, the list confirms that industrious and complex societies were not created in such territories.

The list further shows that the Inca empire was born in the heart of the most disadvantaged, worst-off territory of the Andes, that of central Peru and Bolivia. All the riches the princes of Cuzco had at their disposal came from totally arid coastal Peru where, moreover, the Chimu monarchy also appeared.

The pre-Columbian societies of monument builders thus developed in lands that do not benefit from any rainfall, or scarcely any. This fact leads me to wonder if the compulsion to build big architectural complexes was not the result of a dynamic typical of structures inherent in the societies of arid lands, a dynamic that led to the formation of autocratic systems.

Let us recall that to produce food with the help of a single annual flood would have obliged the peasant to accumulate food reserves for the next twelve months and also to set aside seeds to sow the next crop. Not to operate in this way meant the death of the coastal farmers. Such conditions may have favored an evolution that led to concentrating power in the hands of a small group or a single man, leaders who could then command enough manpower to build large monuments.

Furthermore, the rhythm of agricultural life in arid lands regulated as they are by a single annual flood, as in Egypt and the poor Peruvian valleys, must have meant for the peasants a well-ordered existence marked by a long period of inactivity during which the fields required almost no care.

The Egyptologist M. Mendelssohn has formulated an interesting theory about such situations. He thinks that the pyramids were built as massively as they were because the princes of the Nile Valley were obliged to feed their people all year round, distributing wheat to them little by little in stages, in order to prevent immoderate consumption that would lead to famine at the end of the year. Until the next crop could be harvested, and while they were feeding the people, why not have them work, constructing mausoleums, pyramids, palaces, or even cities? I think the Andean agricultural societies may have experienced a comparable development. This would explain the existence of the enormous palaces in Chan Chan, the ziggurats of Moché made of 20 million unfired bricks, and many other monumental complexes.

We know the Andean societies must have struggled to survive and counteract the destructive forces of earthquakes, torrential floods, and dry seasons. Let us not forget, however, that these elements were not the only causes of their weakening and even destruction.

I have already discussed the exhausting effects of tribal battles. By drastically reducing the number of able-bodied men, these battles must in some cases have brought about the destruction of the group by famine because they did not leave enough people to do the farming. There is a point between what an environment can produce and a minimal number of farmers that cannot be exceeded without endangering the survival of the group.

As an example of other factors that should be considered, let me mention plagues and epidemics. All too often, European-centered attitudes still burden the study of the problems of prehistory. For most people now, epidemics and diseases are synonyms for phenomena resulting from the discovery of the New World by Mediterranean peoples. In my opinion this is too shortsighted a view of the question. Smallpox and malaria, to mention only two diseases we know of, are not the only plagues that decimated the Andeans. Who can assure us that invaders from the Caribbean Islands or the Orinoco Basin did not bring to the western slopes of the Andes diseases as deadly as those imported by the Spaniards and Portuguese? Let us remember the disappearance of the bean planters of Peru, who vanished without leaving any traces, when the corn planters arrived, around thirty-five hundred years ago.

In the beginning of the twentieth century, various indigenous and endemic viral diseases were still ravaging Peru. Leprosy, of dubious origin but perhaps imported from Africa along with tuberculosis and malaria, was still endemic. Then there were Chagas' disease (a trypanosomiasis), Uta (a skin leishmaniasis), and verruga peruana, a leontiasis that ravaged even the Mexicans, as indicated by the portrait vessels that have been found in Central America showing faces covered by pimples.

Also very much debated is the case of syphilis, which many authors think was brought to Europe from America, where they consider that the disease was endemic. Let us not forget, however, that syphilis appeared in Europe in the fifteenth century, under the name of "the Naples disease." Now the French had been waging war in Italy since the fifteenth century, and the Turks had conquered Byzantium in 1453. Why should we discard the possibility that syphilis could have been brought from the Far East? I see it as a Mongolian disease more than as an American disease.

Alcoholism, on the other hand, that scourge of the Andes, seems to have been a disease resulting from the European invasion. Europeans introduced into America the process of distilling sugarcane.

The pre-Columbians drank, of course, in order to relax during festivals or to practice rites. *Pulque* in Mexico and *chicha* in Peru, the fermented corn of the Andes, are not colonial inventions. However, as Soustelle teaches, isn't it better to get drunk occasionally or to trip on a hallucinogen than to kill oneself by drinking *cañazo*, a bad alcohol made from sugarcane, every day? Cañazo is the downfall of America south of the Rio Grande. In Colombia, people kill each other with machetes or guns in the villages, their spirits set on fire by methyl alcohol blended with low-grade rum. In Ecuador I have seen country people sitting on cases of beer bottles. Being able to buy a case and get completely drunk for two days establishes the social status of an individual. In Otavalo I have seen natives lying inert in the fields or being dragged home by their families. Every three or four months, festivals keep people away from work for several weeks. Once when I was looking for laborers for a trip, the administrator of a big farm answered me, "Labor? Unthinkable! The festival begins today. They won't come back for a week!" (Oddly enough, festivals generally coincide with the *Intiraimi,* the Inca festival of the summer solstice. Thus the penetration of a sun cult as far as Quito is attested.) This could, of course, be an instinctive reaction against the requirements of modern life, which demands too regular and too continuous work. Nothing, however, is more painful than seeing the degeneration caused by alcohol and coca in places like Pisac in the Urubamba Valley, a much-visited tourist resort in Peru.

In Lima my gardener and his wife, both of whom came down from the upper Andes fifteen years ago, are ruining themselves with alcohol and coca, despite all my efforts to create an agreeable life and environment for them. This couple, quite small themselves, have now given birth to midgets.

Although alcohol ravages the Andeans, they have on the other hand a great resistance to a host of infections that make European-born people seriously ill. The Andeans' children die easily of scarlet fever, measles, and whooping cough, but if they survive these diseases, they have nothing much left to fear except appendicitis. Drinking water from a canal that carries cattle dung or the dead body of a pig is not at all dangerous to them. Instead, they are frightened by stagnant water or water from faucets, "poisoned" by modern chemistry. Why would the canal water be bad, since it lives, moves, and is renewed? Anyway, among Andeans the unhealthy treatment of open wounds does not give rise to the blood poisoning that threatens Europeans. One of my fieldworkers had a long, thick cactus thorn implanted and broken off in his knee. To make it come out he applied to his knee a nice compress of excrement; in draining, the pus eliminated the thorn.

The metabolism of these people is also different. Andeans go from the hot coast to the puna dressed in just a cloth shirt; they do not feel the cold. My chauffeur will never wear a coat, even when driving at elevations up to seventeen thousand feet. Wearing a shirt with unbuttoned cuffs makes him feel less stuffy and more at ease. But in the meantime I will be wrapped in fur and wool and be shivering, not from the cold, but from lack of oxygen.

If my friends the fieldworkers are not bothered by the cold, they are, on the other hand, half frozen with terror when they have to face a slight hail or snow cloud, but most of all when they hear thunder. It is true that in the bleak, treeless puna lightning often strikes at cattle or the herders for lack of anything else that conducts electricity, but I have a feeling that magic also has to do with these people's terror.

I have a feeling that the strength of Andeans also lies partly in a total intuitive acceptance of the fact that they live permanently in a hostile milieu and must accept it. When I recently told a colleague how worried I was about the future of the city of Lima, which is built on a geological fault and, to quote the geophysicists, "may any day disappear into the sea," he replied, "But without the earthquakes, it would not be 'our' environment!" Earthquakes form part of the Peruvian milieu; nationalism does seem to adopt the strangest appearances.

People with critical minds go a little further, to say that the Andean has been educated to accept the notion of too strong a natural environment against which people are virtually powerless. Critics maintain that this attitude has made the Andean passive and, to a certain extent, lazy. But I cannot forget that these central-Andean populations created enormous agricultural complexes, remarkable irrigation systems, and immense monuments as well as several cities. They also developed unique weaving techniques. This means that, having lived in isolation from the rest of the world, and living as Neolithic tribes, they were highly original creators, craftsmen, and builders. And yet their chaotic territory, cold in the highlands, desert or inundated by flash floods in the lowlands, is certainly not very favorable to human enterprises. Only abstemious and tenacious populations could have survived there.

This abstemiousness is especially noted among the inhabitants of arid lands. According to ethnologists, big holidays as occasions of great gluttony and drinking are more typical of hunting peoples or inhabitants of rainy forests. An excellent example is offered by the Kwakiutl and other nonagricultural peoples of western Canada. Among these peoples, as among their cousins the Polynesians, social rank was expressed by the degree of generosity practiced during big festivals, during which the powerful individuals squandered their fortunes on presents distributed to the crowd. Going backward a few millennia, let us imagine the festival that the capture of an elephant or whale, and the eating of its flesh and fat, must have represented to a group of hunters. But what do we really know about the festivals of the Mochicas and Chavíns?

Among forest peoples, the lack of concern over food, a perhaps unconsciously voluntary lack of anticipation, appears in another form. In the Amazonas, thirty-six hundred square yards planted with manioc easily produces enough food to feed a family of five people for a year, for one acre of virgin earth planted with manioc yields a crop of two tons per year. However, the people's negligence is such that ants, wild pigs, and bad weather destroy a good part of the crop, so the group sometimes suffers from famine at the end of the year.

As discussed, in arid lands the water factor is undoubtedly predominant. When water is absent from a territory, man is too; and scholars looking for his traces will be confronted with a void. However, if water is present, though invisible, even the simplest people know how to find it.

I cannot be persuaded, therefore, that the South American societies were shaped by the environment, that the practice of a technologically advanced agriculture (indispensable in sustaining a large population in very arid lands) could have developed locally by adapting to the environment. I do not see how pre-farming groups accustomed to collecting their food from a dry land could have suddenly turned into farmers practicing irrigated agriculture in the desert without undergoing any transitional stage.

Furthermore, the notion that evolving societies succeeded one another in the same arid territories, clung to these lands, and were able to survive all crises there by improving their agricultural techniques does not correspond to archaeological facts. The best example to support this thesis is the one provided by the Chilca

Basin in Peru, where at least nine societies succeeded each other, but where each society practiced agriculture in a different way. Thus, techniques did not develop in Chilca in order to enable the survival of a single group of inhabitants. Rather, this occurred because Chilca suited varied techniques that quite diverse peoples tried to adapt to what is in fact an inhospitable area.

It is one thing to say that these societies did their best to adapt to the environment to make it produce, and perhaps even modified their milieu. But it may be going too far to imagine that the Andeans were able actually to control their future and destiny. I willingly recognize that the advances made (usually quite temporarily) by certain groups were the result of human effort. But if we analyze the cold reality, we must admit that their lives were subject to too great a number of variables for their leaders ever to determine their future.

As far as the Andes are concerned, we may consider among these variables the climatic factors that periodically weakened the societies living in arid lands. Once weakened, such groups suffered the attacks of warlike bands that came up from the Amazonas. Similar circumstances would also have favored the Inca conquests.

But a lean year of agricultural calamities does not explain everything. Although usually it was bands moving up from the forests and attracted by women, booty, and good farming lands who went up to attack the cold, high plateaus already developed by industrious societies, the opposite occurred as well. The Incas, for example, seized the Chimu kingdom and the rich coastal basins of the Cañete and Chincha rivers.

Thus, success or failure seem beyond the power of either the individuals composing a society or of its rulers. Success results from the internal structures that rule groups of human beings. History is full of examples of self-destruction paralyzing the best-worked-out plans for development. The history of the Andean societies brings this process particularly to light, since this history is dominated by continual intervention by destructive or, culturally speaking, simply very different elements. Dynamic groups that were often much less gifted, apparently, than those forming the locally established societies were continually fighting either to neutralize the latter's efforts or simply to settle in their place.

Along the Pacific, twenty-four miles north of Lima, lies an enormous dune called the Pasamayo. It was well known by motorists who were blocked every day on the Pan-American Highway that intersects this mountain of sand here. (Today this road has been rerouted.) The Pasamayo dune is made of beach sand carried to a high altitude by winds that blow continuously from the ocean. These sands fall throughout the year and flow again toward the beach in countless streams. The more the sand rises, the more it falls; the movement is endless.

The process of this dune symbolizes Andean history, a history of ten thousand years of cyclical migrations, abandonments, and occupations of territories, of appearances and then sudden and complete disappearances of societies who seemed well equipped for survival.

Although we should not overemphasize the effect of foreign, even extracontinental, influences, it is more than likely that they made themselves felt in the

Andes. I am thinking in particular of African influences, which have not received enough attention from anthropologists except from Rivet, who was the first to suggest that there were Australian and ultimately Negroid traits in pre-Columbian South America. Everyone knows the epic of the Polynesians, and one cannot help thinking of southern Asia when looking at Maya temples.

However, in regard to repeated population movements let us not think only of immigrants foreign to the continent; we must also look in the neighborhood. Then we shall see the Andes in both north and south invaded by forest peoples, by Arawaks or Caribs, by Tupis and Guaranis. We shall have to recognize the presence of Arawaks on the Pacific Coast and Guaranis (perhaps even Arawaks) as far southwest as on the coast of Chile. The Jivaros went up to Cuenca in the high inter-Andean valleys of Ecuador, and the Mojos went to the shores of Lake Titicaca.

An intense nationalism, endemic in South America as in Europe, inclines Peruvian, Colombian, and Chilean archaeologists to refuse to admit that the appearance of societies like those of Paracas or the Mochicas could have resulted from distant migrations. What does it matter to us whether the Paracas were Arawaks or the Nazcas were Diaguites, who had themselves come from the Orinoco Basin? It is what these vanished peoples bequeathed to us that is important, and not the fact that they were Peruvians or Caribs.

I wonder if the source of these migrations wasn't ultimately the northeastern part of the continent, an inexhaustible reservoir of people in search of good lands. South America may have experienced the phenomenon opposite to the one observed in the Far East, where the Mongolian nomads hated and despised the peasants of maritime China. The almost total absence of nomadism also seems to me to be one of the dominant characteristics of South American history. The continent was essentially inhabited for millennia by small tribes that were deeply rooted in the land and emigrated in hopes of farming better fields.

In South America the farmers from the forests constantly went up to attack others, certainly because of their wealth, but also, if not especially, because they thought the upper-valley lands were better than their own. We need only to recall the chronicles to visualize how the well-farmed territories were objects for continual assaults by terrifying warriors armed with poisoned arrows, who came from the forests and hot plains east of the Andes.

Today we are experiencing a comparable phenomenon in different forms and in a geographically inverse sense. The Andeans are again rushing toward the good lands, which this time are found along the coastal strip. The high valleys are now totally ruined and unproductive, with used up, eroded farmland.

The farmland found along the coast was developed by immigrants who had usually arrived barefooted, or at least in extremely reduced circumstances. By dint of tenaciousness, they succeeded in transforming into productive property some 1.5 million acres of land that had been cultivated before the Spaniards landed. This land returned to desert sands after the pre-Columbian societies collapsed, and has not been cultivated for four hundred years.

This colonization of the dry lower valleys had a dramatic effect in the sense that it created a situation in which less than 2 percent of Peru's total population came to control more than 95 percent of the productive acreage. It was inevitable in those days of radio, and later of television, for the situation to become explosive, with 95 percent of the Andes populations remaining marginal. So this time, as may have happened at the time of the Tiahuanaco invasion, the people from above grabbed the land below. One can understand why.

Clearly, it is more tempting to take a green patch of ground than to create a field oneself, or to wait for the state to develop the immense acreage that remains still to be exploited in Peru and Ecuador. Programs such as the retimbering that is necessary to ensure a rehydration of land that has dried out and been covered with sand, or the reutilization of the lomas, are understood by very few people, and it takes a long time to retimber and prepare new farmland. The efforts of the United Nations in this regard are hardly known or taken seriously. Furthermore, such programs are too subtle for the Andean peasant, who is no longer able to live on his impoverished plot. He combines forces with other peasants and their families and comes to take the luxuriant lands they see spread out before them in the coastal oases. In all sincerity these people consider these lands theirs, without realizing that the people who developed them are not descendants of the sixteenth-century conquerors who destroyed the pre-Columbian social structures and depopulated the Andes.

Colonial history is not my field. Let me simply recall that in citing the success of those who created modern industrial agriculture in the temperate lower Andes, I in no way wish to justify the methods by which the natives were formerly deprived of their lands.

One of my latest discoveries would certainly create serious reactions in Peru if widely publicized in the press, but let me describe it nevertheless, since this work is written for educated readers.

Peruvians consider that their national territory extends deep into what is now northern Chile. The settlement of 1929, which gave the harbor, fortress, and city of Arica to their hereditary enemies to the south, was poorly accepted. The referees' ruling was considered unjust, and the cry "Arica is ours!" is still heard from time to time, mainly during periods of international tension.

How will Peruvians react when they read that (speaking in terms of pre-Columbian cultures) it is difficult, if not impossible, to find coastal Peruvian traits either in Arica or, alas, even farther north! After a thorough study of the Far South's coastal desert, I have to admit that a culture typical of Chile is found up to Camana in Peru at about sixteen degrees of south latitude, but on the other hand, no coastal Peruvian culture (like the Nazcas, for instance) is found between Camana and the Loa River at twenty-two degrees south latitude. This is so despite the fact that the northern bank of the Loa is considered to be historically the southernmost limit of the Inca empire, when the rulers of Cuzco tried to colonize Chile. Culturally speaking, the Camana-Tacna-Arica-Iquique coastal range is Diaguite or Atacamanian, and nothing else. Nazca remains are still being found just north of Camana—not south of the river. If we adjust the political frontier to the archaeological situation, we would have to cut off some 180 miles from the so-called Peruvian coast. Let us hope nobody makes such a foolish suggestion!

What will the Andeans do with the haciendas they have taken over? Will they be able to exploit them? Is a pioneering elite going to form—a society equipped with the capable administrators without whom all logical, organized production and distribution remains merely a goal? Time will tell.

This being so, I have unquestionably witnessed during the last few years what undoubtedly has once again been the self-destruction of a society. The pioneering elite who developed Peru and Chile in the beginning of the twentieth century neither knew how nor wanted nor understood the necessity to undertake reforms to integrate the peasant mass into the country's economic life. To integrate is not to return to the Stone Age. I have always struggled for integration, distant as I am from the indigenous school of thinkers and poets like Luis E. Valcarcel and José Maria Arguedas (to cite only the heads of the movement) who wanted to revive an Inca society. But the elite did not assume the useful role they could have played by entering into partnership with this mass and giving it the administrators it lacked. They might have been able to maintain the Andeans if not at the forefront, then at least in the mainstream of the changes that have recently overrun the country like the floods of mud that carry boulders down the fifty-two main Andean watercourses.

Although styles differ now—people no longer wear trophy heads—the underlying psychological mechanisms are still the same. Unsuccessful people want to take the place of those who have succeeded, to punish them for having what they themselves do not have.

As a result of the dramatic demographic pressure plaguing Peru at this moment, when once more it has to give birth to a new society, the present crisis may well result in a long period of poor and vegetative life. However, Andean societies have shown so much vitality and such an aptitude for surviving in the most adverse situations that I do not doubt that history will see them emerge once more from a momentary shadow and play a creative role again.

Impregnated with Christianity, bearing the stamp of Rome and of Spanish formalism, the Andeans can no longer turn back. Once again, the citizens of Cuzco and Lima must create, by themselves, a new and original world.

INDEX

Page numbers in *italics* refer to illustrations.

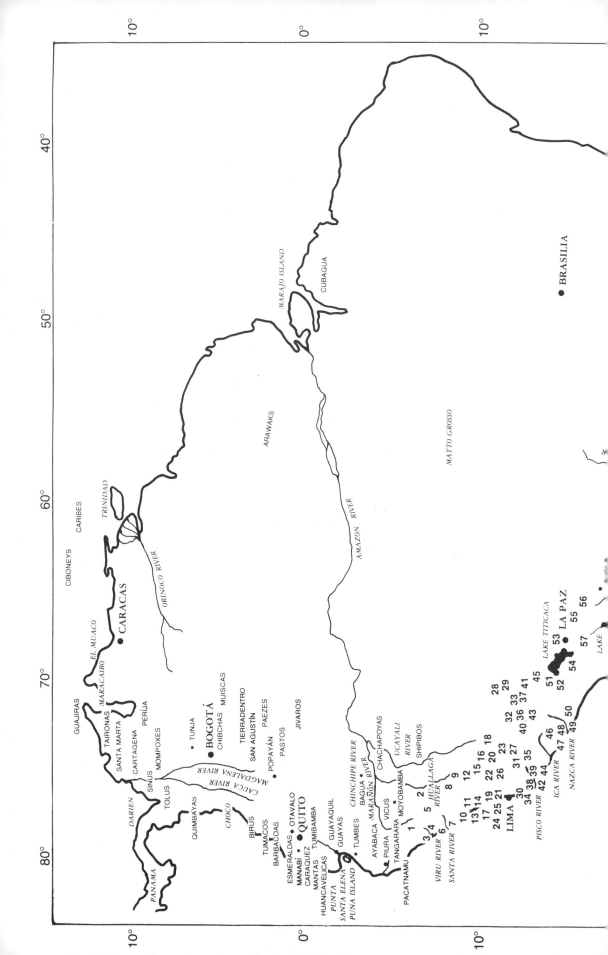